Eyewitness Falklands

Robert Fox was born in Warwickshire in 1945
and grew up on a farm outside Taunton in
Somerset. He was educated at Blundell's
School, Tiverton, and Magdalen College,
Oxford, where he read History. He joined BBC
Radio as a producer in 1968 and became a
reporter with the Radio News department five
years later. As a reporter he has worked
extensively in Northern Ireland and Italy,
covering major terrorist cases and four
earthquakes in five years. In 1982 he won a
Churchill Fellowship to study community radio
and television in remote rural areas. He was
awarded the MBE for services rendered in
connection with the South Atlantic Operation
in the special honours list of October 1982. In
1987 he joined the *Daily Telegraph* as special
correspondent. Since then he has reported from
Afghanistan, the Middle East, the Gulf War
where he was accredited to the 1st UK
Armoured Division, Operation Safe Haven in
Kurdistan and the civil war in Yugoslavia.
Other books include '*I Counted them all Out*'
(with Brian Hanrahan, 1982), *Antarctica and the
South Atlantic* (1985) and *The Inner Sea: The
Mediterranean and its People* (1991).

Eyewitness Falklands

A PERSONAL ACCOUNT OF
THE FALKLANDS CAMPAIGN

ROBERT FOX

Mandarin

TO
MARIANNE, ALEXANDER AND EMILY
AND
ALL WHO ENDURED THE CAMPAIGN

A Mandarin Paperback
EYEWITNESS FALKLANDS

First published in Great Britain 1982
by Methuen London Limited
This revised edition published 1992
by Mandarin Paperbacks
Michelin House, 81 Fulham Road, London SW3 6RB

Mandarin is an imprint of the Octopus Publishing Group,
a division of Reed International Books Limited

Copyright © 1982, 1992 Robert Fox

A CIP catalogue record for this title
is available from the British Library

ISBN 0 7493 1215 7

Printed and bound in Great Britain
by Cox and Wyman Limited, Reading, Berks

Contents

Illustrations

MAPS

PLATES

1a. The SS *Canberra* at Ascension
1b. A Rapier anti-aircraft missile; HMS *Antelope*
     burning in San Carlos Water
2a. HMS *Fearless* at Ascension
2b. HMS *Fearless* in San Carlos Water
3a. A Lieutenant-Commander of the Argentinian
     Marines after his capture at San Carlos
3b. Robert Fox listening to himself broadcasting on
     the BBC World Service, with members of 2 Para
4a. 'H' Jones giving orders for the move to
     Camilla Creek
4b. Camilla Creek House
5a. Clearing Argentinian dead and prisoners from
     Boca House
5b. Argentinian prisoners marching away from the
     surrender ceremony at Goose Green
6a. Goose Green airfield, showing a napalm bomb,
     a damaged Argentinian Pucara and a Sea King
     helicopter
6b. A member of 2 Para and two settlers on Goose
     Green airfield; woolsheds containing
     Argentinian prisoners
7a. Rescuing personnel from the burning *Sir Galahad*

Plates 1a and 2a were taken by the author. Acknowledgements and thanks for permission to reproduce the other photographs are due to David Nicholls for plates 1b, 2b, 3a, 6a, 6b, 9, 10c, 11a, 11b, 13a, 14 and 15; to Chris Keeble for plates 3b, 7b and 13b; to the 2nd Battalion the Parachute Regiment for plates 4a, 5a and 5b; to Steve Hughes for plates 4b, 7a, 8 and 12b; to Cassidy & Leigh for plate 10a; to the BBC for plates 10b and 16b; and to Pete Holdgate for plates 12a and 16a.

The maps were drawn by Neil Hyslop.

Preface and Acknowledgements

On 1 March 1833 and on 16 March 1834, the *Beagle* anchored in Berkeley Sound in East Falkland with the young Charles Darwin aboard. The islands did not attract the zoologist, who wrote in *The Voyage of the Beagle*:

After the possession of these miserable islands had been contested by France, Spain and England, they were left uninhabited. The government of Buenos Ayres then sold them to a private individual, but likewise used them, as old Spain had done before, for a penal settlement. England claimed her right and seized them. The Englishman who was left in charge of the flag was consequently murdered. A British officer was sent, unsupported by any power: and when we arrived, we found him in charge of a population, of which rather more than half were runaway rebels and murderers.

The theatre is worthy of the scenes acted on it. An undulating land, with a desolate and wretched aspect, is everywhere covered by a peaty soil and wiry grass of monotonous brown colour.

That nearly thirty thousand British men and women should be involved in a war for these islands 'of wretched aspect' in 1982 could scarcely have crossed the mind of anyone living north of the River Plate at the beginning of the year. The origins of the claims of Britain and Argentina to the sovereignty of the Falklands are tangled, to say the least. The beginnings of the crisis that led to war had a distinct flavour of Gilbert and Sullivan about it. On 19 March, Argentinian soldiers posing as scrap-metal dealers raised their country's flag on South Georgia. Within a fortnight, an Argentinian army had landed on the Falklands and Britain had to prepare and mount the most complicated amphibious operation since the Second World War.

I was sent to see the leading ships of the Task Force, the carriers HMS *Invincible* and HMS *Hermes* and the assault ship HMS *Fearless*, sail from Portsmouth. I thought it was a weekend assignment. It was to last three months – six weeks at sea, three and a half weeks following troops at the front, a fourteen-hour battle under artillery fire and night battles in the snow under moonlight and mortar fire.

This book is my account of what happened to me in the battle for the Falklands. It is an account of what the men and women I was with said and did. It is a piece of reporting and observation, taken from memory, and nothing more. I have spoken of the way operations appeared to be planned, or not planned, as the case may be, where equipment and communications seemed to succeed or break down, all as I saw it at the time. This is not a history or a piece of dispassionate analysis: I simply do not know enough of what went on elsewhere, particularly in Argentina and at the UN, to attempt that. Historical judgements will have to wait for years to come, I suspect. The journalism of today can only hope to make up some of the materials which historians may use for their more permanent works tomorrow.

I hope this book describes something of what went on in the three months of the campaign to those who were not there. I hope it says something of the ordeal of the islanders, particularly those who suffered most at Goose Green and Darwin, Teal, Douglas, Estancia and Stanley itself. I hope that it suggests something of the dilemma they face now. I hope it also explains something of what was happening to those who had most to endure, the wives and families at home, for whom it is hard to offer adequate words for the weeks of apprehension and, in the cases of many, bereavement.

I would like first to thank my employers, BBC Radio News, for the help and support they have given me throughout the campaign and in preparing this book. In particular my thanks go to my editor, Larry Hodgson, and Bob Kearsley and Ray Gowdridge, News Editor and Foreign Editor respectively. I am grateful for permission to use some of the interview material recorded while I was on assignment in the Falklands. I would like to thank my wife Marianne and our two small children, Alexander and Emily, for enduring first the campaign and then the book.

My profound gratitude goes to those I was with in the field – Lt.-Col. David Chaundler, Major Chris Keeble and the Reverend David Cooper of 2 Para; Lt.-Col. Hew Pike of 3 Para; the commanding officers of 40, 42 and 45 Commandos, Lt.-Col. Malcolm Hunt, Lt.-Col. Mick Vaux and Lt.-Col. Andrew Whitehead, the 'best yomper in the business'. I would like to thank the masters of the *Canberra* and the *Norland*, Dennis Scott-Masson and Don Ellerby, and their Naval officers, Captain Chris Burne and Commander Chris Esplin-Jones, for their hospitality. I thank the settlers of Goose Green and those I lived with in Stanley for their friendship. Major-General Jeremy Moore, Brigadier Julian Thompson and Captain David Nicholls gave me invaluable help and guidance.

One man is not here to be thanked – Lt.-Col. 'H' Jones. I formed a friendship with him in the last ten days of his life which was one of the most unexpected and rare I have experienced. In other circumstances, such is the similarity of our temperaments, I expect we would have quarrelled on sight. His generosity, impatience and humour were infectious and they changed almost everyone I know who was close to him in the campaign. He was a chivalrous man; no other senior officer was as scrupulous in his instructions about the fair treatment of prisoners. He made his men exceed their own limits of achievement and this ensured that his battalion did not lose the battle at Goose Green, for he knew that if it had been lost, the British might not have recovered the Falklands and the Task Force may have been destroyed. I would like to thank his widow, Sara, and his sons, David and Rupert, for the company of this extraordinary man, one of the old-fashioned heroes. His spirit infused the whole campaign from the moment he died until it was done with.

Introduction

The memory of the Falklands conflict ten years on is gilded by distance in time and place. Even as the extraordinary expedition unfolded, it seemed like an episode from a previous era of British colonial and military history. A tiny expedition of well under 10,000 troops initially, a flotilla of ships and a handful of aircraft, was despatched a third of the way round the world to liberate and defend a colony of about 2,000 souls, and five times as many sheep, penguins, seals and other forms of wildlife.

The wildness of the terrain and the remoteness of the battleground seemed to have more in common with an expedition on the North-West Frontier a hundred years ago than anything to do with warfare in the late twentieth century. Operation Corporate, for the romantics in the military historical fraternity at least, was the heir of the Malakand Field Force, subject of the young Winston Churchill's first book, or Lord Roberts' march from Kandahar to Kabul in the Second Afghan War, for which he needed a train of 120 camels to carry his personal wardrobe and effects.

The critics, too, have described the Falklands expedition as the last of Britain's colonial wars. Certainly with yet another round of defence cuts in train, it is hard to envisage a similar operation being mounted with ease. The politicians have now forced on the armed services the stratagem of Marlborough – they can only project military power in support of British foreign policy as a partner in a coalition, and as a very junior partner at that.

The opponents of the Falklands War complained that it was unnecessary and should not have happened – a criticism of a startling lack of originality, and which could be applied to most modern conflicts. Those with a weakness for conspiracy went further: the whole thing was got up by Margaret Thatcher, the Prime Minister of the day, to salvage her reputation in the face of plummeting opinion polls and win the general election a year later in 1983. This is simply too pat. The evidence is that the British and their American allies were taken unawares. The administration most desperate to save itself was the military dictatorship of Leopoldo Galtieri in Argentina. Only a matter of days before, a fortnight at most, did it become evident that the military regime in Buenos Aires was prepared to gamble its fate on an invasion and occupation of the Falklands and South Georgia.

The conspiracy theorists firmly believed that the Argentine occupiers could be negotiated off the islands, and that it was Mrs Thatcher's obduracy that finally pitched British forces into fighting to recover the colony. The indulgence by the left towards the regimes of Viola and Galtieri seems a classic piece of British political eccentricity. The military dictators of Argentina ran one of the more unsavoury regimes in a part of the world which specialised in them. Even the Italian critics of the Falklands war, such as Bettino Craxi the then Socialist Prime Minister in Rome, were horrified at the policy of institutionalised murder revealed in the months after the conflict: at least 20,000 Italian citizens alone were found to have been tortured and killed or 'disappeared' by the hit squads of the different factions supporting the Buenos Aires juntas. Mr Craxi, with characteristic expansive gesture, formally called on the British Ambassador in Rome to apologise for criticising the Falklands expedition in parliament.

At the distance of ten years the Falklands conflict seems to be of greater historical importance than it appeared in the immediate aftermath. When the troops came home, the nation burst out in a rash of red, white and blue – and the mood of jingoism and celebration was likened to the celebration of England's victory in the World Soccer Cup of 1966. 'It's the only two things we have won as a nation since 1945,' said a cynical journalist colleague of the tendency that was prepared to give General Galtieri the benefit of the doubt over Mrs Thatcher.

The comment misses the mark. The Falklands campaign and its conduct was to set a pattern for the way Britain, its foes and allies, were to address conflicts and diplomacy for the years ahead, and its legacy will be with us well into the twenty-first century. For Britain it held lessons in the narrow sphere of the management and mounting of military expeditions, on the projection of force in support of diplomacy, of the perpetual tension between the military, government and the media in times of war. On this point the Americans, with characteristic exaggeration, believed it showed them how to win where they had lost with the media in Vietnam. Misreading the way the journalists were handled in the Falklands they tried their best to put reporting under military discipline in Grenada, the Panama Operation and Operation Desert Storm in the Gulf. At Grenada, with a sally the Duke of Wellington would have admired, the American admiral in charge threatened to shoot any reporters who aimed at landing on the island ahead of him.

For these and many other reasons, then, *Eyewitness Falklands* is being published again on the tenth anniversary of Operation Corporate. For this I offer no apology, but I believe some explanation for its reappearance is due. The account here is a notebook from the mind. It was written down within a few months of the campaign itself, written in the heat of the moment. In many respects it is the record of an innocent – it was the first time I had witnessed set piece battles and warfare of this kind close to, the first time I (and many of those around me) had come under sustained mortar and artillery fire. Ten years on, and in the middle of covering my seventh conflict, (in Yugoslavia), I recognise I am a very different person from the chronicler of these pages. Some of the conclusions and inferences in them, I now realise are mistaken through misinformation or sheer ignorance – but they are the convictions I held at the time. What I learned and experienced in those few weeks in the Falklands has served me well on many occasions since, and once or twice might have helped preserve my life as well as my livelihood.

Some of the episodes I can hardly recall, even as I reread them in these pages. Some images, the burning of the farmhouse at Burntside in the opening phases of the battle for Darwin, the shelling of the Gorse Line and pulling back the wounded, the explosion of the *Antelope*, the soldiers carrying down Colonel Jones' body at dusk, will live in my mind for the rest of my life. And that I think is the value of this record – it is what it appeared to be like at the time, a dimension which has been lost in so much of the subsequent writings where memory has been burnished by the gift of hindsight.

In the ensuing years some excellent books have appeared on the air and sea campaigns, and on the diplomacy of the crisis. There have been two or three outstanding vignettes from combatants – particularly a collection of interviews by Max Arthur entitled *Above All Courage*. Much less satisfactory have been the accounts which have attempted to shift the gears from mere journalism to contemporary history. None I have read captures the atmosphere and the emotional climate, the swings of mood between fear and tension, and relief and elation which gripped us all.

This is an affliction of our age where the journalist or popular historian is impelled towards instant judgement for fear of losing the attention of an audience whose concentration span, apparently, barely exceeds the length of a television sound-bite. The interior landscape of the mind is as individual as a birthmark or a thumbprint – and almost none of the hindsight accounts of the war on the bleak moors of the Falklands conforms to the mental picture I now retain.

A curious episode some four years after the conflict showed how hindsight can twist and reorder perceptions made in the heat of battle. We had been invited to the Islands to attend the funeral of an Argentine pilot whose remains had been found near his crashed plane on Mount Usborne a few weeks before. Diego Angel Gimenez, if I remember the name correctly, had been on a mission in his Pucara piston-engined aircraft during the battle for Darwin and Goose Green when he was downed in thick fog. Indeed he and I may have caught a glimpse of each other on 28 May 1982 – he might have been one of the two planes diving out of the mist towards Major Chris Keeble's Tac2 HQ of 2 Para, recorded in this book. One of the Pucaras then shot down the Scout helicopter of Dick Nunn, and one was destroyed in turn by British fire.

The father and sister of the dead officer were invited to attend the funeral and burial – the first time Argentines had been allowed back to the Islands since hostilities. The father Isaias Gimenez had led the campaign for the Argentine war dead to be repatriated from their temporary resting place in a cemetery on the downland across the bay from Darwin.

It was the last time I saw the Islands, though I had been back two or three times since the war ended – once to take passage aboard HMS *Endurance* to Antarctica. Quite a lot had altered in those few years – farms and businesses had changed hands, and international fishery breathed a hint of new prosperity. But that wild and moody landscape seemed as it always had been that bright blustery September afternoon in 1986.

The funeral itself was conducted with the utmost decorum and dignity. The last post was sounded across the glittering waters of Falkland Sound, and garrison troops fired volleys of shots, according the dead pilot full military honours. The senior officer on parade was Rear Admiral Kit Layman, Commander British Forces Falkland Islands. He had captained HMS *Argonaut* when almost without all power she stood in San Carlos Water under the air raids of the Argentines in the days after the British landings in May 1982. For more than a week the crew struggled to get a large bomb – ironically labelled 'made in Great Britain' – from the ship's forward magazine, which had been flooded with fuel as an added complication.

At the end of the funeral and interment the sky-blue and white Argentine national flag which had draped the coffin was handed to the family, and Admiral Layman shook their hands before escorting them to his helicopter.

As we turned away I was greeted by a scene which stopped my thoughts of the ceremony in their tracks. Across the inlet from the Argentine War cemetery I could see a piece of ground roughly the size of the average municipal golf course in Britain – which from that distance it resembled with its gentle knolls rising to a line of gorse clumps at the western edge. This was the battlefield of Goose Green, the undulating piece of peat I had witnessed the men of 2 Para take nearly eighteen hours to fight across and secure. On this rustic handkerchief of ground the paratroopers, pitifully outnumbered, had nearly lost the Falklands campaign in an afternoon; but their persistence there had virtually ensured that it would eventually be won, come what may. At the time it had seemed a huge space, and now it seemed smaller than a Devon hill farm. In that brilliant afternoon light I could easily pick out the spot by Coronation Point where we had halted in the drizzle to be shelled and mortared for hours, the spot on the Gorse Hedge where we had swum through brushwood and pinging shrapnel to try to survey the battle for the School House on the slope beyond. Further along the line of gorse was the gulley where Colonel H. Jones led his last desperate attack to get the forward troops of 'A' Company on to high ground before their ammunition ran out, and died in the attempt.

Colonel H. Jones remains the outstanding personality of the British military commanders I met in the whole episode of the recovery of the Islands. It was his example, if not his achievement in the battle for Darwin, that was to galvanise the rest. He had been faced with the awful prospect for any commander of his battle plan going completely wrong, one of his leading companies stuck in low ground with ammunition running low. The intelligence, not least that provided by the SAS, had been proved hopelessly adrift – he was faced with more enemy forces than he had been led to expect, and more civilians in the target area, to complicate matters further. He decided to lead an outflanking raid while he felt he had half a chance, rather than wait for more forces with the risk that by then matters may have become irretrievable.

In death the colonel and his actions became as controversial as he had been in much of his military life. In subsequent years soldiers and officers have questioned me about his last hours with ill-disguised hostility, particularly the more sedentary kind of officer used to the more sedate ways of British Army peace-time soldiering in Germany, the march and counter march of leisurely and unreal exercises, balls and polo. His action appeared to be an inconvenient reminder of the question all professional soldiers must face, of how they will respond when they and their command are brought to full battle – would they be prepared to risk all for themselves and their men, their country or their cause?

H. Jones has remained an indelible presence in the recesses of my memory – and in the short time we were acquainted he taught me some valuable lessons that have changed my attitude to some fundamentals in life. He taught me to use my aggression to the full, to be decisive in the heat of action when it was required – to move and act without hesitation. This, though, has had its negative side. Unlike 'H' my origins are predominantly Scottish and Irish, or not so English as my education and upbringing might suggest, though my red hair does give the game away. While I have learned to be decisive when action really calls, I have become the opposite, and quite distractingly indecisive, when it does not. Too frequently only the ghosts of deadlines past can stir me to arms with pen or typewriter.

In the ten years since, promotion has come to many of the officers who commanded with Colonel H. Four fellow battalion commanders have made it to the rank of Major General. All three of the Royal Marine commanders, the then Lt Colonels Vaux, Whitehead and Hunt, became Generals as did the commander of 3 Commando Brigade, Julian Thompson. The commander of 3 Para, Hew Pike, has also made the rank of General and was to become the first commander of the new British Strategic Reserve Division under the new NATO doctrine.

Of the hacks who joined 3 Commando Brigade the highest promotion came to Max Hastings, who became editor of the

Daily Telegraph in 1986 and is now my boss. In the campaign he could read the battlefield and the order of battle better than any of us. He showed by example the need to get to understand the grammar of working with forces on operations – a feature so lamentably lacking in much of the reporting of the Gulf conflict (tactically an infinitely more complex affair than the Falklands), and the near anarchy of the Yugoslav civil war.

Under the influence of Max and many of the soldiers I first met in the Falklands my working life – no serious news hack should talk of having a career – took an unexpected turn. In 1987 I left the BBC after nineteen years, and joined the *Telegraph* – the first full-time job I have had on a newspaper in Britain, (though I enjoyed a memorable interlude of five months as guest columnist on the *Corriere della Sera* of Milan in the winter of 1976–77). Becoming a print journalist was a liberation for the mind and spirit after the strictures of news broadcasting. And by accident I have tended to follow the drum, reporting on five wars and military operations in the past half dozen years.

A number of the soldiers have become good and close friends. Very few of our conversations nowadays touch on the South Atlantic past at all. Some of these friends have discovered a literary or academic bent, and some, God forbid, have even tried a bit of journalism. Major General Julian Thompson, now retired from the Royal Marines, has written three books – one an evocative account of the campaign itself, while a second is a highly readable history of his brothers in arms, the Parachute Regiment.

Most interesting of the three, however, is his study of logistics, once regarded as the most dismal of military sciences. In it he draws a series of crucial lessons from Operation Corporate, the Falklands expedition, and makes damning observation about the way it was commanded by remote control from London. Logistics, he says, was to be the key to a successful advance across East Falkland to inflict defeat on the occupying Argentines garrisoned at Stanley. Despite their claims to the contrary, the naval commanders at the Ministry of Defence and Fleet Headquarters in North-wood knew very little of the science of logistics, and the only experience they had of it in war was as very junior officers in World War II, and possibly Korea.

Lack of adequate logistical preparation nearly led to disaster – and much the same applied to the deployment of the 1st UK Armoured Division in the Gulf conflict. The lessons of the Falklands are still not fully understood in Westminster and Whitehall. At the time such an 'out of area' operation (ie outside the NATO area in Europe) was seen as sport of history – indeed the last colonial war that should not have happened, and would not happen again.

Apart from the purely colonial aspect, the Falklands campaign seems to be more relevant to future operations and conflicts than anything learned from British forces deployed in Europe for NATO over the past forty years. Joint expeditions with allied forces to the ragged fringe of the European neighbourhood and places of vital interest beyond are likely to be the order of the day. They will be components not so much of the new world order, as the Bush administration hopefully term it, but the new world disorder, as the realists would put it.

A brief comment on the place of Operation Corporate in recent military history was given me a few years ago in Jerusalem of all places. I was interviewing Moshe Arens, who has served his country as Foreign and Defence Minister as well as head of Israel's Defence Industry. I had described the whole conflict as a minor affair, of little significance beyond the British Isles and Argentina itself.

'No,' replied the minister, 'I think you're wrong there. The logistical achievement alone in delivering a force so quickly across 8,000 miles makes it one of the most astonishing military feats of our time. On that aspect alone, our commanders here are fascinated by it.'

Robert Fox, London, November 1991

1. *Sailing*

It was dusk when the great white ship, the *Canberra*, finally slipped her cables at Berth 106, Southampton Dock, and shifted gently into the chilly spring night. From the ship thousands of arms waved, streamers flew and farewells were shouted from soldiers and crewmen alike. Ashore the two bands from the Royal Marines and the Parachute Regiment were locked in private contest to be the one that played its own regimental march at the minute of departure. Also in the programme were 'Land of Hope and Glory' and 'Rule Britannia', all brass and nostalgia.

The whole scene of the departure of three leading elements of the assault troops of the British Falkland Island Land Force resembled a newsreel of forty years before. The patriotism, the red, white and blue, was a little self-conscious, the boast and swagger of a nation that had not needed to prepare for this kind of conflict for a generation. There were a few contemporary touches to the departure of the *Canberra*, too. Television crews and reporters came aboard, adding to the uproar as they grabbed the last interviews before sailing. Two well-upholstered young ladies sported the latest T-shirts, their ample frontage bearing the slogan: 'Don't cry for me Argentina, we're going to knock the **** out of you.'

The day was Good Friday. The departure had been delayed for twenty-four hours while work to add two flight decks for helicopters and fittings for refuelling at sea was hastily begun aboard the liner. Until late in the afternoon on Maundy Thursday, the troops from 42 and 40 Royal Marine Commando and 3rd Battalion the Parachute Regiment had been boarding. In all there were some 3,000 military personnel aboard, including gunners, Army signallers, RAF technicians and the Royal Naval Party. They seemed like giant snails carrying mountains of equipment on their backs, water-bottles, shovels, pick axes, sleeping-bags and scruffy rolls of foam rubber, their vital under-matting, were slung every whichway across the bergens, or rucksacks. As the men barely managed to make the top of the gangplanks, it was hard to envisage them storming ashore from landing craft in true newsreel style.

In the bustle of getting aboard there was little sense of what was to lie ahead, a journey of 8,000 miles ending with a beach landing by all 2,500 assault troops aboard the *Canberra* six weeks later. As the *Canberra* headed down the Solent late that Good Friday evening, the shores erupted with cheering crowds. A ferry passed ablaze with lights, and again the shouts and cheers exploded across the still water. Aboard the liner there was only the barest thought that we all might be going to a war.

Like most people, I had become involved in this enterprise by accident. From the first, the Falklands crisis seemed some dotty fantasy of history, a bizarre postscript in the chronicle of the Empire in which the Marx brothers appeared to have a hand. Working in the BBC newsroom at Broadcasting House throughout the previous month, the report of the landing of Señor Davidoff's scrap merchants on South Georgia, the raising of the Argentinian flag there, seemed *opera buffa*. The main preoccupation in March 1982 in the foreign news headlines was El Salvador, followed closely by the Middle East and the rebel South Africa cricket tour. With the Falklands it was as if fate, to paraphrase P. G. Wodehouse, had crept up on the editors of Fleet Street and hit them collectively over the head, if not with the lead piping, a large chunk of scrap metal from South Georgia. No one really took the South Atlantic crisis seriously until the week of the Argentinian invasion of the Falklands itself, which happened before dawn on 2 April.

Once this happened, the BBC, like other major news organisations, despatched correspondents and reporters to the points of the compass, rather like the alarums and despatch of forces to defeat the Percy rebels in *Henry IV*. Punta Arenas, Ascension, Montevideo (later to be renamed Monty Video on account of the television crews), were to be staffed with reporters and the sentinels in Buenos Aires redoubled. I was eventually sent to watch the departures of the leading units of the Task Force from Portsmouth, with the vague catch-all instruction to be prepared to go with one of the ships.

On the Monday morning of 5 April the two aircraft carriers, the *Invincible* and the *Hermes*, their decks lined with Sea Harriers and Sea King helicopters, hauled slowly past the old harbour entrance at Portsmouth and turned down the Channel. On the walls of the harbour there were banners and flags, tears and final waves. There was quite obvious apprehension, too, as most of the people with relations aboard the ships knew there could be no hope of a battle without loss of lives and ships. One trawlerman with war service turned to me and said: 'I'm concerned about the men of the Merchant service going down there. I hope they know what to prepare for.'

Those with sons and nephews in the carriers knew how young the crews were, a conspicuous feature of most of the Naval ships' companies throughout the campaign. Many had joined the Navy never expecting to witness shots fired in anger. The day before sailing I spoke to an engine-room rating from HMS *Hermes*, whom I found wrapped in an untidy embrace with his girlfriend beside the dock gates at Portsmouth. I asked him about morale aboard. 'All right I suppose,' he replied. 'It all depends if we get a run ashore tonight. The ship's in a bit of a mess, though. Her main boilers were in pieces until four days ago.'

The day following the departure of the carriers, the assault ship HMS *Fearless* set out. Her sailing had a graceful and balletic quality. Passing through the old harbour, she was followed by her four larger landing craft. Once off the Isle of Wight, the ship lowered herself in the water and, flooding her stern, took in the four craft like a mother hen sheltering chicks under her ample plumage.

The signal for my departure came a few days later. I had been given my light-blue passport as an accredited War Correspondent with a British operational force at the weekend of the first sailings. There was a little green manual of World War Two vintage, carelessly updated for Korea and Suez with helpful suggestions about correct dress (War Correspondents could have shoulder flashes denoting their status in brass or woven lettering according to choice), discipline, and conduct in the field. There were badly stencilled forms in quadruplicate saying I do remember the Official Secrets Act after all, and discharging the Ministry of Defence of responsibility for my life.

I was told that I was assigned to the liner *Canberra*, newly requisitioned as a troopship and making all speed with her complement of cruise passengers from Gibraltar for Southampton. I was told that the BBC was not allowed to get a correspondent onto Ascension Island, so I would be their man with the troops. I accepted this charge with ill grace. I was convinced that the main action would take place with the carrier force, and an amphibious assault would be very much a last resort in the tactical planning of the campaign. I thought there was a good chance that the *Canberra* would go as far as Ascension and wait there for weeks while a diplomatic settlement was achieved with the junta in Argentina. Besides, I felt I had enough to do in the coming summer. First there was the reporting of the Pope's visit to Britain in May and then in June and July I expected to go to Newfoundland and Western Canada on a Churchill Travelling Fellowship.

I was to be proved partly right in this surmise. The *Canberra* did spend weeks at Ascension while laborious negotiations were carried out between Buenos Aires, Washington, New York and London. Once these talks failed, the *Canberra* and her embarked force were to become one of the most important tactical cards in the pack, and by the beginning of June I was to find myself firmly established in the landscape and community most similar to Newfoundland in the Southern Hemisphere – the Falkland Islands.

The journalists were asked to report at the Post House Hotel, which stands next to the gate to the West Dock at Southampton, the day before *Canberra* sailed. There was still some argument about who was accredited to go and who not; and there were last-minute negotiations to get three Sunday paper writers and an ITN television news team signed up.

Captain Christopher 'Beagle' Burne, a tall, spare figure who was to be the Senior Naval Officer aboard *Canberra*, arrived to state what the rules would be. He made it clear that he had better things to occupy the space in the ship which would now be taken up by fourteen journalists foisted upon him at such short notice. He suggested the fourteen of us might best be accommodated in the quarters for the Goanese crew on 'G' deck, well below the waterline and, as I subsequently discovered, liberally infested with cockroaches.

The night before departure most of the journalists, now to be dubbed for ever more the 'hacks', went out for a meal together. In the restaurant we drew up a sweepstake at £5.00 a head for the date on which the crisis would be resolved or the *Canberra* be turned for home. I chose 25 May, which was regarded then as ludicrously pessimistic. Surprisingly, I was to win by many furlongs.

The morning of Good Friday, three of us decided to visit HMS *Victory* at Portsmouth to while away the last hours before sailing. At Portsmouth we saw a Royal Marine advance party going aboard the assault ship HMS *Intrepid*, sister ship to HMS *Fearless*. Two destroyers were being victualled and stored ready to swell the Task Force. Max Hastings of the *Standard* and *Daily Express* suggested we have lunch at the village of Alresford in the Hampshire countryside. It was a day of limpid, early spring sunshine. As we followed the sleeping stretches of river, Max said wistfully, thinking of his great love: 'I wonder if there's time to hire a rod for a couple of hours' gentle fly-fishing.' On the car radio we listened to yet another retired admiral on the BBC's 'World at One' programme applying his wit and wisdom from the studio chair to the tactical perils lying ahead of us. After lunch I made a final call to the BBC for a 'two-way' interview with the Radio 4 'PM' programme. I mentioned the preparations of *Intrepid* and the two destroyers at Portsmouth. 'Well, you could say, then, we are seeing a second Task Force, possibly for a Second Front?' said the radio interlocutor. The jargon of the armchair admirals was becoming contagious.

The return to Southampton was a scramble through Bank-holiday traffic. Within hours, *Canberra* was in the Solent, her siren, somewhat inappropriately called 'the ship's whistle', booming into the empty darkness. Below deck the jumble of bodies and equipment resembled the Hall of the Mountain King, and it looked as if it would take weeks to learn the geography of the new kingdom. My fellow radio reporter Kim Sabido of Independent Radio News and I were assigned a shoe-box which was laughingly called Cabin A281, complete with broom cupboard for clothes, gurgling wash-basin and a lavatory and shower which leaked progressively as the journey went on and the crisis deepened. It says something for my room-mate's kindly disposition and forebearance that we quarrelled once only in the entire two-and-a-half month deployment, and that was over the trivia of filing facilities.

The first day at sea brought an iron-grey swell and sky and a sharp wind as the *Canberra* ploughed steadily westward down the Channel. It was time for the first test in her new role as troopship. Helicopters flew out from Cornwall to bring essential stores and take away mail and newsfilm. Several times the Sea King helicopters, looking like huge, angry hornets, hovered above what used to be the liner's main swimming-pool, now sheeted over with steel plates shored up by scaffolding, and renamed the midships flight deck. On the first runs the helicopters did not land on the ship. They lowered the stores and hauled the mailbags in by winch. Landing midships on the *Canberra* was a very tricky operation, as I learnt later from the Royal Navy pilots. The landing area was midway between the bridge superstructure and the main funnel stacks aft and could be hit by sudden gusts of cross-winds. The pilots much preferred to use the forward flight deck, perched somewhat precariously immediately forward of the main bridge structure. Landing on this deck always looked a far more dangerous manoeuvre, but the pilots could predict easily the kinds of winds there. From that Saturday in the Channel on, there must have been thousands of landings by helicopters on those two decks, some under threat of air raids. It is one of the minor miracles of the campaign that there were no accidents at all with aircraft on the liner.

The other important new drill which had to be learnt was replenishing fuel at sea (known as RAS or 'rassing' for short). A Naval tanker came alongside and at a distance of a few hundred feet a line was fired across by rifle and the hoses hauled aboard the liner to be connected to fittings on the promenade deck. The Royal Navy has always taken pride in the precision with which this is carried out. The Ferrymasters' *Elk*, the container ship accompanying the *Canberra* south, was less fortunate than the *Canberra*. She tried first the method of replenishing by picking up fuel from lines trailed astern, which proved a total failure, and eventually she adopted the alongside fuelling method like the *Canberra*. No other luxury liner had ever tried this means of replenishment before and it was successful from the first.

Hardly had the first connections been made with the Royal Fleet Auxiliary tanker *Plumleaf*, than we had our first visitor. A Russian intelligence-gathering vessel, or AGI, of the Primori class appeared over the horizon. Refuelling at sea by NATO ships has an endless fascination for the Russians. At one point their curiosity got the better of them and they passed less than a quarter of a mile down the *Canberra*'s side. On the bridge, men could be seen glued to binoculars and cameras with telephoto lenses. The Russians' attentions from the air and the sea were never to be far away from the *Canberra* until she was well south of Ascension. An AGI intelligence-gathering ship followed the little convoy across the Bay of Biscay and down the coast of Africa. 'Bear' reconnaissance aircraft often flew overhead in the tropical latitudes, despatched probably from Conakry in Guinea Bissau, or even Cuba.

The mood on Easter Sunday was subdued. At the church service in the ship's cinema only passing reference was made to the conflict with Argentina. Afterwards the ship's captain, Dennis Scott-Masson, spoke to the journalists in a brief press conference. It was a strained affair. The captain, known to his crew as 'the Squire', appeared a shy man, probably more ill-at-ease with the press than any of the senior men in the *Canberra*.

He explained that he was still responsible for the ship's discipline and received orders from the Ministry of Defence through the senior Navy man, Captain Burne. He said it was his job to get his ship home safely and would not hazard her unnecessarily. He demurred at the suggestion that two-and-a-half thousand paratroopers and marines doing physical training and assault drills day after day would do permanent damage to the liner's structure and decking.

The abiding impression of that first week at sea was the tattoo of hundreds of feet pounding mile after mile round the promenade deck. Men swung like monkeys from available bulkhead and beam. As the sun became hotter as the ship approached Africa, the paratroopers broiled as they trained with wooden beams on the decks, rolling them and raising them from shoulder to shoulder in teams of fifteen men. 'Pick up the log,' became the cry heard all over the ship, and the men shouted back in chorus, 'Pick up the log,' mimicking the local accent of the Physical Training Instructor of the moment – Geordie, Scots, Liverpool, Midlands or West Country.

Physical fitness was almost a fetish with the troops. Even the commanding officers turned out and ground out the miles round the promenade deck with the men. The general standard of fitness in the rifle companies of the paras and the Marine Commandos appeared to put that of the average First Division football team to shame. Some of the workouts seemed excessive, judging by the number of serious ankle and shoulder sprains the physiotherapists had to deal with. Down in the sick bay I saw something I never expected to see in my life – shoulders and legs literally locked by muscle fatigue. The fitness cult was infectious. A group of the hacks quickly joined in with one of the gentler sessions for a Commando HQ Company. It was clear some preparation was called for if we were to go ashore with the amphibious forces. By the time the landings took place, only four of the hacks had resisted the temptation even to go for a run.

As the *Canberra* nosed towards the sunshine, relations became more cordial between the different elements of the embarked company. The main gathering-point for the officers was the Crow's Nest Bar, with a splendid vista over the ship's bows and foc'sle. The bar was the realm of its two veteran waiters, Taffy and Geoffrey, men of a certain sensibility and a waspish turn of phrase, an argot which was a mixture of Larry Grayson and Dick Emery. Quite early on I was buttonholed at the bar by Major Martin Osborne, who commanded 'C' company of 3 Para.

'I was a journalist once,' was the opening shot of the jolly, red-faced major, 'and I'll tell you why I gave up. You are vultures and live off people's misery. I think your way of life is dreadful.'

From such an inauspicious beginning began one of the lasting friendships I made with the men of the Falklands expedition. Martin Osborne had worked for some years on the *Leicester Mercury*, doing a bit of weekend soldiering with the Territorials. When the opportunity came, he decided to go for a regular commission. Despite his oft-vented scorn for the press, he was fascinated by it, and probably had a better idea of how a sensible press policy should have been run for the entire campaign than the Ministry of Defence Press Department and the Royal Navy put together.

From the outset, the information and press policy was chaotic. It appeared to come from at least four different sources at once. The instruments for imparting each change of rules to the hacks themselves were the unfortunate MOD press officers, known as 'the brain police' or 'the minders'. Their job was to act as censors and to supervise the means of transmitting broadcasts and copy. This was done through the Maritime Satellite, or Marisat, which was linked to a telephone and telex. Part of the difficulty was that the minders had received no training in censorship, and, though ex-journalists themselves, had little idea of how newspaper and broadcasting reporters worked on big running stories. As the senior officers came quickly to recognise, the minders enjoyed the confidence of neither the military forces embarked nor the press. Individually they were to be kindly, helpful, indifferent, childishly tyrannical and irrelevant by turn. My criticism is not aimed so much at the individuals, as they were victims of circumstance, but at the system or lack of system in the policy that put them there. The four different sources generating their own rules for the information snakes-and-ladders game were the Ministry of Defence, Fleet (the headquarters of the Royal Navy operations) at Northwood, the Task Force Commander, Rear Admiral Sandy Woodward, and the Senior Naval Officer of *Canberra*, Captain Burne. One day we were allowed to name individual ships and the state of the weather at sea, the next we were not. One afternoon I was allowed to mention the frigate HMS *Antelope* by name, but two hours later my colleague Kim Sabido of IRN was not. A confidential message sent to the press officers aboard by C-in-C Fleet in mid-April, which I was shown, could not have been written better by Humpty Dumpty in *Alice Through the Looking Glass*. It said that speculation about future movements, reports about deployment, tactics, training and equipment were forbidden. No mention of equipment defects or capabilities should be allowed. It then stated grandly: 'It is important that all correspondents on board should continue to feel free to file their stories and material. We rely on public opinion in UK being kept informed but it is also vital that nothing is published which puts at risk lives or success of operation. ... Commanding officers should ensure ... that all correspondents ... are reminded of the need for responsible reporting. ... Speculation by correspondents aboard about operational plans is very dangerous since it will seem more authoritative.' The injunction to be free to report, but nothing of much news value, became like Henry Ford's offer to allow his customers a car of any colour provided it was a shade of black. The restrictions aboard became increasingly irritating in view of the wide range of discussion and speculation being invited and encouraged by the Ministry of Defence itself in London.

Captain Christopher Burne came to take his press responsibilities almost too literally. He had a small day cabin beside the chartroom on the bridge, where the Marisat receiver was located. Often as a report was being filed to London by phone, he would spring out of his cabin like a jack-in-the-box to add his observations and criticisms. 'Beagle' Burne was a figure of marked eccentricity, a trait he did not attempt to disguise. The nickname 'Beagle' came from his renown as a distance runner and his organisation of the beagle pack when he was an instructor at Dartmouth. It could also have stemmed from the rather doleful hang of his jowls. His mannerisms on the bridge were akin to the more frenetic portrayals by John Cleese of Basil Fawlty. So 'Captain Fawlty', he became to the hacks, and to many of the senior officers aboard, so much so that the BBC World Service inadvertently referred to him once as Captain Basil Burne and on another occasion as plain Captain Basil. He was a very widely read man, much given to quoting Von Clausewitz and hugely enjoying throughout the voyage Norman F. Dixon's *On the Psychology of Military Incompetence.* Though at first confusing in the abruptness with which he put new limits on the press, he was a kindly man, evidently a first-class seaman, and in combat proved a cool and courageous commander, winning the devotion of the entire ship's company.

Captain Burne articulated most clearly of all the senior Naval men in the Task Force the Royal Navy's profound distrust of the press. In this, the Navy was very different from the Army. Many senior officers in the Navy have felt that the Americans had lost in Vietnam because of the continuous sniping by the liberal press in the United States. This should not be allowed to happen in Britain, ran their argument, not realising anyway that while in America there is the Freedom of Information Act, Britain has the Official Secrets Act.

If the Navy found it hard to take the hacks into its confidence, the Royal Marines and the Paratroops, with a history of dealing closely with the press and television in Northern Ireland, did not.

The commandos and the paras organised special visits or miniature 'open days' to see their training. They demonstrated the panoply of infantry equipment from Milan anti-tank missiles to General Purpose Machine-Guns, Laser rangefinders, mortars, '66 and '84 shoulder-launched rockets, and the Wombat anti-tank gun normally used only by 3 Para, but never taken ashore because of lack of helicopter facilities to lift them. Much of the practice was simulated. One group of marines used a toy tank with a huge paper blue-and-white Argentinian flag shoved in its turret for the Milan simulator, to give a touch of realism. But whatever else the Milans were used against in the Falklands, not one was fired in anger against an Argentinian military vehicle. Much of the time was spent on rifle drill, so the rifleman could strip, maintain and load his weapon as a routine, almost without thinking. One young lieutenant, Chris Whiteley of 42 Commando, told me that sometimes stripping and cleaning his rifle could take up to half an hour as he would have to think his way through every step of the procedure: the same job would take one of his men ten minutes or less, working by reflex.

At the end of the exercise the hacks were invited to take part in stripping and loading the rifle. In the glorious sunshine we all banged away with target ammunition at a steady flotilla of paper sacks dropped from the stern. Max Hastings advanced to the firing position with a gleam in his eye as if the Glorious Twelfth had come four months early. His grouse may safely graze; he only hit two sacks.

The star of the press visits to the units was Corporal Jeremy Phillips of 3 Para's Patrol Company. He was a sniper, trained to work in two- or four-man patrols. He was a quiet man, an obvious loner, and looked like an orang-utang in his extra-ordinary garb consisting of a festoon of hessian strips hanging from his camouflage tunic and helmet. His main weapon was a heavy-barrelled L42 rifle based on the old Lee Enfield, the barrel specially balanced and the sights adjusted to each sniper's requirements. Corporal Phillips said he liked a quiet life and did not care for shooting as a sport either in target competitions or for game.

'My job is to go out ahead of the main units to get informa-tion – sometimes staying out for up to four days in the wild. I would also pick prestige targets – a man with a map or an officer, who you can usually tell by his binoculars. Part of the job is to demoralise, so I'd get them when they were going to eat or shoot them when they're on the toilet: that tends to get them down a good bit.'

During the Falklands campaign the specialist forces like the SAS, the Special Boat Squadron and the Mountain and Arctic Warfare Cadre won a good deal of glamour and fame. But each of the main infantry units had their own snipers and reconnaissance groups who did a large share of the basic intelligence-gathering, for which they got little public credit. Jeremy Phillips was to be badly injured in the arm and shoulder on Mount Longdon in the bitterest battle of the campaign.

The commanding officers of the ground units showed themselves more than adept at tuning the press. Each wanted their battalion or commando recognised in print and on television, not only for vanity but as a boost to the morale of the families at home. Lieutenant-Colonel Hew Pike of 3rd Battalion the Parachute Regiment went a step further. He used the occasion of the press tour to make a public plea for the restoration of the old 16th Parachute Brigade, a parallel formation of assault troops to the 3rd Commando Brigade in which his battalion was serving for the Falklands Campaign. We were forbidden to print or broadcast his remarks. 'Hew Pike is being politically naive,' was the judgment of the head minder from the MOD, Martin Helm, in one of his quirkier decisions.

The arbitrator in such matters was Colonel Tom Seccombe OBE, Royal Marines. As the Military Force Commander he was the man directly responsible for all the embarked troops in the *Canberra*. He played opposite Captain Burne on the military side, and they made an unlikely couple. Known affectionately as 'Uncle Tom', Colonel Seccombe had dealt frequently with the press throughout his military career, particularly in Northern Ireland where he had won the OBE. He broke up a nasty riot among Loyalist prisoners in the Crumlin Road jail by leading a patrol of Marines wielding pick handles. In his Cyprus service he had to deal with Nicos Samson, then a dubious Eoka informant and later puppet president of the Greek officers for three weeks in 1974. Colonel Tom's company was a source of delight for reasons quite apart from his fund of military anecdotes. I have rarely come across anyone with such a comprehensive knowledge of the classics of light English literature. He could quote Evelyn Waugh and P. G.

Wodehouse by the yard. I once asked him about the difficulties of his job aboard *Canberra* and he replied with Bertie Wooster's reaction to one of his Aunt Agatha's nastier phone calls: 'It's a bit like being hit in the small of the back by the 4.45 from Paddington.'

One of his favourite sources for quotation was Evelyn Waugh's *Sword of Honour* trilogy, and much of the atmosphere aboard the *Canberra* was like the world of Brigadier Ritchie-Hook's Halberdiers in *Men at Arms*. Waugh himself was a Royal Marines Captain and the Halberdiers thinly-disguised marines. As the *Canberra* sailed past Dakar we drank a silent toast to Ritchie-Hook's ill-fated expedition, though no one in the *Canberra* seemed to be talking much of 'biffing' Argies in the way that Waugh's brigadier spoke of 'biffing' his enemy.

Slipping down the African coast, the *Canberra* put into Freetown in Sierra Leone for refuelling ten days after leaving Southampton. It was a sticky, overcast day. A couple of nubile English girls, inexpertly escorted by their father, had come down to the refuelling jetty to wave to the troops. No one was allowed ashore except the party carrying mail and the dockyard workers from the shipbuilders Vosper Thorneycroft, who had by now completed the forward flight deck. They had rivetted and welded through the rain storms and choppy seas of Biscay and beyond, and with their departure *Canberra*'s metamorphosis was complete. On the side of the liner away from the jetty the troops were doing a roaring trade with the bumboats. Knives, skins and spears were traded with the slender figures in the hollowed-out tree trunks serving for canoes; the currency was empty polythene water and chemical containers. Some of the superior canoes offered monkeys and parrots. But the barter was brought to an end on the order of the medical staff. They said the skins carried a risk of anthrax and rabies. As the attentions of the frustrated traders became more persistent, the water-hoses were turned on them from the liner.

The day after leaving Freetown, the second Sunday of the voyage, the *Canberra* was ploughing through heaving, oily, equatorial seas. The clouds seemed to fall apart under the weight of their moisture, great ragged lumps in a livid sky. Spirits sank under the heavy atmosphere, and this was one of the most depressing moments in the whole enterprise. No one seemed to know what the *Canberra* and her forces were intended for. The political news on the World Service of the BBC seemed as confused as ever. In the steam and sweat of that day, most men stayed in their cabins, and the inter-unit sports contest had to be cancelled because of the weather.

By the evening the gloom had lifted. Against a tropical sunset the Royal Marines band beat retreat on the midships flight deck. There were the regimental marches and much ruling Britannia again and 'Pomp and Circumstance'. It was after one of these performances that a senior marines officer turned and said to me jokingly: 'I think dying for Queen and Country is rather a different proposition from dying for Mrs Thatcher.'

The man most cautious about what lay in store among the *Canberra*'s own company was the purser, Maurice Rudderham. He confessed to being utterly shocked when he was told that the ship was to be requisitioned for the Task Force. At fifty-seven he was probably the most decorated officer aboard. On 10 June 1943 he had been torpedoed in the hospital ship *Talamba* off Sicily. 'I gave up being a hero in 1945,' he told me, 'and I never thought I would go to war again.' He had served with P and O troopships well into the 1950s, experience which had stood him in good stead for the victualling of the *Canberra*. Much of the P and O fare had been taken off the ship at Southampton. Catering was worked out with the MOD and the NAAFI, who even suggested the numbers of Mars bars the ship needed to stock up with. This is the staple for the soldiers' survival in the field. After a week at sea, Maurice's audit revealed that consumption of canned beer had gone up from 2,500 on a cruise voyage to 6,000 a day, but in almost everything else consumption was down. The troops ate less and wasted less. They used far more water for showers and laundry than cruise passengers, however. The purser said this was the main difference from his memories of the old war-time troopships. 'The blokes this time are cleaner and brighter. The

abiding memory of those old ships was the stench of stale
sweat on the foot decks.'

The change of appearance in the ship was none too appeal-
ing to the P and O officers; for them the princess had meta-
morphosed into a frog. The main decor in the Crow's Nest Bar
was now a pergola of scaffolding holding up the forward flight
deck. In the gloom of the lower decks, mortar troops practised
crawling with their weapons and kit on their backs like
creatures of the night. In the Bonito Room, where former
World Ballroom Champions Syd Perkin and Edna Duffield
ran the Fox Trot Social and escorted the cruise-line clientele
through the basics of Samba, Cha Cha Cha and Jive, the
medical team were preparing a casualty reception area. In the
Stadium Room they had set up a four-table operating theatre,
with recuperation facilities of more than forty beds in one of
the adjoining open spaces. Where the grannies once would join
the P and O hostess to 'stroll a mile with a smile' round the
promenade deck, troops were running like whirlwinds six
miles at a time, often wearing boots and light kit. Despite
official denials, the deck was beginning to break up.

Of all the groups aboard the *Canberra*, the medical team
stood apart. They often gave the appearance of considering
themselves an elite. Some doctors seemed more militarist than
the rest of the military personnel, and particularly prickly in
dealing with the press. Part of the trouble seemed to be their
uncertainty about their role in the event of combat. Would
they go ashore, or stay in the *Canberra*? If they stayed, would
the *Canberra* be close enough inshore to be of real assistance?
And besides, was not the *Uganda* now the main hospital ship
for recuperation? The Executive Officer of the medics was
Surgeon Commander Rick Jolly, who had the jaw-line and
outlook of comic-strip space hero of the 'fifties like Dan Dare.
He had already left the Navy once, had a stab at writing a
novel, was mad about helicopter flying and talked endlessly
about his four-month tour in Northern Ireland. He seemed a
restless soul, looking for one true role in life: and he found that
role at San Carlos when he got most of his team ashore to the
field hospital at Ajax Bay where the Navy and the Army

surgical teams worked tirelessly from an old mutton refrigeration plant throughout the fighting. The most remarkable figure of the medical team was the psychiatrist, Dr Morgan O'Connell, an Irishman from Connemara. He knew exactly what lay ahead. 'Psychiatric casualties will out-number the physically wounded by five to one,' he told us early on, 'and the most vulnerable group is the press. You are all individuals, and work against each other, so you cannot support yourselves as a team.' Could he also have been talking about the medics?

Quite early on in the voyage, Dr O'Connell was called to the bridge to be consulted about the worrying mental state of one of the yeoman signallers. It was arranged that the yeoman should be asked by Captain Burne to take a file to the psychiatrist's cabin, so they could have a chat. A few hours later a clearly worried doctor returned to the bridge to report the patient in a dreadful mental condition and suggest that he be sent home immediately. Captain Burne later summoned the yeoman and opened with: 'I gather you have had a long chat with Dr O'Connell.' To which the unexpected rejoinder came, 'Oh no, sir, that wasn't me. I sent my mate. I was too busy to take the file myself.'

The most popular adjunct to the medics was the band, whose members were meant to act as stretcher-bearers. They were trained in decontamination techniques for chemical and nuclear warfare, they told us proudly. Their true role was psychological, in which they were universally welcome. Like all military bandsmen they were remarkably versatile musicians. Many sported crew-cuts and dark glasses which portrayed a pedigree back to the Glen Miller era, or Buddy Holly at least. The most surreal sight of the whole voyage was on the first Sunday when I saw a bandsman with a violin under his arm creep into a deserted ladies lavatory on the stadium deck, and soon the steady scrapings of arpeggios and scales came drifting from the fanlight. Since there were now only a dozen women crew aboard – officers, secretaries and cabin staff – the ladies lavatories were rather underemployed and bandsman Andy Clarkson had found the ideal practice room. 'I love the violin,' he said, 'I'm not much good at it yet. I've been with the band ten years and I'm proud of it.'

But the band, like several other elements of the Task Force, had been put under sentence in the 1981 Defence Review. Colonel Tom Seccombe remarked publicly that this was a pity, but again this remark was considered politically inopportune by the minders.

By the second week at sea, the paras and the marines had learnt to live with the press, if not love them. They even began to play jokes on them, which had near disastrous results. In one visit to a tactical instruction period, the sergeant instructor, spotting the arrival of the reporters out of the corner of his eye, started asking his group about the treatment of prisoners.

'What do we do to prisoners?' he asked.

'Kill them if there are no press and television around.'

'And if there are press?'

'Treat them like brothers,' came the rehearsed reply. Unfortunately this story was relayed at second hand to a reporter from the *Daily Express* who was not even aboard at the time. So on 2 July there was an 'exclusive revelation' in that paper that paratroop sergeants instructed their men to kill prisoners. Milder were the planted stories of the killer leopard seals on the Falklands which bit unwary humans and decoyed them into enormous pits filled with their dung.

After ten days at sea, the new company of the *Canberra* was thoroughly shaken down and worked in together. But the air of unreality persisted. On a brilliant clear morning the 42,000-ton liner dropped anchor off Ascension. The huge red pile of volcanic dust was to be the backdrop for a fortnight to come. In the anchorage lay supply ships and HMS *Fearless*, from which the amphibious assault on the Falklands would be commanded and controlled. Aboard the *Canberra* at least one of the unit commanders, Lieutenant-Colonel Malcolm Hunt of 40 Commando, was still privately advising his officers that if there was to be a landing on the Falklands at all, it was more than likely to be 'for administrative purposes only'.

2. Ascension

The great volcanic heap called Ascension was to have a strange allure in the two and a half weeks that the *Canberra* was there. At times the liner was anchored within a mile of the shore, but civilians, and particularly the hacks, were forbidden to land. Soon the pile of red soil and rock, topped with its fringe of greenery, the home of its miniature farm, began to mesmerise like Tantalus's grapes.

When *Canberra* arrived, most of the amphibious force was already there, with the *Fearless* surrounded by the five LSLs (Landing Support Logistic ships) named after the Arthurian knights. The sixth, *Sir Bedivere*, was making all steam from the West Indies, we were told. These ships are not graced with the most beautiful lines. They have a high stern with a ramp, bows that can open sideways and a fat bottom; an incongruous profile now made famous by the images of the bombing of two of them, *Sir Galahad* and *Sir Tristram*, at Fitzroy Cove. The flat bottoms made them 'roll like an elephant on wet grass', according to the marines, and the commandos had a particularly uncomfortable ride south in them.

The LSLs and the supply ships like *Stromness* and *Fort Austin* had been loaded in haste, and their cargoes had to be reorganised at Ascension. The skies would buzz with helicopters, with nine or ten hovering above the ships at a time and then hauling like aerial tractors across the skies with cargo nets swaying beneath them. Within three days of *Canberra*'s dropping anchor there was a sudden frenzy of activity as ammunition was transferred or 'cross-decked'. To add to the perils of leaking wash-basin and lavatory in cabin A281 on the liner, we now had about 70,000 rounds of 7.62 mm rifle and machine-gun ammunition stacked on the deck immediately above. Next to the ammunition were Milan missiles, grenades and rocket-launchers, and mortar bombs. With the panic of reloading and switching stores between the ships came the rumour that we were to proceed south at top speed to join the carrier group which was approaching the Exclusion Zone round the Falklands. I wrote my first news despatch about departing Ascension. I have it still: it is dated 22 April. I was to write at least two more about leaving Ascension over the next fortnight and was not permitted to send any of them. We were never allowed to mention Ascension by name, though everyone clearly knew where the *Canberra* was.

The absurdities over the restrictions in reporting this came quickly to strike Captain Burne. He tried to get Fleet in Northwood to rescind the order, pointing out that it would be better to take the hacks into their confidence, and if they broke this they could still be despatched home by plane from the island, which one of our number was, on medical grounds. Captain Burne's pleas on our behalf, on a secure telephone line from the American Wide Awake Base on the island (nicknamed somewhat predictably by the RAF, 'Fast Asleep Base'), merely brought further restrictions on reporting, and in one signal Fleet suggested that some of us might elect to return home for all the detailed reporting we would be allowed to get through henceforth.

Captain Burne, with his natural sense of courtesy, did take the trouble to explain unofficially what he saw the difficulty to be. It was simply that any assistance the Falklands Task Force was getting from the Americans should not be made public. Technically, Alexander Haig was claiming still to play the honest broker between two friendly powers to America. Though Ascension is a British possession, the airstrip and its facilities are leased to the United States. From the first this had been made fully available to Britain. But what else could be there on the island, we wondered? A nuclear stock-pile, a squadron of Panavia Tornados or Phantoms? What secret piece of surveillance equipment was among the domes and aerials which topped every ridge like the strange vegetation of the Lost Planet in a science-fiction serial? The answer to the mystery was before our very eyes, like the emperor's clothes.

As *Canberra* circled the island on her frequent shifts of anchorage, the airstrip could be seen plainly through binoculars from her decks. We could count the number of Victor in-flight refuelling tankers, the lines of GR3 (ground attack) Harriers, the odd Vulcan bomber, the Hercules and VC 10 transports and the Nimrod anti-submarine patrol aircraft. As Alistair MacQueen of the *Daily Mirror* pithily remarked: 'Well, if they wanted us to start writing stuff about "The Mysteries of Spy Island", they couldn't have gone about it better.'

The day after arriving off Ascension we were summoned to HMS *Fearless* for the first briefing on the plans for an amphibious landing on the Falklands. Below decks the *Fearless* seemed at once grander, more warlike and strangely more dainty than the *Canberra*. Her cabins were more cramped yet proclaimed the ancestry of the ship's name well back into the eighteenth century in pictures and prints from every wall. We were served coffee from china that might have been more in place in a home counties' tea party. The briefing was led by Commodore Michael Clapp, RN, Commodore Amphibious Warfare, whose flag flew in *Fearless*, and Brigadier Julian Thompson, commander of 3 Commando Brigade, who kept mostly silent throughout the presentation.

Commodore Clapp was a large man with a big face and sunny manner. Just turned fifty, he had been with the Navy in Korea and spent much of his service with helicopters. He had come to amphibious warfare rather late in life. As a branch of the services, it has given recently a somewhat run-down appearance. Both the *Fearless* and the *Intrepid* were due to be sold under the Conservatives' Defence Review initially put forward by John Nott. It was rumoured in the Task Force that *Intrepid* had been, or was about to be, sold to Chile, and that the Argentinians themselves had expressed an interest in buying HMS *Fearless*. It was also said that the disposal of these two key ships and the plan to get rid of the Antarctic Survey Ship HMS *Endurance* may have helped to tempt the Argentinian junta into attacking the Falklands, as the reduction of amphibious capability by the Navy suggested that Britain would hardly be in the mood to retaliate.

Commodore Clapp gave a short assessment of the strengths of the Argentinian position in mid-April. He explained that their two German-built short-range submarines were not to be underestimated. Indeed, they were to be a worry throughout the campaign, though they appear to have made only one serious attempt to attack the Task Force. In the jargon of sub-mariners and underwater warfare experts, sonar devices have low efficiency in the seas round the Falklands and Cape Horn because these are 'sonically confused' waters. There are so many different temperature layers in the ocean and the tur-bulence from storms is so great that it is hard to establish a clear pattern of signals for detection. The air threat was also emphasised, and for the first time the Pucara piston-engined counter-insurgency aircraft was commented upon. It was thought that up to seventy could be deployed for hitting troops on the ground in the Falklands. No mention was made of the threat of Exocet missiles launched from Super Etendard aircraft, though the deployment of Exocets on the surface ships, particularly the British-designed destroyers Type 42, *Hercules* and *Santissima Trinidad*, was well understood. Details of how the Argentinian ground forces were faring were sketchy. It was thought that they could not get vehicles across the island and that the water supply had broken down in Port Stanley, causing a spread of disease. This was almost certainly not true, as the Argentinians never appeared to have trouble with water throughout the campaign. Many of their soldiers drank water from pools and streams in the hills, which the British were warned against for fear of the liver fluke which infested the sheep throughout the islands.

The main tactical conundrum was air superiority, and much would depend on the Sea Harrier as an interceptor, very much an unknown quantity at this point. It was stated firmly at the beginning that no beach landing could be contemplated with-out 'local air superiority, at least'. The concept of air superior-ity was reduced first to 'air parity', and then the idea of a 'CAP' (Combat Air Patrol) provided by Harrier patrols over the Task Force was adopted. This is an old Second World War idea where patrols of aircraft keep the skies clear above the ships themselves. In the event, while the Sea Harriers could keep the carrier group covered for long periods, they could offer no permanent shield over East Falkland because the planes had such a limited range. The need for frequent refuelling meant that Harriers could patrol over the islands themselves for ten minutes at most. The Harriers could only hope to get at Argentinian planes after they had made their raids, and the British ground forces would have to rely on air-defence missiles such as Rapier and Blowpipe as their first line of protection against air attack.

The question of air cover, or lack of it, would dictate the timing of any landing on the Falklands themselves. Commodore Clapp revealed that they were looking at eight possible places for a beach landing. Already by mid-April, I learnt later, one option had been ruled out. This was to land the bulk of the forces of 3 Commando Brigade on South Georgia and carry out a series of raids and attacks on the Falklands group of islands, building up to a full amphibious operation which might involve an additional brigade, the 5th Infantry Brigade under Brigadier Tony Wilson, which was already exercising with three battalions in Wales. But it became apparent that South Georgia was too far away, eight hundred miles off East Falkland, and well beyond the range of the Harriers; the weather at this time of the year was at its worst, with snow, sleet, winds with a chill factor of $-20\,^{\circ}\mathrm{C}$ and below, and frequent 'white-outs' where blinding snow would reduce visibility to nothing.

The landing-sites that were now being looked at closely were, apart from Port Stanley itself, Berkeley Sound from which a position on Mount Longdon, Mount Kent and Two Sisters would be established on the heights looking eastward into the capital, Port Salvador and San Carlos Water, all in the northern part of East Falkland. Port Salvador Water was ruled out because of the narrowness of the mouth of the inlet, which was prey to bad weather in winter. Both Berkeley Sound and Port Stanley were discarded because of the high loss of life they would almost certainly bring. The idea of a direct assault on Stanley from the east and the south was rejected by the Cabinet because of the risk to civilians in the town itself. Commodore Clapp and his staff made it plain that the Prime Minister would take all the final decisions and that she was maintaining great personal interest in the detailed planning of the landings. 'Her directives are that we are not in the game just for the sake of killing Argentinians. We want a minimum loss of life.'

There were three more possible landing-sites on East Falkland, at Fitzroy on the southern route to Stanley, and at Goose Green and Darwin where it might be possible to use the grass airstrip. Strangest of all was the suggestion of landing somewhere on the peninsula south of the Darwin Isthmus, called Lafonia. Lafonia is a landscape of miles of flat boggy grassland, with hardly any cover and well observed from the snowy mountains across the narrow strip of water (Choiseul Sound) to the north. Not only would forces on the ground be exposed to driving winds and rain, but they could have been spotted from miles away. The Argentinians had several observation posts well hidden in the upland snows of Mount Usborne which looks directly on Darwin, Goose Green and the rolling plain to the south of them, and they were effective throughout the campaign.

Two more possibilities were looked at for landing on West Falkland. One was to take Port Howard or Fox Bay in the sheltered waters of Falkland Sound, which runs between the two main islands. Both places would afford a safe anchorage and some jetty facilities and the Argentinians were expected to be there in battalion strength – about 600 men – at most. The other choice was to land on the west side of the island, as far away from the main concentration of Argentinian troops, which was in Port Stanley, as possible. The idea would be to tempt the enemy to come out to attack and wear them down by attrition. But a bridgehead on West Falkland would be closest to aircraft coming from the Argentinian mainland, and the whole campaign might degenerate into two forces watching each other from the furthest extremities of the islands. Eventually any British force would have to retake Port Stanley, and if they had to move from the westernmost point of the islands, bad weather and extended lines of communication might make it a second Siege of Sebastopol.

The landing operation was ultimately the responsibility of the Navy, through the Task Force commander, Rear Admiral Woodward, and Commander-in-Chief Fleet at Northwood, Sir John Fieldhouse. The Navy saw their responsibility as 'getting the troops ashore, and for them then to get on with the job as quickly as possible'. In organising the landings there appears to have been a good deal of friction between the sailors and the land forces. Admiral Fieldhouse and Major-General Jeremy Moore, Royal Marines, later to become Commander Land Forces Falkland Islands, flew out to HMS *Hermes* at Ascension to begin plans for the landings, and had to spend some time at first trying to resolve the differences between the services. The imperative for the Navy was not to hazard their ships unduly, particularly the two carriers which carried all the air cover the British possessed. This meant a 'deep fleet' policy, keeping the carriers and their escorts well out into the Atlantic, usually to the north and east of the Falklands, thus giving the Harriers little time to cover the ground forces. The caution of the Navy can be the only explanation for the bizarre notion of landing in the peninsula of Lafonia.

Much of the detailed planning of the landing, the assessment of tides and currents, the state of the beaches and the terrain beyond, was done by one of the most extravagant figures in the whole campaign, Major Ewan Southby-Tailyour, Royal Marines. The son of a major-general, he wore his style as a black sheep of the Royal Marine family like a blazon on a medieval escutcheon. He had done two tours with the Royal Marines in the Falklands and knew the islands and the islanders from almost every angle, topographically and socially. His job was running the marine crews of the landing craft based at Poole in Dorset. It is rumoured that when this branch of the Marine Corps was being set up, a briefing diagram of the command structure was drawn up on a blackboard. In charge was to be a Marines captain. However, it is said that at the coffee break in the discussion period the word 'captain' was rubbed out and 'major' put in its place. Southby-Tailyour, who was in the audience, found himself the man with the right rank and qualification.

Ewan's credentials were remarkable. A very keen sailor, he had sailed the 1,500 miles of Falklands coastline in his yacht, *Black Velvet*. He had written a book about the navigation of the Falklands, but the manuscript had been rejected by publishers on the grounds that no one would be interested in the detailed geography and navigation of the Falklands in 1982. Throughout the voyage south, Ewan was getting messages from his wife about yet another publisher wanting to buy the book. His researches, accompanied by some two thousand slides, made him the most diverting travelling circus round the ships of the amphibious force as he lectured with wit and panache about the Falklands and their inhabitants. He was a fund of stories and anecdotes, most told against himself. The clearest image I have is of his mane of white hair appearing round some corridor or bulkhead in the *Canberra* with the invitation, 'I say, come and share a glass of port in my cabin.'

Ewan had to do the full navigation plot for the main landings, working out tides, currents, the weather and the moon from his own knowledge and from information provided by SAS and SBS units put ashore at the end of April. Luckily there were no Southby-Tailyours on the other side.

The choice of San Carlos Water for the landings was a compromise, and it did not please anyone particularly. It meant there would be a long march, across the width of East Falkland, to Port Stanley. 'I knew that we had to end up in Stanley, and some of the plans were like going to London via John O' Groats,' said Brigadier Julian Thompson of 3 Commando Brigade, who was the main architect of the landing itself. The advantages offered by San Carlos, said the Brigadier, were that it was a sheltered anchorage where troops could be put ashore unopposed and at night. The surrounding high ground could be defended by batteries of air-defence missiles, the Rapiers. 'I realised that the Argentinians had been trained in amphibious assaults by the Americans. You know, very much the Iwo Jima approach; down the ramp, a charge up the beach with fighters roaring overhead, plenty of noise and usually in broad daylight. I knew we would have to do it differently.'

The Argentinians did land with a noisy beach assault before dawn on 2 April, going into Moody Brook Marine barracks and blasting the building with phosphorous grenades. They expected a British assault on the beaches around Port Stanley to the end, leaving their best regular infantry unit, the 25th Infantry, guarding the beaches west and south of the capital and never engaging British forces in the entire campaign.

Julian Thompson set out to avoid fighting at the beachhead itself, for military tacticians from the Second World War on have stated that in any opposed amphibious landing, the assault forces must try to have an advantage of three to one, and at least 30 per cent casualties should be expected.

Brigadier Thompson's style of leadership was very different from that of Commodore Clapp. During our initial briefing with them both, the Commodore said: 'Brigadier Thompson always wants to see his commanding officers to consult with them. My commanders in their ships are often well over the horizon, and it does not bother me particularly if I do not see them at all.'

Somebody remarked that one of the peculiar disadvantages of the modern Royal Navy is that it has Nelson in its ancestry, though I seem to recall that Nelson was rather keen on getting his captains round the table to talk tactics. There is still more than a dash of tradition aboard the larger ships like HMS *Fearless*. The day we went aboard to meet the Commodore and the Brigadier we were invited to witness the twenty-one-gun salute for the Queen's birthday fired from antique saluting guns.

If it might be the disadvantage of the Navy to be descended from Nelson, the disadvantage of Brigadier Thompson, according to commanding officers under him, is that he is a Royal Marine. Many people see him a possible future Commandant-General of the Corps, which is quite a small family, but if he had been in the Army he would have the prospect of rising to be Chief of the General or Defence Staff. He is a neat, lean figure, belying his forty-seven years in looks and, like all the senior marine and paratroop officers in the Task Force, extremely fit. He is the model of a modern brigadier, well-read, and something of an intellectual. He is also surprisingly nonchalant about his past achievements and his future in the services. 'I joined the Marines because there were still lots of bits of Empire to see in those days,' he told me, and he has seen service in Cyprus and Aden as well as in Northern Ireland, where he commanded 40 Commando in South Armagh in 1978, and for the first time brought a unit home from that area without a casualty. With his mentor and friend, General Jeremy Moore, he shares an enthusiasm for history. 'If I had to give up and retire tomorrow,' Julian Thompson told me aboard the *Canberra*, 'I would quite happily take up teaching history, but it would have to be at a prep school because I don't have a degree.'

Later, Jeremy Moore summed up Brigadier Thompson's qualities as those of 'a man with a lot of drive, energy; anything but rash; a careful soldier. He inspires immense confidence. In the campaign he set the pattern. His brigade fought the first battle and then planned the development of the campaign in the mountains. He set the pattern throughout.'

By the time the main units of his brigade arrived at Ascension – the three Commandos and 3rd Battalion the Parachute Regiment – Brigadier Thompson was already altering the plan of campaign. With the intelligence assessment that there now might be over twelve thousand Argentinian troops on the Falklands, he realised that another Brigade, the 5th Infantry Brigade made up of 2nd Battalion Scots Guards, 1st Battalion Welsh Guards and the 7th Gurkha Rifles, would be needed to help in taking Port Stanley. Already 2nd Battalion the Parachute Regiment under the command of Lt-Colonel 'H' Jones, was sailing south aboard the Hull–Rotterdam ferry, the MV *Norland*.

Aboard the *Canberra* the training routine continued in a pattern of almost unrelieved tedium. The open decks swamped with tropical sunshine still echoed during the afternoons to the chant of the paratroopers' 'pick up the log'. Training sessions were set aside for sunbathing, or 'getting a bronze' or 'bronzy-ing' in the slang of the embarked force. Both the marines and the paratroopers introduced 'interest sessions' to break up the monotony of physical training, arms drill, weapon training and tactics. Volunteers grunted and roared their way through instruction in unarmed combat, in which the instructors reached virtuoso heights in their arias of command. Lance-Corporal Meekins of 3 Para had a charming way of opening his periods of instruction, including, 'I know four ways to tear off a man's ear, could spoil his whole day.'

WO2 Les Gordon of 40 Commando confessed he was an amateur at this kind of training – boxing is really his sport – but he managed to keep up a torrent of guidance, exhortation and abuse for fifteen minutes with hardly a pause for breath. He summed up the whole art of unarmed combat with his final command: 'You've got to go hard for him, kick him in the bollocks, get him in the goolies, a good kick to the crutch that'll finish him off. It's the man who fights dirty that'll get there first; he's the one who wins.' There was less to this devil-ish counsel than met the ear. Unarmed combat is taught more as a recreation, an adjunct of PT, in both the marines and paras, and it is only done on a voluntary basis. It is a strange mixture of the oriental martial arts, of akido, ju-jitsu and judo, and is aimed at encouraging agility and balance. A soldier should hardly ever need to use such skills. If he needed to fight with his hands at close range, it would mean that his position had been overrun and probably lost.

Once the main task of 'cross-decking' ammunition and stores from the supply ships to the *Canberra* and *Fearless* had been carried out, practice for beach landings began. The main vehicle for this was the large landing craft called LCU (Land-ing Craft Utility), the old-fashioned high-ramped open boat which is part of the World War Two iconography in the photographs of Normandy, Anzio, Sicily and the Pacific land-ings. The LCU accommodates one company, about 120 to 140 men, plus their equipment, mortars, machine-guns and infantry missiles. The paras aptly called these ugly craft 'the rubbish skips', and beach assault training was dubbed 'rubbish skipping'. Embarkation in the rubbish skips, the LCUs from HMS *Fearless*, proved a tricky operation in the swell both off Ascension and in San Carlos Water. What might appear a flat calm from *Canberra*'s bridge would turn out to be a fifteen-foot swell at sea level, and in such conditions no small boats could go ashore at Ascension. Loading a company of assault troops into the landing craft in a big sea would take up to half an hour.

The biggest hazard for troops disembarking from *Canberra* was not the beach landing itself, though this is always risky as troops running off the ramp can be knocked over as the craft is carried forward on the current. *Canberra* had a special obstacle all of her own, known as the galley-port leap. Troops would have to go out through the galley port on 'D' deck aft, which in the swell could mean a few inches or a few yards. Sometimes this was practised at night. Arms and legs were cracked and twisted here daily, and at least three unit commanding officers were victims. This may have been why the *Canberra* was not used to disembark the first wave of units that went ashore at San Carlos on 21 May, though in many respects she proved highly adaptable to her amphibious role.

Day after day the landing craft embarked the marines and paratroops from the *Canberra* and would take them a mile and a half to English Bay near the BBC station on Ascension. This was the only way the journalists, the hacks, could set foot on the island itself, though this was only for an hour or so and to paddle from the beach. The troops would practice getting in and out of the craft, swim, sunbathe and then return to the *Canberra* in various states of undress. A variation was the seven-mile march across the island to Wide Awake Base to be picked up by helicopter. This was made unpleasant by the peculiar local atmosphere of Ascension. The fine volcanic dust always in the air made it particularly difficult to breathe freely under normal conditions, and even more so if you were carrying up to eighty pounds of kit on your back.

In the assault drills there was a good deal of inter-unit rivalry, and the paras took pride in the fact that they could manage the embarkation, galley-port leap and all, quicker than

most of the marines, to whom assault craft drills were supposed to be second nature. The different approach to physical
training between the paratroops and the marines was quite
apparent. The marines were much bigger men, with heavier
muscles, whereas the paras were smaller and lighter. Size is
seen as a disadvantage for a paratroop recruit, and men over six
foot are rare in the Parachute Regiment.

Some of the assault training was carried out by helicopter.
Six Sea Kings would land in succession, three on the forward
flight deck and three midships, to carry a company to the
shore. Each helicopter carried a 'stick' of twenty men at a time.
The men would wait below decks until summoned to their
assault stations. To the notices indicating the sun decks and
games areas were now added the signs 'Assault Route Starboard' and 'Assault Route Port'. Watching each group come
out onto the flight decks to embark in the helicopters, the
collective expression 'stick' seemed particularly apt. Looking
up at the huge white hull from a small boat three hundred
yards off, I once saw the men moving forward, bent double to
avoid the down-draught of the helicopter's rotor and swathed in
camouflage nets, resembling nothing so much as a stick of ants
intent on some aggressive patrol. Embarkation in the helicopters proved remarkably swift. In under ten minutes all six
machines were loaded and would marshall out at sea, about
fifty feet above the waves, and then sweep across the open
water in formation to land at Wide Awake. The possibility of
the landing on the Falklands being carried out by helicopter
had long been ruled out by the time assault training started at
Ascension, but the drills aboard the *Canberra* showed that
reinforcements could be air-lifted quickly ashore from the
liner.

The methods of amphibious warfare being followed at
Ascension appeared very old-fashioned, the rubbish skips
churning slowly to the shore with only Naval guns for cover
seeming years out of date. Julian Thompson's reply to such a
suggestion was, 'Yes, it is very old-fashioned, but we are operating so far from home that these tactics are the only option.
The main difference between today and the Second World

War is the helicopter – and it is a very big difference.'

From early on, Brigadier Thompson took the view that most of the helicopter force would have to be kept for heavy haulage work, shifting guns, Rapier batteries, supplies and ammunition. This was the principal task of the Sea Kings and the Wessex 5s at Ascension. Day after day they droned lazily from ship to shore and back again with nets of ammunition, light field guns and the occasional small tank slung beneath them. Later they were joined by four of the twin-rotor Chinooks, a relatively new acquisition by the RAF, which squatted down on the *Atlantic Conveyor* for the journey south.

The light tanks and the guns had some much-needed shooting practice on the ranges on Ascension. There were eight small tanks, Scimitars and Scorpions, manned by men of the Blues and Royals. They were commanded by two young aristocratic lieutenants, who provided some of the most delightful company aboard the *Canberra*. No one was quite sure what the small tank contingent was supposed to do on the Falklands, and it would not be unfair to say that the two officers were not exactly the happiest warriors with the force. The younger of the two was Lieutenant Lord Robin Innes-Ker, who loudly lamented the ruination of the polo season brought about by the Falkland crisis. 'Not only have I missed the beginning of the season, but the Argentines produce the best riders and ponies.' His companion, Lieutenant the Hon. Mark Coreth, was more concerned about whether a bronze portrait sculpture he had entered for the Royal Academy Summer Exhibition had been accepted than what might lie ahead in the South Atlantic.

The journey south was difficult and uncomfortable for the whole tank contingent. Most of their equipment had been packed away on the freighter *Elk* and it was difficult to organise training and maintenance schedules. It was surprising that this little unit had been given to two such young and inexperienced officers, but according to Robin Innes-Ker no more senior officers were available. Apparently they all had too much to do at Windsor before thinking of going to war.

When the tanks were moved ashore to the Ascension ranges, the Blues and Royals contingent was given a new base aboard

HMS *Fearless*. The two officers left *Canberra* with much regret; they had got on particularly well with the hacks, and of all the officers aboard seemed most adept at talking on any non-military subject. Rather predictably, they were giggled at a great deal by the marines and paras, who saw them as P. G. Wodehouse characters. In the field they belied this image. At the Brigadier's 'O' (Order) Groups they were the most junior officers present. They rarely took a note while earnest unit commanders took down pages of scribbles in their notebooks, but at the end both Mark and Robin could repeat verbatim everything that had been said. The tanks were to prove valuable in the Falklands, and in unexpected ways. Their great advantage was that at no point was their ground pressure heavier than that of a man, which made them ideal for crossing the marshlands of the islands. In conventional infantry warfare they are intended primarily as reconnaissance vehicles, and have high rates of acceleration and a top speed of about eighty miles an hour in good terrain. (Robin Innes-Ker told me that they were once returning from an exercise in Aldershot and taking the motorway back to Windsor. The general was cruising at a gentle 60 mph in the middle lane when he was overtaken by Lord Robin's troop, well exceeding the speed limit. The troop was banned from taking the motorway again.)

The Ascension ranges did provide the Blues and Royals with some light relief. 'We had a terrific time firing away live ammunition,' Mark told me later, 'we were popping off at old petrol lorries which went off with an enormous sheet of flame. The trouble is, unfortunately, we shot a sea bird which got in the way, very sad.' The last I saw of Robin before the Falklands was in the tank deck of HMS *Fearless* where the tanks were jammed together streaked with the all-pervasive dust from Ascension. He said his men were 'customising' the vehicles, adding their own accessories such as stoves and spotlights, which is permitted in war. The crews were trying to sleep draped over the decks of the Scorpions and Scimitars in what appeared in the gloom to be considerable discomfort. I asked Robin how they were getting on, and he gave me the frankest interview on the journey south. 'They are all right, I

suppose. It's a bit cramped and they're pretty bored. I suppose
the thing they miss most is sex. But they're fine as long as
they're fed and watered.' He might have been talking about his
polo ponies.

As Robin and Mark and their men left the *Canberra*, the ship
received new visitors. The most notable was Lt-Col. 'H' Jones
(he was always called 'H' because he hated his Christian name,
Herbert) commanding officer of 2nd Battalion the Parachute
Regiment. He came aboard *Canberra* for about a fortnight,
accompanied by his Battery Commander, Tony Rice, and his
Intelligence Officer, Alan Coulson. They had three of the most
individual faces in the British Army. Alan Coulson had a
lugubrious moustache and a deliberate slow speech with his
Scots accent. In battle he always wore an old tin pudding-basin
type of paratrooper helmet which, with his moustache and sad
eyes, made him look like a melancholy Good Soldier Schweik.
Tony rice had a long nose with a bump in the middle, earning
him the nickname 'Concorde'. Not that 'H' did at all badly as
far as noses went. It was straight and humorous, above a
curling mouth and a ruddy complexion that was a mass of
crinkles.

Of all the officers he was the most outstanding that I met in
the entire campaign. He was something of an oddity, and
aboard *Canberra* seemed to stand apart from the others. He
was clearly a soldier for the love of it, for he had considerable
wealth inherited from his American father, who died when he
was sixteen. Though he never liked mentioning it, he was an
Etonian, and though possessed of a great deal of charm, was
shy and never found small-talk easy. I learnt later that he far
preferred the company of children to the tedium of the social
round of adults, and at dinner parties he would remain almost
tongue-tied. Soldiering was his life and military history his
hobby. I saw him at his most animated locked in argument
with Max Hastings and Colonel Hew Pike of 3 Para about the
latest assessments of the Earl Haig as a commander. The conversation became heated and ranged far and wide. The torrent
of detail was impressive. To add a bit of spice I tossed in the

names of Hannibal and Suvorov, which threw the conversation, but 'H' seemed to like that.

How 'H''s battalion ever came to be despatched to the Falklands was something of a mystery in itself. His family say they were on a skiing holiday when he decided to return to England and lobby for 2 Para to be sent. The battalion was due to leave shortly for a six-month deployment in Belize. 'H' used his considerable powers to change a few minds in the Ministry of Defence, and the battalion was embarked in the Hull–Rotterdam ferry *Norland*, with its guns and equipment in the *Europic Ferry*. Unlike 3 Para, the other parachute battalion in the Task Force, 2 Para had guns and sappers. It appeared one of the best prepared units for the campaign. The way in which 2 Para joined the Falklands Force seemed typical of the flamboyant streak in 'H's' character, and very much in the pattern of his whole career. He started as an officer with Devon and Dorsets and went later to the Parachute Regiment. Apparently when a member of another regiment joins the Paras, hardly anyone talks to him in the mess for the first few weeks. With perfect timing, 'H' arrived at the depot as most officers were looking out of the mess window after lunch, drinking their coffee. The new officer had turned up in a maroon-coloured vintage Bentley, the perfect conversation piece.

The show in 'H''s character was to some extent camouflage. Despite a marked tendency to choler in his nature, he was very reflective and thought out each move for himself and his unit very clearly. 2 Para had a reputation for being stylish and expensive. The Battalion had been at Arnhem in 1944, had missed Korea and Suez, but was involved in bloody and costly skirmishes in the Radfan Hills in the Aden crisis. An eighteen-month deployment in Northern Ireland began with the ambush at Warren Point, the day Earl Mountbatten was killed, in which 2 Para lost sixteen men. In the rest of the tour more died patrolling South Armagh, and shortly after handing over command, 'H''s predecessor, Lt-Col. Colin Thompson, died of cancer. When 'H' took over he told his men that he was going to train them in their principal role, as an infantry battalion. He put them through their paces in full battalion attacks on several exercises. In one in Kenya in late 1981, according to an officer present, they were so bad that they could barely manage company attacks by day or night, and they were considered so dangerously unprepared that they were forbidden from exercising with live ammunition. Many of the junior officers thought their CO was little short of crazy to spend so much time practising such tactics.

'H' was to die at Goose Green leading the first attack by night and day by a single British battalion since the Second World War. It was an outstanding feat of arms.

Another arrival aboard at Ascension was Major Mike Norman with Naval Party 8901, the Royal Marines detachment he had commanded in the Falklands for only four days before the islands were invaded. The marines had surrendered after a considerable fight in Port Stanley in which they shot away 6,500 rounds of small arms ammunition. Mike was a genial bear with one of those well-worn faces that looks as if it is encased in a stocking. He spoke in an accent which he described himself as 'pure Southend'. He confessed to being the intellectual of the family (his brother was a much-promoted and demoted NCO in the Royal Anglians). It says something for his mental equilibrium that he could be back with his men a bare three weeks after the fight in Stanley. His men brought with them a tattered Falklands flag from Government House in Stanley, lifted by a marines officer some years before. Despite the bravura about 'itching to get back and see the old flag flying again' most of the men were disarmingly frank about their return to the islands.

'We were volunteered,' one of them said.

'I suppose they had not got anything else for us to do,' one of the NCOs recalled. 'I was pretty glad when the fighting was over. We knew we didn't have much of a chance, and I wanted to make sure I lived. After all, I have got a wife and two children to think about.'

Mike Norman was to take over the supervision of the press for 3 Commando Brigade. Colonel Seccombe and Captain Burne had become fed up with the squabbles over filing arrangements and the petty rules now being laid down by the MOD information officers, the minders.

Mike was far from enthusiastic about his new role, but he nearly always did it cheerfully. The hacks welcomed someone capable, at last, of correcting errors of technical detail, and Mike enjoyed hugely pointing out the slips of grammar he spotted in the copy of the quality press. His courtesy was extraordinary in view of the amount of work he had to occupy his time beside his responsibilities as 'super-minder'. He was suddenly ordered to work up Naval Party 890I into an extra company for 42 Commando, and this was given the title of 'Juliet' company. In the daytime he had chores like keeping up with his own fitness training and going ashore to zero his rifle on the ranges; his own gun was still in Argentinian hands in Stanley. Mike always looked the same, toothy grin and 'Saarthend' accent, wherever I met him – after the battle at Goose Green, in the hills approaching Stanley and outside Government House hoisting the tattered flag in the pouring rain.

The arrivals and departures in the *Canberra* were matched by a parade of ships coming into the anchorage at Ascension and leaving for the south. There were the grey-hulled supply ships and tankers of the Royal Fleet Auxiliary, and a string of commercial tankers and freighters. The most extravagant in appearance was the *Stena Seaspread*, which looked like a floating fairground coming over the horizon with her array of derricks and helicopter deck perched high above the stern. She is a North Sea maintenance ship with a workshop aboard equipped for servicing oil rigs at sea. The crew had stripped a number of repair shops due to be closed under defence cuts, at Portsmouth dockyard, and put their best lathes and cutters aboard. The *Seaspread* repaired nearly a dozen warships and supply vessels hit during the sea and air attacks, and was one of the most valuable of all the ships taken up from service in the Merchant Fleet. As she moved closer to the Ascension roads, her cranes and hoists looked like the balustrading and iron fretwork of an old Mississippi river boat, and one almost expected to hear a cotton-picking banjo band from her flight deck.

Another outstanding member of the merchant fleet was the

P and O Ferrymasters container ship, the *Elk*, an anonymous roll-on roll-off container ferry normally plying the North Sea. She turned out to have all the buccaneering spirit of Francis Drake. The *Elk* accompanied the *Canberra* south, carrying guns, ammunition and the Blues and Royals' tanks. The 6,500-tonne capacity freighter was in the charge of Captain John Morton, with Commander Andrew Ritchie as his Senior Naval Officer. John Morton had served several times with the Antarctic Survey in South Georgia aboard the *John Briscoe*, and because of his experience in southern waters was chosen to captain the *Elk*. Andrew Ritchie, a tanned, athletic figure with hollow cheeks, whose favourite headgear was a US Navy baseball cap, was going to take over command of the Type 21 frigate HMS *Alacrity*, but she sailed with the Task Force the day before the change of command was due to take place.

Between them, these two generated an extraordinary spirit of enterprise in true *Boy's Own* style. John Morton was a quiet Yorkshireman with a sly sense of humour, Andy Ritchie far more outspoken and extrovert, the *Elk*'s Eric Morecambe to John Morton's Ernie Wise. In the space of a week or so they transformed the appearance of the *Elk* and a great deal of the thinking about the role of the merchant ships in the amphibious force. One of their tasks was to bring ten Bofors anti-aircraft guns south from England to be installed on the LSLs and other ships at Ascension. No sooner had they clapped eyes on the ageing weapons than they requested two for the *Elk*. They were of 1941 and 1942 vintage, and had been discovered at the RAF base at Leuchars in Fife. Fortunately, or perhaps unfortunately in the view of Morton and Ritchie, they were never fired at Argentinian aircraft during the campaign. The other notable acquisition was one of the forbidden parrots at Freetown. They were never sure what sex the bird was, so it was always called Lady Hamilton and/or Lord Nelson. The ambivalent attitude to the Nelsonian tradition seemed an apt reflection of the eccentric spirit of the *Elk*, one of the happiest ships in the entire Task Force.

Commander Ritchie suggested that the Navy should have bought the *Elk* outright for experiments. He said she proved remarkably manoeuvrable compared with many RFA supply ships. This was because of her variable-pitch propellors, which allowed fine adjustments of speed and the use of bow-thrust propellors as an aid to steering. Purchase, he surmised, could probably prove cheaper than hire, judging by the leasing rates paid to P and O.

The most outstanding innovation aboard the *Elk* was her adaptation to take helicopters, and she could house up to three Wessex 5 helicopters under her forward canopy. To make landing easier, several hundred feet of side decking, seven feet high, were taken down. It was estimated that the job would take at least a week. A troop of Royal Engineers was summoned from *Sir Percivale* under a Corporal Pascoe, 'a wizard with a blow torch' according to Andy Ritchie, and the task was done in fourteen hours.

The *Elk*'s command, with all the gusto of appearing to run their own buccaneering merchant venturing operation, submitted list after list of ideas to HMS *Fearless* for further innovations. 'We managed to slip quite a few ideas through,' said John Morton, 'but they turned down the idea of putting a Sea Harrier on the front ramp. We're thinking of applying for the Space Shuttle next. They said we couldn't have the Harrier because its jets in the downthrust position would burn the plates and could set off the ammunition underneath.' With those two you could not be entirely sure that they were joking. Under all the fun and schoolboy larks aboard the *Elk*, there was considerable personal bravery. She was one of the main ammunition carriers of the amphibious force. Often she lay at anchor in broad daylight in San Carlos Water, calmly disgorging tank and artillery shells, mortar and rifle ammunition. An explosion aboard or a direct hit might well have meant every ship at anchor in the inlet being lifted out of the water by the blast.

There was always at least one guard ship for the merchant ships at Ascension. For much of the time *Canberra* was there, this was HMS *Antelope*, a Type 21 frigate, her name fitting to her graceful lines. She first appeared swishing across the bay in a gentle curve to the characteristic high-pitched whine of her

Olympus gas turbines. Each night she would head out to sea on routine anti-submarine patrolling.

I spent an afternoon aboard the *Antelope* as she was practising Naval Gunfire Support, or shore bombardment, with her main Mark 8 4.5-inch gun. The Naval Gunfire branch of the services has been somewhat discredited of late and the Gunfire Support unit was due to be closed in 1982. On the Falklands, shore bombardment was to be particularly successful as a deterrent. One Naval 4.5-inch gun is the equivalent in fire power of one battery of 105 light field guns. The Naval gun can fire further (22 kilometres as against about 17.5) and throw a heavier projectile, though in the Falklands the Navy could never be quite as accurate as land-based artillery.

The *Antelope* ploughed steadily out to sea and aimed at a Dan-buoy target over the horizon, using the reverse bearings from landmarks on shore. Normally the land features, mountains, inlets and promontories on the coast would provide the coordinates for the target to be bombarded, and the bearings would be called by Naval Gunfire Support Forward Observers already ashore. For the purposes of the exercise, the NGSFOs (or Nigsfoes, as they were known) were flying overhead in a Gazelle helicopter. The gunfire teams did much of their work under hazardous conditions. Sometimes they would land in enemy territory to set up their radio links. I was to meet one of these itinerants several times in different parts of East Falkland. Captain Kevin Arnold, Royal Marines, a round-faced officer in his early thirties, always smiling and with a breezy line in banter, his pointed nose seeming to have been fashioned in the same workshop as Pinocchio, spent several hours at Pebble Island and South Georgia on the foreshore guiding the Naval guns while he was directly in the path of fire of the enemy.

The exercise aboard the *Antelope* was a relaxed affair. The range and bearings would be relayed from the helicopter, the command 'Call for Fire' given and then the order 'Fire'. The bridge windscreen would then be filled with a cloud of smoke and the boom of the gun pounded the ear-drums. Sometimes you could sense an almost audible 'click' as the gun misfired or failed to fire while the Weapons Officer muttered about 'that bloody microswitch again'. But all in all the view of the commanding officer, Commander Nicholas Tobin, was that it was 'a good day's shooting, gentlemen'.

The most impressive feature of the ship's company was its youth, with most of the ratings little more than twenty and few of the officers over thirty. The executive officer was a jolly, freckle-faced Lieutenant-Commander, Robert Guy, all dimples and baggy white shorts. He extolled the virtues of the Royal Naval Polo Team, which kept its ponies near my home town of Taunton. I asked him how he considered the skills of my former shipmate Robin Innes-Ker and the team of the Blues and Royals. Clearly he did not consider them, and then proceeded to remonstrate with the oldest serving man aboard, Fleet Chief Petty Officer Ashton, serving as a Marine Engineering Officer, who had a wonderful line in non-stop Yorkshire misanthropy. He complained of his age, his length of service (he had been in the Navy since Suez) and the youth of modern serving officers. Much of his service had been in the Leander-class frigates, and he found the temperamental nature of oil-fired ships and the greater space in the older frigates more congenial. In his control-room he looked as if he was in the cockpit of a modern aircraft. 'Mr' Ashton, as he was always called, was frank about the difficulties he had acclimatising to the Type 21 frigate, but his witticism and music-hall grousing suddenly turned to glowing praise when he was talking about HMS *Antelope* and her company: 'This is one of the best companies I have ever served with, and certainly they are the most cooperative. You know all the ships have had difficulty with fresh water supplies. I have never known a ship's crew to be so conscientious about rationing and conserving water, so thoughtful for each other. They're a very good bunch, and I'll tell them that before we get much further south.'

While we were on the bridge for the gunnery practice, a freighter with a tall superstructure and high derricks was sighted from the west of Ascension. She was the Argentinian transport, *Rio dela Plata*, 10,000 tonnes. Later the *Canberra* raised the alarm and was ordered by HMS *Fearless* to put to sea

immediately. It was known that the Argentinians had taken a
recent interest in miniature underwater warfare equipment
and it was believed that they had purchased the latest two-man
midget submarines from Italy. For the next fortnight the
Canberra was to sail at night and return to anchor during the
day, for fear of a nocturnal attack on her hull. Frogmen were
put into the sea from HMS *Fearless* to check all the ships for
limpet mines. During the day the Argentinian freighter would
appear at regular intervals for a peep at the Ascension arrivals
and departures, and at sea the *Canberra* was pursued during
refuelling operations by yet another Russian Primori-class surveillance ship. Above, there were now the latest Cosmos satellites. Quite what intelligence the Russians were gathering has
never been made plain. Judging by the solemn manner in
which Argentinian ambitions in the South Atlantic, and particularly towards Antarctica, were being denounced by
Moscow, it appears that not much of what the Russians were
discovering was being passed on to Buenos Aires. Nor was
there much evidence that the *Rio dela Plata* was doing anything but watching.

In the middle of one brilliantly sunny morning there was a
sudden stir aboard HMS *Antelope*. Her blue-painted Lynx
helicopter, baptised Norman by the air crew, roared towards
the land only to head out to sea again accompanied by a Royal
Marines Gazelle helicopter. They started dipping and diving
over the sea, giving every indication of a positive contact with a
submerged object. As they were about to attack, they discovered the target to be a metal container a few feet beneath
the waves. The *Elk*'s crew had been throwing empty containers overboard to clear the decks for her new role as heli-
copter-carrier. By drilling holes in the huge metal boxes, they
had hoped that they would sink.

There was much in the anti-submarine and air-raid drills at
Ascension that was play-acting. But on 1 May the make-
believe atmosphere was dispelled for good; after that, no one
had any doubt that the amphibious force would sail south soon
to attempt to retake the Falklands by force of arms.

3. Into the War Zone

I. SOUTH FROM ASCENSION

With her nocturnal sailings to avoid underwater attack in the
Ascension anchorage, *Canberra* appeared to be moving in a
world of her own. It seemed that the liner was looking for her
own southern version of the Bermuda Triangle to disappear
into, and one of the paratroop majors started a whole series of
letters home with the words, 'Arrived at Ascension again this
morning'. The atmosphere aboard was a mixture of the last
days of habitation on the *Mary Celeste* and the 'Good Ship
Lollipop'. There were parties as one unit entertained another
and guests came for the night from other ships in the amphibious fleet. One night Captain Chris Burne found an SAS
colonel lurking between the containers lashed to the sundeck.
Members of the SAS do not wear unit flashes or badges of rank
and 'Beagle' Burne welcomed his distinguished guest with the
words: 'Who the hell are you skulking around on my ship?
And why aren't you dressed properly?'

The visibly shaken SAS man appeared later in the doorway
of Colonel Tom Seccombe's cabin, muttering, 'I have just met
a madman masquerading as a Naval captain.'

One of the greatest challenges in the *Canberra* was to find a
decent cup of coffee. It may have been the coffee beans
shipped in by the NAAFI, or it may have been the hours kept
by the kitchen and waiting staff, but it was almost impossible
to find a warm cup of coffee in mid-morning, and what there
was tasted of sawdust. The solution to this local difficulty lay
in two small offices opposite the main ship's office or the
Bureau as it was called, on the promenade deck. These offices
were the lairs of Helen Hawkett, the Ship's Accountant, and
Lauraine Mulberry, the Senior Assistant Purser. Helen

possessed a coffee percolator, such a prized object that she concealed it in a bag when she went to fill it with water. It provided the best cup of coffee in the South Atlantic. The girls' offices became known as 'the coffee trap', and a strange coterie began to congregate there, with Helen and Lauraine, Martin Osborne, Pat Butler and Adrian Frere of 3 Para being the founders and the membership committee. Pat, Martin and myself came to be called third, fourth and fifth girl, though in what order of precedence we never worked out. The friendships formed in the coffee trap were the most cheerful and lasting of the expedition. To our company was added the presence of Malcolm Chappell, Nigel Horne, the Deputy Purser, and the Executive Officer of *Canberra*, Martin Reed, whose nose looked as if it had been smashed when its owner was swept down a scupper, which is exactly what had happened to cause it to bend it in on itself. The trap was an invaluable source of gossip and minor detail about the ship and what was to happen to her next, and it was well away from the eyes and ears of the three MOD press officers – the minders.

The coffee trap set would also gather of an evening either before or after dinner. Occasionally there would be a 3 Para party in which a lethal mixture called Rocket Fuel would be prepared in an insulated Norwegian food container normally used for Arctic warfare. It contained about two gallons of liquid which could be advocat, gin, brandy, exotic liqueurs and fruit juices. Two mugs of this high-octane fuel sent the drinker into orbit. The other diversion was playing marathon games of scrabble in the Crow's Nest Bar.

After a week or two at Ascension, it was difficult to work out what was going on further South in the Atlantic and on the diplomatic front. Nearly all our information was coming from the BBC World Service, which even 3 Commando Brigade Headquarters in HMS *Fearless* used as its principal source for news of what was going on elsewhere. The lack of communication between the different elements of the Task Force seemed quite surprising by this stage.

On 25 April British forces from the SAS and 'M' Company, a

Royal Marine unit with special Arctic training, which had been detached from the rest of 42 Commando, now in the *Canberra*, recaptured South Georgia. As the SAS had tried to establish themselves ashore, they had encountered terrifying onslaughts from the weather, with winds of up to a hundred knots and 'white-outs' as the snow drove in. Three Wessex 5 helicopters had crashed in trying to fly the SAS patrols off. The final action had started with the sighting of the old Guppy-class submarine, *Santa Fe*, on the surface. A Wasp helicopter hit her with a torpedo, which failed to go off because it was fused to detonate at least twenty to thirty feet beneath the surface. The operation had been conducted from three ships, the destroyer HMS *Antrim*, the Type 12 Rothsay-class frigate HMS *Plymouth* and the Antarctic Survey ship HMS *Endurance*. Once the operation ended with the *Santa Fe* wallowing half-sunk in Grytviken Harbour and with almost no casualties received on land, Guy Sheridan of 'M' Company sent a message to his unit commanding officer, Lt-Col. Nick Vaux of 42 Commando aboard the *Canberra*.

'Our unit flag flies high over Grytviken,' it ran, 'have much to tell you when we rejoin which we look forward to.'

'All ranks from here send congratulations on the outstanding success achieved in most daunting circumstances,' replied Colonel Vaux. 'Did you have the right wax?' (Apparently there had been some argument about the right kind of ski-wax necessary for South Georgian snow conditions.)

The attack on South Georgia had been the subject of speculation in the British press and on the BBC World Service. The fact that two ships had split from Admiral Woodward's force and were racing south had been commented on publicly as the operation began. But the first that the senior military commander aboard the *Canberra*, Tom Seccombe, knew of the recapture of South Georgia was when he was told by John Shirley of the *Sunday Times* that it had been announced on the World Service. His reaction at the way he received the news would be described as 'expletive deleted' in Watergate jargon.

The press conference that subsequently took place in the *Canberra* was pure farce. Colonel Vaux naturally wanted to talk about the role of 42 Commando, as there had been no press reporters with the units that retook Grytviken. This led to endless trouble in terms of rival claims between 'M' Company and the SAS as to who did the lion's share of the work, an example of the irritating and often childish inter-unit rivalry which was to plague the campaign and its aftermath. No sooner had Nick Vaux's press conference been convened, than the minders handed down the Ministry of Defence edict that no sub-units or individuals could be mentioned by name. The colonel gave me an interview in which he detailed the various sporting achievements of both Major Sheridan and his second-in-command in the operation, Chris Nunn, mentioning the various mountains they had climbed in the Himalayas and the ski championships they had won, a mass of information which would have made it quite possible to indentify them by the most cursory glance at a sporting year book. Finally the minders refused any mention of 42 Commando by name. All the main Fleet Street dailies printed names and ranks the following morning, with photographs of Nick Vaux himself, and his displeasure was further incurred by a large photograph of Lt-Col. Tim Donkin, Royal Marines, a rival of both Commando COs in the *Canberra*, standing before a huge map of South Georgia at Fleet Headquarters at Northwood where he had described the Grytviken operation in detail.

The minders' interpretations of censorship were reaching new heights of folly. Each morning they spent nearly an hour on the phone to the Ministry of Defence in London, the Kremlin as one of them called it. According to Ministry policy, we were to preserve the fiction that no one knew where the *Canberra* was, and all mention of Ascension was forbidden. Unwittingly I had been allowed to give the clearest indication of where we were in my report of Naval gunfire practice aboard HMS *Antelope*. On the tape could be heard quite distinctly the landmarks of Ascension being called out – 'Portland, English Bay, Wide Awake' – as the bearings were picked up for the target, and these were allowed through for broadcast without demur.

The news of South Georgia's recapture was met with envy

and some indifference by the troops aboard the *Canberra*. 'They're the lucky bastards,' was the view of one marine sergeant clearly impatient to be on the move, a mood which was beginning to affect the timing of an amphibious assault on the Falklands themselves. With weather conditions worsening to the south, particularly for the members of 45 Commando and the Logistics Regiment aboard the LSLs, there had to be a limit on how long 3 Commando Brigade could be kept at sea in the motley flotilla of the amphibious ships.

The operation to retake East Falkland began on 1 May with the dawn bombing raid by an RAF Vulcan from Ascension followed by Fighter Ground Attack by RAF Harriers GR3s on Stanley airfield. The settlements of Goose Green and Darwin were bombed by Harriers, and Lieutenant Nicholas Taylor, RN, was shot down over Goose Green by anti-aircraft fire on 4 May. He was buried with full military honours in a ceremony of considerable dignity by the Argentinian garrison.

Canberra had been at Ascension for ten days and would be there for a week more. From the Crow's Nest Bar we could see the returning Vulcan and the relays of Victor tankers which had refuelled the bomber ten or eleven times on her round trip. Some of the tankers had to fly out to refuel yet more Victor tankers which were taking station furthest south.

The BBC World Service reported statements from the Ministry of Defence that the Stanley airstrip had been bombed. It was only when some of the hacks were visiting HMS *Fearless* for the landing on 21 May that they saw the air reconnaissance pictures which indicated that only one of the pattern of twenty-one bombs had actually hit the runway. Despite repeated Vulcan raids, the Argentinian pilots, with skill and great courage, managed to use the Stanley airfield till the day their forces surrendered on 14 June. Hercules transport planes continued to land almost nightly, and occasionally fighters and Pucara counter-insurgency aircraft put down there after the British forces had landed on the islands.

News of the first aerial battles round the Falklands was still coming in when it was announced on the World Service that the Argentinian cruiser *General Belgrano* had been torpedoed by a British submarine outside the Total Exclusion Zone. The *Belgrano* was an ancient American cruiser, laid down before the Second World War, but had been modified to carry Exocet missiles. She also carried the heaviest guns of any warship in the conflict, five- and six-inch guns, and these could be a considerable menace in shore bombardment. At first it was reported that she had been torpedoed in the bows and was taking water, and then, three hours later, she sank. Aboard the *Canberra* there was at first some ghoulish 'gung-ho' talk, but when it became apparent that hundreds of lives had been lost, many of our company were appalled. One unit commanding officer said frankly that he thought it a mistake to have sunk the cruiser outside the Total Exclusion Zone, and that Britain should not appear to be bending at her own convenience the rules she herself had laid down.

Later in the week, copies of the *Sun* arrived, and by that time the garish headlines of 'Gotcha' and '1,200 Argentines Dead' received no applause in the *Canberra*. The *Belgrano* was sunk by the nuclear-powered submarine *Conqueror*. Contrary to reports about the new secret 'Tigerfish' torpedoes being used for the first time, the torpedoes were of a type that first went into service in the late 1930s. Much of what led up to the sinking will be kept secret for thirty years, but it is certain that the decision to fire the torpedoes was not taken suddenly and had been referred to the Task Force Commander, Sandy Woodward; and it is now known that Margaret Thatcher and the inner cabinet discussed it at Chequers the Sunday before it happened.

I learnt later that the *Conqueror* had been watching the *Belgrano* and her two destroyer escorts for three days. The cruiser had been skirting the TEZ (Total Exclusion Zone) to the south and several times appeared about to engage the Task Force. In gunnery she had huge fire power and her escorts also had Exocet. At the time she was hit, her group was steaming east and appeared to be making a run at full speed towards the British Force.

At this stage one can only conjecture what kind of threat this posed to Admiral Woodward. Frequently his force was split up into small groups, each with a limited frigate escort. The first weekend in May, the carrier force was engaged in air battles over the Falklands and ground attacks on Stanley and Goose Green. This would mean little cover for the small force on South Georgia. If the *Belgrano* had eluded the main Task Force and the submarine shadow, she could have flattened Grytviken and Port Leith on South Georgia with her big guns in a matter of hours. Superficially, the sinking of the cruiser outside the Exclusion Zone seemed diplomatic ineptitude, but on closer examination it indicates how vulnerable the whole of the British sea operation was at this stage.

For two days after the sinking, the BBC reported the fearful conditions of the rescue operation, with mountainous seas, blizzards and gales. No one could have lasted more than a few minutes in the Atlantic in those latitudes. For a day or more it was not known how many men had been aboard the *Belgrano* when she sailed: the complement was well over a thousand and there was almost certainly a marine contingent embarked. By the middle of the week, Argentina announced that more than 700 men had been rescued and nearly 350 lost.

The sinking of the *Belgrano* was discussed by soldiers and sailors alike aboard the *Canberra* like so many armchair admirals. Marine and paratroop officers explained the deployment of the British submarines over the cornflakes and toast at breakfast in the Atlantic Restaurant. They knew the weapons used and the firing procedures in detail. But it all turned out to be largely fantasy, and they knew no more about what had gone on than anyone else in the *Canberra*.

It was just as supper was being cleared away in the Atlantic Restaurant that evening, 4 May, that one of the waiters came up to me and said, 'I think one of our destroyers has been sunk. It came on the eight o'clock news of the BBC. I think they said it was the *Sheffield* and she was hit by a missile from an aircraft.' The news was confirmed surprisingly quickly, and as it came to be known throughout the *Canberra* it was as if the temperature had dropped by ten degrees. Most of the younger officers and serving men were shocked that any British ship could have been crippled so unexpectedly, still less a Type 42 destroyer, one of the mainstays of the battle-line. The journalists started quickly writing pieces about the reaction to the news aboard the *Canberra*, and my colleague Kim Sabido typed his in the Crow's Nest Bar in the presence of some forty or fifty officers. Some worried artillery officers accused him of being ghoulish and threatened to throw his typewriter overboard and him along with it.

As I was phoning over my report to the BBC, Captain Burne came into the chartroom, where the Marisat apparatus was installed. He was courtesy personified and quietly took me aside for a chat. What he had to say and the way he said it was typical of this extraordinary, generous man. He said that the air-delivered Exocet, a sea-skimming missile that travelled well above the speed of sound, would continue to be a major threat throughout the campaign, and he thought more ships were bound to be lost, such was the nature of the conflict. The lack of long-range air warning systems would prove a weakness against aircraft of the quality of the Super Etendard.

Captain Burne knew the Type 42 destroyer well, as he had seen HMS *Coventry* through the last phases of her construction and had been her first commanding officer. There is a delightful story about her working-up trials when he ordered a man to jump into the sea to test 'man overboard' drills. When the man refused, he hopped over the side himself. Quite apart from his experience in seamanship, Christopher Burne had spent some time in gunnery studies of new weapons and their procurement. He knew well the weakness of the Type 42, which was known to be too lightly armed with anti-aircraft weapons. The main armament, the Sea Dart missile, is a long-range, high altitude weapon, and it could only reach a target coming in high to attack provided adequate radar warning had been given. This was conspicuously lacking in the Task Force. There was little by way of AWACS or Aircraft Early Warning System, and the Nimrod AWAC long-range reconnaissance aircraft was not available. Hitherto, anti-aircraft warning had been provided by the old Fairey Gannet aircraft operating from a Fleet Carrier like the *Eagle* or the old *Ark Royal*. If such a carrier had been available, it would have been much easier to track the Etendards, and Admiral Woodward would also have been able to deploy the Phantoms and Buccaneer bombers embarked in *Ark Royal*, which would have made an enormous difference to the campaign. All of this was already plain to Captain Burne as it must have been to the Admiral's staff itself. The attack on the *Sheffield* made it a priority to build up some kind of makeshift AWAC system, which was done with ingenuity and some success.

The *Sheffield* had been in a line of frigates and destroyers acting as an anti-aircraft picket to the carrier *Hermes*. Her main radar was switched off when she was hit in the area of her Control Room by an Exocet which was only spotted fifteen seconds before it struck. The radar was not in use because its signals could have attracted the homing device of missiles, and, according to another source, because the ship was using a satellite to transmit signals back to Northwood. The radar was working in the next ship in the picket, the frigate *Yarmouth*, one of the oldest warships with the Task Force. Heeding the warning, she fired 'chaff', or strips of metal, which did decoy the second approaching Exocet which turned away and hit the sea harmlessly. The missile that struck the *Sheffield* did not explode but the fuel in its rocket ignited and soon the ship was burning uncontrollably. Much of HMS *Sheffield*'s misfortune could be laid at the door of repeated defence cuts. It is said that when Denis Healey was Defence Minister, as an economy measure twenty feet was cut from the overall length of the Type 42 destroyers in the original specifications, and this meant a corresponding reduction in air defence weapons. Repeated parings of defence budgets meant cheaper PVC materials being used for insulation in the main cable ducts. In the *Sheffield* this material appears to have caught fire quickly, giving off clouds of black smoke and poisonous fumes. Ship designers aboard the *Canberra* also spoke of their disquiet at the amount of aluminium in the more recent British destroyers and frigates, particularly the Type 21 frigate, and the Type 23 which the post-Falklands Defence Review has indicated will be the replacement for the Type 21s and Type 42s lost in the Falklands. At very high temperatures aluminium can melt, and according to some reports may even ignite.

Two days after the *Sheffield* was hit, it was announced that two Sea Harriers had disappeared on a mission. They were seen flying into cloud and may have collided. It was the first and only loss of the Task Force's main interceptor aircraft, but three Harriers, including Nicholas Taylor's GR3 shot down at Goose Green, had been lost in three days, and only twenty-two of the planes were left aboard the two carriers. Reporting the reaction to such developments from the *Canberra* proved a delicate task, and the journalists were closely watched by the press liaison officer from 3 Commando Brigade, Captain David Nicholls, Royal Marines, who came over to *Canberra* from HMS *Fearless* every afternoon to give briefings to the press on the latest developments. Captain Nicholls had clear, light-blue eyes above a boyish mouth draped in a droopy moustache and one of the coolest temperaments in the brigade. Like Major Mike Norman he did not find his role as press officer entirely congenial. He was one of the most distinguished mountaineers in Britain and until recently had commanded the Royal Marines Mountain and Arctic Warfare Cadre. Despite his reluctance, he was an excellent information officer and earned the trust and respect of nearly every member of the press with the Task Force. His briefings were thorough and helpful, and he was always courteous enough to say why certain pieces of information could not be released immediately for fear of jeopardising future operations. I was to meet him on and off throughout the campaign, aboard HMS *Fearless*, high in the hills above Estancia Settlement, and we walked into Port Stanley together on 14 June. He had a quiet, unhurried, almost unassuming manner, but this belied the steel in his character; he was not easily thwarted, or circumvented by wily hacks, and it was quite clear that he had the complete confidence and respect of his superiors, General Moore and Brigadier Thompson, and far more so than any other officer of his rank.

My first report on the air battles and bombing raids over Port Stanley brought a hurried visit by David Nicholls from HMS *Fearless*. In the report I had talked about reaction to the news of the attacks on the Falklands aboard the *Canberra* and among the amphibious force. I added that detailed plans for a landing on the Falklands were now being laid, and that the options for where the beachhead would be were narrowing and the timing would depend on the weather and the state of the seas round the Falklands. For some reason Brigadier Julian Thompson had not been listening to the World Service much until then, and he was less than pleased at my public line of speculation. He wanted to know where I had taken this approach from. The answer was remarkably simple. Only three days before the broadcast, his opposite number in the Navy, Commodore Clapp, had given me an on-the-record taped interview saying that the options were narrowing, which seemed a remarkably anodyne statement.

Julian Thompson was not the man to make an undue fuss or to dwell over-long on such things, and when we met a few days later we had an agreeable conversation about the way the World Service worked, a matter on which the MOD press officers seemed conspicuously incapable of informing him or David Nicholls. Strangely, Julian Thompson was pleased about a line I had put into a report about reaction to the sinking of HMS *Sheffield*, the notion of Captain Burne's that the *Sheffield* incident could mean 'a bloody and difficult campaign ahead'. Julian Thompson more than anyone wanted to dispel the nineteenth-century jingoism and 'gung-ho' of the Fleet Street tabloids and the idea that the battles to come would be a 'walkover' in the unfortunate phrase reported from an interview with Sandy Woodward, which the admiral was said to have subsequently corrected.

In *Canberra*'s last week at Ascension the options for the landing-site were indeed being narrowed. The number of possibilities had been reduced from eight to four. The notion of building a fortress on West Falkland still appeared to be in play, as did the use of the settlements on either side of Falkland Sound, the two at San Carlos, and those at Fox Bay and Port Howard on West Falkland. Some unit commanders continued to favour the idea of getting closer to Port Stanley and attacking the main group of Argentinian land forces quickly.

But the San Carlos anchorage was fast emerging as the favourite because of its sheltered waters and high barrier of hills. There
was another priceless advantage. The wife of the Falkland
Island Company manager at Port San Carlos, Mrs Miller, a
close acquaintance of Ewan Southby-Tailyour, was in England
and could give minute details of the land surrounding the
settlements. Quite a bit was known about the kind of Argentinian forces in the area as local amateur radio operators had
managed to transmit for quite some time after the Argentinians
landed at Port Stanley on 2 April. San Carlos, too, would provide the ideal base from which to strike the Argentinians'
mobile force, known as 'the strategic reserve'.

The strategic reserve came to have an almost mythical significance. It was thought to be about a thousand men, an
infantry battalion with several companies of specialised forces
attached to it, and to be the only force that the enemy could
deploy rapidly by helicopter. For a long time it was supposed
to be based at Goose Green. The first prize of the land campaign would go to the unit which made 'an advance to contact'
the strategic reserve, to engage it in battle, and win the first
victory, which would be vital in psychological propaganda
terms. The lucky unit chosen first for this was the glamour
outfit of 3 Commando Brigade, Colonel Nick Vaux's 42 Commando.

Whether the Argentinians themselves had any concept of a
'strategic reserve' I am not sure, and certainly in the event it
was not to be 42 Commando that made the first contact with a
major concentration of enemy ground forces, but 'H' Jones's 2
Para at Goose Green. In *Canberra*'s last few days at Ascension,
the first week in May, I began to learn in detail of the landing
plan. How I came to discover it was by a curious string of accidents.

By this stage nearly all the hacks had been doing some form
of physical training or jogging round the promenade deck.
With Kim Sabido I could manage twelve circuits, about three
miles, with ease, and then, for no very good reason, my ankle
gave way. In the ship's sick bay I found LMA Tony Dawes, a
trained physiotherapist. With his colleague Steve Hardwicke

he discovered that my left ankle was a mass of bruised tendon from an accident when I fell down the stairs in Broadcasting House five years before. With some malicious pleasure they decided to break up all the scar tissue and set the foot to healing anew. This proved extremely painful as first the tendons were rubbed raw on three consecutive days and then the foot was shoved into a bucket of ice for half an hour. Apart from the pain, the episode proved highly rewarding. Not only was the company of the two Medical Assistants excellent, but I received first-class physiotherapy daily for nearly a fortnight, which would not have been possible under the National Health. The sick bay also proved an extraordinary exchange and mart for rumour, speculation and good solid information. Not only were brúisers of every rank and size appearing regularly for treatment, but also three injured unit commanding officers came down and talked quite freely.

The doctors were talking to their staff about what lay ahead, too, and they had as much to prepare as anyone for the land campaign. In the last week in May they started taking a thousand pints of blood from the troops. The optimum period for keeping fresh blood was roughly two to four weeks. The donors had to work back to full strength and fitness before getting ready for disembarkation, so from 7 May, say, this would give a landing date of about 21 May. 'I hope not too many of the Toms [paras] and boot-necks [marines] have realised this. I know some of them have been doing their sums right, though,' one of the anaesthetists, Steve, muttered to me at dinner one night. Another worry for the doctors was the need to have their operating theatre in the Stadium, just aft of the Crow's Nest Bar, and their main recovery ward on the deck below. Rick Jolly's Medical Squadron had rigged an ingenious chute from the flight deck to the main ward on which they lowered stretchers lashed to a trolley from the helicopters. They had several practice runs at Ascension as 'casevac' ('casualty evacuation') patients were brought in from other ships, men with complaints varying from acute appendicitis to a foot crushed by a passing Land Rover.

Another emporium for soft gossip and hard information was

the monkey island bridge, where officers went for a quiet 'bronzy' in the last of the sun before heading south. The monkey island is the highest deck on the Canberra, above the bridge. There officers of all units would gather to read, sleep and swap gentle banter. Some of the hacks made Herculean efforts to chat up the attractive deputy ship's doctor, Susy West. Take the information from the physiotherapy sessions in the sick bay, the chat of the monkey island, the odd tit-bit from the coffee trap, add a dash of seemingly casual cross-examination in the Crow's Nest Bar before dinner, and one had the outline of the landing plan.

The planners knew almost the exact number of inhabitants in both San Carlos Port and San Carlos Settlement. The two Parachute battalions would be landed at either end of the anchorage to secure the high ground, Sussex Mountains to the south and Cerro Montevideo above Port San Carlos. Commando units would go ashore at key points east and west in San Carlos Water, at San Carlos Settlement and Ajax Bay. 42 Commando would be held back to make a helicopter-borne attack against the mythical 'strategic reserve'.

Much good did the knowledge I had gained of the landing plan do me. I had to endeavour to reveal to the minders as little as possible of the detail I possessed, for fear of blowing my cover and giving away my sources. There was nothing I had gleaned, from sick bay or coffee trap, monkey island or Crow's Nest, that I could possibly have used in any report or broadcast at that stage or for a long time afterwards. Because of the risks involved in the landing operation, I felt incapable of doing the jolly 'Look at Life' or 'Pathe News' style of reports that the ITN news team were still doing and the 'hometown boy' stories of Kim Sabido was being asked for by his radio news office. *Canberra* was now a month out of Southampton and I knew the forces aboard her would have to land soon or morale would drop.

A week after the first bombings of Port Stanley, the *Norland* with 2 Para aboard, HMS *Intrepid*, the *Atlantic Conveyor* and the *Europic Ferry* with the 105 guns and ammunition aboard, dropped anchor off Ascension. Twin-rotor Chinook helicopters landed on the *Conveyor* from Wide Awake. Ground-attack Harrier GR3s inched forward above the freighter's decks and then swivelled gingerly and lowered slowly onto the foredeck.

The Harriers were to reinforce those already aboard *Hermes* and the *Invincible*. Some with Indian Air Force markings had been spotted by visitors to the Ascension airstrip, as they had been requisitioned direct from the British Aerospace factory for the Falklands Task Force. New Harriers were in short supply, as the subsonic versions had been written off by many of the world's air forces as too slow and with too short a range, which made their success in aerial combat over the Falklands the more surprising. One of the most frightening experiences in all the time *Canberra* spent at Ascension was on 1 May just after the bombing of Stanley was made public. Two Harriers painted grey all over dived out of the cloud at the liner, passed a few feet above her mast and, banking steeply, tucked themselves behind the volcano on the island to land on the airstrip.

With the arrival of his battalion in the *Norland*, 'H' Jones left the *Canberra*. 2 Para had only a day or two to practise 'rubbish-skipping' with *Intrepid*'s landing craft, whereas 3 Para had nearly three weeks using the craft from *Fearless*. The *Canberra* left Ascension anchorage on a limpid, cool evening of bright sub-tropical sunshine with a calm sea and almost no clouds in the sky.

We passed along the ships riding at anchor as if at a miniature Spithead Review. There were waves and cheers from the *Fearless* and *Intrepid*, and the Type 21 frigate HMS *Ardent* weighed anchor to escort the liner. Other escorts like the frigate *Argonaut* continued to loll lazily in the bay surrounded by merchantmen and supply ships of all sizes, the ferry *Norland*, the *Conveyor* and the tankers. On the port beam the radio masts bristled on spy island and the radar dishes glinted in the evening sun. The airstrip seemed more crowded than ever with Nimrods, more than a dozen Victor tankers, VC 10s Harriers in their anonymous grey livery, the Vulcan bomber and the maid-of-all-work both for Britain and

Argentina, the C 130 Hercules Transports. In keeping with the mood of departure a medley of marches blared over the ship's tannoy. Jammed somewhere between 'Pomp and Circumstance' and the selection of Sousa marches, I heard distinctly the strains of the 'Horst Wessel' song.

II. THE SOUTH ATLANTIC

As the Ancient Mariner would have been able to tell, the really difficult period in a long voyage begins in the fifth and sixth weeks. It is then that the hallucinations and depression begin and the company starts to get on each other's nerves. It was the longest period most of the ship's company had spent at sea. At Ascension about a dozen crew members took their pay and booked their flights back to England. Many of them had not thought that the ship would be going further south than Ascension.

The man directly responsible for the administration of the crew was the Deputy Captain, Sam Bradford, a bluff, jolly fellow who had spent most of his life with P and O. He often served as the captain of the *Canberra* and the other ships of the company, and like Dennis Scott-Masson carried the rank of full captain in the Royal Naval Reserve. Sam had no doubt about the outcome of the conflict with Argentina. The evening we heard that the *Sheffield* had been hit, I expressed my fears about the vulnerability of the British escorts to Exocet attacks launched from the Super Etendards. Sam would have none of this. 'Lucky shot I'd say, and one is always bound to get through. No, we've got the finest ships and finest men, the true bulldog breed. I don't think their air force is going to give us much trouble.'

This was the mood at one of the very few unit intelligence briefings I was allowed to attend, a general background brief to all the men of 42 Commando, given in the ship's cinema. Most of the talking was done by teams of senior NCOs, sergeants and corporals, who seemed to run both the commandos and the parachute battalions in much of their training. The lecture was given in five sections: the state of the Argentinian forces on the ground in the Falklands, their weapons and their armour and vehicles, their air force, the command and personnel, and their navy. Considerable detail was already known about the defences round Port Stanley, the heavy mining of the beaches and the ridges running into the little town from the west, like Sapper Hill, and to the north of Moody Brook. There was a good deal of information about the vehicles they were using, the Panhard armoured car and the tracked vehicles used in the landings on 2 April. The litany of the capabilities of each was concluded with the invocation, 'but our anti-tank weapons, the Milan, the '66 and '84 missiles, are better'. There was an accurate assessment of the missile air-defences round the port, the American Roland, an equivalent to Rapier, and the British Tiger Cat, the land-launched brother of the Sea Cat, the old-fashioned visually guided air-defence weapon in the majority of the frigates and the *Fearless* and the *Intrepid*. Neither Roland nor Tiger Cat was to bring down a single British aircraft, though the Argentinians did shoot down one of their own Mirages in the first air attacks on Stanley airfield.

The Argentinian airpower, however, was underrated. The exact number of Super Etendards, which had a range of over 600 miles, was not known and there was a great deal of bluff about 'we believe they had only seven air-launch Exocets, and they have fired two already' (at the *Sheffield* and *Yarmouth*). Careful mention was given to the Pucara, the twin-piston-engined counter-insurgency aircraft built by the Argentinians for operations in the countryside against guerrillas. The marine giving the brief indicated that they could be a menace to ground troops caught in the open, and their slow speed (about 300 knots maximum) would make them hard for a jet fighter to intercept. There was considerable respect, too, for the Mirage IIIs, the 'A' version built by Dassault in France and the 'C' or Dagger built by the Israelis. With a top speed of Mach 2 (twice the speed of sound, or some 2,200 mph), these planes were much faster than the Harrier. But the brief had every confidence that the Harrier could 'hack' (handle) the question of air superiority and air cover, despite the fact that the Sea Harrier had only just received its first taste of aerial combat. There was optimism, too, about the balance of strength between the British and the Argentinian artillery. The Argentinians used in the main the 105 mm pack howitzer, an efficient weapon but one which was now obsolete with British forces. It had a shorter range and threw a lighter shell than the 105 mm Light Field Gun, which was the standard artillery weapon for both British brigades on the Falklands.

There was an important gap in the intelligence about the Argentinian artillery, since it was unknown whether or not they had brought to the Falklands any 155 mm guns, which could outrange the Light Field Gun by at least five kilometres and fire a much heavier shell. Four or five of these positioned in Stanley could make it very difficult for British troops digging in on the high ground to the west. Many of the casualties suffered by 3 Para on Mount Longdon were due to the heavy shelling by one of these weapons alone. Major Mike Norman asked if it was known whether the Argentinian gunners had the help of radar surveillance equipment like the American 'Green Archer' which could help to locate enemy positions, particularly those of opposing artillery, from the discharge of their shells. Not much was known about this, but it was thought that the Argentinians did not have much sophisticated targeting equipment. This turned out not to be the case; their field night vision aids and signals interception equipment, some of it British-made, turned out to be good, as good if not better than that of the British forces moving towards them. The two British brigades had the Cymbeline radar for tracking incoming mortar fire and fixing the location of the enemy mortar line, but in the battles on Longdon, Tumbledown, Mount William and Wireless Ridge it had very limited success.

The most fascinating part of the briefing was the background to the senior Argentinian officers believed to be on the islands. The most prominent was Major Patricio Dowling, who was well known for his activities with the detention of political prisoners and the campaign against the guerrillas after the military returned to power in the mid-1970s. His name had long been associated by human rights organisations with the campaign of 'disappearances'. He claimed Irish grandparents, which accounted for his pathological hatred of the British. His police methods met with small success among the islanders and we learnt later that he had himself disappeared back to Argentina by the time the fighting started round the Falklands. Not much was known about the rest of the command in Port Stanley and the other garrisons, and nothing useful was given about the military governor, General Mario Benjamin Menendez, who had been a close associate of Leopoldo Galtieri in the later stages of their military careers. The lack of knowledge about some of the senior officers was the more surprising as some of them had been to the Falklands in the recent past with the LADE mission which ran the air link to Argentina. One of the most popular was Air Commodore Carlos Blumer-Reeve, the deputy governor under Menendez, a man of British and German extraction and great humanity who won the respect of most of the Falklanders in Stanley during the occupation.

Information about the state of the garrison in Stanley was also patchy. The soldiers were believed to be roughing it in the open in considerable discomfort, short of food and victims of dysentery. This was a greatly exaggerated picture. Food and ration supplies did get through till the end via Hercules transports landing on the airstrip and a freighter is known to have slipped through the blockade and into Stanley harbour under cover of fog. The rations supplied to the troops were often better than those given to the British soldiers, and the paras and marines that entered Stanley on 14 and 15 June plundered eagerly the row of metal transport containers on the shore road, which were packed with tinned meat (with the almost obligatory corned beef in abundance), rice, spaghetti and ravioli. Reports of starvation and disease amongst the Argentinian conscripts circulated quite frequently among British forces throughout the campaign but there was little evidence to support them.

Some of the information for the intelligence briefings now being given to the commandos and para units was coming from SAS and SBS (Special Boat Squadron) patrols already ashore in the Falklands. Some had been moved south with the carrier group and gone ashore in small boats. Others had travelled on supply ships like the *Stromness*, where they were annoyed that there was a member of the press embarked, David Norris of the *Daily Mail*. The SBS men disappeared one night, according to David, and were taken aboard fast frigates (a Type 21 could do nearly forty knots) and some later went to submarines.

In the weeks before the main landing at San Carlos, the SAS carried out surveillance patrols in different parts of East Falkland, one group spending several weeks observing Port Stanley from the high ground north and east of the harbour itself and from Port William. Throughout the campaign it was found to be practically impossible to penetrate the port itself undetected and much of the intelligence about what was happening there came from the settlers going out to the countryside or 'camp' and the scraps of news reaching the outlying settlers by telephone or the Citizens Band radio link used for consultations with the doctors in the capital each morning.

The other important role of the SAS and the SBS was to prepare the landing beaches at San Carlos, to warn of enemy activity in the area and to provide a screen of observations posts and patrols on the morning the landing craft touched down. The SBS would be by the beaches themselves, to flash warning lights to marshall the LCUs, the 'rubbish skips', before they lowered their ramps. Not the least of their jobs was to warn the settlers in San Carlos and San Carlos Port an hour or so before the landing took place.

The SAS and the SBS won more of the limelight and publicity in the world's press throughout the Falklands campaign than they did in any other single action. Before the marines and paras were landed, the *Canberra*'s notice boards were covered with the crude drawings of SAS and SBS soldiers in the guise of 'action man' which had been in nearly all the Fleet Street tabloids, and these caused much hilarity with each of the mistakes of fact and detail in the accompanying copy neatly underlined. There was a certain amount of resentment towards the SAS, and any ostentatiously glamorous unit is bound to attract such odium and envy.

Much important reconnaissance work was done by the Patrol Companies of the commandos and the paratroops. A captain, Matt Selfridge from Pat Butler's Patrol Company, was sent forward to reconnoitre the route of march across East Falkland at the time of the main landing. He marched almost the breadth of the northern part of the island and then reported back on his secure radio that he thought he had been followed for much of the way by a patrol of Argentinians. He said he could hear them shuffling through the tussock grass in the dark. As he was calling in, he said he thought he heard them again, lurking in a hollow below where he was hiding. He edged forward and then in the moonlight saw a group of penguins like portly waiters, their beaks pecking at the white bibs on their chests. They had followed him for nearly twenty miles, as he had first heard them down by the coast before setting out.

The weekend after the final departure from Ascension, the long-postponed inter-unit sports contest was held. The evening before, Colonel Tom Seccombe had a small dinner party for somebody's birthday. I cannot recall whose it was, and I think it was never stated; clearly it was an excuse to have a last party. The company was Tom himself, Helen Hawkett and Lauraine Mulberry, with myself as gooseberry. We ended up watching a video-cassette of *Patton* with Tom declaiming the opening monologue in unison with George C. Scott. Earlier Tom had mentioned his fear that reality was beginning to imitate fiction and that he suspected his clerk, Corporal Page-Bailey, was preparing to write a novel. 'I am sure he is keeping a diary,' said Tom. 'Every time he appears with yet another signal about some cock-up with the embarked force he has a horrible sickly leer all over his face.'

It was now clear that the *Canberra* would go into the war zone, and that she would to in close to the Falklands themselves at the time of the landing. The two girls, Helen and Lauraine, and the rest of the company took this news with equanimity despite the fact that when the ship was first taken up from service they had been told that it was unlikely she would go into battle area and might not even sail south of Ascension. Helen's reasons for agreeing to sail with her were straightforward. 'I had just been appointed to the ship, and she was, after all, my ship now and I could not face the idea of her going without me.' Lauraine Mulberry was never enthusiastic about the *Canberra*'s new role. 'I don't like the talk of war all the time and people losing their lives and being terribly injured. I was never formally ordered or asked to go with the *Canberra*. I listened to the radio all the time before she sailed, and when they said some of the women crew members would be going, I just turned up.' Lauraine had thought she might have been of more use aboard the *Uganda*, a ship she knew well.

The morning of the sports day I awoke to the continued slamming of heavy doors all down the starboard side. I thought we must have hit a gale and some of the watertight bulkheads had swung loose. Struggling on deck, we found that the noise had been HMS *Ardent*, another Type 21 frigate now serving as the *Canberra*'s escort, firing practice rounds from her main 4.5-inch gun a few cables off our starboard side. It was a gesture of salute and friendship to the 'great white whale', as the *Canberra* was now known throughout the fleet. She was also called 'the gin palace' by the more ignorant souls in the fleet who still thought we were dining off cruise-line fare. The white whale's rival was 'the black pig', the *Queen Elizabeth 2*, which had just been requisitioned to bring the 5th Infantry Brigade south. As the *Ardent* glided along through the gentle swell, her turret wreathed in white smoke from the gun, hundreds of cameras clicked from the *Canberra*'s decks. Among them were the last official pictures to be taken of the *Ardent* at sea.

It was a grey, damp day, hardly the best conditions for thundering round the promenade deck for the sports competition. The almost childish competitiveness of the units and their officers became tedious after a series of officers and men had whined in my ear like pleading prep-school prefects that the rules and individual events had been fiddled to favour the opposition. The important event was the 10,000 metres, twenty-four times round the promenade deck, predictably won by the 3 Para team, which had won the Army cross-country championship. The great delight of the entire competition was the performance in the race by Frank Taylor, a lean figure who normally served as a leading laundry hand in the *Canberra*. His chief cheer-leader was his wife Anna, a dark, attractive young woman who helped out in the Bureau, the ship's office. Frank Taylor came fourth in the 10,000 metres, saying later that this was not really his event, which was the marathon. He had competed with success in the first of the New York marathons. Many of the officers, and all three unit COs, had been entered in the London marathon which took place the following weekend. It was astonishing to see the singlemindedness with which men in their early forties managed to keep fit and run three or four miles at least three times a week, as all three colonels did habitually even when they were doing their desk jobs in Whitehall.

Not too surprisingly, Nick Vaux's 42 Commando won the overall contest and received a cheque for their welfare fund, which was donated by the hacks. 42 was emerging as very much the favourite son of 3 Commando Brigade, and, outwardly at least, seemed the smartest of the three main units embarked. Nick Vaux, the commanding officer, was a dapper figure, slightly older than the other lieutenant-colonels, with a curiously clipped manner of speech, his words seeming to be squeezed out from one side of his mouth. It gave him a slightly pompous air, which was totally deceptive, and in the field he was a quick, tough and humane commander.

The sports contest brought the last ludicrous passage of arms with the minders aboard the *Canberra*. It was decided that we could report that there had been such an event, but there was to be no mention of units or individual performances. By this time all the London papers had reported several times that 3 Para, 40 and 42 Commando were aboard *Canberra*, frequently mentioning their commanding officers and precisely what kind of equipment they were taking with them to the Falklands.

For most of the journey through the grey South Atlantic, the *Canberra* appeared to be dawdling, doing no more than a bare twelve to fifteen knots. She was sailing well out into the ocean to reduce the risk of surveillance flights by Argentinian aircraft – they had been using Boeing 707s to watch parts of the carrier force earlier. Moreover, the threat of submarine attack was increasing, and for much of *Canberra*'s deployment south of Ascension it was never known for sure where one of the Argentinians' new German-designed Salta submarines was hiding. *Canberra* had two important rendezvous before moving south and west towards the Falklands group. First the ferry *Norland* with 2 Para and the *Europic Ferry* had to catch up, and then there was to be a meeting with the LSLs, the Arthurian knights, which had sailed a few days before the liner from Ascension as they could only wallow along at twelve to fourteen knots.

There were only a few days left to catch the sun and the last scrap of gossip and information on the monkey island bridge. On the last day of fair weather – and the beginnings of a gale were already whistling through the ship's wireless aerials and halyards – we saw from the monkey island the *Norland* and her escort. As the ferry ploughed along we could see the water astern erupt in plumes of spray as the men of 2 Para let fly with machine-guns, rifles and sub-machine-guns from her stern in their live firing practice. She seemed a floating shooting gallery. As we watched, we noticed sudden activity on the *Canberra*'s bridge wing. It had been reported by a lookout on HMS *Intrepid* that a periscope had been sighted astern. We never knew what caused the alert, and the minders were conspicuously assiduous in not checking what had happened, despite repeated requests for information.

The Russians were being especially attentive to the *Canberra* again. One afternoon two 'Bear' reconnaissance aircraft swept out of the low grey clouds and had a close look before wheeling away back to base, which in that latitude could have been either Conakry in Guinea or Cuba. We had friendlier visits from Nimrod anti-submarine patrols from Ascension, which could drop mail in canisters parachuted into the sea, though much of this work was done by Hercules C 130 transports, and letters and newspapers arrived with surprising regularity. But there was little besides to relieve the boredom. At least at

Ascension there were several visits to other ships, and runs across the anchorage in the fast boats used by the SBS, the 'rigid raiders'. These are fibreglass boats driven by powerful outboard motors, which give them a top speed of forty knots. The collection of raiders the commandos had were pretty threadbare as they had seen hard service in the Arctic exercises in Norway. They gave a thrilling but excruciatingly uncomfortable ride, as the passenger had to hold on to the wooden struts of the boat's frame and try to bounce with the craft as it hit each wave. If you mistimed the bounce, your behind and spine was jarred as if riding a motorbike with no springs across country. The raiders could carry an armed patrol of six to eight marines, though how they managed clandestine operations from boats with such noisy engines beats the imagination.

Major Mike Norman did his best to alleviate our boredom by organising a series of lectures and instruction courses. He gave two himself about the formation of a brigade in attack, and how to bivouac, dig a trench or shell-scrape, or construct a 'sanger', a defended position, out of stones if it was not possible to dig a dry hole in the earth, which it was not for 90 per cent of the time on the Falklands. One of the lectures he set up was about survival by a Sergeant Pennington. It was almost a pantomime. The sergeant appeared not to have any teeth of his own, and each time he made a point, his mouth, all gums yawning wide under a beaky nose, would yell: 'And what do you do next, Tommo? If you don't think faster than that, you are going to be dead. You won't survive more than a couple of minutes in those waters if your ship's sunk or the helicopter crashes.'

His first aim was to shock the younger marines and paras, and he had some useful tips about surviving in an open boat after a helicopter had ditched. He explained how to get out from the troop-carrying compartment of a Sea King, though this must have been wishful thinking. In the two Sea King crashes over water in the Falklands, only one crewman got out alive, and in one of the accidents eighteen SAS men lost their lives. Instructions about survival on land moved into the realms of fantasy. First there were some practical hints about always sterilising water because of the prevalence of liver fluke in the Falklands streams. I discovered that the Argentinians took no such precautions and took most of their drinking water from pools and rivers near their forward positions. Liver fluke can be nasty in humans, though its prime target is sheep, and the liver can be severely damaged from infection after three to four months. One wonders how many of the young Argentinians are suffering now. Frostbite, according to the sergeant, was another major hazard, appearing in great white patches of dead skin at first on face, feet and toes. 'Well, what do you do about that Tommo?' roared the delighted sergeant, who could not wait to give the answer himself. 'You get your oppo [mate] to put his warm hands on your face as soon as it starts going white. And if it's the feet, well, what's the warmest part of the body? Well, we all know, it's the crutch: so you shove your feet in your oppo's crutch.'

This was followed by advice on clothing, wearing as many layers as posible, keeping one pair of socks dry, by storing it in that ubiquitous source of heat, your crutch, at night, and the usefulness of wearing a pair of women's tights if you are moving across country and fording streams and lakes. 'If I were you, Tommo, I'd get around quick and ras [from Navy RAS, Replenishment at Sea] a pair of tights from the shop. No one's going to call you a poof now.' Soon after the *Canberra* shop ran surprisingly low in women's tights, as too did the dining-rooms of spoons and knives. The troops were advised to take the minimum of cutlery, best being a spoon with its steel handle sharpened down one side to serve as a knife. The P and O management decided to call an amnesty and asked for the cutlery to be returned, and 800 more assorted spoons, knives and forks vanished instead.

The sergeant concluded with his *pièce de resistance*: how to live off the land. He explained how to set snares for rabbits and garrot birds and beasts of the field already snared. Unrolling a huge diagram, he showed how to slaughter a sheep, hang it to drain the blood through the throat and then skin it. Everything had some zany purpose. Use the fat to grease your lips against wind chill. The fleece would be part of your bedding. Cut the meat in strips as you needed food day by day. His imagination soared to new heights. You might find cattle, and you could kill them and hide in them like Buffalo Bill did with the bison on the American plains. What was the most common bird on the Falklands? The penguin. Well, you could eat penguin eggs, and make penguin soup and stew, but you had to be careful about skinning the birds as 40 per cent of the meat was poisonous, particularly the giblets. The tour through the fantastic workings of this latter-day Kit Carson's mind concluded with the recommendation: 'Don't kill too many animals, or more than you need for a few days' survival at a time. I don't like killing myself, and I try not to go in for it too much.'

Major Mike Norman was furious at the comic-strip style of the survival expert. Solicitous of the journalists' welfare and that of his new 'J' Company, he wanted information of real value to those who would be digging in after the landing, their first experience of life in the field with an infantry brigade. The kind of preparation Sergeant Pennington was most interested in was for pilots ditching in wild country and patrols operating in enemy-held territory. Some of his wisdom was useful for the Falklands, and would that many of the islanders could share it. They clearly did not believe in bleeding slaughtered sheep quickly, judging by the coarse, dark, sanguinated texture of almost all the mutton we were to be offered in the settlements. Later, settlers at Goose Green told us of an Argentinian pilot who had followed survival drills to perfection. He had baled out of his Mirage in the wild region near the justly named 'No Man's Land', ringed by high mountains of the Mount Usborne range. With an injured leg, he managed to limp to a shepherd's hut where he corralled four or five sheep, killing one, skinning it and stripping the meat for his daily food. Each morning he would set out in a different direction and return to the hut at night. Eventually he met some forward patrols from Darwin and Goose Green, and he was sent home some time before the British landed. His skill in skinning, hanging and dressing the sheep's carcase impressed the settlers greatly, and they said it was carried out more delicately than most of them would have done. The pilot spoke English well, with a distinct public school accent, and the few settlers he met were impressed by his kindness and courtesy.

The wildlife in the South Atlantic, what we saw of it, was fascinating and it was sad that there was so little time to appreciate it. Round Ascension we were haunted by all kinds of gulls, skuas and albatross. One afternoon Tom Seccombe felt sure that a para company at firing practice on the *Canberra*'s stern was about to down an albatross, and, quite clearly having had enough of the Navy already on the expedition, did not want to condemn himself to a life sentence as Ancient Mariner. He ordered that all live firing should be curtailed for the afternoon. In the sea there was all manner of living thing, glinting, gliding and slithering. Once the ship hit a whale, whose sonar had gone awry, and occasionally the sea would boil with dancing dolphins. Despite the onset of winter skies and squalls as the ship ploughed steadily south, the flying fish continued to attempt ever longer and more daring leaps. On the last day we could go up to the monkey island with any sense of comfort, Martin Osborne and I saw one flying fish skim above the waves for over three hundred metres.

At this time I was sunk in deep depression. It may have been the sensation of the shades of the Ancient Mariner and the Sargasso Sea at my shoulder, but Martin Osborne said: 'You don't seem to have been on net lately, Foxy,' using a straight-up-and-down World War Two expression, of which so many are still in use in the British Army. 'On net' refers to wireless slang, 'being on the network' or tuned in to the right wavelength. He was right; I was definitely not 'on net'. I had caught the *Canberra* bug, a nasty cold and sore throat which lurks deep in the bowels of the ship's plumbing, and, even worse, I had caught a fierce dose of superstitious premonition that I was going to die in the campaign ahead. The premonition was tied up with the superstition because I thought we might land on 17 May, my daughter Emily's birthday. About the time she was born two years previously, four friends and colleagues had been killed within a short time of each other. It was a dreadful and depressing time, and as the anniversary came round it began to dominate my thoughts. One evening Kim Sabido returned to A 281, now known as 'the grot' (from slang for 'grotto') and found me miles away listening to a Haydn Mass on the headphones of my cassette recorder. It was ju-ju, as the paras put it, warding off any thoughts that I would go ashore on the 17th, the following Monday. Kim said he was pretty depressed too about what lay in store. It was more difficult than ever to work out what was going on beyond the assault force. On the World Service we heard that diplomatic talks were still in play as the UN Secretary-General, Perez de Cuellar, searched more frantically for a peace formula.

I realised quickly that the mood of gloom and depression was not confined to our 'grot', despite the fact that the leaking lavatory and basin in A 281 were becoming noisier and pouring water over the floor by the bucketful. This state of affairs was made worse by the first and only major storm the *Canberra* bucketed through before the landings in San Carlos. Martin Osborne and some of his fellow para officers also felt that they might not make it through the fighting on the land. 'I feel I have had too good a life up to now, Foxy, and the luck has got to run out sometime,' he said. Conversation at breakfast became almost tongue-tied, even at the table Martin, Pat Butler, Peter Dennison, and the other 3 para officers usually sat at. It was served by a delightfully witty Irishman called Damian who came from the Ardoyne in Belfast and whose family had known parachute units well, from the other side. Some of the hacks were showing the strain, too. The scrabble games had long become poker sessions in Max Hasting's cabin, but the frenetic pace of the games and Max's conversation had worn out most of the other players. Max had been the great conversationalist all the way down, and helped to keep us diverted and entertained through the stretches of Ascension boredom. He summed up the mood aptly: 'I wish to bloody hell they would get on and do something, or go home.'

By the time each of the hacks had been told which unit he would go ashore with, I had made some tentative arrangements to disembark with either 3 Para or 40 Commando, as I had got to know officers and men in both well. I was appalled to discover that I was to cross to the *Norland* to go with 2 Para, of whom I knew only 'H' Jones and the Battery Commander, Tony Rice, slightly. I thought this was a malevolent act by the minders because of the amount of information I had been getting from the paras and marines in the *Canberra*. It turned out not to be so, but the plan had been worked out by David Nicholls and Brigadier Thompson. They thought I would be one of the first ashore with 2 Para and would have a commanding view of the anchorage, being able to get despatches back for the BBC and World Service quite easily. This calculation turned out to be broadly right, and, despite much counter-propaganda about 2 Para aboard the *Canberra*, I was never to regret travelling with 'H' and his men.

Reports about 2 Para in my last physiotherapy sessions in the sick bay were not favourable. 'OK I suppose, but a bunch of psycopaths,' said a 3 Para lance-corporal also receiving treatment. 'They tend to lose a lot of men. They're a good bunch, but expensive. You watch yourself with them, mate.'

Most of the marines were calm about the prospect of landing, and many were looking forward to action at last. In the remaining days of sunshine they polished and sharpened their bayonets on the aft deck, with clear instructions not to serrate the edges as this was against the Geneva Convention. Others oiled and checked their rifles and submachine-guns. After one of the last physical training workouts by the empty swimming pools on the stern, I overheard Marine Hobbes of 40 Commando telling his mates about what he was going to wear ashore. 'The real problem is the wet, more than the cold, so you have to wear lots of layers of clothing that can be dried out quickly. I'm not going to wear too much heavy stuff, like big jerseys. I'll wear Mao quilts and a teddy-bear suit, if I can find one. You've got to be able to get the stuff off at night and dry it for the morning.' A teddy-bear all wool and nylon undergarment is favoured by the SAS. Marine Hobbes had already done a year's tour in the Falklands, and his approach to preparing mentally and physically for the campaign across East Falkland was to be unsurpassed.

Equally calm and instructive were the words of LMA Terry

Bradford, the medical assistant who had been with Mike Norman's Naval Party 8901 on the Falklands. He gave us five talks on 'Battlefield First Aid'. The hacks proved rather dull pupils, but Terry Bradford did impart useful information about morphine, particularly when not to use it, and burns in battle. The initial response to burns seemed to be to douse them with water, except where they were caused by phosphorous shells and grenades, which many were to be in the land battles, because water would make the phosphorous burn even more. We were warned not to wear the green-coloured nylon trousers we had bought from one of the commando's stores, for the plastic in the fibres ignited by phosphorous would burn into the limb and into the bone. Terry Bradford explained all the basic first aid rules clearly, concisely and with authority, belying his appearance as an innocent abroad. When the Argentinians had invaded the Falklands on 2 April, he stayed with the marines defending Government House, and though he had never been trained as a rifleman he conducted himself with courage. Once the fight was over, he went to the hospital to help in the operating theatre, but arrived to see the death as he was undergoing surgery of the only Argentinian casualty to die there.

Terry had been told to go to the Falklands at the very last minute as the medical assistant first selected had dropped out. 'Do you want to go to the Falklands?' his commanding officer asked him. Replying that he wanted to go away and think about it for an hour or so, his superior added, 'Come on, son, no one turns down the possibility of a year in the sun.' He had no idea where the Falklands were.

In one of the last exercises in Terry's course of lectures, I had to treat David Norris of the *Daily Mail*, who was also going with 2 Para. He feigned arterial wounds and burns of all description and I made a messy job of tying them up with field dressings and feeding him the right dope. 'Fat lot of use you'll be as a companion,' said David, more than a little perturbed at the prospect that his life could be in my hands in the near future. He turned out to be the ideal companion in the field, calm, not very talkative, but very kind and a very good hack.

At the end of that last week aboard the *Canberra*, Major Chris Keeble, the second in command of 2 Para, came across from the *Norland*, and he, David and I had lunch. Tall, and with a thin face and aquiline nose and a scar on one cheek, Chris looks like a medieval monk who has long finished his novitiate. His iron-grey hair is cropped in the manner of a Florentine fresco of St Francis of Assisi. He turned out to be a devout Roman Catholic, and part of his reason for coming to the *Canberra*, I suspect, was to have his confession heard by the Catholic priest aboard, Father Noel. On first acquaintance, Chris is not the easiest conversationalist, and the talk at lunch was stiff and rather formal. Both David and I tried to find out something about the unknown battalion of alleged psycopaths. Chris Keeble recalls that I behaved as if I had been kidnapped by the Wild Bunch.

The end of the week saw the rendezvous with the LSLs and the last few despatches relayed back to London before the total news blackout was imposed as the time for landing approached. On one interview from the 'Today' programme, I was asked how it felt now that the Argentinians had made it plain that they regarded the *Canberra* as a legitimate target. We had known for some time that she would be a target, and from leaving Southampton it was understood that she was a troopship and, despite having a sizeable hospital facility aboard, could not claim status as a hospital ship. The Geneva Convention did not allow a ship to change its role in mid-voyage, and a hospital ship had to register for protected status at the outset of its deployment. Furthermore, I could not say to the questioner, one of the older staff reporters of the BBC, that I knew the *Canberra* would go right in to the beachhead. If he asked me how I felt about the ship being a target once, he asked it four or five times. In the radio interview business, the 'how do you feel' questions are the killers, all too easy to ask without thought and all too difficult to get a response of any value to. The 'how do you feel' questions from London were to be a plague and a curse throughout the campaign. In gentler vein, a 'PM' interviewer asked me about the battlefield first aid course, and concluded by asking if I was going to carry a weapon with me. Pompously, I replied, 'I wouldn't dream of it.' Besides, I claimed, 'The only weapon I would be likely to get hold of, a 9 mm Browning automatic, would be useless in my hands, and, anyway, it is not my job to think about killing Argentinians.' I now know that I was kidding myself with this high-minded clap-trap. If the Argentinians had shown any sign of counter-attacking and overrunning our positions at Goose Green, I would have grabbed the nearest weapon to hand and used my limited knowledge to make it fire back at an advancing enemy.

The conversations with London showed that we on the *Canberra* and our offices in London were in different worlds of reality and they were fast diverging. While they were asking about training, torpedo threats and carrying weapons, we were becoming obsessed by another threat, from the air. Soon we would be in range of the Super Etendards and at the moment we were going ashore we knew there would be limited air cover. As long as the carrier group could protect us there would be CAP (Combat Air Patrol) from the Harriers but once the dawn arrived over East Falkland, the troops digging in would be vulnerable to Fighter Ground Attack (FGA) from the Argentinian Mirages, A-4 Skyhawks and Pucara. It could take a day at least to establish the Rapier batteries ashore, as they had travelled 8,000 miles in the ships and would take time to settle down; furthermore they had never been used in battle before. The image many of our imaginations locked onto was of heavy strafing of the troops on the mountainside, scraping off men by platoons as they struggled to find cover in a treeless landscape of bog and rocks.

As the skies grew darker and the sea a dull, grey, heaving waste, more urgent air-raid drills and lifeboat assemblies were called, some in the night. Machine-guns were placed on the bridge wings and on the rails at the stern. The lifeboat drills were a helter-skelter into the main restaurant and open lounge areas, many of them in positions impossible to reach if the ammunition had started blowing up on the main decks. We crammed like sardines on the floors in simulated air-raids and then shuffled to the lifeboat muster stations. There was a brief homily in a slow drawl by Sam Bradford on the tannoy; in the tropics this task had fallen to Commander Rick Jolly, who once proposed to charge men for getting sunburnt to the extent that they had to skip some training sessions. If *Canberra* had been hit, since the passageways and stairs were so narrow and choked with a heaving stream of green and maroon berets in the lifeboat exercises, I suspect the scene would have been more like the last hours of the *Titanic* than the well-ordered disaster drill at which Sam Bradford aimed. The last 'abandon ship' practice, which was late at night, ended in considerable displays of frustration and bad temper.

Some of the marines kept themselves cheerful with home-grown entertainments. 40 Commando had a band night in which they sang a turgid ditty to a Cliff Richard number about going off 'on a Malvinas holiday, to kill an Argie or two', the nearest we got to sentiments of 'biffing the enemy'. I kept away from such things, as I avoided writing a will, which most of the other hacks did in the last days before the landing. I did not want to tempt the Fates too much; I was depressed and worried about how many aircraft the enemy had capable of FGA over San Carlos and its ring of high ground. The ITN reporter Jeremy Hands enjoyed the concert hugely, but admitted that much of it seemed 'straight out of the National Front song book'. It is surprising how the old saw held good, that the men with the big hearts and mouths amongst fighting soldiers in times of peace rarely became the big performers in the fighting, when the quiet, almost awkward individuals shone.

The coffee-trap set threw a last party with Rocket Fuel on the excuse that I was about to leave to join the *Norland*. I still was not 'on net', suffering from the *Canberra* bug and wanting to get moving. In the Crow's Nest Bar the tension had dulled the edge and Welsh charm of Taffy, the waiter, and was undermining the bonhomie of his colleague Geoffrey's corpulent and sensitive nature. 'I wish we could get on with it. I can't stand all this tenseness.' Few people showed up in the bar throughout the weekend.

On 15 May we were all called up for active service on MOD

and government instructions. Every civilian embarked was now at war, though no official declaration of hostilities was made then, nor was ever to be so. Curiously, the minders did not inform us of this, out of a mistaken sense of kindness, I suspect, not wishing to frighten the horses amongst the sensitive hacks. It was important in one respect, that we were now under the orders of the commanding officer of whatever unit we were with, and this meant we no longer had any choice as to where we went. Later we were each given a slip of paper saying that if taken prisoner we were to be treated as British officers of the rank of captain. This caused much mirth amongst the troops we went with during the fighting.

The weekend brought more news of action on the Falklands with the announcement of the SAS raid on Pebble Island. They slipped ashore in the dark under heavy Naval bombardment, Captain Kevin Arnold going ashore as the NGSFO to guide the guns of HMS *Glamorgan*. The raid met with success, with several Pucara damaged and destroyed, the enemy routed and light casualties amongst the SAS. In the Crow's Nest Bar, Ewan Southby-Tailyour showed me on the map the strategic importance of Pebble Island; it guarded the entrance to Falkland Sound, the passage between the two main islands, which led to the entrance of San Carlos Water on the northeast side. Ewan had not been told anything of the raid beforehand, despite the fact that he was now working on the last-minute timings of the main landing. He complained bitterly that he was finding it difficult to get helicopter lifts back to the *Fearless*, and he had been stranded for two days aboard the *Canberra*.

Later the BBC World Service said that all Argentinian ships were now prevented by British Naval forces from sailing between East and West Falkland and the west island was now cut off. On Sunday the 16th, the frigate HMS *Alacrity* sailed between the islands bombarding enemy positions on either side of Falkland Sound, and she was not attacked. This, I suspect, was accomplished at night, as there were no air strikes against her, and the importance of the exercise was that the frigate had shown the passage clear of mines. With this information it was clear that the landing could only be a few days away, despite the repeated announcements of further toings and froings at the UN.

On the morning of Monday the 17th, we were all put out of our misery. David Nicholls appeared from HMS *Fearless* with a roll of maps under his arm, and he was accompanied by a scruffy looking lieutenant-commander with a heavy five o'clock shadow from Commodore Clapp's staff. Immediate news blackout was imposed and no notebooks were allowed at the briefing, despite repeated protests from John Shirley who had already been told to prepare for the 'Insight' book of the campaign by the *Sunday Times* and who pleaded failing powers of memory. The plan was that the amphibious force would soon meet up with the carriers and would be escorted to a point of no return some fifty miles north of San Carlos. If everything went to plan, the ships would then move into San Carlos to land the troops four or five hours before dawn. 2 Para would land at San Carlos settlement, turn south, and walk the eight kilometres to Sussex Mountains where they would take up position. 45 Commando would move to the west arm of the Water at Ajax Bay and take up position on high ground looking over San Carlos and Falkland Sound on the other side. 40 Commando would land at San Carlos Settlement flanked by 2 Para, and they would secure the Settlement, move north and hold the hills looking east. 3 Para would take Port San Carlos on the northern stretch of the anchorage and move to the steep hillside above, looking north-east across the island. 42 Commando would be in reserve to move off later. Nearly all of this had been known via coffee trap, monkey island, sick bay and Crow's Nest for a week before. I did not know the extent of Naval cover, with guns from several ships, among them HMS *Arrow* and HMS *Ardent*, shooting at Argentinian positions on Fanning Head, the headland guarding the entrance to San Carlos, Goose Green and Darwin and at the concentrations of enemy troops on West Falkland at Fox Bay and Port Howard, for it was now believed that the mythical 'strategic reserve' was to be found there. Later we discovered that there was an intelligence report that it had crossed the Sound to the West Island a day or two before the landings, as the Argentinians believed the first assault would be on West Falkland. There were to be hit-and-run raids on Port Stanley with heavy Naval gunfire for cover and more diversions on the Darwin Isthmus.

There then followed much rigmarole about filing facilities and the need for delays in releasing material. Only the broad-casters should aim to come back to the ships with their material and the rest of the newspaper copy would have to be passed through Brigade Headquarters once they were estab-lished ashore at San Carlos from HMS *Fearless*. There were homilies about not wasting too much time of senior officers and that commanders in the field had too much to think about to be worried by itinerant pressmen, so we were not to trouble them with our requests. We should wait till the man appointed as press-liaison officer could help. We should also rely on the MOD officers, the minders, to help shift copy, and they could play the cassettes from Kim Sabido and myself over the Marisat. They would also see whether we could move round the beachhead, but this was not to happen at first as heli-copters were much too precious. But the minder's hour was past. In the event the arrangements did not work out on this pattern, if at all. Both Max Hastings and I, subscribing firmly to the cock-up theory of history, had already resolved not to leave any arrangements for communication to them that we could possibly manage ourselves.

One other important detail was the allocation of ships of dis-embarkation. 40 Commando would go from *Fearless* and 3 Para from HMS *Intrepid* at the head of the anchorage. 45 Commando would leave from a variety of stations, LSLs, the lead assault ships and the vessels with the Logistics Regiment under Lt.-Col. Ivan Helberg, which would also base itself at Ajax Bay. This meant journeys to *Fearless* and *Intrepid* and uncomfortable stays there for a day and a half for 40 Com-mando and 3 Para. 2 Para would disembark from the *Norland* herself.

After the briefing there was a noticeable air of hilarity, as if the end of term had come unexpectedly. Max threw a cham-pagne party in the Crow's Nest on which he spent my winnings from the Southampton sweepstake for the prediction of the nearest date to decision day. With my guess of 25 May I was only four days out on the landing. I went to A 281 for the last clear-out and to pick up kit on the way. The marine quartermasters had procured camouflage trousers, windproof smocks and, most important of all, the down-filled Arctic sleeping-bags. Some key items would still have to be obtained from the units to which we were assigned, but what Captain Geoff Whitely and Captain Dennis Sparks of 40 and 42 Commando did manage to round up for us was remarkable, particularly in comparison with the paltry supplies given to the press who eventually went ashore with 5th Infantry Brigade. In A 281, the basin and lavatory leaking still as if there was no tomorrow, I kitted out in camouflage trousers and smock and stowed away my civilian clothes. I threw all that I thought would be useful in the bergen, or rucksack, and went to find out about the Sea King to take me and David Norris to the *Norland*. Going up to the flight deck I met Colonel Tom Seccombe, who looked at me and said, in a typically warm farewell, 'Not bad. You'll get on all right, but do the straps up tight.' On the flight deck we stood chattering like a drey of nervous squirrels. In the weak early afternoon sun we took off for *Norland*, and on the ten-minute flight my camera broke down for the second time, this time irretrievably.

A few minutes before leaving the *Canberra*, I had run into Martin Osborne and said, 'Well, I'm off to the *Norland*. I don't know about you, but I think 'H' Jones is going to do something really loony.'

4. Assault

The ferry MV *Norland*, 13,000 tonnes, normally plies between Hull and Rotterdam. On this route she rarely spends more than a night at sea and more than forty-eight hours on the longest of her journeys. She is very much a home port ship, with strong ties to the community of Hull, and many of her crew come from the surrounding region, South Yorkshire, or what the Post Office now insists on calling Humberside. By the time the ship entered San Carlos Water, she had travelled more than 10,000 miles without docking. Her captain had been concerned that her engines would not last the journey, and the Royal Navy party aboard had been worried that the fierce storms of the South Atlantic would tear her plates apart, as she was designed for the bucking, short swell of the North Sea. None of these fears was realised. The engines seemed to thrive on such a long run with none of the shunting and stopping and starting of the quick turn-round needed in Rotterdam and harbour, and she managed the rough weather round the Falklands like a veteran.

The *Norland* is one of the most unsung heroines of the whole campaign. She was deployed for longer than the *Canberra* and the *QE2*. Like the *Canberra*, she sailed into San Carlos for the beach landings and accompanied her back to South Georgia to pick up prisoners, and she took the first of these into Montevideo. Long after the *Canberra* had turned for home, she shuttled between Ascension and Port Stanley with supplies, returning Falklanders and the garrison troops of the Queen's Own Highlanders. Though the appearance of the *Canberra* below decks was by now becoming pretty warlike with most of the watertight bulkheads closed up all the time, the appearance of the *Norland*'s car decks and cabin quarters was of an overcrowded barracks, with every available bunk and space in the accommodation sections taken up. All officers of whatever rank had to share cabins with one or two others; and this applied to Colonel 'H' Jones, too, although his cabin had to serve as a private office as well as sleeping quarters. The food was predominantly that of a ferry cafeteria, and the menus were never outstanding for their sense of variety. The biggest privation for 2 Para was the lack of exercise space, particularly for distance running. A circuit of the deck would be more like an assault course, swinging down ladders, through blacked-out cabin doors, down companionways and across the flight deck on the stern, usually as slippery as a skating rink from a thick film of grease, water and aviation fuel. When the ship was at flying stations, this valuable piece of deck was out of bounds for exercise. Despite these local difficulties, the *Norland* was a united community, far more so than the *Canberra*, simply because of the size of the company and the fact that only one major unit was embarked, 2 Para. There were about 1,000 military personnel on the *Norland*, only about a third of the number in the *Canberra*. There was a strong bond between the paras and the Yorkshiremen, and they followed each other's fortunes keenly throughout the land fighting. *Norland* did not get away unscathed; and in one of the air raids she was hit by shrapnel and splinter which caused superficial damage to her superstructure.

The afternoon we arrived from *Canberra*, we were greeted by Major Chris Keeble, who was to be our guide and adviser for much of David Norris's and my own attachment to the battalion. We were offered tea or coffee in the lounge of the main bar on the stern, which was where the Royal Army Medical Corps doctors and the medical staff attached to the Parachute Regiment had to do much of their office work and briefings. It was also used by the RAF Harrier pilots whose GR3 (Ground Attack) planes were stored in the *Atlantic Conveyor*. With them in the *Conveyor* were the four twin-rotor Boeing Chinook helicopters, and their pilots and ground crews were also in the *Norland*. The Harrier pilots spent much of their time mooning about, looking very bored. They had an obsession with the space-invader machines on which they tested their manual reflexes over and over again. Very skilful they were too, racking up mammoth scores which must have made the games very cheap but terribly dull.

The coffee we were offered by Chris Keeble was little better than that in the *Canberra*, but there was plenty of it, and it came from a pantry just beyond the bar which served much the same purpose as a general exchange for gossip and information as the coffee trap in the *Canberra* accountant's office. The atmosphere was more relaxed and informal than on the *Canberra*, and members of each different unit, the Chinook teams, the Harrier pilots, the gunners and medics, would tell us quite freely what they were doing and how they thought each of their operations would develop once ashore.

We were taken below to 'H' Jones's main briefing room, a pokey little office off the main assembly area where the men queued with endless patience for pay, letter forms and stamps. Frequently 'H' had a slightly flustered appearance, but his natural politeness never left him unless he was in a complete paddy. He excused himself and said he could not see us for a while, as he had an Orders Group (always known as an 'O' Group) with his company commanders, implying that there was still a great deal to be ironed out in the battalion's landing plan. After stowing our kit in a cramped cabin we shared with a sergeant photographer, Ron Hudson, we returned below for our first discussion with 'H' about the landing plan. I sat opposite him looking at the map of Falkland Sound, and like so many of my subsequent conversations with 'H' he seemed to be probing to find out how much I really knew of what was going on and what was planned. Then he would ask what we thought about it. We repeated all we had been told in our last briefing aboard the *Canberra* and, to our surprise, we seemed to have more of the overall picture than 2 Para had been given, with more detail about what the individual Commando units would be doing, and the kind of Naval gunfire cover available. 'H' and Chris Keeble mulled this over, and then we talked about the political setting against which all this would happen. The talks set up by Señor Perez de Cuellar were still just about active and had not been broken off officially, though the news

from London and Buenos Aires was of continuing divergence
between the British and Argentinian positions and it was clear
that no diplomatic solution would be found quickly.

Despite his later, much publicised, image as a schoolboy
hero, 'H' seemed to understand the diplomatic and international setting in which the Falklands crisis was unfolding
better than almost any other officer with the landing force
except Brigadier Julian Thompson, now his superior as 3
Commando Brigade commander. The characters of the two
men were complementary, though 'H' yielded to his
impetuous streak where Julian Thompson took the cautious,
thorough approach. 'H' saw the process of decision-making in
the land campaign in highly personal terms; the order to 'go'
for the landings was all down to Mrs Thatcher, always referred
to by him as 'Maggie'. Would Maggie have the nerve, or the
'bottle' as the paras and marines put it, to go for the landings
on the first night with favourable weather, or would the
cabinet be caught on the hop at the last minute by diplomatic
manoeuvres at the UN? Evidently, where the Prime Minister
was concerned, 'H' was a fan, and he thought she had to give
the order to move ashore now: the men had been embarked for
long enough and would now get stale and he was concerned
about the fitness of his battalion with their severely restricted
PT sessions aboard the *Norland*.

So, what did we think of the landing plan? He left us in no
doubt that he considered it a pretty poor compromise between
the political and military expedients, being miles away from
Port Stanley which had to be the final target. He was in favour
of a quick, bold thrust to take the capital. Landing at San
Carlos would mean a big build-up of supplies and logistical
arrangements and a long and risky helicopter hop to get the
troops across East Falkland to attack the capital, and if the helicopters were not available, it would mean 'a pretty long "tab"'
(para slang for march, the equivalent of the marines' 'yomp').
'H''s feeling about the plan being a compromise was still
shared by everyone, including, I suspect, Brigadier Thompson
himself. 'H' also underlined the vulnerability of troops on the
ground to air attack, and was worried about the distance 2 Para

would have to move in the dark to dig in on the heights of Sussex Mountains. From San Carlos Settlement Beach, it would be a distance of five miles, most of it along the track south to Darwin.

The zero hour, or 'H' hour, for landing was 06.00 GMT, or Zulu, two o'clock in the morning local time, which would give about four and a half hours to sunrise. I was astonished to be told that 'H' thought the battalion would be lucky if it moved at much more than one mile an hour in that terrain, which had been compared to Dartmoor or the Brecon Beacons where the paras did much of their training. With progress estimated to be as slow as this, it meant a very tight timetable with every possibility of the battalion being found in the open in daylight if there was a delay in the landing or a hold-up on the track. It still was not known for sure if parts of the track and the beaches round the anchorage, at least, had been mined.

After these discussions with 'H', there was a guided tour of the ship by the Senior Naval Officer, Commander Chris Esplin-Jones. One of the strangest features of the modern Navy is the number of serving officers with double-barrelled names, often ending in 'Jones'. Chris was a helicopter engineer by training, and had been summoned to the *Norland* only two days before sailing. He had a genial round face, with heavy glasses and balding red hair. He was as relaxed and informal as all the Navy staff officers we had met in HMS *Fearless* at Ascension seemed stiff and awkward in the presence of the press. 'I am just an engineer,' said Chris after the formal introductions had been made, 'and I suppose you could say my politics are well to the right of Genghis Khan.' He proved a marvellous guide and a fund of information on all manner of aspects of the campaign, particularly on the deployment of the helicopters. His forte was playing the devil's advocate for the Argentinians, and in the most alarmist way.

'If I were them now, I'd wait till we started approaching the Falklands, and then throw everything they'd got in their air force at us. Swamp the Task Force, that's what I'd do, and they'd be bound to get some of their planes through. That's what should happen once we get in and start landing. If they throw everything at us, it's going to be pretty difficult.'

Despite such Cassandra-like predictions, his face beamed as he thought up each new and more terrible possibility. Taking us round the ship, he pointed out how the troops would disembark, the equivalent of the *Canberra*'s galley-port leap, only in the *Norland* this looked like a gaping hole in the hull on one of the car decks, which were slippery with oil and grease and scattered with heavy chains and cables, easy to trip over in the dark. In the main canteen he apologised for the squalor, but fifteen hundred men had to eat in each meal-break of an hour or so. Sometimes there were queues for half an hour, with no privileges in this for officers and senior NCOs. The menus were even more restricted since the *Sheffield* had been hit, as this had led to an order to stop all deep-frying in the Task Force. When the fuel of the Exocet missile in HMS *Sheffield* ignited and started the fire amidships, it soon spread to the galley where the deep-fry vats exploded. Five catering staff were among the dead.

To round off the tour, Chris took us to the bridge, a much less grand affair than the *Canberra*'s, where the navigation plots had to be made by the Naval Party behind a thick curtain as a blackout, as there was no separate chartroom. In the wireless room there was a Marisat link and it was nothing like the sacred totem it was on the liner, where the P and O and the Naval signals staff frequently bickered about its use, and occasionally made their own attempts at censorship.

In the early evening, 'H' called the whole battalion together in the ship's Continental Lounge, as he wanted to give them his view of what lay ahead. They were crammed in, row on row, but looked as disciplined as if on a parade ground. 'H' stood in front of a large map and indicated the main phases of the landings. He told them of the timings, first the convoy assembling at the rendezvous point north of Falkland Sound, the run-in past Fanning Head with the *Norland* anchoring off the mouth of San Carlos Water, and then the disembarkation and the landing at San Carlos Settlement, Blue Beach One. The address was one of the most extraordinary and dramatic projections of a personality I have ever seen. It was quite unselfconscious, clearly the work of a man who was in his element. 'H' leaned forward, showing the profile of his long nose and jutting chin, with the curling, wrinkling, almost Punch-like mouth in between. He told the battalion that the assault would be soon, in the next day or two, and that they must be ready to move quickly. On the last two nights aboard they must sleep in their clothes, not least because of the threat of air and underwater attacks. The theme of his talk was the need for aggression when the time came. 'When Maggie gives the order to go, which she will soon, I want maximum aggression. If we hit the enemy hard, then he'll fold. So far their forces haven't put up a fight. They didn't on South Georgia, and they didn't on Pebble Island. So perhaps they won't at all. But you can't rely on that. You've got to go in hard against them.'

That evening we were taken to meet the captain, a wry Yorkshireman, Don Ellerby. He had been worried about taking the ship so close to the Falklands, because nothing of this had been mentioned when the *Norland* was requisitioned. Some of the crew had not thought the ship would go beyond Ascension and had been alarmed at the call-up to active service that weekend.

At supper in the ship's officers' dining-room, the Navy men and the *Norland*'s officers ate at separate tables. There were no Royal Naval Reserve men in the ferry's command and, unlike the *Canberra*'s hierarchy, the men of Hull made no claims to the Nelson Touch.

At supper we met the second in command of the Naval Party, Lieutenant-Commander Ian Hughs, a roly-poly character who was working on electronic warfare when he was called to serve under the ensign of North Sea Ferries. He did try to add a dash of tradition in one institution, the 'pipes' to get the men out of their bunks or 'pits' in the morning. Each morning the pipes became more elaborate productions, blasts on a bosun's whistle followed by a piece of doggerel. One morning this was substituted with strains of 'Rule Brittania'.

My second day aboard the *Norland* was grey and dull, the weather to the south becoming fouler. Most of the company seemed irritable, as there was no indication of when the decision to land would be taken. Tony Rice was trying to get a helicopter ride to the *Europic Ferry* where one of his gunners had blown some fingers off his hand after tossing a live grenade about in one of the ammunition holds. The flotilla was building up as we had caught up with the LSLs and we had the *Conveyor*, the *Stromness*, the *Europic* and *Elk* as transports of equipment and the two assault ships or LPDs, the *Fearless* and the *Intrepid*. Ahead was a heavy screen of destroyers and frigates. Helicopters roared overhead on anti-submarine patrols, the blue Navy Lynxes from the frigates, with their dolphin-like bulbous noses, carrying the silver-painted torpedoes and missiles.

The task of the day was to scrounge the kit that we were not given in the *Canberra*. In this we were helped by Lieutenant Alex Ward, who was to look after us in the landing and see that we dug in with the rest of the battalion on Sussex Mountains. Back at the Depot in Aldershot he had been in charge of the motor pool, and was only too grateful to have found some job that would enable him to join the battalion for the Falklands. Because of the terrain, there were to be no battalion vehicles, except for the Volvo BVs or 'Bandwaggons', tracked vehicles for Arctic snow which the marines had brought and would administer. The principal job for Alex was to be a spare pair of hands at Battalion HQ, particularly in manning the radio watches. He was a calm, enthusiastic, fair-haired man of twenty-five, strong as an ox, but surprisingly on the chunky side for a paratrooper, whereas men like Chris Keeble and the company commanders looked positively ascetic. In the Falklands campaign he met his moment, and he was made second in command of 'A' Company after Goose Green.

As we were escorted round the Quartermaster's Stores on the lower car decks, we were laughed almost off the ship. No, there were no trenching shovels, puttees, waterproof coats, ponchos or over-trousers, particularly for the press. Some of the older sergeants looked at us as if we had come from Mars, and 'young Mr Ward' was only to be pitied for the rotten deal he had been given in looking after us. Eventually the kit did appear in generous supply, with several pairs of thick, white, woollen Arctic socks and the thin, light Arctic underwear, very different from the civilian thermal underwear and much easier to move in. Equally vital were the quilted 'Mao' suits, which were to be worn under combat trousers and smock. 'They're great,' warned Alex, 'but the problem is that they only come in two sizes, and fit either Chinese dwarves or giants.' I had drawn a dwarf's pair of trousers and a Goliath's quilted jacket.

With all this came the first issue of field rations, Arctic and GS (General Service). Both had alternative menus, and the two favourites were the ones with chicken supreme and curry. Alex Ward was particularly keen on curries and took extra curry powder with him. Most of the troops thought the Arctic 'rats' were more edible and had greater variety, but their drawback was that they needed more water on the understanding that in the Arctic there was plenty of snow. On the Falklands there was always a shortage of water whenever it was most needed, and what there was appeared to be stagnant or frequented by sheep carrying the omni-present fluke. Round the packets of dehydrated vegetables, chicken, curry and rice, there would be bars of chocolate and glucose sweets, 'the nutty' we munched endlessly on the march, and materials for breakfast such as porridge and dehydrated apple and apricot flakes. Often we threw in all the dehydrated foods together if time was short and night coming on or hunger driving us to desperation. Curry with peas and rice and apricot flakes tasted surprisingly good. There were materials for eight or nine 'brews' a day, tea, coffee, chocolate and beef stock and soups, Garibaldi biscuits and dry AB biscuits with a small tin of paste which was also supposed to act as a counter-laxative. All this was to be cooked, stewed, boiled and brewed on a rickety open tin box with a flaming hexamine block, the Army's 'hexy' stove', whose prototype must go back to the beginning of the century. More experienced hands like David Nicholls brought his Swedish camping stove which he took on his mountaineering expeditions, neat little pieces of kit with tiny gas cylinders attached.

The whole object was to travel as light as possible, and items of heavy kit were ditched or thrown into a second rucksack which would be brought ashore when the quartermaster set up his base, known as the 'B' Echelon. So there were no spare shoes, though commandos tended to carry gym shoes with them, and only one change of underwear and socks, the mess tin and spoon with a knife filed in the handle, waterproofs, quilts, a ground sheet, Arctic sleeping-bag, camouflage net, Arctic underwear, 48 hours rations, and a shovel and poncho if I could find them. In addition I carried spare batteries and two cassette recorders, and together this came to about 60 or 70 lbs in weight. Some of the mortar troops would carry nearly twice as much, particularly the man carrying the base plate and tripod of the weapon.

The most difficult things to find were puttees, which gathered in the trousers at the bottom, preventing them from getting wet and flapping round the GS, or General Service, boots. A kind officer gave me his second pair of puttees, but I lost one the first morning scrambling through the tussock to Sussex Mountains in the dark.

Many of the pieces of kit we managed to get from the stores on the car decks were for the photographer sergeant, Ron Hudson, who did not seem well equipped for going ashore. He spent long periods lying on his bunk in the cabin and confessed to David Norris that he did not much care for what was about to happen, and that he did not particularly hate the Argentinians as a people. The stretches of boredom taxed all of us, and for David it led to pilgrimages for cigarettes, a need that preoccupied him greatly when we were ashore.

The tedium of the morning was broken with a brief talk on how to disembark from the landing craft by Sergeant Phil Atkinson, who had been in the marines for three years before signing on in the Army and coming to the Parachute Regiment. The burden of his lecture was that troops in a landing craft must file out quickly by moving to the sides of the craft. Once on the ramp, you must jump to the side and not forward off the lip of the door, as a sudden surge forward by the boat on the tide would grind the landing troops under the ramp and hull. On the diagram I noticed that the shore-line was always spelt 'beech' and the last had the rousing motto: 'We can show that we can do it better than them' (the marines).

On a return visit to the stores on yet another hopeless quest for a trenching tool, I met Sergeant Atkinson, who said, 'You are the most unmilitary-looking person I have met in my life. Look at the way you're wearing those trousers and puttees. My eight-year-old daughter could do better than that.'

I did not know whether to take this as a compliment or an insult, but added, 'At least I can spell beach.'

'I joined the Army to fight, not spell,' rejoined the Sergeant.

On the World Service News there was much speculation about a landing on the Falklands taking place within a day or two. It was reported that the *Canberra* and the other troop-carrying ships had met the carrier group of the Task Force, which surprised us, as no one with the Task Force was allowed to mention details of position and deployment in such precise terms; this was reported by defence correspondents and sanctioned by the Ministry of Defence. It was speculated on three days running that the landing was likely to be at night and somewhere between the two main islands of the Falklands Group.

'H' became frantic at the lack of clear orders to go ahead with the landing. His refrain now, and for a week to come, was: 'It's about time Maggie got a grip of her knickers. We've got to go now. How can we get on to Downing Street? It looks as if the weather is OK. She's got to get a grip now and take the cabinet along with her.' If he could have found some way of speaking to Downing Street, I think 'H' might well have done so. With him it was always the personal touch that won through; after all, it was how he managed to get his battalion attached to 3 Commando Brigade for the landing.

He was at his most relaxed at meal-times, the only time when he would pause for conversation about anything outside immediate military matters. He talked about his children and their education, and at one point seemed on the brink of a theological clash with Chris Keeble. The second story in the British news at this time was whether the Pope would go ahead with his pastoral visit to Britain, due to start in ten days' time on 29 May. It had been reported that Popes in recent times had tried to avoid visiting nations at war, and in this case the Pope was bound to favour Argentina as a nominally Catholic state and a country with a high level of religious observance. The Vatican would almost certainly be bending the Pope's ear not to visit Britain for fear of offending the Catholic military regimes in Latin America; and many of the curia would be working from first-hand knowledge, as the priesthood in many areas of Argentina, and particularly in the armed forces, is predominantly Italian. Chris Keeble as a devout Catholic was plainly disappointed that the visit looked like being cancelled. With the later news that a compromise was emerging, Chris was obviously delighted, and said he had every faith that the Pope's visit would lead to some kind of peace formula being devised. A firm Anglican, 'H' did not disguise his distaste for the Papacy and the Roman Catholic Church, and scorned Chris Keeble's hopes for the Papal peace mission in the most caustic terms.

In the evening, 'H' ordered a full drill for embarking in the landing craft, just in case the landing should be set for the morning of Thursday 20 May. In the Continental Lounge each group formed up by boats, about 150 at a time, in ranks of eight. David Norris and I were with the heavy weapons platoon of Headquarters Company, the mortars, the padre and the Regimental Aid Post which would be responsible for first aid in the forward area of a battle. With us was the Forward Aircraft Controller, Squadron-Leader Jock Penman, who had joined the RAF in 1946 and was about to retire. He was a crusty Scot whose job was to guide the RAF Ground Attack, GR3 Harriers onto forward targets, a highly skilled task requiring physical courage, as he would have to operate ahead of the main battalion when it dug in on Sussex Mountains. He was a fund of good information about the state of the air battles.

We were in No. 3 Boat, which would be one of the nearest to San Carlos Settlement. Riflemen in the forward part of the boat were told that they might have to go ashore to support 'D' Company in Boat 4 if there was a fight in the settlement. A bigger concern was not shooting the 40 Commando flank company nearest 2 Para, the unit due to take San Carlos itself. The problems of avoiding shooting friendly forces in the dark were to be uppermost with company commanders in 3 Brigade throughout the campaign and in the murky winter darkness and unpredictable terrain of the Falklands it was recognised that this was bound to happen. The responsibility of making sure 'D' Company did not fire on 40 Commando or the settlers fell to Chris Keeble, while 'H' went with the forward two companies to get them moving up the track to the positions on the high ground of the mountains.

Once formed up, the companies moved in single file down to the disembarkation port on the lower car deck, shuffling through the dark, stumbling over bollards and chains, holding onto the man in front. In one part of the ship the men walking up a ramp were silhouetted by a dim red lamp, their shadows on the walls like those of a ghostly race of giant miners, with the picks and shovels protruding from their packs. As we passed the port from which we would slide down into the landing craft, we felt a blast of cold wind. 'When you feel that, you'll know we're really going and there'll be no turning back,' said Chris Keeble at my side.

By the following morning most of the Harrier pilots had departed for the *Atlantic Conveyor* to prepare their aircraft, which had been packed in huge black polythene bags as if they were toy construction models. Many of the Chinook team wanted to cross-deck to the *Conveyor* as well to put their helicopters together. Their commanding officer, Tony Stables, explained that it took roughly a day to bolt on the huge rotor blades which had to be packed away to make space on the container ship. He extolled his machines, 'Marvellous things really. It's surprising that the RAF have only just decided to have this kind of machine again.' The design of the Chinook goes back well into the 1950s, when twin-rotor helicopters were already quite commonplace in Western air forces. Wing-Commander Stables claimed that the RAF order had just about saved the helicopter section of Boeing from going bust. The machines would give the Task Force the ability to lift the light tanks ashore and carry huge quantities of artillery ammunition.

Another favourite with the helicopter men was the old Wessex 5, a bit long in the tooth now and overshadowed by the more glamorous Sea King. The Wessex had about half the capacity of the bigger machine, and could carry about ten or twelve assault troops to the Sea King's twenty. They seemed to be from the sticks-and-string biplane era compared with the Sea Kings, with wires and struts plainly visible inside the fuselage. The air crew loved them for this. They were much easier to maintain than the Sea King, where large pieces of fuselage were moulded together, rather in the manner of a mass-produced car, so when one piece had to be replaced, large sections had to be dismantled as well. The Wessex belied its 'Paraffin Parrot' image and worked throughout the storms and blizzards of the Falklands land campaign with very little incident or need for maintenance.

In the cabin opposite ours lived Petty Officer Steve Wooley, an aircrewman of the Wessex Squadron. We had met six years before in the Cod War of 1976 when he was serving as the crewman to the Wasp in the Leander frigate HMS *Scylla*. In the four-week patrol round Iceland, I used to go up in the Wasp almost daily to relieve the boredom, and frequently met Steve in the hangar. He had the philosophy of Sancho Panza: sane, reasonable and downbeat. He did not care too much for the idea of fighting round the Falklands, and later, when we met in the *Fearless*, referred to the whole thing as a 'big nause'. One of our successes with the Quartermaster was to purloin a paratrooper's helmet, which being made out of reinforced glass fibre was much lighter than the steel helmet of the marines and fitted better. When Steve saw me with it, he asked if I was serious about landing with the paras. He thought I was quite barmy to even contemplate it.

Another mine of information about the helicopters was Chris Esplin-Jones, who had been closely involved in planning the replacement for the Sea King. One of the outstanding features of the campaign was the durability of both the Sea Kings and the Wessex helicopters. In peacetime the machines undergo hours of maintenance after relatively few flying hours. Many of the Sea Kings, the Wessex and the smaller machines

– Lynx, Wasp, Gazelle and Scout – had almost no full service for the duration of hostilities; this was the true import of the term 'wartime maintenance schedules'.

Chris Esplin-Jones remarked: 'I suppose they'll just shove them in the hangars for the return journey, and the ground crews will work on them non-stop. And that'll be when the trouble will start. As soon as they begin flying again they'll begin breaking down regularly.'

The Sea Kings had a great asset in their specially reinforced and coated blades, which gave them a longer flying life before replacement than any equivalent helicopter in the world, and it meant that they could operate in temperatures of ten degrees lower than Sea Kings with other air forces.

One afternoon the coffee pantry brought a meeting with a mild man with a rounded face, all curves and no angles, which bore a constantly puzzled expression as he spoke hesitantly in a soft Yorkshire accent. He was the padre, the Reverend David Cooper, who for some years had been the only parachute-trained priest in the British Army. Next to 'H' Jones, he was the most outstanding personality in the battalion, and probably the man the Toms respected most. He says he became a priest 'through the back door', because his friends went to church when he was a teenager, 'and this was the best way to meet the girls, as it was the only time their mums and dads would allow them out by themselves'. He grew up in Leeds where he first worked as a curate before joining the Army, 'which I did on a suck it and see basis, and if I didn't like it I'd get out'. He wanted to join the Army because of what he calls 'the hobby', championship target shooting. A couple of days after his return from the Falklands he won the individual Army rifle target-shooting trophy at Bisley and 2 Para won the team event. He probably knew more about rifle fire power in the Falklands than any other man in his battalion, and he took a particular interest in the training of the snipers, frequently giving them target-shooting instruction on the ranges. He concluded that throughout the land campaign the Argentinian snipers were better than the British ones, and had more suitable weapons for the terrain. 'Nobody took sniper training really seriously in the battalion until Chris Keeble arrived last Christmas and as second in command reorganised the instruction schedules,' David Cooper told me later.

David Cooper's greatest ability was to communicate with the men round him in a way I have never seen in any other priest. He could talk to them at their own level, individually, and in his sermons he held them all in the palm of his hand with a mixture of humour, whimsical anecdote and blunt talk, of 'telling them like it is'. His whole approach is summed up in the Yorkshire expression 'think on', but the way he gets you to 'think on' is subtle and beguiling. Something of the First World War's front-line priest-poet Woodbine Willie lives in the work of the unassuming and mild man from Leeds.

Our first conversation was about the Argentinians. What kind of army were they? How hard would they fight, and how much did they care about the Malvinas being Argentinian? I said I knew they were a mixed bunch, many with Italian origins, a people I knew well. This was one of the few discussions of any kind about the other side during the voyage south, and the most illuminating thing I had heard about contemporary Argentina was a talk by V. S. Naipaul on the World Service based on his collection of essays on the same subject published ten years previously. He described the people as the poor, hopeful migrants from Europe a hundred years ago looking for a new life and fortune in South America, but Argentina today, he said, was a desert of disappointed dreams.

Instead of the usual pipe on Thursday 20 May we were blasted from our bunks with a tape of the full orchestral rendition of 'The Ride of the Valkyries', the paras' regimental march. For the rest of that Thursday you could hear young paras whistling the 'Ride' up and down the passageways of the *Norland*. The music was accompanied by a piece of doggerel on the lines of 'Wakey, Wakey, Rise and Shine, it's time to sock the Argentine'. With an overture to the day like that, both David Norris and I thought the order was bound to be given to land.

For hours there was no sign of the command being given. The *Norland* was now one of a tight convoy bowling along in a box formation flanked by destroyers and frigates, some less than a hundred yards away. There were heavy rain clouds and a hint of mist, ideal conditions for making a run into the Falklands. At the rear of the convoy the carrier HMS *Invincible* could be discerned dimly through the mist, turning to the east to launch a Harrier patrol, and the day before we had seen the outline of HMS *Hermes*. The sight of thirty ships ploughing along through the curling waves was one of the most dramatic in the sea war. Overhead roared the Harriers and the helicopters droned out to the flanks to begin 'dunking' their sonars into the waves on anti-submarine patrols. The destroyers and frigates, the *Antrim, Broadsword, Brilliant, Argonaut, Plymouth, Yarmouth* and *Ardent*, signalled with their Aldis lamps. Still there was no news that 'D' Day was on the morrow, and 'H' was getting in a frenzy.

The signal arrived in mid-afternoon, seven hours late. It had been sent in the morning from HMS *Fearless*, but the machine for transcribing the message, known as a 'literaliser', had given out half-way through. The *Norland* asked for the message to be retransmitted, but the staff aboard the *Fearless* declined to do so.

In the afternoon, 'H' sent a message by lamp to HMS *Broadsword*, a Type 22 destroyer on the *Norland*'s port quarter, asking if she had received any orders. She replied that she had and came alongside to fire a copy by a gunline between the two ships. The refusal of the *Fearless* to repeat the order seems extraordinary, and 'H' was fuming at getting the instruction seven hours later than he should have done.

Just before lunch, Captain Kevin Arnold gave an 'interest' lecture on Naval Gunfire Support, in which he described his own work in the bombardment of Pebble Island. In the *Canberra* we had similar talks about mortar and artillery cover, though much of the mathematics was Greek to me. Kevin Arnold described the two principal types of Naval 4.5-inch gun, the Mark 6 semi-automatic, mounted in the twin turrets of older ships like the *Plymouth* and *Yarmouth*, and the faster-firing Mark 8 automatic rapid fire in the Type 42s and Type 21s. With a rare sense of prophecy, he concluded, 'I prefer the Mark 6, which though slower-firing is more reliable. The trouble with the Mark 8s is that they tend to fall over when you need them most.'

In the afternoon the bar was shut up and the space-invader machines switched off. The RAMC medical teams and the paras' Field Ambulance men started sawing off the legs of the tables in the lounge round the bar, as this was to be an operating theatre and they wanted to set up their own table. On one of the tables I saw a submachine-gun, stethoscope, a plumber's spanner and a screw driver side by side, four symbols to sum up the campaign.

The doctors in the *Norland* were as friendly as many of their Naval colleagues in the *Canberra* had seemed stand-offish. Most senior was a mild and shy Scot, Colonel Bill MacGregor, whose surgical achievements at Ajax Bay and in Port Stanley are worth a chapter on their own. One of the most cheerful was Rory Waggon, a balding man with gold-rimmed glasses through which he goggled disbelievingly through the round lenses. Youngest was Steve Hughes, who at twenty-five had finished training only a year before.

The afternoon was a rush to scrounge the last items of kit; and I still could not persuade anyone to provide a shovel to be shared between two journalists. 'H' insisted that there should be some digging facility for the press and offered me his shovel as he said he thought he would be too busy to use it himself. Alex Ward was searching vainly for the armourer to cut his binoculars in two, a task which obsessed him. He said it would make them much lighter to carry as he would use the one half as a small telescope. This accomplished, the next obsession was to find his missing cassette of the Fauré Requiem which he intended to take ashore with his miniature cassette player as his main entertainment between 'stags' in the Battalion HQ tent and seeing the journalists properly fed and watered.

Supper was early and there I met WO2 Bob 'Buster' Brown of the Royal Marines' Police, whom I knew from the *Canberra*. He had come over to prepare the *Norland* as a prisoner of war ship. Like Steve Wooley, he gave me a look of pity when he heard that David and I intended to land with the paras and climb Sussex Mountains with them.

In the evening we spent an hour or so on our bunks, and later were asked to an informal service conducted by David Cooper in the Continental Lounge. It was an occasion to sing a few hymns together and say a prayer or two before we landed, he said. There was Bunyan's 'He who would valiant be' and 'One we've got to know quite a bit on our journey south,' as David put it, 'Eternal father strong to save', as well a favourite with the troops, 'I vow to thee my country', whose tune they found hard to retain. David himself gave a short address: 'I think I should say a few words now and you probably might say I would say what I have to say now, otherwise I would not be here.' He gave one of his short, sharp sermons, direct and warm and never dodging the main issue. This sermon has received very little publicity, but it is really the first half to the address he gave later in Stanley Cathedral on 16 June, which was broadcast to great effect with its references about 'thinking on' and 'thinking of what you valued most, your wife, your girlfriend or your dog, or maybe life itself.'

On the *Norland* he told the paras: 'I don't think God is over-concerned with causes, as much as He is with people. Some of you will face fear and death. Some of you will die. I have to say this, because this is what I believe in, I want you to know that you will not be alone. God will be with you, and whatever happens this is not the end.' The address lasted barely five minutes, and everyone listened. I was at the rear of the congregation with Chris Keeble and Chris Esplin-Jones, and in the middle of the throng I could see 'H' sharing his hymn sheet with a para. That group of people in the lounge called together by David Cooper was united in a way that I found no other in the entire campaign. Services in the *Canberra*, however ecumenical, were very much a meeting of officers and senior ranks, with very few junior ranks and serving men present. In gatherings organised by David Cooper, there are very few distinctions.

The convoy appeared to reach the rendezvous point fifty miles north of the Sound on time, but then there was a delay which was difficult to explain. The formation for the approach was not in the right order, and HMS *Fearless* was astern instead of ahead in the column that had to pass Fanning Head. As the landings began, there was to be a diversionary attack on Fanning Head where there was thought to be a company of Argentinians overlooking the narrows.

The previous night, 19/20 May, a troop of SAS, which had been involved in the successful Pebble Island raid, was cross-decking in a Sea King helicopter from HMS *Intrepid*. According to some reports, an albatross hit the tail rotor of the helicopter as it took off and it plunged into the sea, killing eighteen of the SAS men and two crewmen. It was the worst single disaster for the SAS in their recent history. The setback may have accounted for a change of plan for the Fanning Head operation and the forces who would accomplish that would now have to leave from a different ship.

After an hour the convoy set off for the coast, with the *Fearless* leading the landing forces. 'H' Jones invited David Norris and me onto the roof of the bridge to watch as the ships slipped down the straits, and to see if we could spot any Argentinian lights on the foreland. Our faces had been 'cammed up', covered with sticky camouflage paste. As we climbed up onto the roof with Chris Keeble and Chris Esplin-Jones, 'H' told us to keep away from the ship's sides in case the enemy opened up with heavy machine-guns. For some time we could see very little on the headland, despite the assistance of a night-vision telescope with an image intensifier. Before us we could see the *Fearless* with one light burning dimly inside her tank deck. For a moment we thought we could see one light on Fanning Head, perhaps a bonfire, but there was no sign that we had been spotted by lookouts on either side of the water.

The night was cool and still, starry but with a few clouds, and the waters were dead calm. Our conversation was casual, and 'H's' main worry was still the operation's vulnerability to air attack. The principal weapon the battalion had against aircraft was the Blowpipe shoulder-fired missile. 'A lot will depend on the nerve of the gunners themselves,' 'H' said. 'It takes a lot to stand up and fire at a plane with your body exposed from the waist up.' Again he speculated on how his men would face up to strafing from the air, and, he said, neither he nor anyone else in the battalion had had any previous experience of such attacks. During the evening he spoke to me of his Christian belief and said he did not believe in any unnecessary killing of the enemy.

As we passed Fanning Head we prepared to go below. Eventually our boat numbers were called to assemble in the main lounge where there was a scene like a street market. Sergeants were handing round rubber contraceptives to cover the muzzles of the rifles to keep out mud and water. As we were called into ranks boat by boat, Alex Ward swung his bergen on his back and walloped me across the face, splitting my top lip, the only scratch I was to receive in the entire campaign. One of the RAP orderlies quickly slapped on a plaster, though the wretched lip continued to bleed throughout the day. We seemed to wait for eternity in our rows for embarkation, and later we were told the delay had been due to an accident with the first boat. A man had slipped between the landing craft and the *Norland*, crushing his pelvis. By now the operation was well over an hour behind schedule. Suddenly the order to move was given, and we pushed forward, stumbling in the dark, grabbing the pack of the man in front, now stopping abruptly and now moving forward with a jerk. Round the maze of the car decks we went, with their tangle of chains and cables and only a dim red interior light on one corner. The blast of fresh air was a relief as we came to the hole against which the landing craft was nudging gently. It was not so much a leap as a slither as two marines helped me down a short ladder, and then David Norris and I crammed against the aft end of the landing craft, Chris Keeble between us.

The first thing we were told was that the landing craft's radar, a primitive little instrument at the best of times, was faulty. We shoved off, and seemed to motor round in circles, with the hulls of the *Norland* and the *Fearless* looming over the sides from time to time. The night was still, clouded and not bright. We set off towards the entrance to the south arm of San Carlos Water. As the four craft began to move together, the firing of Naval guns at Fanning Head ripped the air and became louder as we moved into San Carlos Water. There would be a thud, the sound of tearing cardboard and the report of the shell landing. As the landing craft turned south, I could smell cordite heavy in the air.

At this time the raid on Fanning Head was going in. The party of special forces and marines had at their head Captain Rod Bell, chosen for his expertise in Latin American Spanish. Having grown up in several South American countries, he had joined the marines speaking better Spanish than English, recalls Julian Thompson, who ran the training company with Jeremy Moore at the time. When Rod lost his temper, he often swore in Spanish, and whenever he referred to the locations on East Falkland, he gave names like San Carlos and Cantara a distinct Spanish twang. As the attack began on Fanning Head, he stood up and shouted through a loudhailer in Spanish: 'Come out and surrender, we have you surrounded.' The trick did not work. The Argentinians, about a company strong, fought back despite heavy shelling from the ships, and when the fight died down many retreated along the spur towards Port San Carlos. A few did give up to the marines, but 'H' Jones's prediction was being proved wrong: the Argentinians could and would fight back. With the failure of Rod Bell's appeals through the megaphone, Brigadier Thompson was reluctant to try again with 'Psy Ops' (Psychological Operations), if the ruse can be graced with so grand a title.

As the landing craft moved down San Carlos Water, Chris Keeble gave a running commentary. We expected the enemy to be around the anchorage in very small numbers, but latest intelligence was that they were not there at all, though 2 Para would wait until 40 Commando had made sure there were no Argentinians in San Carlos Settlement. 'It's all just as I envisaged it from the intelligence photographs,' Chris exclaimed. 'We'll pass a headland soon and turn in in about twenty minutes.' He continued to ask if the radar was working, and then if there were any lights from the SBS patrol. The

Naval guns boomed and thudded steadily behind us.

In the landing craft we were cramped and jammed shoulder to shoulder, our bergens stuffed behind us. David Norris said he was dying for a cigarette, as he was to repeat a thousand times in the days ahead.

In the run towards the landing-site we appeared to have made up time and were about half an hour behind schedule. The sky was getting steadily brighter as the moon began to rise and some of the most brilliant stars appeared in the south. The landing craft swung sharply to the east, and moved into the beach. The red light had appeared from the SBS and the order to haul on bergens was given. 'What was that?' Chris Keeble asked sharply. 'I am sure I heard a shot.' I had not heard anything, but later we discovered that a rifle had gone off when the order was given to release safety catches and a para had shot the edge of his neighbour's boot accidentally. In another craft a submachine-gun had gone off, causing a flesh wound in the leg of the man in front.

I had been muttering into my tape-recorder, but such commentaries are always too long for broadcast. As soon as the ramp went down, I made the simple statement: 'This is the moment we have been waiting for . . . the ramp is down . . . we are going forward . . . I'm in the water,' and at this I kicked the water for evidence and the men round me looked at me as if I had lost my marbles.

The water did not seem particularly cold and the distance to be waded was a bare twenty yards, followed by a scramble across some soft, peaty soil. We crouched down to wait for enemy response, which was hardly expected. In the huddle of small houses, vague shadows on the nearby hill, dogs barked. To our left there was the drone and crashing of gears of the marines' landing craft. We had landed on the Falklands.

5. Ashore

I. 'IF THE GRACE OF GOD ...' SAN CARLOS, 21 MAY

The men sat in small groups on the matted grass, waiting for further orders. Through the damp we heard the clatter of the ramps and the men of 40 Commando wading ashore. Still no sound from the houses, apart from the yowling and barking of the dogs. The moon was becoming brighter. The men of Headquarters Company and the Regimental Aid Post began to sort themselves into some order of march, and Chris Keeble departed to make sure no assistance was required by 40 Commando. To the right, higher up the track, 'H' Jones was preparing to move off with his two leading companies, once the signal was given from the assault engineers that the path was clear of mines.

The signal for the main group of the march to move off was a long time coming. At first we heard that there was an obstacle on the path and the engineers were dealing with it. Once the column did start moving, it went desperately slowly. We were now more than an hour behind schedule, and the sky became lighter as a brilliant star rose over the ridge.

Time-spans in the land campaign are difficult to report. At any point where the body and brain are seized by fear or excitement, time appears to be elastic, now passing agonisingly slowly, now accelerating with the drama of events. When recalling such passages of the past, the memory naturally appears to excise irrelevant details. Reporting the times of particular events in the Falklands after the landings has another hazard, the fixation in the British Task Force for posting operational times in Greenwich Mean Time, or 'Zulu' time as the Navy calls it. 'The Navy does everything in Zulu,' was the only explanation I ever got for this. It made conversation with

the Falklanders almost impossible in recalling events accurately, and it was to bedevil all my radio reports until hostilities
were over. Local Falkland time was four hours behind GMT,
and Port Stanley time was three hours behind GMT. By the
time the main body of 2 Para was moving along the track to
Sussex Mountains, it was about eight o'clock GMT/Zulu or
four o'clock in the morning local time. Dawn was two and a
half to three hours away and the pace was still mournfully
slow.

The obstacle was not anything on the track, but the weight
many of the men were having to carry on their shoulders. The
biggest difficulty was that of the Blowpipe missile crews, who
had to carry the heavy firing stands and the missiles in cases
which made them look like huge green milk bottles. After a
mile or two the first Blowpipe teams had collapsed under the
weight and two men had to be allocated to carry each of the
missiles which were to be the battalion's main air defence that
day. Whoever imagined that these weapons were man-portable
over rough ground for any distance must have been dreaming.
Eventually many of the missiles were dumped and brought up
in daylight by helicopters. But the delays caused by the Blowpipe crews and the twisted ankles in the tussock grass were
beginning to raise tempers as the sky became a streak of grey
and then a deepening blue over our shoulders.

The landscape revealed by the dawn was oddly familiar. It
looked like the gentler rising ground of Exmoor or Dartmoor
as we trudged up the ascending scale of ridges. Looking back at
the anchorage, it might have been a loch in the quieter parts of
the west of Scotland, and the outcrops of rock punctuating the
peat, rough grass, bracken and heather could have been
anywhere from Caithness to Donegal. The unusual feature was
the lack of trees, and there was not a bush bigger than a stunted
clump of gorse. It has not been the fashion to praise the subtle
beauties of the Falkland landscape, and more the habit in the
reporting of the winter campaign to revile it for its harshness
and the climate for its perversity. Perhaps for most who disembarked at San Carlos that Friday in May there was never to
be time enough or opportunity to pause to take in the tran-

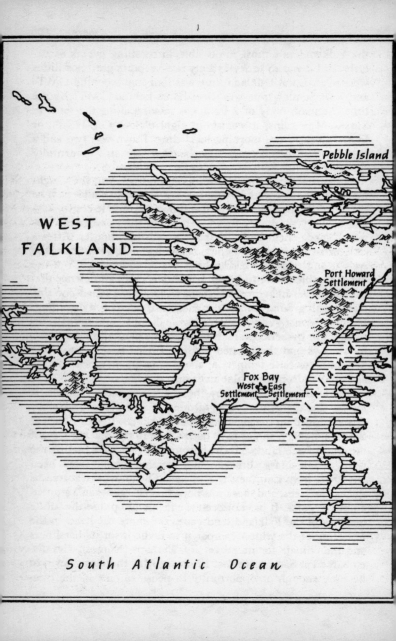

Pebble Island

WEST
FALKLAND

Port Howard
Settlement

Falkland

Fox Bay
West ★ East
Settlement   Settlement

South Atlantic Ocean

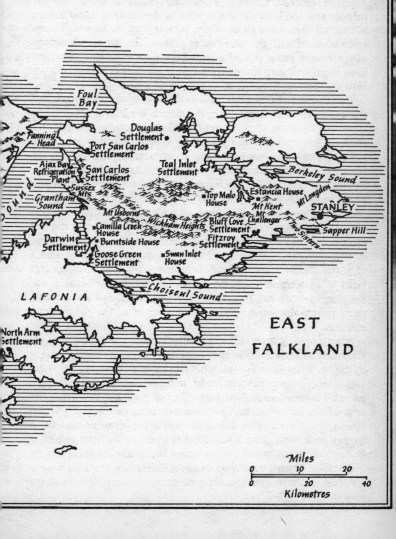

South Atlantic Ocean

Foul
Bay

Fanning
Head

Douglas
Settlement

Port San Carlos
Settlement

Ajax Bay
Refrigeration
Plant

San Carlos
Settlement

Teal Inlet
Settlement

Berkeley Sound

Sussex
Mts

Top Malo
House

Estancia House

Mt Longdon

Grantham
Sound

Mt Usborne

Wickham Heights

Mt Kent

Mt
Challenger

STANLEY

Camilla Creek
House

Bluff Cove
Settlement

Two Sisters

Darwin
Settlement

Burntside House

Fitzroy
Settlement

Sapper Hill

Goose Green
Settlement

Swan Inlet
House

Choiseul Sound

LAFONIA

EAST
FALKLAND

North Arm
Settlement

Miles

0   10   20

0   20   40

Kilometres

quility and the wild and romantic displays that nature made
there. The landscape was a continuing drama. The weather and
wind was never the same for more than half an hour on end
and the colours across the hillside changed shade by the
minute and the hour. The morning of the landing it was a deep
autumnal hue, with most of the country up to Sussex Mountains covered with the pale coarse grass of the island. Occasionally spongey moss coated a peat bog, deceiving the marching
men like small elephant traps as they squelched up to the knee
into the oozing grey mess.

To anyone used to wilder hill-farming country in Britain and
the moorlands of Yorkshire, the South-West and Wales, the
terrain was not strange. It reminded the paratroopers of their
training grounds in the Brecons in Wales. It reminded me of
the famous cross-country course at school, known as the
Russell after its founder, the Devon parson Jack Russell,
breeder of terriers. In the Russell we had to ford rivers seven
times in as many miles and drag up steep ridges of rough grass.
As we topped each rise there was always yet another crest
ahead. The trick was to take shorter strides the steeper the hill
and to be careful of pocks and holes in the ground made by
horses and cattle. This was the technique to use now, and I
took the line of march where the going seemed to be surer and
risks of turning ankles least. I was amazed to find that I was
keeping up with the rest of the battalion HQ, as I knew I had
done much less fitness training than most of the men in the
column.

After crossing a small bridge, the battalion was due to leave
the track and move up to the rocks on the top of the mountains
to dig in. It was hard to tell what the landmarks were; the track
was scarcely obvious for most of its length and the only feature
to work by was a small stream. By the time the sun rose, the
rear of the battalion had just started to leave the flat ground
round the shore. The schedule for the operation had been
highly optimistic, and it was hard to cover in an hour one mile
of such difficult ground with heavy loads like Blowpipe.

Another hazard was map reading. Many of the maps were
incomplete or inaccurate. Despite famous names like William

FitzRoy and Captain James Cook being associated with the cartography of the Falklands, maps of the islands still look remarkably empty. They do have a plethora of names, probably twice as many place-names as there are inhabitants outside Port Stanley. Distances and locations of minor features were sometimes wrong. To expect 2 Para to make the five miles from San Carlos to Sussex Mountains in four hours or under now not only seemed optimistic, but it appeared we were taking the long way from San Carlos water itself. As we started to move up from the stream and above the track to Darwin, Chris Keeble muttered to me, 'This is disastrous.' Five hundred men of the battalion were strung out across a bowl of open ground in bright autumn sunshine. It looked like an invitation to ground attack from the Argentinian air force.

In the distance there was the drone of an aircraft. 'Pucara?' asked someone. Men began digging hastily and getting down in the long grass. Chris Keeble yelled: 'Get up, you bloody fools, don't you know the sound of a Scout helicopter yet. It's one of ours.' The helicopter hopped over the rise below us and Chris went back to herding the rear of the column like scattered sheep. As we climbed up the steepening slope, the photographer sergeant said he did not like the way things were turning out.

By an outcrop of rock I came across Major Tony Rice, the battery commander, with his wireless operators. His seemed the only calm voice at the moment. Looking down the valley ahead suddenly I said, 'Somebody's opened fire.' We saw a cloud of blue smoke and a piece of material fluttering like an autumn leaf. Dangling underneath was a body; it was the parachute of a pilot whose Pucara had been shot down. 'At least the Navy can do something right, they've just brought down that Pucara,' said Tony Rice as he became busy with establishing the battalion headquarters.

The Navy had not shot down the aircraft. It was brought down by an SAS patrol which had been covering the landings. They had fired a shoulder-launched American missile called a 'Stinger'. Brigadier Thompson was enormously impressed with this weapon as it was lighter to carry than the Blowpipe

and did not require the operator to expose himself so much as a
target. It works on the 'fire and forget' principle, as the missile
itself is heat-seeking and does not have to be guided visually
and manually by joy-stick like the Blowpipe, which calls for
considerable dexterity as well as steady nerves. At the end of
the campaign, Julian Thompson summed up the sentiments of
most of his field commanders when he said: 'I think Blowpipe
should be binned after this.' Blowpipe did claim eight hits on
Pucara, but its missile was too slow (under Mach 1, the speed
of sound), to be used against jets unless they were diving
straight at the gunner and at a speed of under 300 knots.

After the Pucara was shot down, there was a shout of 'Air
Raid Warning Red, Take Cover.' We nestled into some
bracken-clad rocks and watched the anchorage. In the distance
I could see the *Canberra*, her white hull gleaming in the
autumn haze. As I watched, I saw two huge splashes by her
hull, but it was too far to see the aircraft attacking the ships. At
first I did not realise that they were being bombed and I said: 'I
think something is happening down there.' We could not
believe it as it looked so calm. Turning to look up the valley, I
saw two Aermacchi jets two miles away, appearing to drift
almost lazily towards us. Both had drop tanks on their wings
glinting in the sun. They were coming straight at us and the
apprehension in that moment of strafing from the air was the
most frightening experience I had in the entire campaign.
After several minutes the planes drifted away to the east and
were hidden by a spine of hills running up to Mount Usborne
in the south.

I felt our luck could not last and that the Argentinian air
force must start attacking soon while the men were still spread
out in the open. Few had started digging in and most were
trying to find their positions. But their difficulties were
nothing to those of the landing force elsewhere.

The landing craft which had 'rubbish skipped' 2 Para ashore
at Bonner's Bay close to San Carlos Settlement were the grey-
and-black camouflaged LCUs from HMS *Fearless*. By a
curious paradox these four boats now had to go back the length
of San Carlos Water to disembark 3 Para from HMS *Intrepid*

and land them at San Carlos Port. In the first wave of the operation, the four LCUs from HMS *Intrepid*, which were painted a vivid tiger stripe camouflage of black and green, went to HMS *Fearless* to carry 40 Commando ashore on the left flank of 2 Para at San Carlos Settlement. The *Intrepid* boats then returned to take 45 Commando to Ajax Bay, where Ivan Helberg's Commando Logistics Regiment was also to set up its base, the Brigade Maintenance Area (known as the BMA), at Red Beach. The LSLs also began disgorging their argosies of men, materials and vehicles. In between them ploughed the smaller landing boats, the LCVPs (Landing Craft Vehicle Personnel, with the capacity of an infantry platoon or a Land Rover and trailer), the rigid raiders and the Navy's Gemini dinghies powered by outboard motors. Soon after daylight, the Sea Kings began lifting ammunition for small arms and the mortars ashore with the field guns and the components of the Rapier missile batteries.

Because the disembarkation of 2 Para had been so long delayed, troops going ashore at the head of the anchorage to San Carlos Port were now likely to be ambushed by the dawn before they could move off the landing beach. It was broad daylight when 3 Para went down the ramps into the little port. In one of the boats there was a delay due to the language barrier between the paratroopers and the marines. The normal marine order for disembarkation from a landing craft is 'Troops Out', and when the Marine sergeant gave this order the Paras did not move. The sergeant repeated the command quietly, and then a Para sergeant realised what was happening and yelled 'Go!', the normal paratroop command for a parachute jump from an aircraft, and the men jumped into the water and dashed for the beach. There was some ill-feeling towards the marines because some of the paras in the landings at either end of the anchorage found themselves jumping into water up to their waists. The rock formations in the water were extremely variable and there was no smooth shelf on the beach.

At Port San Carlos 3 Para came closest of the landing troops to opposition as they moved towards the houses. According to one report, part of the company of Argentinians that had been holding Fanning Head had retreated to the little settlement. Some of the young soldiers had been trying to make breakfast of onions boiled in saucepans of water in the community hall when they heard the paratroopers arriving. The Argentinians moved back quickly into the hills. Two Marine Gazelle helicopters flew forward to look for sites for Rapier batteries, and rounding a hillside were caught in machine-gun-fire. The helicopters had been surprised and had exposed themselves too high above ground, a constant problem with this kind of spotting and reconnaissance work where the helicopters had to rise up to get a good view of the terrain. In the Gazelle there was an added difficulty if the crew wanted to fire their SNEB missiles slung on brackets outboard of the cockpit. The sights were a primitive 'H' shape, like an old-fashioned television aerial, and worked on the principle of a simple battle gunsight on a rifle. To release the missile at a group of men or machines on the ground – and they are intended particularly for destroying enemy helicopters – the Gazelle pilot has to lift the nose of his machine so that it rears up, and again this exposes the helicopter as an easy target for marksmen on the ground below.

The two Gazelles crashed into the water, and the crew of one were seen to bail out. One man was machine-gunned from the hills as he struggled with his dinghy and lifebelt. The three bodies and the survivor were ferried back to the hospital in the *Canberra* along with a dozen or so young Argentinians captured by 3 Para fleeing from Port San Carlos. One of the prisoners was wearing a British Royal Marines pullover taken from the kit of Mike Norman's Naval Party 8901 at Moody Brook Barracks at the beginning of April. The photograph of the young conscript being brought in by a moustachioed para became one of the most famous of the campaign.

Four hours after sun-up, 3 Para had still not secured their objective above Port San Carlos, though it was not to take them much longer. Hearing of the firing above the settlement, Brigadier Julian Thompson decided to order in his reserve 42 Commando led by Nick Vaux. They went from the *Canberra* with little fuss and as speedily as any of the disembarkations from HMS *Fearless* and HMS *Intrepid*. When these marines arrived at Port San Carlos, they were not required to fight, and prepared to dig in round the little settlement.

The Argentinians who made their get-away from Port San Carlos started a long cross-country march back to Port Stanley, following the route that Brigadier Thompson's 3 Brigade would take a week later through the settlements of Douglas and Teal. At Douglas the Argentinians shut the settlers up in a hall for a day, and robbed them of food, before setting out across the hills to the capital. Others of the group that had fought on Fanning Head and retreated through Port San Carlos on 21 May tried to live off the land out in the rough country, graced with such exotic names as 'Cushy's Flats' and 'Home Flock', and were brought in as prisoners by marine and paratroop patrols over several days after the landings.

On Sussex Mountains the leading companies of 2 Para were beginning to dig in. Once the turf was removed to the depth of two feet, the trenches filled with water, and this was nine hundred feet above sea level. The most popular form of shelter, 'bivvy' or 'basher' was a combination of trench and 'sanger', a barrier of stone laid like a dry-stone wall with a poncho or tarpaulin overhead. These seemed extraordinarily open to air attack, but I was assured that unless the plane was going very slowly, there would hardly be time for the pilot to pick out the shelters which would be yet more blobs of green on the landscape. A bigger giveaway was a cluster of faces looking skywards, which would stand out like a crop of pink mushrooms; hence the need for 'cam' cream.

As the afternoon approached and we watched between two rocks for more attacking aircraft, David Norris and I began to consider how to get our copy and radio despatches back to report that the troups had now landed on East Falkland. Sergeant Hudson was more keen than ever to get back to his darkroom on the *Norland*, though had he known what was happening in the air round the ferry at the time he would have been less enthusiastic. I agreed to take David's copy back and add a few paragraphs for the pool despatch. I did not have enough faith in the minders' dexterity to play the tape-recording of the landing over the Marisat without mishap and I wanted to know what was going on with the other units, thinking that nothing could be such a terrifying shambles as the 2 Para landing operation. 'H' Jones had been more than generous in his provisions for getting our copy back, and said we could use his Scout helicopter if there was no priority requirement for it. When the helicopter arrived at Battalion HQ next to a thick outcrop of rock with quite a luxuriant growth of bracken and weed covering it, I was told it would be going back to *Norland* to refuel and might manage to hop over to *Canberra*. I then made my first big mistake, and one from which I was never to learn. I left my bergen behind with the breezy assurance that I would be back later that afternoon. The old adage for troops in the field is never get separated from your kit. Sergeant Hudson knew better and hauled his in beside him as he scrambled aboard the Scout.

As we took off, I saw written on the helmet of the pilot in front 'Lt R. Nunn' and his blood group. He was to be our chauffeur on dozens of trips over the next week, a member of the Royal Marines Air Squadron, known as the 'Teeny Weeny Airways', a pun on the initials TWA. They were a tiny outfit compared with the Army Air Corps, the RAF and the Royal Naval Air Service, but popular individually in inverse proportion to the size of their unit. As we swooped down across the mountain, the co-pilot told me I would be lucky to get back to *Canberra*. At one point the pilot took the machine down in a hollow where we seemed to crouch like an animal being stalked. I was told that there was an air raid warning and we could not move for a few minutes. Then we made a dash for the *Norland*, and no sooner were we down than a ground crew appeared with fuel hoses. The sergeant photographer got out and we did not meet again until days after the surrender in Port Stanley.

Richard Nunn asked me if I still wanted to go to *Canberra*, and when I said I did, he replied that he would see what he could do. This was typical of many of the pilots, friendly, obliging and extremely brave. Much of our communication was by grunts and thumb signals. Many of the Teeny Weenies and the Air Corps' pilots regarded the hacks as fellow itinerants, and asked for news of what was going on with other parts of the force and at home whenever they gave me lifts from the ships. As we landed on the forward deck of the *Canberra*, a hand grabbed me and practically threw me under the bridge wing. All round were sandbags and men with helmets and long white anti-flash masks. It was only when I got below that I realised that the *Canberra* had already suffered four or five air attacks, and she would see at least as many more in the remaining part of that day.

The machine-gunners and Blowpipe teams on the bridge wings had been busy throughout the morning. They recorded no hits, but Blowpipe and tracer from the machine-guns proved a deterrent to the planes diving onto the ships at anchor. Colonel Tom Seccombe watched one of the attacks on the *Canberra* from the bridge of HMS *Fearless*. He said that as the Pucara began its run at the *Canberra*, there was a salvo of small arms fire and tracer from the liner's decks and a Blowpipe was fired from the bridge. The pilot saw the fire coming at him and pulled his plane up, dropping its bombs short so they splashed in the open water, throwing up a column of spray. Against low-flying aircraft, the jets as well as the propellor-driven Pucara, machine-gun fire was to prove as effective as any other weapon. The pilots could see the streams of tracer coming at them, which they could not with Rapier missiles, and it intimidated them.

Below decks *Canberra*'s appearance had changed in the five days since I had last seen her. From troopship she had become air-raid shelter, with all crew ordered to lie on mattresses in the bigger open lounges and stairways while the air raids were on. Throughout the attacks Captain Burne kept up a running commentary over the tannoy from the bridge. He interpreted when an 'Air Raid Warning Red' alert meant that the planes were coming in to bomb the anchorage or were attacking ships out in Falkland Sound. The commentary was interspersed with whimsical jokes. 'He's really kept us going,' said Anna Taylor who, with her husband Frank, had begun work as a ward orderly for the injured prisoners. 'Fawlty's been magnificent,' was the comment of Martin Helm, the MOD Information Officer still on board.

I went up to the bridge to find Captain Burne sitting in his captain's chair talking to some of the younger P and O officers. He greeted me as a lost traveller returned and asked how the landing had gone. He told me that the fighting had been heaviest against the frigates in Grantham Sound and he feared that the *Ardent* had been crippled. The cruiser *Antrim* had an unexploded 500-lb bomb wedged beneath her Sea Slug 2 missile battery aft, and HMS *Argonaut* had been hit. He said it had been a particularly bloody fight for the frigates, many of whose commanding officers he had trained at Dartmouth, and said he would not be surprised if one or two were not lost by the end of the day. He ordered that I should be taken below to the Ops Room, which was collating the information from the three main units which had travelled on the *Canberra* and were now ashore. I left him still standing by his chair, where he had been since dawn broke. If any Argentinian plane had taken a direct strafing run at the *Canberra*'s bridge, he was bound to have been killed. It would be too easy to use some cliché such as 'acting in the finest tradition of the Service', but it was an extraordinary performance of courage and leadership by a man who became a very good friend, which he proved by many small, and some big, acts of kindness throughout the campaign.

The Ops Room was at the aft end of the bridge superstructure, in a completely blacked-out chart room. Wireless operators and watch keepers were trying to collate messages from 40 and 42 Commando and 3 Para and from Ajax Bay. Not that there was much fresh information to gather at the time. 3 Para reported that there had been enemy in Port San Carlos but they appeared to have fled, and 40 Commando seemed well established in San Carlos Settlement and were taking up positions on the hills above, the Verde Mountains, where they were selecting sites for Rapier batteries.

On the deck below, the doctors were dealing with the first casualties, about twenty pathetically young-looking Argentinians from Port San Carlos. Steve, the anaesthetist, looked at my lip and grubby face plastered with peat and camouflage cream and asked if I needed any attention. Everyone was more

than willing to help. Frank Taylor passed by in surgical overalls and mask. He and Anna had thrown themselves on the
beds of the younger prisoners when the air attacks were on to
shield them from shrapnel and splinter. They were joined by
the substantial figure of Franco Tamburini, one of the waiters
in the Pacific Restaurant, a native of Venice who now regarded
himself as British as Yorkshire pudding. Franco could manage
some Spanish, which proved a real help with the recovering
patients. One young Argentinian looked thoroughly bewildered as Steve and a Naval Medical Assistant, Rex Barker,
tried to speak to him in phrase-book Spanish. Most of the
soldiers looked as if they came from the country and had a
swarthy colouring, and with straight, black, oily hair. Some
had thick lips and Indian features. They sat up hesitantly on
their mattresses as the men and women of the P and O crew
gently spooned soup to their mouths. The doctors were sad-
dened by the youth of the Argentinians, some, by Commander
Rick Jolly's estimation, being only sixteen. They were under-
fed because they had been out in the country for some time and
were badly frostbitten. They had broken legs and wounds to
the face. One would lose an eye. They had swollen toes and
feet with thick, black crusts of skin from severe frostbite. One
boy seemed starving and had suffered a leg wound at Fanning
Head, so the limb would have to be amputated. He was nicknamed 'Stumpy' and the doctors thought he would be lucky to
survive. In one corner of the ward the bodies of the three air
crew from the Gazelles shot down at Port San Carlos were laid
in bodybags.

Martin Helm tried to explain to me what the information
policy was now. He insisted I stayed aboard until I had written
a pooled despatch for the newspapers and allowed me to make
one broadcast later in the evening on the understanding that it
would be delayed even further by the Defence Ministry in
London. There seemed an almost complete lack of coordin-
ation between the Ministry of Defence and their officers with
the troops. It was on this occasion that Sir Frank Cooper, the
Permanent Secretary of Defence, admitted practising a 'disinformation' policy. His staff released to correspondents in London

the news that a number of raids had taken place on the Falklands but did not say there had been a full amphibious landing. The thinking behind such a move in the short term is obvious: the intention was to delay for as long as possible informing the world that the main elements of 3 Commando Brigade were ashore at San Carlos. Rapier batteries would take at least a day to get working properly, and indeed most were not installed fully until the evening of the day after the landings, Saturday 22 May. But the Argentinian Air Force already knew where the main group of amphibious ships was by midday on the day of the landings, and some of the British troops had been watched by Argentinian observation posts on the land. It is now known that one of the Argentinian officers at Port San Carlos, a Lieutenant Rais, did not retreat immediately to Douglas and Teal but stayed in the hills above the anchorage where he hid for some days and drew detailed maps of the British positions. This intelligence information, which was well documented, was taken off this enterprising officer after the surrender in Port Stanley by Major Pat Butler of 3 Para's reconnaissance company.

In the longer term, the MOD disinformation policy had a bad effect because it led to confusion about what was speculation, what fact, what sensitive information which could endanger future operations, and what common-place knowledge. In one week, London newspapers reported that Goose Green had been captured on no less than three separate occasions before the settlements of Goose Green and Darwin were surrendered to 2 Para on 29 May. Some of this must have been a product of the MOD's 'disinformation' policy on the day of the landings. On 21 May there was diversionary activity by the SAS near the Darwin Isthmus which was the target for heavy Naval bombardment, but none of the settlers in Goose Green recalls a land attack anywhere near the houses there that morning. On Monday 24 May both the *Guardian* and the *Daily Telegraph* carried pieces from their correspondents with the ships of the Task Force saying that, according to 'unconfirmed reports', British troops had taken the Goose Green airstrip following a heavy Harrier bombing attack. On the

Thursday and Friday of that week, London papers reported the imminent capture of Goose Green, again with the *Daily Telegraph* to the fore. The newspapers were still anticipating events on Saturday the 29th, the day Goose Green did finally fall. As Chris Keeble's party was moving down the track to the airfield to negotiate terms of surrender of the Argentinian Air Force and Army units in Goose Green, late editions in London had been on the streets for more than half a day reporting that paratroops were now well established in the settlement. In this climate of chaos on information policy, it must have been hard to know what was sensitive information whose early release could cost lives, what had actually happened and what was about to happen. The politicians in London seemed to have been as confused as anybody; hence the release of news at Westminster that 2 Para were about to attack the Argentinians holding the Darwin Isthmus thirty-six hours before it happened.

During the afternoon on the *Canberra*, Martin Helm fed me useful information about the fighting with the other elements of the Task Force, the bombardments of Stanley and the settlements on West Falkland. He also explained about the loss of the SAS troop in the bird strike on the Sea King taking off from HMS *Intrepid* on the night of 19 and 20 May, but added he could not foresee us ever being allowed to report this. Similarly, there would be restrictions on anything we tried to say about the crash of a Sea King helicopter on the Chilean coast, which he said was almost certainly part of an SAS operation aimed at the Argentinian air base at Rio Grande in Tierra del Fuego. The permutations and combinations of possibilities as to what happened are varied and intriguing, and so far all that I know and have read about the raid is based more than 50 per cent on conjecture.

The first possibility is that the helicopter was stripped of all inessential fittings, was given extra fuel tanks and flew a considerable distance from the Task Force with an SAS troop to attack the Etendard bases at Rio Gallegos in Patagonia and Rio Grande in Tierra del Fuego. The helicopter was supposed to ditch after landing the troops and the air crew intended to escape on foot through Chile. There are two slight variants on this story. One is that that targets were not so much the Etendard aircraft but the stocks of Exocet missiles to be fired from the planes, as it was known that the Argentinians were searching the world markets for more of these weapons, an indication that they had few left. The other variant is that the SAS troup was landed from the patrol submarine HMS *Onyx*, the only conventionally powered British submarine deployed in the South Atlantic during the hostilities. She was chosen because her electric motors are said to be less easy to detect than the noisier nuclear-powered submarines like the *Valiant* and the *Conqueror*.

According to 'Rumour Control' in the Task Force, the raid was said to be a success, with the aircraft and missiles destroyed. This was certainly untrue, as the Task Force was to be attacked by Etendard for some days to come. Weeks after hostilities ceased, Etendard patrols were flying out to look at the formations of British ships patrolling round the Falklands. It is known that parts of the Task Force, among the ships being the carrier HMS *Hermes*, did make a run into the Argentinian coast and came to within 150 miles of land at one point, and that this was in support of some clandestine operation before 3 Commando Brigade landed at San Carlos. It is possible that both helicopters and submarines were used, with only the abandoned Sea King left as the visible sign that the raid had taken place, like a fingerprint inadvertently left behind by a cat burglar.

The intention is likely to have been more subtle and long term than a hit-and-run raid to destroy aircraft and a few missiles on the ground. The problem that bedevilled British air defences continued to be the lack of early warning radar, now needed more than ever as the troops were about to go ashore on East Falkland. The intention of the helicopter raid seems as likely to have been to set up some early warning system on the ground in Tierra del Fuego, possibly leaving a forward patrol of SAS with surveillance equipment. This is pure speculation on my part, but it is known that early warning of air attacks improved steadily throughout the campaign, and sometimes over twenty minutes' prior warning was given before the Skyhawks and Mirages attacked land targets. The fleet became better protected, too, with the fitting out of two Sea Kings with radar which allowed them to fulfil something of the early-bird role that the old Gannet AWACs planes did once from the fleet carriers like *Ark Royal* and *Eagle*.

I set to work to write the despatches on the landings, but my mind was numb. It was hard enough to get my fingers to work the typewriter keys, let alone to recall the important events since I had last spoken to London a week ago. As I was wrestling with these problems, an air raid warning was given, accompanied by the forlorn mooing of HMS *Fearless*'s siren, which meant that the attack was aimed at the anchorage. Martin Helm told me to get down, as these warnings were not given lightly.

Over the tannoy from the bridge Captain Burne's voice warned calmly that the aircraft were about four minutes away, and then later yelled, 'This one's coming straight at us. Get down!' There was a roar and a whoosh down the port side, a chatter of machine-gun fire, the explosion of a Blowpipe missile being launched, a bang and a splash as the aircraft dropped its ordnance into the water. On another occasion there was a bang and a mighty wind as every porthole, door and bulkhead blew open.

Canberra sustained a dozen air attacks that day, and escaped without a scratch. HMS *Antrim* came into San Carlos and turned slowly before the liner as explosives technicians worked to defuse the bomb jammed beneath her Sea Slug mechanism. The scarred *Argonaut* also arrived in the anchorage as the LSLs continued the patient work of unloading rations and ammunition for troops at the different beaches – Blue for San Carlos settlement, Red for Ajax and the BMA (Brigade Maintenance Area) and Green for Port San Carlos. The surprise was that the aircraft seemed to be aiming at the escorts, the destroyers and frigates and not the transports. Later, General Jeremy Moore was to remark, 'I would say that where the Grace of God comes in is that on the first days in San Carlos the pilots went for the escorts and not the amphibious ships, and that might have stopped us altogether.' This was to be the biggest mistake by the Argentinians in the land campaign.

Towards evening, Captain Burne told us that HMS *Ardent* had been so badly damaged that she would have to be abandoned in Grantham Sound. Her main weapons were out of action and she had suffered a number of killed and injured. HMS *Yarmouth* had been despatched to pick up survivors, who would be given accommodation in the *Canberra*.

HMS *Ardent*, who had been bombarding Goose Green before dawn and then after daylight came, volunteered to support the ships patrolling Grantham and Falkland Sound. Her last stand was witnessed by the men of 'B' Company 2 Para as they dug in on Sussex Mountains, a superb view across the Sound. The *Ardent* was attacked by no fewer than three raids of Mirages and Italian-built Aermacchi fighters. The Argentinian pilots showed that they knew their business as they passed low over the frigate from opposite directions, performing a scissors movement in the sky. In doing this, and aiming to fly over the mast and the main stack, they found the blind spot between the arcs of fire of the ship's main armaments, the 4.5-inch automatic gun forward and the Sea Cat missiles mounted aft. Soon the main power supply was out; the gun and the missiles would work no more. Men were turned out on the decks to fire small arms and machine-guns. On the flight deck, Lieutenant-Commander John Sephton is reported to have commanded the flight and ground crews, firing a sub-machine-gun himself at aircraft passing so low that they broke the tip of the main mast. He died in one of the attacks, and was awarded a posthumous Distinguished Service Cross. The hero of the machine-gunners on the rails was a civilian, the NAAFI manager, who had been in the armed services and was more than familiar with the firing and cleaning drills of the GPMG (General Purpose Machine-Gun, known affectionately as 'Gimpy'). He told two young petty officers I met soon afterwards in the *Canberra*: 'The only time I felt really scared was when the belts of ammo ran out.'

From the hills above the Sound, a para corporal described the last attack. 'We saw the ship moving slowly north, out to sea, plenty of smoke pouring from her. As she got to the place where the land juts out, she was attacked again. They came in really low and were pretty good. Then we saw two huge balls of flame above the ship and we thought she had had it this time. Then we realised it was two Sea Harriers which had come right in behind the five aircraft attacking the ship. Two blew up immediately and at least two more had black smoke pouring from them.' The Sea Harrier was more than proving its value as a close interceptor. Though they could not maintain a constant CAP above the anchorage during the landings, Admiral Woodward was holding the carriers close enough for the Harriers to be brought in to catch Argentinian planes striking against the ships in the Sound and as they turned for home. While troops were concentrated round San Carlos, Admiral Woodward endeavoured to keep some air patrolling presence west of the Falklands at least, so the returning planes could be caught on their way back to Ushuaia, Rio Gallegos and Rio Grande, the three principal southern bases in Argentina.

The transfer of the *Ardent*'s crew to HMS *Yarmouth* was carried out quickly and calmly. The *Ardent* had lost more than twenty killed and thirty injured. The *Yarmouth* was able to come alongside the *Canberra*. Coffee, tea, rolls and beer were provided as the men were given a 'survival kit', a full change of clothes and washing materials. In one of the assembly rooms, the Meridian Room, Helen Hawkett and Lauraine Mulberry sat at a table quietly taking names and addresses of next of kin and allocating cabins. There was very little sign of emotion. Some of the younger ratings talked quite casually about their experiences, and the psychiatrist, Morgan O'Connell, later organised them into group therapy sessions on the journey to South Georgia.

A lieutenant-commander, a weapons officer, whose face was white and green in patches from the fatigue and shock of the battle, told me a little of what happened, how the ship had made her way up the Sound with power failing and nothing to drive the gun or the missiles. He spoke of his pride in his men: 'They fought like young tigers to the end.' Captain Burne said he would like to greet the men of the *Ardent* but would only come down from the bridge if their captain, Commander Alan West, wished it. In the middle of the room Captain Burne talked quietly to the men and shook hands with Alan West, not thrusting his presence on anyone. He looked sad and moved that after thirty years of service he had now seen the fiercest day of action for the Royal Navy since 1945. That evening he gave a short address over the tannoy which set the mood exactly. It had been 'a sad day, but one of gallant deeds, particularly by the frigates'. As a serving officer of the Royal Navy, he said he was proud to have been with the men of the amphibious force and the escorts at San Carlos on 21 May.

In the evening we all ate in the Pacific Restaurant; I was sitting next to two young petty officers from the *Ardent*. They talked excitedly but quietly about the fight, the NAAFI manager leading the machine-gunners, and who among their mates had been lost. They were surprised to be getting waiter service, and just beginning to experience the relief that succeeds survival of battle. The *Canberra* waiters were now wearing blue sweaters and trousers in Naval style. They felt very much part of the force, they said. Throughout the day of air raids and alerts, all meals had been cooked and served to everybody – prisoners, injured, the gunners on deck – and all on time.

With Captain Burne's help, I was given permission to make a broadcast that evening, and he asked to make a comment about the fighting round the frigates. He calculated that six had been damaged badly, apart from the *Ardent* which was now blazing fiercely, abandoned off the suggestively named Wreck Point. Many of the ships would have been damaged worse or even sunk but for the fact that about half the Argentinian bombs did not go off. This was partly due to the use of old stocks of American, and, it is said, some British iron bombs, and partly because the bombs had to be released so low that they had not time to detonate. The great skill of the Argentinian pilots was to come in beneath the British local radar. Their talent and training was astonishing in the way they hugged the tricky contours of East and West Falkland, sometimes keeping less than twenty feet off the ground, as they made their final runs to attack. The news that Argentinian bombs were not going off was released in London, and eventually the Argentinian Air Force commanders learned from their errors and adopted small French retard bombs, whose descent was delayed by small tail parachutes. The release of information about incorrect fusing of the ordnance enraged the bomb disposal team led by Flight Lieutenant Swann at Ajax Bay.

When I got through to London I was told that Brian Hanrahan had already reported from a warship in the Task Force that the landings had taken place. One of the ladies in the Traffic Section, which deals with the despatch and reception of all foreign news messages and reports in the BBC, said with some sense of irony that she did not think I should bother with filing. I put over a straight despatch about the run-in to the landing, some recordings of Naval gunfire, the short commentary of splashing ashore and some shouted air raid warnings against Pucara. It seemed pretty run of the mill stuff compared with the momentous events happening to the *Canberra* and the *Ardent*. I was astonished to hear of the play this was given both in the British papers and abroad, particularly on the American TV networks. My boss, Bob Kearsley, who had managed much of the BBC's television and radio coverage of the closing years of the Vietnam war with success, thanked me warmly for the work, and with characteristic generosity asked if I was now able to get some rest.

I was under notice to move ashore as quickly as I could as the *Canberra* would be sailing that night to avoid dangers of underwater attack. She was ordered not to try her luck against air attack for another day, too. I went to say goodbye to Captain Burne, who chatted over the day's experiences and said that he thought more ships might be lost if the Argentinians kept up the pressure of air attack. Everybody who did not want to sail with the *Canberra* to South Georgia was told to leave the ship by midnight. In the medical wards there was a rush as Commander Rick Jolly prepared to move as many as possible of his No. 2 Naval Surgery Support Team, the Commando Medical Squadron, and the Parachute Clearing Troop from *Norland*, ashore to Ajax Bay. He had discovered there the abandoned Mutton Refrigeration Plant, and felt it would be ideal as a field hospital. It was an inspired decision. There would be ample space for recovery wards and room for an operating theatre with six or even eight operating tables working at a time. There was enough flat ground outside for helicopters to land and be turned round quickly when a flood of casualties was brought in from a battle. The decision nearly earned him a court martial from a surgeon captain on the Admiral's staff, who insisted that the field hospital should be set up on HMS *Intrepid*, which would have been awkward as the stretchers would have to be carried below down narrow companionways and stairs from a restricted flight deck which would also be used for other missions. Rick Jolly had the full support of his superior, an easy-going and jovial surgeon captain, Roger Wilkes, who had won the MBE for ingenious chest surgery on a casualty in the mutiny of the East African Rifles in Dar Es Salaam. The Ajax Bay field hospital was to be a brilliant success story where scores and possibly hundreds of lives were to be saved by Jolly's teams and the surgeons led by Colonel Bill MacGregor. Of all the casualties flown in to Ajax, only four or five died subsequently.

I worked my ticket ashore by descending to the galley in *Canberra* to negotiate with the rear parties of 42 and 40 Commandos. I was given camouflage cream and told to jump into a rubbish skip that would be heading for San Carlos Settlement. I waited for nearly an hour in the freezing wind as stores, mostly rations and ammunition, were loaded aboard. As the craft turned to the south, there was a huge blue and red flame on the western skyline above the ridge of hills which seemed to flare up for more than a minute. It was followed by a distant rumble, the sound of HMS *Ardent* exploding before she finally sank.

This time the landing craft tied up at the jetty at San Carlos at the place where 40 Commando and 2 Para had landed. The Quartermaster of 40 Commando, Geoff Whiteley, was there to meet us. I was told there would be no chance of returning to 2 Para that night and I should not try to make the four or five miles in the dark for fear of being shot by a patrol or jumpy sentry. I helped stack the stores for 40 Commando by an old Nissen hut used for storing wool. With the rear party of 40 Commando's 'B' Echelon, we decided to sleep in one of the huts. I lay down on some galvanised tubing, used for pipes for the farm animals' water troughs. I had some old sacks to cover myself with but my quilt underjacket and trousers and sleeping-bag were with my kit high up on Sussex Mountains at Battalion HQ of 2 Para. After about twenty minutes of trying to get to sleep, Major Andrew Gowen, the second in command of 40 Commando, in an act of Samaritan generosity offered to unzip his sleeping bag and share it with me and gave me his quilt jacket. In the morning I thanked him for this noble deed. He replied: 'I had to do it for all of us. We didn't want to be kept awake by the sound of your shivering rattling those pipes all night.'

II. RAIDS

The men were turned out of their sleeping-bags half an hour before dawn with the order 'stand to'. This is a custom which is said to go back to the British Army's campaigns in Africa following the defeats by the Zulu Impis at Isandlawana. Units in the open should stand their men to at dawn and dusk, times when the enemy might use changing light to attack. It does serve the purpose of making men adjust their eyes to rapidly approaching daylight or darkness.

At San Carlos we were told to get away from the buildings and to find some shelter in case the Argentinians should stage a dawn bombing run over the anchorage. Many of the men had already dug elaborate trenches and shelters near the sheep pens by Blue Beach. One of the best had a thick layer of roofing made from turf, soil and wooden stakes. The occupants said they were Royal Engineers, hence their superior skill at dug-out building, and they generously extended their hospitality to

passing marines and journalists. As an Air Raid Warning Red
alert was sounded on the sergeant's whistles and the sirens of
the *Fearless* and the *Intrepid*, men jumped for the nearest hole
in the ground for shelter. In time, matters became more
relaxed, as few of the air raid warnings were followed by
enemy planes appearing over San Carlos.

One of the sheep huts on the edge of the settlement was the
temporary headquarters of Lt.-Col. Malcolm Hunt, the CO of
40 Commando. The shed was a simple building with wooden
gates for the pens, hay racks and nets dangling from the walls
and a packed earth floor. Malcolm gave us a cheerful greeting
as he appeared from his bedroom suite, a loose box at one end
of the shed, and offered us a cup of tea. He asked after 'H' and
2 Para and said his two companies in the hills were having the
utmost difficulty in keeping dry in the trenches. Positions
almost on the crest of the hills were filling with more than two
feet of water. One marine had tried to sleep in his trench
despite such discomforts and had to be evacuated by helicopter
suffering from acute hypothermia. At one time during the
morning his heart had stopped.

Malcolm showed us his headquarters. Royal Engineers with
their earth-movers were digging out an underground Operations Room and Brigade HQ would work from there. 40
Commando's base area had the most permanent look of any I
had seen of the units in the field. At one point Malcolm had a
sharp exchange with a company commander who had sent out
a number of patrols in the night. One patrol had only just
reported seeing men dragging objects from the water in a bay
further north in the anchorage. Though they had watched the
two men through night-vision aids, which revealed that one of
those observed was wearing a frogman's outfit, their suspicions
had not been aroused. They thought elements of the Special
Boat Squadron were still in the area, so had not radioed back to
headquarters. There were so many men from the specialised
forces, the SAS, SBS and Mountain and Arctic Warfare Cadre,
that they almost seemed in danger of tripping over each other.
As Martin Osborne of 3 Para remarked, the 'naughty boys'
club' of SAS and SBS seemed to have been let out of school.

Martin Osborne's 'C' Company of 3 Para on the high land above Port San Carlos had suffered the opposite misfortune to the bemused patrol of 40 Commando. Two patrols of different companies of 3 Para had collided in the night, which was dark and cloudy, making map-reading very tricky. One was off course and, contacting the second patrol, thought they had met the enemy and called down mortar fire. Three men were seriously injured and others suffered light wounds. Such encounters are termed in Army jargon 'blue on blue' and were to happen several times across East Falkland.

Who the men spotted by the 40 Commando patrol were not established at the time. In the anchorage no chances were taken in preventing underwater attacks on the ships by frogmen with limpet mines. The Argentinian Specialist Forces were known to have had extensive training in sabotage by one- and two-man teams. For the time she was anchored in San Carlos, HMS *Fearless*'s crew threw 'scare charges', a form of stun grenade, into the water two or three times each hour to deter frogmen.

Two sheds in San Carlos had been commandeered by Lord Robin Innes-Ker with his troop of four light tanks, the other four having gone to Port San Carlos. Robin offered us a warm-up by the radiators of his vehicles if we got too cold. As each air raid warning was given, his tanks roared and bucked their way out of their temporary garages and stood on a small knoll, though what chance they would have had against attacking aircraft I do not know. At about this time Max Hastings appeared with camouflage cream still smeared on his face, with a typewriter in one hand and a walking stick in the other. He had dug trenches the afternoon before and spent the night in one, having cooked the evening meal for the four companions with whom he shared his bivouac. 'They didn't seem to have much clue, so I told them to get on and dig and I would do the cooking.' He was impatient to move on with the campaign or go home. There was little sense of momentum, despite having landed only twenty-four hours previously. Most of us felt that it might be a long, dreary affair of minor clashes for months to come.

After a couple of hours' delay, Malcolm Hunt managed to get me a ride in a Scout up to 2 Para. Like most of the unit COs in the field, he wanted to make sure the press moved about as much as possible and got their reports back with the minimum of delay and official interference. Returning to Sussex Mountains, the hillside appeared bleaker than ever. Most of the tent roofing at the Battalion HQ was in danger of blowing away, and there was a constant threat of rain as the wind speed rose steadily. Everywhere was slippery grass, bracken leaves and black, shiny mud. Huge grey clouds batted across the sky. The Falklands weather was being its most perverse, and this was a great advantage. There were no serious air raids over the anchorage that day. The Rapier batteries were installed, the artillery bedded in and the machine-gunners on the high outcrops of rock and in the sangers and trenches could check their arcs of fire. This was a second opportunity missed by the Argentinian Air Force. The 'ring of steel' of air defences, as Julian Thompson termed it, was now all but completely in place.

I arrived at the HQ tent to be told that my bergen had again eluded me and had been taken back to San Carlos by David Norris, who had spent a particularly dreary and wet first night in the open. Chris Keeble was sorting out the watches in the Operations Room. I moved up to the high ground on the right where 'A' Company was dug in. The commander, Major Dair Farrar-Hockley, gave me a formal greeting, asked me to take a seat and 'have a brew', and wanted to talk over what was going on in the rest of the world. How bad had the fighting been with the frigates? What was Maggie saying? Were the government still going to negotiate? Most of his trenches, he said, were under water, but the lads were quite cheerful, and the fierce wind at least meant that their clothes would dry out quickly. Many of the 'bashers' and 'bivvies' resembled school changing rooms on a wet afternoon after a very muddy football match. The Rapier batteries had suffered from the rain as well as the sea water on the voyage down, and one of the batteries on the 2 Para position required a new generator that afternoon.

On the way back to the Battalion HQ, I met 'H' Jones, who

said he thought the landing had been 'a shambles'. He had just been to 'B' Company in the most exposed position of all, looking into Grantham Sound. He said he thought the Pucara patrol was coming straight at him immediately after the landing and would have bombed the two forward companies of the battalion had it not been downed by the SAS 'Stinger'. Soon after, Brigadier Thompson appeared from the direction of 'B' Company and expressed satisfaction at the way the landings had gone and that all the main units were now in position. But both Jones and the Brigadier knew the men could not endure the conditions in the open of the forward trenches of 40 Commando and 2 Para for long; physical fitness would decline rapidly after a week or so. 'H' was anxious to break out from the beachhead quickly, and was preparing aggressive patrolling to Port Sussex House and Cantara House, where local farmers said some Argentinian troops had been spotted a week or so before the British landings.

At the head of Bonners Bay, the southern tongue of San Carlos Water, there was a flat land of about three hundred acres with a bright-red-roofed house with white walls, Head of the Bay House, which stood out in most weathers in light pastel colours. By the house, Tony Rice's battery of six guns was set up. In fine weather there would be a sudden puff, then a drift of a small white cloud and then nearly half a minute would elapse before the report of the gun would be heard on the top of Sussex Mountains. The guns were 'bedding in', sinking in to a manageable level in the soft peat, and the ranges were being calculated. The ground was so soft that this would have to be done three or four times a day, and when the guns fired as few as six rounds in some positions, they would have to be hauled out and bedded in afresh because they had ploughed back so far from the line with each shot. As the gunners carried out their ranging exercises, the machine-guns would start up without warning to establish their arcs of fire. On my way from 'A' Company I was warned just in time as two began firing above me.

Opposite the Battalion HQ, men of the Regimental Aid Post and the 'A' Echelon were clinging like molluscs to a line of rocks where they established their stores and their living quarters. Moving from 'bivvy' to 'bivvy' like a whirling dervish in the gale now blowing was David Cooper, dispensing comfort in the form of the remains of a bottle of whisky I had given him just before we left the *Norland* together. He strapped it into his bergen along with two crosses (wooden, collapsible) of his own pattern and making that he thought he should carry, but for what useful purpose he was not clear. He looked purple at the lips, and frozen, but said the lads were of good cheer, particularly after a drop of whisky. The medics did not recommend alcohol in the field because it gave a false illusion of warmth; in reality it tended to lower the body's temperature and made it more vulnerable to cold.

'Bare-arsed' was the way the Blowpipe team described their living quarters on the saddle of hillside above the RAP and 'A' Echelon's stores. 'We're soaked and half blown away, but we are here,' they said. 'Come and have a wet, mate,' and they thrust a mug of what passed as tea into my hands. The main thing to be said for it was that it was wet and sweet, and with it came the perpetual nutrient and oral fix, some 'nutty', either chocolate or something sweet, Spangles, mints or Army issue glucose sweets which always appeared covered with peat, fluff or some other part of pocket lining. 'You are the first bloke we have seen in a couple of days,' said the Blowpipe sergeant. 'What's going on in the rest of the world?' I said what I had heard via the World Service, and we talked about the loss of the *Ardent*, which he had seen passing up Grantham Sound. My presence was now becoming more accepted throughout the battalion, to whom I was a kind of peddler who, if he had nothing more to offer, had some information about what was going on elsewhere. I became part of the furniture, and while the men knew I would never be one of them, I became familiar like a piece of kit that would end up somewhere in the baggage train as the battalion moved across the Falklands.

From the Blowpipe position there was a view of more than thirty miles across to the West Island opposite the settlement of Port Howard. As patches of blue sky appeared, the sun picked up areas of white like long, shallow, shelving steps of rock and patches of dried grass down to the sea. To the south it was hard to discriminate between cloud and the areas of white tussock grass and rock which had the shapes of pools of colour. Nothing I have seen of Scotland resembles this; it is more like the curiously light-textured oil paintings my parents have of the Baltic Islands like Bornholm, and the southern coasts of Sweden.

Returning to the Battalion HQ, I ran into Alex Ward and discussed culinary matters. The curry powder worked a treat with the curry, rice and apricot flakes, but you had to make sure not to overdo it with the processed peas, he advised. They were as hard as bullets and tended to ruin the meal. In the ops area of the HQ tent, Chris Keeble was arguing with the RSM Malcolm Simpson. A forward observation post (OP) had seen two helicopters down by the coast between Port Sussex and Rookery Point. One report said they were Pumas, Anglo-French-designed troop-carriers used also by the RAF but not brought with the Task Force, and another report said they were Sea Kings. The RSM was trying to establish the bearing, while Chris, snapping occasionally like a school ma'am, wanted a positive identification. Chris was prepared to call for fire from Tony Rice's battery. Confusion at such a distance was understandable. The helicopters might have been a British anti-submarine exercise, and Sea Kings were carrying out a number of sonar 'dunkings' in the Sound as it was feared the *Salta*, one of the two Argentinian German-built submarines, was lurking there. If the helicopters were enemy troop-carriers, they might be landing forward patrols to break into the beach-head.

As this was being resolved, Chris Keeble told me to go back to San Carlos and find the bergen, otherwise it would be impossible to sleep in the open. He said there was no point in suffering for the sake of it, and I should try to get a hot meal at Brigade HQ, spend the night in the dry and return the following day. Such consideration for the press was typical of the battalion, as the personal thought and courtesy of Chris Keeble was typical of the man. It was also part of 'H''s policy to the press. The whole battalion had to look after the two journalists and keep them informed, and the journalists would then be expected to do the job of keeping the world informed about the actions of the battalion – minders, censorship and the MOD permitting. It was part of 'H''s and Chris's home-grown open-information policy, and it worked.

I never did find out what the helicopters were doing. A number of enemy machines were destroyed by Harrier attacks across the island, and by forward SAS backed up by 'sneaky beaky' patrols. British guns managed to hit convoys of vehicles near the settlements across the Sound. The enemy, too, had reconnaissance patrols out. Some penetrated ground held by 40 Commando, and 3 Para and the marines continued to pick up prisoners outside Port San Carlos days after the landing. Settlers at Hill Cove on West Falkland found an Argentinian pilot who had baled out of his plane returning from a raid on San Carlos Water.

The Scout helicopter returned to San Carlos as dusk was gathering. Round the houses the marines were continuing to dig trenches, and a water purification plant was being built by the Royal Engineers next to the cattle pens. Most of the drink-ing water was still being fetched from the farmhouses, where water was continuously boiled in huge kettles on the stoves. The people seemed tired, hospitable and uncurious. They offered all visitors mugs of tea and cake, said little about them-selves but invited all to sit a little in the kitchen to benefit from the warmth. The colours were the dark creams, mud browns and chipped greens of most farmhouses, the floor trailed with mud, as at this time of the year the only serviceable article of footwear indoors and out is the wellington boot. The family in the nearest farmhouse was particularly welcoming because they had heard my voice on the BBC World Service and in reports relayed on the 'Calling the Falklands' programme which had been broadcast daily since the first week in April. But the farmer and his wife had little news of what was going on outside San Carlos, and after filling my water-bottle and pouring a mug of tea we sat in silence.

My bergen had been dumped in a potting shed at the

northern end of the settlement, and in the shed David Nicholls had set up his base camp with his mountaineering primus and stocks of food. The hacks at San Carlos decided to sleep in a large sheep-shearing shed with white wooden walls and a corrugated iron roof. It was the biggest farm building in the settlement and as it stood on a knoll above the jetty it was an obvious target for air attacks. During the frequent air raid warnings and 'stand-to' at dawn and last light, we hid beneath a dry-stone wall at the end of the concrete collecting yards. The wall appeared to be part of a sheep-dip, which like so many things on the Falklands farms seemed only three-parts completed. Inside the shearing shed, the floors and the wooden dividing partitions were matted with dried dung and looked as if they could do with a good pressure-hosing. Round the sides were the huge bales of wool, wired tight in reinforced plastic sheeting. The building was drafty but offered shelter from the driving rain. We put down our Arctic sleeping-bags on their foam-rubber mats and set about cooking meals in pairs: the system was that one would prepare the 'scran', as the marines put it (the army slang was 'scoff'), while the other did the washing-up and prepared the 'brews', the hot drinks.

My partner was Max Hastings, and he certainly got the worst of the deal. He was an experienced hand at camping and understood the mysteries of preparing Army rations. He had located a small shop in the settlement, and promised to share some baked beans and tinned meat he had purchased there at exorbitant prices if I did not broadcast the fact that this emporium existed to all and sundry. Max said his caution was fear of a stampede if the shop was found by 40 Commando.

As we knocked together the evening meal, Max kept up an animated monologue about how the landing had gone, and how the campaign would develop. His observations were witty and shrewd as usual. Max had perhaps the best grasp of the shape of the campaign of any of the journalists, being an accomplished military historian. Before leaving for the Falklands he had been working on a book about the Normandy Landings, looking at the campaign from the German side. He had just had success with a recently published book about the workings of the SS as a fighting unit. As a reporter he had seen the Yom Kippur War in the Middle East and fighting in the late 'sixties and 1970s in Vietnam, though he was not as given to trumpetings about past achievements in this field as some of the others accredited for the Falklands Operation. That evening in the sheep-shearing shed, Max was cautiously optimistic about the outcome of the Falklands campaign. 'I think the worst might be over, now. Don't you think? They have allowed us to land unopposed, and that's a considerable achievement.' There was also the fact, we agreed, that there had been no heavy air raids over the anchorage the day after the landings, which had allowed the Rapiers to be installed.

The novel feature of the campaign for all the reporters was its rural aspect, no phones or telex, no running water or facilities for laundry and showers. The principal modes of transport were rigid raider and landing craft, helicopter and feet, though occasionally one could thumb a lift on a passing tractor and trailer and Volvo BV snow vehicle. The fact that there was no perspective on this little war from the bar of the Intercontinental or nearest Hilton seemed strange to many of the hacks. The thinking of the military seemed a Byzantine mystery at times, full of weird, hidden rituals, hierarchies and taboos. My understanding was about as much or as little as the soldier in the fighting units, and I knew only what they did out in the field, despite my itinerant role peddling knick-knacks of world news gathered from the BBC's World Service broadcasts and odd scraps gleaned from my office when I could reach them by Marisat from the ships. One aspect of the campaign was very familiar to me, however. For the first twenty-one years of my life in school and university holidays, I had lived in an environment where the most common features were cows, chickens and tractors. The fact that there was not even a pub or bar near did not even worry me; it was like being home on the farm.

Morning came with a call to stand-to, and not to show lights until after sunrise. We were rebuked by a marine sergeant who said that the shearing shed looked like Blackpool Illuminations at night as we groped around with torches and lit the hexamine stoves for a brew. Max cursed me for the particularly disgusting breakfast I had prepared. Outside, the digging continued, with children from the farms now sporting a variety of military clothing, hats and gloves, and helping in the trenches. Up at the potting shed David Nicholls gave a briefing about the previous day's events, unit by unit and sector by sector. It was very thorough and unhurried and the picture seemed to make sense, though he apologised profusely and unnecessarily for the muddle. We were now allowed to mention the destruction of HMS *Ardent*, and I helped the pool with what information I had learned from the survivors in the *Canberra*.

David Nicholls had arranged for us to cross to the *Stromness* to file our reports by Marisat. As the landing craft chugged away from the jetty, an air raid warning was given. Arriving at the *Stromness*, we were told to get under cover as quickly as we could, Max Hastings legging it smartly to the wireless room, whence he had the decency to return as quickly to tell me that they were already on the line to the BBC, and I should take advantage of this right away. In the wireless room I met Brian Hanrahan, my colleague from BBC Television News, for the first time since we had watched HMS *Hermes* loading at Portsmouth the day before she sailed. Brian looked at me with a bemused expression and later explained that I looked as if I had stepped out of the jungle with mud on my clothes and a good deal of camouflage cream still on my face. He handed over the phone to me and I started filing the script already prepared about the troops digging in on the hills round San Carlos. Brian told me some of his adventures in the fighting at sea, some of which he said had been 'bloody frightening'. With him was Mike Nicholson of ITN, greying blonde hair, sharp, aquiline features, prominent nose and blue eyes, very much the action reporter and the doyen of the broadcasters in the campaign. He began talking nineteen to the dozen to his office, at one point lifting chunks of my script about the *Ardent*. His style made up in passion and vigour what it lacked at times in syntax.

As he spoke, we were told that the Argentinian planes were heading for the anchorage. I rushed out on a bridge wing and missed the first pass. When the Skyhawks and Mirages came

over again, I ran out on the starboard side, heard a crack and
looked up high to my right and saw above the hills guarding
Ajax Bay a cloud of black smoke where a Rapier missile had
been fired. Turning to look in front through the main windscreen of the bridge, I saw a crescent of roaring flame plunge
into the water between two of the LSLs.

I returned to report exactly what I had seen to the BBC. The
experience of seeing the plane destroyed seemed detached from
my emotions: the first thing was to get the job done and report
what I knew. It was only after a minute or two's reflection that
I registered that the Argentinian pilot had been incinerated in
the explosion. During the raids, the BBC cameraman, Bernard
Hesketh, with his sound recorder, John Jockell, had stood on
the bridge wings and the top decks filming the planes attacking.

Bernard's energy matched that of any of the younger
reporters. He was fifty-five and due to retire in a year or so.
Some eight years of his time in the BBC had been spent covering Royal events and overseas tours. In the brief period I
worked with him on the routine television training attachment
undergone by the BBC's national radio reporters, he was
always turned out with a far more sober and dignified appearance than I. So he was always taken by strangers to be the
senior representative and the correspondent or reporter. He
was responsible for most of the television film and tape of the
entire land and sea campaign. There was only one other crew,
from ITN, and they were dogged with bad luck and broken
machinery. One significant disadvantage Bernard suffered
with the use of the new ENG cameras was that the weight of
the equipment made it virtually impossible to walk any distance with the units that had to 'yomp' or 'tab' across the Falklands or march to battle. Bernard had to work with both Brian
Hanrahan and Mike Nicholson, and had to maintain a firm
sense of his own purpose with the whims of two correspondents to cater for. Bernard had a fiery spirit and a sharp tongue
when he wanted to use it, and I found it a relief to have a quick
disagreement which was soon completely forgotten. By this
time the three TV correspondents were also working for radio,

which was particularly important in the deployment of our resources for the World Service. Brian Hanrahan had got a brief from the World Service people at Bush House before leaving, and I had worked for them on and off for most of my fourteen years with the BBC. For the ITN journalists, the radio became the myth of Echo revisited, and sometimes it was hard to tear them away from the Marisat phone. Brian Hanrahan took the hard-headed approach that he would file in voice for television and radio whenever he had the material and could reach a satellite outlet quickly. His radio pieces were particularly fine, with a sharp, direct style; before becoming a reporter he had been one of the best scriptwriters in the BBC Television Newsroom.

The air raid over and the despatches filed, we were offered showers and a change of clothes. In the dining-room there was a delicious Chinese meal cooked by the galley staff who came from Hong Kong. David Norris decided to spend the night aboard, and visiting the *Stromness* for him was a homecoming, as he had left England aboard her. We were told to get ashore quickly as more air raids were expected. Brian Hanrahan and Mike Nicholson did not come with us as they still had not got full kit for the land campaign and would wait for the arrival of 5th Infantry Brigade, now believed to be approaching South Georgia in the *QE2*.

As we prepared to get aboard the landing craft, we saw HMS *Antelope*, the Type 21 frigate, sister-ship of HMS *Ardent*, steam slowly past us in the anchorage. Steam gushed from her stack and a neat hole drilled in her side amidships, with a curl of smoke coming through the jagged metal. She had been hit by a bomb, but as far as we could tell she seemed to have dealt with the fires by damage-control drills. On her flight deck a group of men stood in orange suits, known as the 'once only' survival kit. Her mast had been snapped and had cannon shell holes in it. As we shoved off from the *Stromness*, the ITN crew asked to go near to the *Antelope* to film her wounds and the crew on deck. There was little sense of emergency, the sea dead calm and the sky darkening at the approach of a winter's evening. As we came within two hundred feet of the *Antelope*, the men on deck started waving. We waved back and cheered. There was a breakdown in communication; for the *Antelope*'s crew it was a case as of 'not waving but drowning'. They were gesticulating for us to get clear as the ship could be about to explode.

The good spirits aboard the landing craft were fuelled by another ludicrous incident. One of the marine crewman was hanging off the upper part of the control compartment of the boat when he slipped and seemed to bounce in the water as his rubber suit inflated. He said he had not intended to do this, but it was worth a swim to test the suit and the water was not too cold.

Ashore at San Carlos, Malcolm Hunt seemed in good humour too. He said that the plan was not to carry out aggressive patrols from the beachhead, and with Rapier and the Sea Harriers out at sea 'to attrite' – the most dreadful expression in the military lexicon of the Falklands Operation – the Argentinian Air Force. The Navy and 3 Commando Brigade were by now issuing figures of aircraft shot down and 'possible' and 'probable' hits at a rate which would mean the Argentinians would have no Air Force left by the middle of the following week. The inflated tally is easy to explain, quite apart from the propaganda need to make optimistic noises wherever possible. So many of the hits or 'splashes' were seen and reported from a number of different places, and the destruction of one plane recorded several times over. Malcolm Hunt also told us that there had been some signals' intelligence of a message sent by the Argentinian commander in Port Stanley, General Menendez, to General Galtieri in Buenos Aires, that he did not think the Argentinian forces on the Falklands would be able to defeat the British.

As we returned to the sheep shed we heard an enormous explosion across the anchorage to the north of the settlement's grass airstrip. It was followed by another report and a cloud of billowing black smoke. 'My God, it must be the *Antelope*,' someone said. Within minutes came the noises of helicopters leaving HMS *Fearless*, their searchlights cutting through the gathering gloom.

The *Antelope* had received a bomb amidships, which had failed to explode. A disposal team had gone to the ship from Ajax, led by Staff Sergeant Jim Prescott of the Royal Engineers. Flight-Lieutenant Swann of the RAF unexploded bomb team told me that Jim Prescott had managed to get the fuse out twice, but had reinserted it because he was not quite sure how stable the bomb was without the fuse. He was in the process of removing the firing device a third time when the projectile 'cooked', or overheated, and exploded. Prescott was killed by the explosion and one of his team lost an arm. An eighteen-year-old steward, Stephens, had been killed in the air raid. No one else was lost or hurt. Commander Nick Tobin, whom we had met briefly on our visit to the *Antelope* at Ascension, had ordered the crew aft and those who had them to get into their 'once only' suits, which made them look like circus clowns in the baggy orange overalls. The ship's Lynx helicopter had been flown off before the first explosion, with tools and spares loaded aboard it.

The ship's magazines erupted again after nightfall, the secondary explosions shooting sparks skyward with the anger of a volcano. The moment was captured by one of the most powerful photographs of the campaign by the Press Association's Martin Cleaver from HMS *Fearless*. Both Mike Nicholson and Brian Hanharan watched the ship break her back and begin to sink. By the morning she was a steaming wreck, bent and twisted, listing to starboard, her sharp bow bent upwards. In the brilliant sunlight she turned slowly and sank, her razor-sharp bow pointing up for hours before slipping under the calm waters.

The death of a ship brings a particular grief. Ships have a personality in the way that newspapers have a personality, an intimate quality that broadcasting stations and television channels lack. Ships are happy or quarrelsome. They are lucky or have jinxes, and these attributes persist despite the change of companies. The quality of *Antelope*'s personality was quickly sensed after a few minutes aboard. She was a happy ship and one that was well disciplined. Commander Tobin ran a 'tight' ship and this resulted in so few casualties in her last action.

The Type 21 frigates, like the *Ardent* and *Antelope*, are beautiful in their line. They are fast with their Olympus and Tyne gas turbines, but the design of ship is generally disliked throughout the Navy, and with reason. The Type 21s were not designed by the Navy itself, but by a commercial builder, Vosper Thorneycroft, who were constructing them for foreign fleets like the Iranian Navy of the Shah. The Ministry of Defence was casting round for a stop-gap replacement to the Leanders and the Broad-Beam Leanders, and found the Type 21, which they bought off-the-peg from Thorneycroft. To achieve speed and reduce weight topsides on the superstructure, much is built of aluminium, which is susceptible to high temperatures, melting in great heat and even appearing to ignite in some circumstances. Both the American Navy and Royal Navy designers are very concerned about the free use of light materials in modern escorts, materials which they suspect add unacceptable fire risks. The other disadvantage of the Type 21 is her armament. The frigates were intended first to be fitted out with Sea Wolf missiles, but these could not be provided in time, so they were given the older Sea Cat, the manually and visually guided weapon. As the Argentinian air attacks on the *Ardent* showed, there is a blind spot between the arc of fire of the main 4.5-inch gun forward and the Sea Cat batteries aft. In the Falklands it was recognised by Naval officers that such ships would benefit from being equipped with more heavy machine-guns for combatting attack from low-flying aircraft. The use of machine-guns against low-flying aircraft was to be vindicated time and again, and is one of the main lessons of the Falklands campaign, though the civilian strategists and weapons buffs in Britain and America, obsessed with the Middle East as the trial ground for modern close-combat weapons, seem reluctant to accept that anything at all can be learnt from the Falklands battles.

Sea Wolf, mounted on the Type 22 destroyers *Brilliant* and *Broadsword*, and the Leander class HMS *Penelope*, was the success many hoped it would be, though it showed some teething troubles. The Sea Wolf is at least a generation further advanced than Sea Cat, and is a point defence anti-aircraft and anti-missile missile. It proved well in both roles in the Falklands, striking down both Exocet missiles and low-flying planes. It is intended to be a close-range weapon, so had the tendency, it was said at Ajax Bay, to defend first and foremost its own whip and not a line or squadron. If aircraft attacked the ship from four different directions, the guidance computer might become 'confused', centralise and start the tracking process from the beginning, losing valuable time as the attackers approached the target. Engineers from Marconi came out from Britain to work on the systems in the *Brilliant* and *Broadsword* to provide a manual override which would allow operators to choose targets and to fire at missiles and planes attacking other ships. The design of one of the Type 22 destroyers like *Broadsword* showed a weakness, too, when a hit on the main cable ducts took the power supply from the weapons systems at one blow.

The morning the *Antelope* sank was like spring, clear, fresh and brightly sunny. Packing up my kit in the shearing shed, I began the tortuous negotiations to get a helicopter flight back to Sussex Mountains and 2 Para. The minders said I would have to wait and that helicopters were not intended for the press. I went across to the Brigade HQ, a cluster of heavily camouflaged tents dug into the ground by Blue Beach Two above the spit of land with the grass airstrip. Ewan Southby-Tailyour emerged from the tents saying that he felt out of place among so many staff officers and that his landing craft crews were still getting stick from the paras. As we were chatting, 'H' Jones and Tony Rice came by on their way to the Brigadier's Orders Group. 'H' immediately offered me a lift back to the unit in his helicopter, which was likely to be a Sea King, a mountain to move a mouse, as only two passengers were scheduled for the ride. As the Orders began inside the tent, there was an Air Raid Warning Red alert, and we jumped into the trenches camouflaged by gorse branches. Shortly after the siren wailing from *Fearless*, the first planes came over. Machine-gun fire swished through the air, thwacking the branches sticking out of the camouflage nets as rounds came back on a ricochet. One of the marines picked a spent bullet from his puttees. Later Brigadier Thompson and 'H's' party emerged from the tent, Julian Thompson saying that it was so crowded inside he could not hear himself think and that if the raids over the settlement continued, the Brigade HQ would have to be shifted. The small party moved to a ditch at the side of the field and were tapping maps animatedly when the second air raid came in. I saw the two Skyhawks like green arrowheads skirting the contours of the green and brown hillside. They banked and then levelled as they hugged the land. Keeping as low as they could, they seemed suspended on elastic like puppets. With the planes moving behind the buildings, machine-guns burst from different directions and guns and missiles fired from the ships. One missile flew horizontally like a red-hot rod of steel and splashed short of the beach. Behind a low ridge the planes dropped their bombs harmlessly, though it was in the area of the rear position of 2 Para and the gun battery. As the plane hauled up the steep hillside to the south, the machine-gunners from 2 Para opened fire and from Brigade HQ we could see two long, heavy jets of black smoke pouring from the aircraft. We jumped out of the trenches and danced like apes, shouting 'Yaaaaah' with delight that the attackers had been hit. Moments later I was disgusted at my animal elation. The flying by the two Argentinian pilots had been wonderfully skilful and brave; from a distance, the aerial display had been a gentle, balletic quality as the planes flitted across the hills like shadows.

Emerging from the edge of the field, Brigadier Thompson was perturbed at the amount of machine-gun fire from the ground. He ordered later that machine-guns should not be fired indiscriminately against aircraft as thousands of rounds were being shot away in each air raid. 'H' and Tony invited me to join them once the 'O' Group was over. As I clambered into the straps of the bergen, a corpulent minder chased after me and said I could not go in the colonel's helicopter as I had not been cleared to do so. As I ran to catch up with 'H' I suggested he tell this to the colonel.

On Sussex Mountains just about every machine-gunner said he had hit the Skyhawks passing twenty or thirty feet overhead from the raid on San Carlos. Each may have been right, as thousands of rounds of ammunition had been shot into the sky. Men of Headquarters Company felt hot fuel spurting from the planes' tanks onto their faces and clothes, soaking their bedding and tents. The men in the forward positions said they saw both planes take a shallow dive across the sea in the direction of Port Howard and that they must have come down on West Falkland. No one saw the pilots bail out. The shooting down of the aircraft fed animated conversation for hours afterwards, and no one seemed keen to heed the Brigadier's orders about conserving ammunition and not firing indiscriminately at aircraft. 'It helps to keep everyone cheerful,' said one officer. But 'H' Jones was keen to get on the move, and he planned to begin a raid on the Darwin Isthmus that night.

'H' had been discussing the plan with the Brigadier that morning. The object was to attack the Argentinians in Darwin and Goose Green at night, to inflict as much damage as possible before withdrawing at daylight. He would not take the full battalion but three to four light companies, who would march to a point just north of the isthmus at Camilla Creek House and lie up there in the long grass for a day to begin the raid soon after dark. It was a march of some fifteen miles from the positions on the Sussex Mountains to Camilla Creek House and then another three to four miles to the neck of land at the head of the isthmus. Field guns would be flown down at dusk on the second night to give covering fire. It was thought that much of the cover would be from the machine-guns. 'It's very much down to the Gimpy,' was the summing up of one of the company commanders after 'H' had given his orders. Chris Keeble was to stay behind with the rear party and the Battalion HQ. 'H' did not invite me to his 'O' Group, but later explained quietly and in detail what was at stake and asked me where I wanted to go. I did not take much to the idea of being with a rifle company in close skirmishes in the dark, but asked if I could be in a position where I had some perspective on what was going on in the whole battle. 'H' agreed to let me ride in the helicopters bringing down the guns to Camilla Creek. I would travel with Tony Rice's gunners and go forward from there as the attack developed.

Some on Sussex Mountains thought 'H' was over-eager to have a go and 'banjo' the enemy, as the paras so quaintly put it, at the first opportunity. Some were not even sure that it was necessary to go into Goose Green and Darwin, where it was still thought there was only a light concentration of Argentinian infantry. The mythical strategic reserve, which many were beginning to doubt existed by this stage, was supposed to be at Fox Bay on West Falkland. The real target was Port Stanley, so why show your hand and lose men before you got there? 'H' had some sympathy with this view. He saw as a first essential that his men should move off Sussex Mountains. He thought a raid on Goose Green was necessary to make sure there was no risk of a flank or rear attack on British troops advancing on Stanley by the southern route which would take them through Fitzroy and Bluff Cove.

'H' foresaw a stalemate developing at San Carlos if 3 Commando Brigade waited there for a further build-up in supplies and the arrival of 5th Infantry Brigade, now not expected until the following weekend (that of 29 and 30 May) at the earliest. If the enemy moved forward from Stanley, with possible airborne support from parachute troops, there could be some difficult and bitter fighting across the central hills and mountains of East Falkland which might last for weeks and months.

'H' gave me a short radio interview about his planned attack, but the tape was lost with half my kit after the battle at Goose Green. It was the last recording of his voice. He was in a very good mood, and as he finished talking about the raid, said: 'I've got to go and finish my farewell letter to Sara,' his wife. He sat outside the Battalion HQ by his bivvy in his quilted jerkin penning a few more lines home, talking cheerfully to anyone passing. At dusk he went to see the lead company, 'C' Company, with the recce patrols as they set off to join the track to Camilla Creek and then he prepared to move out with the rest of his force. Alex Ward and I made yet another curry complete with dried apricot flakes and drained the water from the bottom of the trench, baling with mess tins before getting our heads down after the evening stand-to. We talked a bit about the raid, Alex eager to come along as my bodyguard, for which I would have been heartily grateful.

The Arctic sleeping-bag in the open was surprisingly warm. I listened to the latest World Service News on head-phones with my small pocket radio before trying to sleep. Suddenly a brilliant light shone through the poncho sheet over my head, followed by the crackle of a rocket flare. This was followed by several more and the shuffling of sentries down the valley, which concluded with a short burst of machine-gun fire. In the morning I was told an enemy four-man patrol had been seen in the valley beneath our positions and they had made off after they were surprised. The alert was followed by some firing from the field guns down at Head of the Bay House. Then all was quiet.

At the 'stand-to' in the morning, I was surprised to find most of the battalion still where they had been the day before. They had not set out for Camilla Creek and Darwin. 'H' quickly explained that the raid had been cancelled in the night by the Brigadier. The official reason was that the necessary helicopter assets were not available to lift the guns and their ammunition, as the helicopters were required on a priority mission by the SAS. 'H' also confided that the cabinet had not been keen on the plan as they thought it might risk a level of casualties they did not want at this point in the campaign. He said he was going to have words with his old friend Colonel 'M', the CO of 22 SAS Regiment, and tell him that if it was anyone else in charge of the unit responsible for the hold up he would have been furious. There was some muttering about, 'I wish Maggie would get on with it. How do we get into Downing Street?' and so it went on. He also said he thought the Brigadier was being too cautious. He was angry that he had brought back a company of men after nearly a dozen miles. The men would not be so eager the next time and now we had given the enemy warning we were coming, and much of the element of surprise must have been lost. Later Colonel 'M' told me that 'H' had said to him: 'You ... I've waited twenty years for this. And now we're being held up because of one of your patrols.'

I spent the morning visiting 'B' Company in their eyrie on the highest rocks. Their commander, Major John Crosland, was putting as good a face as he could manage on the previous twenty-four hours' events and said it was still pretty damp and cold in his position but it was not too bad. 'H' had told me earlier that he was getting worried about the men's feet, as quite a number of cases of trench foot were being reported already; this is a mild version of frostbite where the feet soften and peel in the cold and wet. With feet suffering such ailments, it would be hard to get the battalion to march great distances to engage the enemy. I continued the interviews with John Crosland's men, and there was much banter and the kind of cheery chat one might have heard from these men's predecessors on the Western Front in the First World War. John Crosland came from a modern school of soldiering, with a great deal of experience in specialist tactics. He looked a veteran with his camouflage cream now indistinguishable from the peat and mud, a dripping nose, topped by his talisman, a rolled-up blue balaclava perched on the top of his head, the oldest and most famous woolly hat in the battalion. Not far from me a corporal said that life was not too bad and the 'scoff' was good, at least that was the gist of what he had to say, as every other word was qualified with the epithet 'fucking', still the universal adjective and adverb in any conversation in the field.

One of the sergeants, who spoke to me of his love of the countryside, sounded Colonel John Frost's hunting horn which he had used to rally the battalion at Arnhem in Operation Market Garden, the Parachute Regiment's first great battle honour and, like many in British military history, a heroic defeat. The best crack came from Sergeant Lewis, who said that his 'basher' between some rocks was rather like a package holiday in Spain – 'No water, no showers, and miles from the beach. And the hotel isn't built yet – I'm not coming here again.'

The tour was accompanied by Private Nick Lukie, an amiable conversationalist who had taken over as battalion photographer in the place of the missing photographer

Sergeant Hudson. Nick's main interest was finding out how he could market some of his pictures to the national dailies. Nick was very sharp, and far from an 'old sweat'. His father was a schoolteacher and had an old friend who was a schools' supervisor in Port Stanley. He asked me if I got to the capital before him, to look up the family's friend. Nick did get to Stanley in one piece, but blew a hole in his face afterwards when handling a captured pistol – it put him in the *Canberra* hospital for a fortnight.

On the saddle of the hill north of 'A' Company was one of the Rapier installations. The crew were suffering from the cold and damp and had been scared the night before. They had taken a para sergeant as their guide to fetch petrol for their generator. As they reached the petrol dump, they lost their guide in the dark and then could not find the path back. Suddenly they were surprised by rocket flares and a machine-gun opened up on them. They hid for half an hour before crawling nearly a mile and a half back to the battery. So much for the report that an enemy patrol had been in our midst. The first that 'H' knew that it was the mishap to the Rapier men that had led to the previous night's alert was when I told him. On several occasions it appeared that information took a long and tortuous path to get back to the higher levels of battalion command or to the HQ Ops tent from the outlying company positions.

Chris Keeble, who took considerable interest in modern weapons deployment and was an expert, in particular, on the Milan anti-tank missiles, was anxious to move the Rapier position to improve the arc of fire against low-flying planes coming up over the ridge from the sea or the anchorage. The Rapier team was reluctant to move, as it was heavy work to shift the guidance equipment and the battery itself, which resembles a giant, upturned dustbin with the four missiles like barbed harpoons. The sergeant also said that if his battery moved forward it would get caught in the arcs of fire of other weapons such as the machine-guns. Chris had paid a number of visits to the Rapier to see how their visual guidance system worked. 'So what does it mean if it lights up as it is doing now?' he asked at one point.

'Well it means we're under attack, which can't be right because we haven't had a warning.' As the gunner spoke, a flight of attacking Skyhawks roared overhead to bomb the anchorage. They had crept under the radar by flying low across West Falkland and Falkland Sound. In the afternoon's raids, two of the LSLs were hit, and the *Sir Galahad* had to be abandoned for a few hours.

In the afternoon we heard over the radio that there had been heavy attacks on the Task Force at sea and that the Type 42 destroyer HMS *Coventry* had been hit north-east of the islands. Later we learnt that the *Atlantic Conveyor* had been lost, but the Harrier GR3s she carried had been flown off to the carriers. It was thought that all four Chinook helicopters and the squadron of Wessex helicopters and their spares had gone with the container ship. One of the Chinooks was saved by the lucky accident that it was carrying out flying trials at the time of the Exocet attack. It was to be kept running throughout the rest of the campaign with almost no maintenance and with no spares. The pilots flew it for long hours. At one time, flying over Teal Inlet, the co-pilot thought the pilot was nodding off and the machine lurched down to wave level. Following regulation ditching drills, he kicked out the left-hand door, which woke the pilot up. So the Chinook flew without a wheel and a door until the surrender was taken in Port Stanley, where the ground crew took a door off one of the captured Argentinian Chinooks to make good their loss.

The Exocets had been aimed at HMS *Invincible*, which had fired chaff, strips of metal, from her mortars and this had deflected the missiles onto the *Conveyor*, the nearest large target. 3 Commando Brigade had lost their main heavy-lift helicopters and reserve troop-carrying helicopters from the Wessex squadron. There had been spares for the Harriers aboard the *Conveyor* and nearly four thousand tents for the troops. The loss of the *Conveyor* meant that much of Brigadier Thompson's force would have to move across the island on foot to attack Port Stanley. The loss of HMS *Coventry* meant that a fourth warship had been lost in three weeks and, like the *Sheffield*, the *Ardent* and the *Antelope*, one of the most modern in the fleet.

The news that night did not disclose the loss of both the

Conveyor and the *Coventry*. It did say that John Nott had reported to parliament that the important military decisions would be taken by commanders on the ground and there would be no political interference with them. Secretary of State Alexander Haig said in Washington that 'significant developments' could be expected on the Falklands within three days.

The following day 'H' seemed less disappointed about the cancellation of the Goose Green raid. He told me the news from an Argentinian pilot who had ejected over San Carlos the day before and been taken aboard HMS *Fearless*. According to the officer, there were twice as many pilots as planes in the Argentinian Air Force. Many of the squadrons were being brought down from the north to Rio Gallegos and Rio Grande, given their mission orders and told to return to a different base. This was how the extent of losses was being concealed, because each time a mission returned and a pilot asked after a missing colleague, he would be told that his comrade had been switched suddenly to a secret operation and had to land at another airfield. The prisoners also said that initially orders to strike San Carlos were ludicrously vague. They were told to fly over the anchorage and 'hit anything grey', and they were told there were no air defences. He said he realised that losses were much higher than official estimates, which were between 5 and 10 per cent. Accordingly, he baled out while he had the chance to stay alive.

In the morning I decided to return to San Carlos to see if I could play over to London the tapes of the interview with the men dug in on the hills. But there was no ship with Marisat facility and only short scripts could be sent in crypt from the Sat. Comm. station at Ajax Bay where there was still no facility to broadcast in voice, despite repeated assurances from the Ministry of Defence to our offices in London that there would be one available. There never was to the day I left the Falklands, and the MOD viewed from our end never gave the appearance of wanting to provide one.

I went to visit Pat Short, the San Carlos Manager of the Falkland Island Company, and recorded a conversation with him and his wife Isobel and Alice Alazia, a member of one of the great Falklands clans. They talked casually of the days the Argentinians came before the British landings. The troops were poorly fed, and seemed demoralised. There were stories of shootings of mutinous troops, though these were never to be confirmed later at first hand by Argentinian prisoners. They all remarked how young the conscripts looked and said that on the whole they found the officers quite polite. They had expected the British for some time, they said, and when the Naval bombardment first started they knew it would not be long. I found this phlegmatic, almost fatalistic, approach in several of the settlements, and something faintly admirable in the nonchalant way the islanders regarded the landings by the marines and paratroops.·

Wandering around the settlement with nothing much to do, and meeting Malcolm Hunt, who was still talking about 'attriting their air force', I was grabbed by David Nicholls, who said that David Norris and I were to pack immediately and go by helicopter back to 2 Para. The battalion was moving to attack Goose Green and we were to go with them. The sinking of the *Coventry* and *Conveyor* had brought a change of plans, ordered directly from London. 2 Para were to attack Darwin and Goose Green. 42 Commando, 45 Commando and 3 Para were to move out of the beachhead, and north through Douglas and Teal settlements.

We jumped into the helicopter and arrived at Battalion HQ on Sussex Mountains at dusk. A sergeant from 'B' Echelon said there was no point in staying there because the battalion had set out already for Camilla Creek, and the marines were putting in a company to man observation posts on the mountains now. We decided to go back to the sheep shed and take the first helicopter to join 2 Para in the morning. We were allocated to a Gazelle flight at daybreak to fly down to Camilla Creek, where the battalion would be lying up for the attack on Goose Green and Port Darwin.

6. The Liberation of Goose Green

1. CAMILLA CREEK

Camilla Creek House is the only landmark of note to the north of the neck of land which connects the north part of East Falkland and the large peninsula now called Lafonia but in Darwin's day known as Rincon del Toro. The isthmus which bears Darwin's name today is one of the few places he specifically mentions in the description of his visit to the Falklands in *The Voyage of the Beagle*. He marvelled at the magnificent build of the wild bulls he found near the isthmus, as they were far bigger than the Spanish cattle of South America from which they were descended. 'We rode across the island to the neck of land which joins the Rincon del Toro (the great peninsula at the South West extremity) to the rest of the island,' he writes on 17 April 1834. 'From the great number of cows which have been killed, there is a large proportion of bulls. These wander about single, or two and three together, and are very savage. I never saw such magnificent beasts; they equalled in the size of their huge heads and necks the Grecian marble sculptures.' Herds roamed the uplands round Mount Usborne and dotted the plains of Lafonia. The animals on the northern peninsula were brown and white with wide, spreading horns, those to the south black and white, which enabled them to be seen from miles off as their coats could not be disguised against the brown and yellow tussock. Some of the descendants of the northern breeds are still kept in the grasslands round Goose Green and Darwin, and many of the domestic cattle there were to be killed on the minefields sown by the Argentinians outside the Goose Green paddocks.

Darwin's party spent the night within a few miles of where 2 Para were lying up before their attack on the settlements of

Goose Green and Darwin itself. Charles Darwin was amazed that the Gauchos with him, led by the colourful St Jago, managed to find materials to make a camp fire despite the lack of any firewood. 'The valley was pretty well sheltered from the cold wind,' the entry for 17 April continues, 'but there was very little brushwood for fuel. The Gauchos, however, soon found what, to my great surprise, made nearly as hot a fire as coals; this was the skeleton of a bullock lately killed, from which the flesh had been picked by the carrion-hawks. They told me that in winter they often killed a beast, cleaned the flesh from the bones with their knives, and then with these same bones roasted the meat for their suppers.'

As the two helicopters bringing David Norris and myself to Camilla Creek arrived, the men of Headquarters Company were cooking their midday meal, not with the bones of Darwin's cattle but with hexy stoves and other appliances inside the house itself. The flight had taken us back to Sussex Mountains to pick up last-minute supplies and rifle and machine-gun ammunition. The flight from Sussex Mountains was a dash along ridges and down gulleys, our route marked by the few traces of track and the single line of telephone wire across a sea of surging tussock grass and peat. All eyes kept watching for marauding planes, particularly the Pucara which could move slowly enough to get a clear sighting to enable them to turn and engage the low-flying helicopters with machine-gun and canon.

David Norris and I walked through what might pass as a front door in Camilla Creek House. The house itself stood away from a cluster of farm buildings, all deserted now, with a few broken wire fences and yew hedges to mark what must have been home paddocks and corrals for the cows and sheep. It was approaching half-past two Zulu or GMT, half-past ten local time. The company commanders, Tony Rice and Chris Keeble, were in the downstairs rooms and they said 'H' was upstairs and in a rage. Dair Farrar-Hockley said: 'The BBC World Service has announced that 2 Para is outside Darwin, five miles away and about to take Goose Green. Do you know anything about this?' I did not, and I said that if this was true it

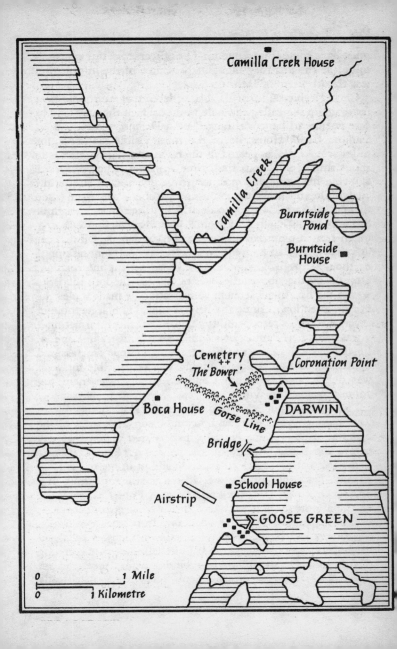

Camilla Creek House

Camilla Creek

Burntside Pond

Burntside House

Coronation Point

Cemetery
++
The 'Bower'

Boca House   Gorse Line   DARWIN

Bridge

School House

Airstrip   GOOSE GREEN

0 ——————— 1 Mile
0 ——————— 1 Kilometre

must have come from London. The officers said this appeared to be the case, as they thought the source of the information was the Ministry of Defence.

Chris Keeble said that 'H' had ordered that we should now try to go up the valley and hide in the folds of the grassland in case enemy artillery was ranged on a Defensive Fire grid on Camilla Creek House itself, the most visible landmark for miles around. 'H' appeared in the room and started his tirade about suing John Nott, the Prime Minister if necessary, for allowing his battalion's position to be given away so gratuit-ously. 'Do you think we could do it, Robert?' he asked. 'Sue them. Tell Sara she's got to do it. I'll write to her.' Much of this was in fun, and 'H''s widow tells me that this was very much a catch-phrase of his, to sue everyone in sight if disaster threatened. I acted as *agent provocateur* at one point, asking if he thought the BBC should have broadcast the information. Once in his diatribe on the lines of 'I'll sue the lot', the BBC was in the list. In subsequent conversation he made it clear he had no intention of suing the BBC, and added that he thought it was the BBC's responsibility to broadcast this information if it was being made public by a Minister or Ministry in London. Furthermore, both he and his company commanders assured me that he did not hold me in any way responsible for what was being broadcast from London and nor was there any animus against the World Service.

The BBC's announcement on the 14.00 GMT news bulletin was cautious in the extreme by comparison with some of the material appearing in the daily papers in London that day before the battle. According to the *Express* and the *Daily Telegraph* that morning, 2 Para were all but in the settlements already. How this came to be written is still something of a puzzle. One source was the Parliamentary Lobby. Apparently, on the afternoon of Wednesday 26 May, Tory backbenchers had been assured that the break-out from the San Carlos Beachhead had begun. Plans of a raid on Goose Green had been openly speculated about in Whitehall since the beginning of the week. On the Thursday, the day before the attack, at least one defence correspondent mentioned specifically

Camilla Creek as a rendezvous point for the attack. This attack was not scheduled to begin until 06.00 GMT on the following morning, Friday 28 May. If they looked at Fleet Street, the Argentinians had more signals about the operation than a troop of Boy Scouts could give at semaphore practice.

Much of the confusion must have been caused by the fact that attacks on Darwin and Goose Green had been reported and speculated about from the moment the troops landed at San Carlos on 21 May. The capture was reported four times before the operation was complete. The last premature report appeared in the papers on the morning of Saturday 29 May, as Chris Keeble's small party of officers and the two journalists was preparing to set off for Goose Green airstrip to discuss terms of surrender with the Argentinian commanders.

In a field of open intelligence operations, what is commonplace information to one side may emerge as the valuable missing clue to the other side. At this time, the Ministry was ostensibly running a closed information policy, with special briefings to accredited correspondents and editors in London and censorship of despatches from journalists in the field. But there appears to have been so much speculation and rumour drifting about London that it was hard to discern what was fact, commonplace information, speculation, innuendo and rumour, and vital strategic material whose publication might jeopardise present and future operations.

Such was the nature of the anonymous terrain where Darwin's Gauchos made their camp fire from bullock bones, and where 2 Para were stretching their ingenuity to find cover to hide in, that an announcement that a British parachute battalion was five miles from Darwin and about to attack could only mean that the troops were at one place, Camilla Creek House. Camilla Creek House marks the point where the track from San Carlos heads south into the Darwin Isthmus. A mile and a half from the house, it turns to pass between a tongue of sea and the lake north of Burntside House. From Burntside, the track divides to run west into Lafonia through Goose Green, and to turn east to form the main route to Swan Inlet, Fitzroy, Bluff Cove and Port Stanley. The Argentinians knew that Camilla Creek guarded the eastern approach to the chain of settlements at Burntside, Darwin and Goose Green. There was no other notable feature near, just miles of heaving bog and grassland.

Whatever the strategic implications, if the Argentinians had perceived the full import of what was being revealed about the 2 Para position that Thursday, and had they been able to use the principal weapon of the British air attacks, the cluster bomb dropped from Figher Ground Attack aircraft, half the 2nd Parachute battalion would have been destroyed in the grasslands of Camilla Creek. The attack on Goose Green would have been defeated before it started, the momentum of the campaign lost, and in 'H' Jones's view, defeat at Darwin and Goose Green could have meant that the Falklands would never have been recaptured.

The information chaos takes on a Crimean War perspective when another fact is taken into consideration, and it is one of which I only received the first inklings three months after the battle at Goose Green. By the day of the battle itself, Friday 28 May, senior military staff officers in London had intelligence that there were about 1,500 Argentinians in Goose Green, and not the three or four companies making up a 'light' battalion of 500 men at most which was originally reported by the SAS surveillance patrols on the ground there. This information never reached the commanders of 2 Para before or during the battle. A senior staff officer told a Parachute Regiment officer some weeks later: 'When I heard that 'H' Jones had been killed and that only one battalion was attacking Goose Green . . . I went to bed that night with a heavy heart.' He said he could not believe only one British battalion had attacked the settlements, knowing the strength of the garrison. The briefings for 2 Para at Camilla Creek the night before the battle mentioned the enemy dug in at company strength. No reinforcements were sent in until after the fighting had died down on the Friday night, when Mike Norman's Juliet Company from 42 Commando was flown in.

'H' told me that the march south from Sussex Mountains had been quite hard going and for a time the Argentinians had tried to shell the track, but rounds had landed several hundred yards wide. During the afternoon he said that the idea of suing anyone about the leak of information about the battalion's position was impossible and he thought about getting a letter to *The Times*, but I suspect he realised even that was not a realistic proposition for a serving officer like himself. He was adamant that we should get well away from the house and spread out across the rough grass.

While hot food and some 'brews' were still available, we were reluctant to get out of the farmhouse. No family had lived there for some time; the owner was away from the area, we were told. It had a crumbling, derelict air, ripped lino floors and decrepit plumbing. The phone was still working and Chris Keeble warned us that once the receiver was lifted, phones in Darwin and Goose Green might ring and the Argentinians would know we were in residence. Their forces had left dozens of indications, like forgotten visiting cards, of their recent occupation of the house. Scattered across the floor were mudstained prayer sheets in Spanish, the *Oraciones* for the forces in the field. The remains of their beef rations had been found and some of the paras tried to heat them up for their lunch.

Moving out to the grasslands to the north, the radio warned that there would be some Harrier strikes on Goose Green and the planes would pass down the valley. They came like grey bolts, skimming the rolling grasslands, like the Argentinian Skyhawks, looking as if they were suspended on elastic as they dipped and rose gracefully, following the contours of the rolling sea of coarse grass, soil and rock. Their flight was a movement of pure elation for those watching, and as they roared to the horizon, the left-hand plane of the pair would seem to kick upwards as they began the run across the neck of land. As they swung south-west towards the target, there would be spurting clouds of blue and grey smoke and then the stuttering roar of cluster bombs and rockets exploding and anti-aircraft fire coming up at them. Twice they rocketed down Darwin's valley and the run was punctuated by the chain of crashes and explosions which crackled again as they made a second attack on Goose Green from seaward. After the second raid, the radio reported one Harrier seen shot down. The pilot, Squadron-Leader Bob Iveson, managed to eject safely and sheltered in an outlying settlement until Chris Keeble despatched a helicopter to pick him up two days later, after the battle.

The veteran of the party at Camilla Creek, Squadron-Leader Jock Penman, had suffered badly from the march from the beach-head. His feet and legs had given him trouble, not surprising in a man of fifty-seven. One of the problems with blistering on the marches was that the tears in the feet and damaged muscles could become infected, with conditions like cellulitis leading to high temperatures. Jock had to return to Ajax Bay for treatment and one of the officers remarked: 'He shouldn't have been asked to tab all that way. It's his brain we're going to need, not his legs.'

'H' joined us in the grass to begin an afternoon 'O' Group. As he was chatting, there came a report through the wireless of a contact with an enemy patrol to the south of the house. Shots were fired and 'H' shouted that we should not give our positions away and the enemy must be shot rather than allow them to flee and give away the battalion to the garrison. Then came the news that all four in the patrol had been taken prisoner; two of them had been injured trying to escape. The Argentinians had a blue and white Land Rover commandeered from Goose Green and their regular recce run was to drive up and down the track from Darwin and Burntside to Camilla Creek. 'H' said he had still not got his plans together, so postponed the 'O' Group meetings to walk back to the house to see the prisoners.

Captain Rod Bell, Royal Marines, who was with us as interpreter, started questioning the two uninjured men, Lieutenant Morales, who said he was leader of the Argentinian Reconnaissance Troop, and a Private Pedro Galva. Of the two, the private was the more helpful. Rod Bell said the lieutenant was a professional soldier and seemed to be dissembling and hiding the truth. The private was a conscript but he knew very little, apparently, of the defences outside Goose Green and Darwin.

In the evening sun I saw the young soldier swaying on his feet with his hands on his head in the pose of the captive, talking quickly as he tried to draw in the soil with his boots, their laces removed, diagrams of trench positions. The Argentinians' weapons appeared to be in poor condition, rusty and with old ammunition. Their food supply looked not much better. They had a polythene container for margarine with a huge slab of margarine fat in it and some scraps of meat. The two younger soldiers seemed glad it was all over for them, at least.

A paratroop sergeant explained how the enemy patrol had been surprised and tried to make their escape in the Land Rover. Once they had been disarmed, the sergeant of the patrol made a grab for one of the weapons that had been dumped on the ground, and was shot through the calf muscle in his attempt to get away.

After all the excitement of the afternoon and morning, 'H''s 'O' Group was calm and orderly and gently good-humoured. We sat in a little bunch beneath a yew hedge as the sun died in the west. 'H' had cordially invited David Norris and myself to listen to the situation intelligence reports and the orders being given to the company commanders and the leaders of the specialist sections like the gunners, Naval Gunfire Support team, Mortar Fire Controllers and those in charge of Heavy Weapons and Forward Aircraft Control.

The Intelligence Brief was given by Captain Alan Coulson, the intelligence officer, with his lugubrious moustache and the pudding-basin helmet. He opened with a paraphrase of Charles Darwin that 'the settlement of Goose Green is surrounded by forty acres of the best pasture in the Falklands'. He might have added that it was just about the only piece of land that could claim to be called pasture in the entire archipelago. There was discussion of the local SAS intelligence reports that the enemy positions were held at company strength and the garrison might be a battalion at most, four to five hundred men. The one comfort was that we would probably be attacking at odds of one-to-one. Nevertheless, tactical wisdom says that in such an assault, where the forces are equally well trained and equipped, the attackers should aim at a superiority in numbers of three-to-one. The enemy's fixed positions of trenches were not thought to be particularly well fortified, lacking overhead cover against aircraft and airburst artillery shells.

'H''s plan was a six-phase assault by night and day which would lead to the capture of Darwin, the nearer of the two settlements, at dawn and the seizure of Goose Green from the airfield in daylight. The plan was a complex one for an attack along both sides of the narrow isthmus, which was a mile and a quarter wide at its narrowest. The battalion would 'tab off' from Camilla Creek at 02.00 GMT and the leading companies, 'A' and 'B', would cross the 'start line' by Burntside at 06.00 GMT. 'C' and 'D' Companies would be fed through the first two at later stages, with heavy weapons giving covering fire across Camilla Creek inlet initially before crossing onto the isthmus itself. The object was to capture Darwin and Goose Green, hold them and stay there. In 'H''s mind this was no raid: it was the capture of a staging-post on the way to Port Stanley.

Once again, the featureless geography of the Falklands posed particular problems. 'H' named the principal landmarks for the attack, the beach to the south, the track leading from Burntside to Goose Green, and a barrier of gorse bushes on a rise above Darwin, which marked the nineteenth-century boundaries between the home meadows of the two settlements. This was to be called the Gorse Line. Much of the line of advance would have to be along the track for fear of mines, and it was not known if the beach itself was mined outside Darwin. Some rolling ground to the north and west of Goose Green was thought to conceal enemy artillery and it was to be a priority for the battalion's three guns and the Harrier attacks to try to knock these positions out. Arrangements were made to find a replacement for Jock Penman to guide the Harrier attacks when they became available. HMS *Arrow* would be off Goose Green for Naval Gunfire Support from the early morning, but she would have to leave the area before dawn to avoid air attacks of the kind that had destroyed her sister-ships, HMS *Ardent* and HMS *Antelope*. Finally, 'H' gave orders for the chain of command: 'If the CO is killed the 2 I/c [second in command, in this case Chris Keeble] will come forward to take charge, and while he is doing that the BC [Battery Commander, Tony Rice] takes over.'

Afterwards 'H' asked me where I wanted to go, and I said I did not know as I had never been in anything like this before and did not know how I would get on. He said that he had not been in anything similar either, and wondered how he would make out. He said I should move up with the battalion Main HQ, which would mean I had some contact with what was happening in the fighting by the rifle companies.

As the light began to fade, we heard an Air Raid Warning Red for San Carlos over the radio. The sun was setting as the crash of a large explosion came from the north. 'They must have hit an ammunition dump,' I suggested. Later it turned out that planes had hit the Brigade Maintenance Area at Ajax Bay with their new French-designed retard bombs. The ammunition exploded for half the night and considerable amounts of 3 Commando Brigade's supplies were destroyed, including the Milan missiles belonging to 45 Commando. Five men were killed, one in the trenches by the sheep-shearing shed at San Carlos Settlement, which received a direct hit into the dug-out itself. In the back of the mutton refrigeration plant at Ajax, where Rick Jolly had set up his hospital, two four-hundred kilogram bombs landed and failed to explode.

After 'H's' 'O' Group at Camilla Creek, Alex Ward, David Norris and I made another of our gourmet all-in-one ration pack suppers. Alex was told he could not come with David and myself, because Chris Keeble had a real job for him back at the gun-line at Camilla Creek House, preparing ammunition and supplies to be brought forward during the fighting. Alex was bitterly disappointed, but he was to appear eventually, on the battlefield before the fighting was over.

As the dusk drew in we heard over the ridge the distinct, slow, rhythmic 'whop, whop, whop' of Argentinian helicopters. 'That's a Huey,' said one para NCO. 'I'd know that sound anywhere.' The Argentinians were moving their forces about, and bringing in reinforcements, it seems. Later,

Lt.-Col. Nick Vaux said that his men of 42 Commando found trenches and positions on Mount Kent abandoned in a hurry by troops of the Argentinian 12th Infantry Regiment. They left debris littered across the mountain, food, containers, old blankets and sleeping-bags. Quite how extensive was the reinforcement of Goose Green is not clear. We heard several helicopters on the move and it is possible they used one or two of their Chinooks, beside the Huey machines, for troop-lifting. There were no big helicopters on the ground at Goose Green when the settlement was captured, though we know a company of reinforcements was helicoptered in to a position south of the settlement the night of the battle itself as the fighting was dying down.

We were ordered to pack our bergens with our sleeping-bags strapped to them and dump them in one of the farm sheds. We could not carry them in the battle. With the moon and stars shrouded in mist, we went into the house to get three or four hours' sleep before setting off for the attack at two in the morning GMT, or ten o'clock at night local time. We curled up on the floor. 'H' was next to me, and talked of the day's events and the battle to come. We slept a bit and then woke up and chatted like schoolboys in a dormitory after lights out. Officers came in and out. 'H' asked a former paratrooper and SAS officer who was now attached to 3 Brigade staff as a liaison officer, what colour beret he was going to wear when the fighting was over – green for the commandos, maroon for the paras or brown for the SAS? However, at the 'O' Group he had already given orders that everyone was to wear helmets, and 'no woolly hats' – a reference to John Crosland's chosen headpiece, his familiar, grimy, lucky blue woollen balaclava. Someone said in the loud, officious tones of a public-school pefect, not realising 'H' was there: 'I say, some of us want to get some sleep.' The talking stopped and 'H' snored in his slumber.

II. THE BATTLE AT DARWIN AND GOOSE GREEN

It was a dark, misty night, heavy with the prospect of rain, as the men formed up at Camilla House to move down the track towards Darwin. They stood in single files which coiled between the buildings, many of the figures stooping with the weight of equipment, radios, pickaxes, shovels and ammunition on their backs. There was a delay while the leading company and 'H' Jones's Tactical Headquarters (Tac HQ) group headed off first. Beyond the houses and the corrugated iron sheds, the gunners prepared the ammunition for the three field guns which had been flown in at dusk.

The night was so dark that we had to hold on to the kit on the back of the man in front as we splashed down the muddy track. I grabbed the radio pack of the man in front of me, as the column suddenly jerked forward and asked him his name. 'Manfred,' he replied, and it was weeks later that I discovered that this was his surname and not his Christian name.

After half an hour on the track, the artillery opened fire from Camilla Creek. The shells tore through the air with the familiar noise of ripping cardboard. We would soon be able to distinguish the different notes of the heavy weapons, the crack of a gun discharging and the crunch, like a huge load of coal being dumped, of the shells landing. The sharper note of discharge was the mortar firing. There were the staccato burts of the lighter machine-guns and the steady bass thud of the heavier 50-calibre machine-guns which the Argentinians used to great effect.

As we marched down the track, the field guns fired steadily two or three rounds a minute, and we could hear each shell rip the air and land twenty seconds or so later. Flashes lit the distant horizon and a building caught fire, white smoke billowing above the flame. 'Poor old Argies, they're getting it now,' said Chris Keeble as the three guns fired at once. 'I wouldn't like to be with them.'

At his 'O' Group, 'H' Jones, using the traditional slang of the World Wars, had instructed the gunners: 'Give them a bit of a stonking before we start. We'll brass them up a bit with the guns if we have to.' From the right of the column a machine-gun opened up firing tracer bullets, red dashes in the sky. The gun was firing high and well out of range.

'A bit windy I should think, a bit of panic there,' commented Chris Keeble as we sat on the peat bank by the track. In the field there was a rustle and a movement of several bodies.

'Hey, I think someone's out there,' said David Norris. 'I wonder if these blokes realise it.' I listened for a few seconds and said we should not worry too much about a herd of cows. 'How do you know that?' asked David. I replied that I had listened to the sound of bullocks snorting and chewing grass for years at home on my parents' farm in Somerset.

We listened to the animals as men flitted by to take up positions along Camilla Creek; the machine-gun platoon and the Heavy Weapons would give cover across the narrow inlet while 'B' Company made its attack against positions on the north side of the Darwin Isthmus. Where the track turned south to Darwin, Chris Keeble told us to move to a small knoll. Over the radio we heard the leading companies prepare to go into battle, crossing the start-line at Burntside, 'A' Company hitting the positions on the southern side of the isthmus, 'B' to the north and 'H's' small Tac HQ. Crashing and banging out of the night roared the blue and white Land Rover commandeered from the prisoners the afternoon before and now used for ferrying the mortars and their ammunition. Chris Keeble told the mortar men to keep the noise down as they shouted for help to push the vehicle out of the mud. 'H' hour for the battle to begin was approaching when we heard over the radio that patrol company 'C' Company had not cleared all the obstacles for setting up the start-line and marking it with tape.

The delay lasted for nearly half an hour and the battle began at 06.30 hours GMT or half past two in the morning local time. The 4.5-inch gun in HMS *Arrow* began firing illuminating rounds, lighting the sky with a yellow flare, adding a theatrical glow to the landscape. Several times the gun fired illuminating shells and then, as it prepared to get down to the serious business of 'brassing up' enemy positions, it went 'click'. Kevin Arnold, the Naval Gunfire Support Officer, lost radio contact with the ship and she was not able to give the paratroopers supporting fire for the remaining hours of darkness. Kevin's words aboard the *Norland* now seemed prophetic. He had said that he did not like the new Mark 8 guns because 'they always fell over when you want them most'. HMS *Arrow*'s gun had done just that, with perfect timing.

Once across the start-line, the leading companies moved quickly through the enemy positions on a line with Burntside and casualties were light. At Burntside, 'A' Company raked the windows with automatic fire and threw in white phosphorous grenades in case the enemy had machine-guns and snipers there. Intelligence reports had said that the civilians had moved out weeks ago. The paratroopers stopped firing when they heard voices shouting from the house. They were calling out in broken Spanish, thinking the attackers were the Argentinians. The family of four had remained in the house; one was a grandmother of nearly eighty who hid under the bed in the one room the paratroopers had decided not to pour fire into.

Running beyond the house, the woolsheds had been set alight by the artillery and blazed like a beacon till dawn. As we passed round the lake north of the house, the still water, the sheds with the bales of wool in flames and the gables of the house itself with the neatly fenced paddocks before it looked like a stage set from *Oklahoma*. Beyond Burntside, Chris Keeble decided that our Battalion Main Headquarters Group should stay on the track, because it was feared that the surrounding grasslands had been mined. Heading up a gentle rise, we were ordered to halt. Flares rose into the air like rockets on Guy Fawkes' night, with the Argentinian mortars firing up to eight in succession to light up the men attacking them. If there was a particularly bright cascade of flares, we froze like children playing 'statues' in a party game. Sometimes there would be a whirr like a Catherine Wheel exploding as the dishes of the illuminating mortar bombs came down near the track. To the right, the jerky bursts of machine-guns broke out and rifles cracked. I felt no danger. I thought they were firing at the company in front of us. Chris Keeble shouted back down the line: 'How's Foxy? Find out if he's OK.' I could not understand why he had asked after us so solicitously, and it was only three months later that he told me that our column was under intense sniper and machine-gun fire. We were quickly distracted by the showers of flame and sparks being thrown up in the peat to our left, ten yards from the track. They were bursts of phosphorous shells from the Argentinian artillery. 'By God, that's close. One of those effing rounds has gone straight into our effing lines,' muttered the RSM, Malcolm Simpson, who was standing close to David Norris.

With the news of the first casualties, medical orderlies from the Regimental Aid Post were called forward. 'D' Company had sustained casualties, with three dead, the radio reported. 'B' Company had moved so fast against the enemy positions on the northern line of attack that some enemy snipers and machine-guns had been bypassed and they had been shooting at us before 'D' Company silenced them. Moving forward with the Regimental Aid Post, the padre David Cooper was urging the men of 'D' and 'A' Companies to keep going. His skill as a marksman told him that the enemy snipers were firing high, so there was no need to go to ground. The enemy sniper rifles were the old German Mausers, of First World War vintage, but they could be accurate at hitting a man to up to two thousand yards. The British sniper rifle, the L42, is based on the old Lee Enfield and is not so accurate, according to David Cooper. 'From the moment we landed,' he told me, 'I knew we had the wrong rifles for that terrain. Even their basic infantry rifle, the Belgian FN, could outrange the rifle carried by most of our men, the SLRs.'

In a quiet moment I asked one of the radio operators how the CO was doing. 'Oh, pretty fine,' was the answer. 'H' had already had two radios break down on him, and the language was getting pretty blue, I was told, but the attack seemed to be going through on schedule.

As the bombardment by artillery with phosphorous lessened, the column started forward once more. It was nearly dawn. At a little stream cutting into the hillocks of turf from the south, marking a promontory called Coronation Point, the stonking from the enemy mortars and guns began afresh. Chris Keeble called us back, told us to get down as low as we could and wait.

It was at this time that the forward companies were beginning to meet unexpectedly tough resistance in the vicinity of Darwin Hill. Hector Gullan, the liaison officer with 3 Commando Brigade Headquarters back at San Carlos, grabbed a shovel and dug furiously. He said I had better do the same, and David Norris began bartering for a shovel, eventually getting one from one of Chris Keeble's men who had dug trenches for the radio operators by a turf bank close by the track itself. The paratroopers began brewing tea in the trenches. Beneath us the little stream ran out to sea in a bay dotted with small islands overhung by low clouds. This could have been anywhere on the West Coast of Scotland or the Hebrides. Watching a flock of geese out to sea, we were jolted by a whizz and a clang of metal like a heavy welding job in a blacksmith's yard.

'What's that?' I asked, staring at the black scar in the turf.

'A mortar, I should think,' said a paratrooper.

The crashes and clangs quickened pace, making patterns in the earth between the trenches. The mortars were well ranged: it was the first time I had experienced a mortar barrage at first hand. I turned to Hector Gullan and said, 'What do we do now?'

'I don't know,' he replied. 'I've never been in anything like this before either.'

In the lulls between the barrages, David Norris attempted to trade the remaining tea bags and sachets of coffee we had brought in our smocks for cigarettes. They were hard to come by: the men would share jokes, advice, a brew and a bit of nutty, but a smoke was as rare as gold dust on that field. Each time we got up to move, the mortars seemed to follow us round, like the eyes of Frans Hals's 'Laughing Cavalier' in a classroom print. We thought the enemy were watching us from observation posts in the mountains across the water; it is just as likely they were firing at Defensive Fire Zones worked out by grid reference on the map, because the rivulets by Coronation Point was one of the few landmarks between Burntside and Darwin Hill.

In the radio operators' trench, the Operations Officer, Roger

Miller, stood gasping on a cigarette and shaking with cold, his face green from the damp and chilly wind. He was swathed in a green Arctic raincoat several sizes too big for him, constantly listening to the reports coming from the other companies. Near him the RSM, Malcolm Simpson, swayed to and fro trying to keep warm. 'By God those phos rounds were close,' he said. 'How're you two getting on?' He said he was worried about getting casualties back for treatment and needed bodybags for the dead. He said that on the voyage out, the brigade did not want to think about bodybags because it would affect morale if it was known they were being carried by the fighting units on the ground, but he said he needed them now for the Argentinian dead as well as the British. He was concerned, too, about the prisoners, as he had heard that he might have to provide escorts for twenty or thirty Argentinians. 'I don't have the men to supervise them in these numbers,' he said.

'Sunray is down,' the radio reported starkly from the 'A' Company position. Sunray is the codename for the commanding officer. His party reported that he had been hit and that Chris Keeble would have to go forward to command the battle. No one knew the extent of 'H''s injuries. Asking what this meant, I was told that 'H' had been injured in the groin but was alive. He would have to be evacuated by helicopter, so Chris Keeble was taking charge. I was requested not to talk about the CO being down to the men, and the news was kept from most of the battalion for some hours to come. Chris Keeble listened to the situation reports from the leading companies and had a hurried conference with Hector Gullen before making his move. He had to decide whether to go forward to the position where 'H' had fallen or to take up another vantage point to direct the battle. The radio reported that the northern line of attack with 'B' Company was in difficulty from enemy positions at a ruined building called Boca House, and the men were under heavy machine-gun, mortar and artillery fire from anti-aircraft guns fired along the ground. The Battery Commander, Tony Rice, reported he could not direct the battle as 'H' had commanded because of the intense fighting around him. Chris Keeble ordered John Crosland of 'B' Company to take over the battalion until he could get forward with Hector Gullen. Chris had no radio of his own because he had sent two forward earlier to replace broken sets with 'H''s party. He took Corporal Kelly as his operator, much to the corporal's surprise, as he usually served as a desk 'gopher', a clerk at the regimental depot. They had to rely on the two radios carried by Hector Gullan for the rear link with Brigade in San Carlos.

Chris Keeble was now acting commanding officer. It was evident by now that 'H''s timetable had gone awry; enemy resistance was much tougher than anticipated and there were far more ground troops in Goose Green than anyone with the battalion had suspected. The mortars were running low in ammunition and there had been no support from the Harriers. At the first request, we had been told that the planes could not take off because of 'fog at sea', and the aircraft eventually arrived over the target thirteen hours after the first troops had crossed the start-line to open the battle. Chris Keeble says he prayed as he left our Headquarters Party that he would not be found wanting. The RSM took him aside to wish him the best of luck and tell him to take his time, and keep calm.

Shortly after Chris left, Malcolm Simpson said the first prisoners would be bringing in their dead. They looked pathetic in the drizzling rain, their dark-green fatigues tatty and caked with mud. They were made to lie down along a shallow gully in the ground. Many of them were shivering and the younger ones whimpering with cold and fright. They had not even the presence of mind to ask to relieve themselves. The Argentinian dead were laid out in a row close to the track, the faces and exposed parts of leg and arm white and green in death. David Cooper came back from the Regimental Aid Post and in his mild, puzzled way asked if we should not do something for the prisoners who wanted to go out to collect their dead. RSM Simpson said the dead should be buried because he had no bodybags, and we arranged to say a few prayers over them. The growing numbers of prisoners and casualties continued to worry the RSM and David Norris and I said we would do anything that was needed to assist the injured and the dying. We were just going to help with some prisoners when the warning 'Pucara, Get Down!' was yelled from the track. I crouched in the gully with the prisoners. In front of me the paratrooper cocked his rifle. With a drone, the two light planes hopped over the ridge ahead and banked sharply towards us. I curled in an even tighter ball, like a hedgehog, to give the planes as little of me to shoot at as possible if they started a strafing run. Every fighting man round me let fly with rifle, machine-gun and submachine-gun, with tracer curving into the sky but wide of the mark.

'Fire in front of the planes not at them,' shouted the RSM and one of the officers yelled:

'Make them fly through your fire.'

Seeing the tracer, the Pucara swung away and dived below the ridge behind us. One fired on a Scout helicopter which was coming forward. It crashed, killing the pilot, Lieutenant Richard Nunn, Royal Marines, and badly injuring his air-crewman. Turning north, the planes started a bombing run on the guns at Camilla Creek. Two units with Blowpipe shoulder-launched missiles operators were positioned there with the artillery. One Blowpipe gunner fired his weapon, hitting one of the planes head on. He was so delighted, he jumped up on his bunker, yelling, 'I hit it. I hit it.'

'Get down, you bloody fool,' screamed his mate, 'there's another one behind it.'

The gunner threw himself onto the ground as another missile destroyed the second Pucara.

Richard Nunn had ferried me round San Carlos and Sussex Mountains several times. After he died, no helicopters would come forward to bring ammunition and take back casualties for some hours. Richard Nunn came from the Royal Marines Air Squadron, the Teeny Weeny Airways, who were vital in the battles for carrying ammunition up to the rifle companies and their wounded back. Often they flew in miserable weather, mist, drizzle and snow, at dusk and in the dark. Both the Teeny Weenies and the Air Squadron were regarded very highly by the commanders in the battles. Lt.-Col. Andrew

1a. The SS *Canberra* at Ascension.

1b. A Rapier anti-aircraft missile in the foreground, with the burning HMS *Antelope* in the background in San Carlos Water.

2a. (*above*) HMS
Fearless at
Ascension with an
RFA tug alongside.

2b. (*left*) HMS
Fearless in San
Carlos Water with
geese in the
foreground.

3a. A Lieutenant-Commander of the Argentinian Marines having been captured by 40 Commando at San Carlos. This was the first evidence of Argentinian ground forces actively reconnoitring British positions at San Carlos.

3b. Robert Fox listening to himself broadcasting on the BBC World Service on Sussex Mountains surrounded by members of 2 Para.

4a. 'H' Jones giving orders for the move to Camilla Creek.

4b. Camilla Creek House, where 2 Para laid up before taking Goose Green.

5a. Clearing Argentinian dead and prisoners from Boca House during the battle of Goose Green.

5b. Argentinian prisoners marching away from the surrender ceremony at Goose Green.

6a. Goose Green airfield, with Goose Green Settlement in the background, showing a napalm bomb, an Argentinian Pucara damaged by British Harriers and a Sea King helicopter.

6b. A member of 2 Para discusses with two settlers the 105 mm Argentinian pack howitzer on Goose Green airfield. The woolsheds containing Argentinian prisoners are marked with the letters POW to ensure that they were not bombed by the Argentinian Air Force.

7a. A helicopter and life-raft help in the rescue of personnel from the burning *Sir Galahad* at Fitzroy Cove on 8 June.

7b. David Cooper, the padre, on the left, and other members of 2 Para help an injured Welsh Guardsman into a helicopter at Fitzroy.

8. Dedication of the memorial to 'H' Jones and those who fell with 2 Para at Goose Green.

9. A Sea King helicopter lifting a 105 mm light gun of 29 Commando from Teal to Mount Kent.

10a. Lt.-Col. 'H' Jones.   10b. Maj.-Gen. Jeremy Moore.

10c. Conferring over a map are Brigadier Julian Thompson (left), Major-General Jeremy Moore (centre) and Colonel Pennicot, CRA adviser on General Moore's staff (standing), on the slopes of Mount Kent just before Thompson gave his orders for the brigade attack.

11a. A typical Falklands landscape, with Mount Harriet in the background, taken from a helicopter.

11b. Aerial view of Port Stanley just after the surrender.

12a. 45 Commando picking their way through a minefield on their way into Port Stanley the day after the battle for Two Sisters.

12b. Moody Brook Barracks after the capture of Port Stanley. The Barracks were rocketed when the Argentinians invaded on 2 April.

13a. Argentinian prisoners outside the Falkland Islands Co. building at Port Stanley waiting to go to the airfield.

13b. Port Stanley from the airfield after the surrender.

14. A land-based Exocet missile in Port Stanley. On the right is the generator, on the left the launching

15. Argentinian prisoners leaving Port Stanley on their way to the airfield. On the left is a line of twelve Argentinian Panhard armoured cars.

16a. Brigadier Julian Thompson walks into Port Stanley with his bodyguard, followed by Robert Fox (centre) and Patrick Bishop.

16b. Major Mike Norman's Naval Party 8901, which fought as 'J' Company 42 Commando, raises the British flag again at Government House.

Whitehead of 45 Commando said that it was their training as soldiers as well as pilots that proved so important because it helped them to understand terrain better than RAF trained pilots, and this was critical in poor flying conditions.

With no helicopters coming forward, there was now a serious shortage of ammunition for the leading companies. Near the position where 'H' Jones had fallen, 'A' Company under Major Dair Farrar-Hockley was attempting to clear the enemy from Port Darwin. On the other side of the narrow strip of land leading to Goose Green and to Lafonia, 'B' Company under Major John Crosland was held down by heavy machine-gun fire from trenches round Boca House and snipers and machine-gunners in the ruined building itself. From the ridge above Darwin, Darwin Hill, the row of gorse bushes cuts across the isthmus. Below the Gorse Line the ground slopes gently down towards Goose Green, rough pasture grazed tight, so open that the paratroops nicknamed it the 'billiard table'. Harassing fire from the Argentinian pack howitzers and the anti-aircraft guns aimed along the ground was accurately directed all afternoon across the billiard table from Goose Green, so much so that the command positions of the companies trying to advance to capture the airfields and the cluster of houses could hardly move for lengthy periods.

The advance on the southern side of the isthmus, led by Dair Farrar-Hockley's men of 'A' Company, was held up when it encountered a group of heavily defended Argentinian positions in the shape of a horseshoe above Darwin. There was a gentle rise in the ground before the Gorse Line with the tiny cemetery for the communities of Darwin and Goose Green on the right. The graves had a rickety fence round them with a solitary bush like a lookout. 'A' Company had moved round to the left in an attempt to outflank positions on the high ground, and at one point some men had moved along the beach, though it was mined. The attempt to outflank led straight into the jaws of the enemy position, which was facing south. As the paras' attack showed signs of slowing, 'H' Jones's party moved towards 'A' Company to discover what was happening.

It was two hours after dawn, about 13.30 hours GMT. The

man closest to 'H' Jones at the time was the sergeant he had
chosen aboard the *Norland* to lead his personal protection
party, Sergeant Barry Norman, a quiet and well-spoken man
who had served ten years with the paratroopers. He gave me
his own account of how 'H' Jones died.

As first light approached, we were up with 'A' Company
and Colonel 'H' Jones was talking to Major Farrar-Hockley,
and they reorganised Company deployment. As we
progressed towards the gorse, 'A' Company came under
heavy fire from the hills off to our right, and the company
deployed to take out these enemy positions. We were pinned
down quite heavily and we took cover on the water's edge,
which provided a steep bank. After twenty minutes or so,
the fire was still quite heavy and the colonel decided Tac 1,
his party, would move up to join 'A' Company and he
would find out what the score was because he wasn't
satisfied the battle was progressing as fast as he wished. So
we crawled back to the water's edge and in the shelter of the
bank moved round behind the gorse. Once we got behind
the gorse there was excellent cover from view but there was
no cover from fire. We had to get white phos. [white phosphorous grenades] to provide smoke. The CO threw one
himself to cover the first part of Tac 1 across this open piece
of ground, and Sergeant-Major Price of 'A' Company threw
the other to cover the remainder of the party. We then
joined the Headquarters of 'A' Company situated on the
rear slope of the first enemy hill. Once we reached there, the
CO, the Mortar Officer, the Gun Officer and the officer
commanding 'A' Company, Major Farrar-Hockley, got
together and discussed the situation. The guns could not be
used because some friendly forces were too close to the
enemy positions. We had to use the battalion mortars.

We used the battalion mortars, but then the colonel
decided we would attack across the top of the open hill and
asked for mortar smoke, which we got. Once we got on the
top, the smoke ran out: we'd run out of the mortar ammunition and we were caught there, about thirty of us, along the
top of the hill, pinned down by quite heavy fire. In fact

Captain Dent, the second in command of 'A' Company, was killed in that part of the action. The CO then shouted out, 'Follow me,' and turned to his right and ran down into the dead ground, which was on the right side of the hill, and headed towards the enemy position. I immediately followed and was followed by Corporal Beresford, others of Tac 1 and 'A' Company.

I was less than twenty metres behind him, but he got a bit away from me because he was a pretty fit bloke. He got round into a re-entrant [a gully of dead ground] and as I went round to follow him, someone to my rear, who I later found out was the BC [Battery Commander, Major Tony Rice] shouted: 'Watch out, there's an enemy position on the left.' I immediately looked left and saw an enemy trench and as I noticed it, it opened fire on me. I hit the ground and I looked up and the colonel was in between two enemy positions in complete dead ground.

I returned fire to the enemy trench, and the colonel took his magazine off his submachine-gun, checked it, reloaded it, cocked his weapon and proceeded up the hill towards the enemy position that we'd just noticed. As he got within three feet of the position, I shouted out: 'Watch your fucking back.' But he took no notice and subsequently was shot in the back from a trench to the rear. I remained there for some considerable time, possibly for ten minutes – it felt for ever – pinned down by two enemy positions. Eventually two 66s [66 mm rockets, fired from the shoulder against armour] were used on the enemy trenches and they surrendered. I believe it was Corporal Abols who fired the successful rocket of the two: all I heard was a bang at one end and an even bigger bang at the other, and I was quite relieved that they surrendered at that particular time.

As the enemy surrendered, I went up to the colonel because I was still within twenty metres of him. I started to administer First Aid with the help of two men from 'A' Company. We removed his belt order and found an exit wound in his groin and I applied a shell dressing to that and then put a shell dressing on the entry wound. He lost consciousness. I applied a drip, and he took a full drip almost instantaneously. I told Major Farrar-Hockley that the colonel would die if we didn't get qualified medical help. Major Farrar-Hockley told us to carry him up to the high ground and he would try to get a helicopter in. I put another drip into him and we made an improvised stretcher out of a piece of the Argentinian trench, a bit of wood and some corrugated tin. It wasn't very satisfactory and half-way up the hill the whole thing fell to bits, whereupon other members of 'A' Company, with their rifles, some quilted material and other pieces of kit, made another stretcher and we carried the CO to where we thought the landing-site would be. He was still unconscious and at this stage I wrapped him up into his quilted jacket to try and get some of the warmth back into him.

We waited there for some time, about half an hour, and I noticed he was dying; and subsequently he died. I covered his body after ensuring that life had gone and went and informed Major Farrar-Hockley that the CO had died for him to tell the rest of the battalion. He asked me and another man to bring in the body of the CO to where the other bodies were laid out, those of Captain Wood and Captain Dent and the others killed in that action.

The adjutant, Captain David Wood, had been killed as the colonel's party had come up to join 'A' Company. He was a Scot with a dry, black sense of humour, one of the most popular figures in the officer's mess. The news that 'H' had been killed reached the rest of the battalion slowly. Major Chris Keeble said he only knew that the CO had died from his wounds some time after he had met Major Crosland of 'B' Company, the Battery Commander, Tony Rice, and, with Hector Gullen, had rearranged the battle plan to clear the obstacle at Boca House on the right flank of the paratroopers' advance.

'H' died in the style with which he had commanded his battalion, impetuous, generous and imaginative, always leading from the front. His character and manner of leadership set the stamp on the battalion for the rest of the campaign;

he was the most forceful figure I met in all the land forces in the Falklands. Meeting today some officers and the men closest to him, like Sergeant Norman and Corporal Beresford, they all now seem to have something of 'H' in them. In the days before he was killed, both David Norris and I had got to know him well; he enjoyed chatting to two civilians stuck on Sussex Mountains, two men who were not strictly under his command. He would rage at the slowness of the campaign one moment, and then be laughing the next. He was furious at Brigadier Thompson when the first plan for the raid on Goose Green was cancelled on the morning of Tuesday 25 May, and the next day he was full of understanding for the Brigadier's position and speaking warmly of his skill as a commander. He used David and myself as his sounding boards, his civilian private ears, and was continuously asking us what we thought was going on in London. It was always a question of 'When will Maggie get a move on?' and 'We've got to hit them hard. If we're told to raid Goose Green and Darwin, there's no point in going in and coming out. If we drive them back, we're going to hold the place and move on from there to Stanley.'

It has been argued that a battalion commander should not have been so far forward as 'H' was in the battle by Darwin Hill. It has also been said that a commander should not have led the kind of attack that 'H' did when he shouted to Sergeant Barry Norman, 'Follow me.' Who can say what was going through his head as he charged across that twenty metre-strip of ground to the enemy machine-gun position? All of us on the battlefield knew that he would not ask anyone to carry out an action that he would not do himself. Chris Keeble says that he had decided to go forward because he needed to see the battle for himself; his intelligence reports before the attack started were now being proved to be badly wrong about enemy positions and the strength of the Argentinian defences. When he discovered that 'A' Company was being held up, that artillery could not be used and there was no mortar smoke left to hide an attack, Chris Keeble thinks he took the calculation, 'Do I use ten men now to do what it might take more than a hundred to do if we wait?' Sergeant Norman describes 'H''s reasoning for his charge at the enemy machine-guns in more simple terms: 'He was a very determined man and he said throughout all the actions and all the briefings that he felt that if we hit the Argentinian trenches hard, they would fold. He wasn't satisfied that the action was going as fast as he wanted it; he was very impatient and wanted to progress through as fast as possible. It was natural for him to say "Follow me", and in every exercise we've done with him he's led from the front.'

'He was a very fair man to work for,' says Sergeant Norman, 'and he always expected the best from everybody under his command, and got it. If people fell foul of him, they got the full force of his wrath, and they probably deserved it. The blokes knew what to expect from him and wouldn't have had it any other way. The battalion knew he was a good tactician and a good soldier and his plan for the battle worked. The plan worked even after his death, so it must have been sound. Before we set off, all the blokes knew the plan, and they knew we were going to succeed: we were a little taken aback by the number of enemy there initially, but in true airborne spirit we progressed through it.'

Major Dair Farrar-Hockley, who knew 'H' as well as any of his officers, describes his achievement at Goose Green in a sentence: 'He provided us with a highly flexible battle plan which we could use afterwards for continuing the attack, and he died in a most extraordinary act of courage.'

As Chris Keeble made his way across the gently rising ground towards the Gorse Line for his conference with the Company Commanders and the Battery Commander, the Regimental Sergeant Major gathered the prisoners together by the stream where we had been mortared for much of the morning. 'I am very proud of the lads,' said the RSM. 'They're doing really well, particularly the young ones. I'll never be able to shout at them again when we get back to Aldershot.' The officers manning the radio, Roger Miller and David Constance, told us to pack up our kit and prepare to move down the track to Darwin. The mortar bombardment had slackened and the sky had cleared. It was a leisurely walk along the path, with puffs of black smoke rising from the horizon before us as the mortars and artillery continued to stonk the Gorse Line. The sea bit into the land before us with a deep, curving bay and steep peat banks above the beach. At the end of the coastline, a mile or so off, we could see the white houses, the first glimpse of Port Darwin. Taking a left-hand fork, the track dipped towards the beach and continued to the settlement. We jumped over the peat banks and crunched along the black gravel of the beach, as the men of 'A' Company had done hours before, in the dark.

I remember looking at the flat calm of the sea and the clouds lifting over the mountains, and thinking that the worst seemed to be over. We had not seen much mortar fire for some time, and the sounds of battle were coming from well beyond the Gorse Line from the direction of Goose Green itself. We climbed off the beach towards the nearest clump of gorse at the bottom of the hill outside Darwin. The bushes were blazing, smoke rising in a thick plume and the fire giving off a pungent smell. Men scurried round the bushes carrying drips and field First Aid kits. Three helicopters stood back from the gorse ready to carry the seriously wounded out to San Carlos. Some of them had been unloading the brown metal cases of rifle and machine-gun ammunition. Puffs of smoke, blue and grey, and the clang of metal above spurts of peat announced the renewal of the mortar barrage. The helicopters were ordered back, and we kept going into the gorse to look for cover. Men lay round the clump of bushes at the bottom of the rise; some were on stretchers, others covered with waterproof sheets. Moving into the gorse, I met the Intelligence Officer, Alan Coulson, who said: 'They say the CO is dead. Do you know if it's true? I can't believe it.' He seemed stunned by the idea. I said I'd try to find out from the medical orderlies, as I'd promised to help them with drips, hugging them to my body to warm them up. At the dressing station where the helicopters had been landing, a medical orderly said it was true that the colonel had been killed, and his body was still at the top of the hill. He said we should not talk about his death too much as not many of the men knew.

Turning away from the medical teams, I met Sergeant Major

Price of 'A' Company, who had come down from Darwin Hill to fetch ammunition. He confirmed that the colonel had been killed and I taped a short interview with him. He said he admired the way the enemy machine-gunners had fought. His company had fifty-eight prisoners to handle now. As we spoke, we were interrupted by rapid bursts of machine-gun fire fifty yards ahead, and the deeper bass rumble of the heavier Argentinian automatic weapons further down the slope. 'It's all right,' said Sergeant Price. 'I think the nearer firing is ours. It had better be. Well, I suppose I'd better get this show on the road and get ammoed up.'

The mortar fires started again, the shrapnel clanging against rock as the bombs exploded. Orderlies yelled at the pilots to move the helicopters back out of range. We were told to go forward into the gorse. The mortar men and the Argentinian gunners were 'bracketing' the position with precision, aiming one moment in front of the gorse, and another to strike behind the line of bushes and peat banks.

David Norris and I crawled forward, flattening our bodies on the ground as the fire came closer, the whistles and pings now only four or five feet from us. On the crest of the hill and behind us in the valley the bushes were blazing, sending off thicker clouds of heavy smoke. In a clearing between the gorse we saw a young, ginger-haired soldier, his back to the direction the fire was coming from. He was rolling a cigarette, cleaning his gun and making a brew on his hexamine stove beside him. He told us he was an assault engineer, from 59 Independent Squadron of Commando Engineers, and his job was to clear the mines in front of the British advance.

'What the hell are you two doing here?' he asked, when he discovered that we were two civilians from the press. 'You scared?' he added.

'Not if you're not,' one of us replied.

He told us that the firing at troops as they crossed the ridge had been very hot. Still the mortar and anti-aircraft bombs and shells burst round us, behind, before, and either side of us. A paratrooper seemed to swim through the gorse towards us, shouting, 'I've just learnt more about myself in the last ten minutes than I knew in my whole life before.' Above us we could see paratroopers receiving stinging swipes from shrapnel on their legs and backs, and then they were obliterated by the billowing smoke that swept across the hillside by the rising wind. Later Major Roger Jenner, OC 'C' Company, came stumbling back to the Aid Post with shrapnel burns across his legs and back. The young assault engineer threw a piece of shrapnel at me. 'This is yours, mate. It missed your head by eighteen inches. It's time to move. This fire's getting too accurate to be funny.'

There was a lull in the enemy stonking and we slid back down the hill. The padre, David Cooper, was talking to the young medical orderlies at the Regimental Aid Post. Steve Hughes, the young doctor who had been in the army only eighteen months, was scurrying from stretcher to stretcher giving what help he could. A young paratrooper was brought in completely grey in the face. The orderlies were talking to him gently, and as they lifted the poncho waterproof from the stretcher I saw his leg had been severed neatly below the knee by shrapnel and the foot was strapped next to him. Across the foreheads of the injured streaked in black crayon or red marker pen was the letter 'M' and barely legible numbers, indicating that morphine had been administered and the time it was given.

Some of the Argentinian prisoners were in a very bad state; one young officer appeared to have most of his abdomen missing. The medical team called for more supplies; the pilots were asked to bring cartons of saline drips and morphine capsules. I asked David Cooper what help I could give. He said he wanted to go over the hill to look for the dead and seriously injured and asked if I could go with him. RSM Simpson said he needed to have some idea of the names of the dead and wounded. The prisoners were still a serious worry to him, as there were now more than a hundred left huddled below the peat hags round the beach. From behind us, Alex Ward appeared in the blue and white Land Rover used previously for bringing up mortar ammunition. The RSM handed over responsibility for the prisoners, and he drove off slowly across the moorland to the rear of our position with a snake of some hundred Argentinians following like a funeral cortege.

The RSM, Padre Cooper and I were just setting off for the ridge when a group of the British snipers came loping in from Darwin looking like long-haired apes with their helmets and jackets strewn with long strips of hessian. 'Could you just wait a minute?' asked David Cooper. 'I just want to talk to these lads, see if their sights were working all right, just to find out how they got on.' He sat down cross-legged in a circle and chatted to them calmly for twenty minutes or so. The RSM and I moved off to tend to some wounded and prisoners. If we three had set out to look for bodies, I learnt later, it was likely that we would have walked into a minefield.

As the light was turning to the orange of sunset, a radio operator shouted that a Harrier ground attack would arrive in ten minutes, coming in from the sea. It seemed half an hour later when we heard the crash and pop of a succession of explosions as the cluster bombs went off and the anti-aircraft guns replied; there was a pause and briefer chain of explosions. I looked at my watch; it showed thirty-five minutes past seven, 19.35 GMT. The small arms firing went on for about twenty to thirty minutes more and then gradually died down. Some men of 'D' Company came back to the Aid Post and said that a Pucara had tried to drop burning chemical over their position, but they could not be a hundred per cent sure it was napalm. It missed the company and the plane was shot down by machine-gun fire.

As dusk approached, a party was sent out to bring in the dead. I saw two soldiers carrying 'H' Jones's body on a stretcher, clearly outlined against the side of the hill. In front of them walked a soldier with the three submachine-guns of the dead officers slung over his shoulder. A quiet, un-rehearsed ceremony, the indelible image of that day. Later Chris Keeble emerged, and there was now only the odd crack of rifles and burp of machine-gun fire. 'I've just had a good look at those positions round "B" and "D" Companies,' said Chris, 'and I think they're just about ready to give in.'

David Norris and I had seen very little of the development of the battle as we never managed to get beyond the line of gorse bushes running north from Darwin. For much of the afternoon, Chris Keeble and Hector Gullan had been about two to three hundred yards further along the gorse ridge from the position where the medical orderlies took such a heavy stonking when David Norris and I and the RSM's party came up with them. Both Major Keeble's Tac Party and the RAP position had taken some of the heaviest artillery and mortar barrage of the battle, but they were still not sure whether the Argentinians could see us there from Observation Posts in the mountains or had worked out where the headquarter elements of the battalion were likely to be and fired at set map references. There is still bound to be some debate about minor details of what happened in the battle itself, but some months later Major Chris Keeble did give me a full account of what happened to him when we parted at Coronation Point after 'H' Jones had fallen and he went forward to take over directing the battle.

'H' had taken his Tac 1 HQ party across to Darwin Hill to assist 'A' Company against the enemy positions dug in on the hill. After the attack in which 'H' died, the enemy positions were cleared by Corporal Abols firing a 66 mm anti-tank rocket. By this time, on the other flank, beyond the Gorse Line, John Crosland's 'B' Company were pinned down by heavy fire from the ruined building, Boca House. Artillery and mortar were very close to his company headquarters, caught on the forward slope into Goose Green Settlement, from which Major Crosland himself was directing the assault on Boca House. This meant that he was unable to move his company across to help 'H' Jones before he was killed.

As soon as Major Keeble, Major Hector Gullan, and their party came up to the Gorse Line, they held a hurried conference with John Crosland who had been temporarily directing the battle from 'B' Company's headquarters, despite incessant fire from artillery and anti-aircraft weapons round the Goose Green airfield. Milan anti-tank missiles were brought forward and set up on the ridge, and the machine-gun platoon came up with them to direct fire into the bunkers round Boca House and at the Argentinian machine-gunners and snipers inside the building. Meanwhile, Major Phil Neame's 'D' Company were moving down the beach, along the shoreline on the opposite side of the isthmus from Darwin. The landscape which had refused cover on the open 'billiard table' grasslands leading into Goose Green now became an ally of the attacking soldiers. The peat hags were high enough entirely to conceal the men of 'D' Company crawling down the beach from the view of the Argentinians in Boca House. The fusilade of Milan missiles from the Gorse Line began to break the bunkers and trenches in front of the house. 'B' Company prepared to move down the slope from the gorse and Phil Neame's men were ordered to move into the house from the sea. 'Thank God for that,' shouted Major Neame over the radio. 'The tide has come in.'

From the slope above Boca House towards the Gorse Line, heavy, sustained machine-gun fire poured into the trenches outside the house. The men of 'D' Company got up from the beach and, in Major Keeble's words, 'just went straight through the building'. The Argentinian machine-gunners and snipers were silenced, and many prisoners were taken. The second major obstacle in the daylight battle had been removed, the first being Darwin Hill where Dair Farrar-Hockley's 'A' House, Major Keeble, Major Gullan, the 'B' Company Commander Major Crosland and the Battery Commander, Major mander Major Crosland and the Battery Commander Major Rice, met to redraw the battle plan. Chris Keeble and Hector Gullen came forward to the area of Boca House. The next objective was the grass airstrip on rising ground above Goose Green itself, which sits on its own small peninsula jutting south from the neck of land connecting East Falkland to Lafonia. The second objective was now the schoolhouse, which stood by itself between Goose Green and Darwin on the southern side of the isthmus. It had been the boarding school for children of secondary school age from the remoter settlements in 'camp', the Falkland countryside. The Argentinian garrison at Goose Green had used the building as a barracks and were defending it in strength. With the airfield and the schoolhouse cleared, the approach to the settlement would be open.

The plan was for Phil Neame's 'D' Company to move across the isthmus, taking the airfield and then attacking the schoolhouse. 'C' Company under Major Roger Jenner was to move down the slope from the Gorse Line to attack the schoolhouse, following a diagonal path across the slope to end up on the left of 'D' Company for the assault on the trenches and the school itself. John Crosland's 'B' Company was to hook round to move towards Goose Green from the south.

Major Keeble says his object was to concentrate effort and firepower on individual targets and take them one by one. He says that the flaw in 'H' Jones's initial plan was that it divided the battalion's resources, simply because 'H' thought he was attacking three to four companies at most. By the afternoon it was evident that the paratroopers were up against an Argentinian battalion, 600 or 700 men at least.

Phil Neame's 'D' Company began attacking the airstrip, in the teeth of fierce firing along the ground from the enemy 20-calibre anti-aircraft guns. The company split, with platoons moving down either side of the grass field. 'A' Company put two platoons forward from Darwin towards the school, and 'C' Company passed two companies through them to attack the building. As the operation began, fierce artillery and mortar barages came from Goose Green itself. Much of the fire was directed at the Gorse Line and began disrupting the command positions of the companies approaching the schoolhouse. Chris Keeble by this time had his headquarters on the Gorse Line about two hundred yards from the Regimental Aid Post where David Norris and I were now sheltering under the clump of gorse bushes known to the local settlers as the 'Bower'. We had chosen badly. According to Chris Keeble, the Bower and the Gorse Line received the heaviest mortar and artillery bombardment of the day. Just forward of where we were, Roger Jenner and 'C' Company HQ could hardly move because of the continuous plastering by shrapnel and mortar bombs.

Despite the heavy fire, 'D' Company kept moving towards

the airfield and as they closed with the enemy defences round
the airstrip, the Argentinians manning the 20 mm guns there
ran off. Two platoons of the company then managed to link up
with two of 'C' Company on their left flank, a very tricky
manoeuvre under such conditions, and they began attacking
the trenches in front of the schoolhouse. It was here that one of
the saddest incidents of the campaign took place. Argentinians
in a trench facing 'D' Company hoisted a white flag. As
Lieutenant Jim Barry got up to take the surrender, a British
machine-gun opened fire to his right; immediately there was
answering fire from an Argentinian position to his left, some
distance away from the trench trying to surrender. Jim Barry
was killed as he stood in the open. Those at the scene do not
think that this was deliberate treachery, with the white flag
being used as a decoy. The shots that were fired at the
lieutenant were in reply to the British machine-gun which had
fired at that moment.

The way Jim Barry died affected soldiers for the rest of the
campaign; and later it made the paratroopers of 3 Para in the
fighting on Mount Longdon far more cautious about accepting
surrenders and taking prisoners in the heat of battle. Surrenders and negotiations are very difficult to manage while
fighting is continuing, and radio communications between
different units in the battle is so limited. Jim Barry died
because of a mistake, though the circumstances were not to be
reported accurately for some time.

Once 'C' and 'D' Company linked up, there were now six
British platoons attacking the school. Milan and 66 rockets
were used to break the trenches outside the house. Machine-
gun fire and phosphorous grenades poured into the windows
and doors of the building itself, and quite suddenly it erupted.
At least fifty Argentinians were killed in the explosion, 'a
ghastly sight', according to Chris Keeble. There had been
about three enemy platoons there, with no escape route. All
that was left of the school was the two end walls blackened
from flames and smoke. The battle had now turned and the
Argentinians used desperate measures to hold the settlement,
with anti-aircraft fire from the little peninsula of Goose Green

and attacks from the air by the slow-moving Pucara. Some men of 'D' Company said there was one attack by Skyhawk jets, though this has not been confirmed. As one Pucara rose in the sky, a Blowpipe missile snaked out across the open ground from the Gorse Line and tore its wing off. It crashed in flames, and the pilot was killed. Later another Pucara swept over 'D' Company dropping two pods of flaming chemical, now known to have been napalm. Heavy machine-gun fire brought the plane down and the pilot was captured. He tore his badges of rank and identification from his flying suit. When he was put with the other prisoners, no one had the energy to ask him what exactly the substance was that had been dropped in front of 'D' Company, and this was to be a mystery for several days to the men it missed by a few yards.

In the early evening the three RAF GR3 Harriers were guided in from the sea towards Goose Green itself. They sprayed the area with cluster bombs, a particularly nasty weapon. The bomb splits into a number of smaller, anti-personnel bombs which spray metal across an area the size of a football field. The raid silenced the anti-aircraft gun, a 35 mm Oerlikon gun with low-level radar guiding it, which stood at the seaward end of the settlement. As the daylight began to fade, the firing died down, and men of 'B' Company close to the settlement thought they saw white flags appearing.

Chris Keeble now returned to the 'Bower' area where the Regimental Aid Post was with the Battalion Main Head-quarters, and began preparing the next phase of the battle. He knew his men were exhausted, now facing a third night without sleep. Artillery and aircraft would have to do much of the work if the attack was resumed in the morning. On the radio to Brigade Headquarters at San Carlos, three more field guns were requested and two thousand rounds of artillery ammunition. Hector Gullen was sent back to the beachhead by helicopter to explain in person to Brigadier Thompson what had taken place in the battle so far. If need be, Major Keeble was prepared to 'flatten the houses of Goose Green with artillery' rather than risk bloody, close-quarters fighting by the paratroopers in the settlement. As the preparations for the artillery barrage were being made, with the extra guns being flown to Camilla Creek at first light, a message came from Brooke Hardcastle, the manager at Darwin, that there were 114 civilians in the houses at Goose Green. Intelligence reports before the battle suggested that there were no civilians left in the settlement. The news that all the inhabitants were potential hostages made a negotiated surrender a priority.

The orders from the brigadier were to 'go firm' for the paratroopers to hold their positions. Mike Norman's 'J' Company from 42 Commando were flown down to the isthmus and they moved in to reinforce John Crosland and 'B' Company on the south side of Goose Green. Overnight the Argentinians too brought in a company of reinforcements. A Chinook twin-rotor helicopter and at least six Hughs helicopters brought the men in from Mount Kent and deposited them further down the isthmus towards Lafonia.

In the twilight, tracked BV waggons arrived from Camilla Creek with food, but no waterproofs or sleeping-bags. The night was becoming frosty. Alex Ward, David Norris and I cooked a special 'all in one' meal in which the rock-hard peas of the Arctic Ration Pack featured strongly. I wondered about hitching a ride on one of the last helicopters out that evening to file a report, but decided against this as I had no idea what the outcome of the battle for Goose Green would be. Helicopters arrived infrequently. The battalion was still short of ammunition and needed two desperately injured men removed, as the doctors did not think they would live through a night in the open. The radio signallers called out again and again with the battalion's coded call sign for more helicopters. There appeared to be little response from San Carlos. In Brigade Headquarters back at Blue Beach, Captain John Greenhalgh of Army Air Corps, who was off duty, heard the increasingly urgent request for help. He walked over to the operations tent and discovered it was a call from 2 Para, a unit he had worked with often. On his own decision he took off for Darwin with his crewman Sergeant Kalinsky, and by the time he arrived it was dark. Without any night-vision aids, he drove his machine over the ridge of the Gorse Line to pick up the two casualties and flew them back to Ajax. As he approached the anchorage over Sussex Mountains, he lost his way in the dark and tried to put down. He had only a few minutes' fuel left, so he called for some of the ships to show a light to guide him in. Lights shone into the sky from nearly every vessel in San Carlos Water as he crossed the shoreline.

Chris Keeble was now trying to start negotiations. He chose two senior NCOs from the Argentinian prisoners to go under a white flag to their garrison commander with a message. On the radio he asked the brigadier if there was any way of getting a radio call to the Argentinians to ask them to receive the two men. The brigadier said, 'Leave it to me,' later signalling that the 'Goss-Miller' axis had been set up and the Argentinians would receive the delegation in the morning. Later we learned that the 'Goss-Miller' axis was a short-wave radio communication between Alan Miller, the manager at Port San Carlos, and the Goose Green farm manager, Eric Goss. In the darkness that evening I recall passing by a small huddle of officers beside the gorse bushes, still blazing and throwing shadows across the men's faces. In the middle of the circle were two Argentinians. I heard Chris Keeble say slowly, 'I am Catholic. You are all Catholics. We are all Christians. I do not believe in killing unnecessarily. I have many, many men here and we will fight again at daybreak.'

There was a pause as Captain Rod Bell translated.

Chris Keeble resumed, 'I have many paratroopers here. Do you know what a paratrooper is?'

There was a hitch in the translation and the explanation began again: 'You know red berets. There are many of these men here. They are finest fighting soldiers in the world.' After this discourse Chris Keeble came over to me and said he thought that a surrender might work. At the least he had to get the Argentinians to acknowledge the rules of siege and let the civilians go, he argued.

The night grew increasingly cold. Stars appeared between the clouds. The prisoners huddled next to the flaming gorse further into the valley. Some were crying; the sergeants were yelling orders. Officers cried out political exhortations. One group were on their knees telling their rosaries and praying. The officer with his stomach missing groaned as death approached.

It was impossible to get warm enough to sleep. I rolled into a gorse bush with a waterproof cover wrapped round me. I got up, strolled down to where the bushes were alight and stamped through the glowing ash to warm my feet. I chatted to a few of the paras about the cold, the battle and whether any more waterproofs and packs would come up from the gun-line at Camilla Creek in the night. The prisoners seemed in a more miserable condition than we were in their thin American combat jackets. Back up on the hill I looked in vain for somewhere to sleep out of the wind. Falling over the padre, David Cooper, I woke up three paratroopers sleeping side by side. 'Here, mate, you get in here. It's the only way you've got a chance of getting warm.' I slipped between the three men and we jammed ourselves tightly together, wrapped in our thin waterproofs like silkworms in green cocoons. I have never been so grateful to my fellow men for physical comfort in my life.

III. SURRENDER AT GOOSE GREEN

The hills were blanketed with mist when we woke, obscuring the view of Port Darwin and the distant hills towards Burntside. Chris Keeble said: 'Wake up. I think they are going to surrender. The plan is working, and I want you to come with me as a witness.' I asked if he was sure that we were not going to have another day's fighting. Chris said the two Argentinian prisoners had gone down to the settlement of Goose Green at first light and the commanders of the garrison had agreed to meet a delegation from the battalion on the airfield to talk about the safety of the civilians in Goose Green, and terms for their forces to surrender with honour.

Chris Keeble was still not sure of the enemy strength, or that the negotiations would be serious. It could be a trap to pick off the battalion command. He was determined to persuade the Argentinians to give up without resuming fighting into the settlement itself. He needed time to bring up the extra half battery of three guns, bed them in on the gun-line at Camilla Creek and supply them with sufficient ammunition. If the Argentinians seemed reluctant to surrender, Chris Keeble and the Battery Commander, Tony Rice, had arranged a 'fire power demonstration'. The Argentinian officers would be asked to observe a piece of ground away from the house and then fire would be called on that map reference, and the spot would be bombed and strafed from the air by Harrier GR3s, now on priority call from the carriers at sea, and all six guns in the battery at Camilla Creek.

David Norris and I were told to get some breakfast and then prepare to move over the Gorse Line ridge to the airstrip with Major Keeble, Major Rice, Major Hector Gullan, who had returned from briefing Brigadier Thompson at San Carlos, Captain Rod Bell as interpreter and Corporal Shaw as the radio operator. We were given a mess tin full of porridge by Kevin Arnold's Naval gunfire support team, and told to dump all extra equipment, webbing belts and helmets. We were to look as least warlike as possible. Attached to my webbing belt was a gas-mask holder into which I stuffed my portable stereo cassette recorder, spare tapes and batteries. I put the belt and the recorder down with the other kit by the gorse bushes in the Bower and asked the Naval gunfire signallers to look after them. I never saw the recorder again on the Falklands, and with it I lost the last interview taped with 'H' Jones, the interviews with 'A' and 'B' Company on Sussex Mountains and the tape-recording of the wade ashore on 21 May. It was returned with the kit of the dead and injured three months later; only the cassette with the interview with 'H' was missing.

As I shovelled porridge into my mouth, more marine reinforcements arrived to move over the ridge to 'D' Company's position. The RSM asked what David and I were about to do as he had heard that we were to go down to the settlement with the acting CO's party. 'I'd rather you than me,' he said, 'you never know what trick they might pull. But good luck and keep your head down if it starts up again.' David and I went to join the four officers at the top of the ridge at a gap in the gorse. We jumped over a bank onto a narrow path. The slope leading into the settlement and to Lafonia beyond, the 'billiard table', lay spread before us.

Moving away from the Gorse Line, I thought that if they wanted to pick us off now we would be easy targets for snipers or machine-gunners. But I thought that the chances they would do so were slight. We talked of how the Argentinians would respond to the proposal to surrender with honour or face a bloodbath amongst the houses. Would they acknowledge rules of siege and let the civilians go rather than hold them hostage? How persuasive would the 'fire power' demonstration be? Earlier, I had said to Chris Keeble that I knew very little about the make-up of the Argentinian armed forces, though I suspected that two things might be important. First, many of the soldiers were conscripts and probably reluctant to fight to the death for the Malvinas, and secondly, I knew that the Argentinians have a very heavy Italian influence in their make-up, about 40 per cent of all Argentinians in the north of the country being of Italian origin. I had spent a great deal of time working among Italians, and I thought that those Argentinian officers of Italian extraction would be looking for a face-saving formula, a proper ceremony of surrender to prove to outsiders that they had fought with valour and then yielded honourably to a superior foe.

Down the track we could see the two chimneys and outer walls of the schoolhouse which was still smouldering. Heavy rain had turned to hail, which came lashing across the bright green grasslands of Lafonia. To our right, we could see the wrecked Pucara aircraft on the airstrip, one with its tail cocked into the air as if it had taken a nose-dive before taking off. Along the cart-track we found oddments of fighting equipment left by the retreating Argentinians. Chris Keeble threw two bayonets in their scabbards at me and said: 'Stick these in your trouser pockets. They may come in useful one day.' We decided to take a short cut to the airstrip across the grass, and then someone shouted, 'Mines!' In the distance there was a bang and a puff of black smoke above it. Nearly half the herd of cows at Goose Green had been killed already on the minefields; the bodies of the animals looking huge and bloated where they had been left for a week or more. None of the mine-fields was marked, so we decided to take the long way round to the airstrip. As we approached, we could not see anybody at the meeting point. Then at a corrugated iron hut by the main-tenance sheds we saw a white flag. A group of men came out to meet us, shake hands and then move inside the hut to begin the talking.

The garrison commander was introduced to us by a tall Naval officer with a heavy black moustache through which he grinned continuously with a gap-toothed, Bugs Bunny expression. The commander was a small man with a soft, rounded face, with a rodent-like demeanour and bushy eyebrows. His name, he said, was Air Vice Commodore Wilson Dosier Pedrozo. The Army commander was a short, deeply tanned, hard-faced man, Lieutenant-Colonel Italo Pioggi. The British officers were introduced by Rod Bell in turn and I explained that David and I were members of the press. The Air Force man did not seem too pleased at this and asked me to put away my small cassette recorder. We all shook hands and then the talking began.

Chris Keeble explained his concern for the civilians. He said that as a man of deep Catholic principles he must make sure of the settlers' safety. Furthermore, he did not wish any lives to be wasted needlessly; the Argentinians had fought well, but were now in a hopeless plight and should consider surrender-ing with honour. But first of all, he said, he must have a guarantee for the safety of the civilians whether the fighting continued or not. The Air Vice Commodore said he would not give separate guarantees, but saw the 'whole thing as a global problem'. He wanted to discuss the civilians and the surrender together. He added that there would be no question of holding the settlers hostage and their safety was assured. As he pronounced this convoluted formula, I realised for the first time that the fighting at Goose Green was probably over. It was quite clear from the first that the Air Force commander was looking for an escape route of surrender with honour; his whole feline approach to the discussions was that of a military

politician. I realised that we had to sell him the idea that he
had given up with great dignity, which would be respected by
his fellow officers in Argentina, and that he had fought
against terrible odds.

Colonel Pioggi, the Army commander, proved a much
harder man to negotiate with. He kept insisting on having time
to decide. If there was to be a surrender ceremony, he wished
to inform his superiors in Port Stanley of what was happening
and the exact terms of the negotiations. He said he needed two
hours to call up General Menendez's staff on the radio net.
Hector Gullan, a practised negotiator, immediately countered
the colonel's plan by saying he could not be allowed such a
long time for consultation and was not sure that either
commander in Goose Green should be allowed to radio
Stanley at all. Hector was not going to allow the Argentinians
to dictate the pace of the talks and the timetable for the
surrender. After some argument it was decided that the two
Argentinians would be allowed to go away before bringing up
their men to the airfield to throw down their weapons. But if
there was to be a radio consultation with General Menendez, a
British officer must be a witness to the conversation. The
colonel said this was unacceptable, so I said I would go as
witness as I was a civilian. This was even less acceptable. It
became clear in the discussions between Colonel Pioggi and
Rod Bell that Menendez had already said that the Goose
Green garrison could surrender 'provided the local commanders deemed their position to be militarily hopeless'.
Colonel Pioggi wanted to confirm that he considered that he
was trapped and further fighting was useless.

As these discussions with Pioggi drew on, Chris Keeble and
I were left with Air Vice Commodore Pedrozo with the young
Naval officer translating in bad English and myself inter-
jecting in Italian when the lines appeared to get crossed. At
one point Chris missed a step in the conversation and said:
'But I need to make sure that the civilans' safety is guaranteed.
I must have that first.' The Vice Commodore said this was so,
but he was worried about being seen to give up with honour. I
drew Chris aside and muttered that as far as I could make out

the civilians were fine, and that we should not press too hard on that point as the Argentinians might sense our concern and use the settlers as a bargaining counter. I felt that, like Italians who want to make *la bella figura* (cut a fine figure), the Argentinians wanted to save face and to have something which would enable them to say they had fought well and surrendered with honour, and this was recognised by the British.

Chris Keeble then moved on to other vital details such as the state of the civilians, the housing of the prisoners after the surrender and the promise that they would be repatriated as soon as possible. The Argentinians wanted to be taken to San Carlos immediately and shipped home. The biggest question was the minefields, and Major Keeble demanded assistance in identifying their positions and advice in how to lift them. We were astonished to be told that the officers did not know precisely where the mines had been laid, the mining being the responsibility of a corporal who had just scattered them about the place on his own initiative. Chris Keeble said the corporal would have to be found immediately after the surrender. As this phase of the talking was unfolding, two mines went off further across the field, but no one opened fire.

The talks were taking place less than two hundred yards from the headquarters of 'D' Company, which was concealed completely from view. The hundreds of British paratroopers were all out of sight and not one shot was fired that morning. As we had approached the airfield, one of the company HQ reported over the radio that a company of Argentinians were straggling up the beach to get to Goose Green. These were the troops dropped by helicopter the evening before, and they had lost their way in the night. The paratroopers were ordered not to fire but to let the Argentinians pass through to the houses, which they did without incident.

As the Argentinian officers returned to the houses, we stood around trying to keep warm. Tony Rice radioed back what had taken place and we tried to look over the hedge to the houses in a little hollow to see what the Argentinian soldiers were doing. There was a gap in the hedge and after about half an hour Hector Gullan said he could see men forming up

beside a building with a wooden spire, the church and community hall. We crossed into a pasture and the Air Force men
marched towards us to form-up in an open square. The Air
Force commander, Wilson Pedrozo, said that he agreed to the
surrender terms and then turned to harangue his men in one of
the strangest ceremonies I have witnessed. I tried to creep close
to pick up some of the speech on my tape-recorder but was
gestured away by the Vice Commodore. I heard bits and pieces
about pride in the fatherland and the cause of the Malvinas,
but not much more. At the end there were shouts of 'Eviva'
and a singularly tuneless rendition of the Argentinian national
anthem which seemed to go on interminably. It sounded first
like a dirge, then the chant of a doleful football crowd. At the
end, the men threw down their arms, some with evident relief.
The Air Vice Commodore stepped forward, came to attention,
saluted Chris Keeble and handed over his pistol and belt,
saluted again and walked away. As the Air Force men sloped
off towards the houses for a meal before the paratroopers put
them in compounds, one of the British officers yelled for them
to come back and take off their belts as well as their helmets.

At first we had mistaken the Air Force contingent for the
entire military garrison remaining in Goose Green after the
fighting. There were about 250 Air Force personnel on parade.
If there was the same number again of Army and special
forces, it would be roughly the strength we had expected to
find in the settlement, about 600 men at the most, for we knew
by the morning of the surrender that over 100 Argentinians
must have been killed and wounded on the battlefield and 100
prisoners were being held on the beach by Darwin.

What Major Keeble's party saw next was one of the most
amazing sights of the campaign. We saw the soldiers coming
out of the houses and the huts, first by platoons and then
companies. There was first fifty, then a hundred and then too
many to count quickly. Hector Gullan could see them being
paraded and harangued by their officers. As they marched up
the slope towards us, we realised clearly for the first time that
the previous day the paratroopers had been fighting not a few
companies of Argentinians as had been suggested at 'H''s

Orders Group, but at least two, and possibly three, battalions. With masterly understatement, Chris Keeble said he was very glad we had not needed to fight in a second day of battle. If the British forces on the ground at Goose Green had under-estimated Argentinian strength in Goose Green, the Argentinians had certainly overestimated the force attacking them, which they thought matched their ground forces in numbers.

The grounding of weapons by the Army contingent was over much quicker than the Air Force ceremony. About nine hundred to a thousand men had formed up by companies. Some appeared pathetically ill-clad, their faces pale, wan and pock-marked. Some seemed not to have been able to hold down a good meal for weeks, others looked cocky and tried to laugh as they passed the British officers. They were followed by three very tired-looking priests who greeted us warmly with a wave and a smile. Among the soldiers was a small Naval party who had commandeered the islanders' freight ship, the *Monseunen*, which was tied up to the wharf, her propellor deliberately fouled by cables and chains. As the large group threw down their rifles and submachine-guns, many of them rusty from poor maintenance, Major Tony Rice called up for the party 'India 9' of 'D' Company to move into the settlement 'to investigate the situation of the civil population of Goose Green'.

Across the islands and the bright emerald green of the flat-lands of Lafonia, a series of rainbows broke out in the autumnal sunshine. Major Keeble and the Battery Commander started walking towards the houses. Two Gazelle helicopters with Sneb missiles outboard on their brackets besides the cockpits came in to take away the senior Argentinian officers to Brigadier Thompson's brigade head-quarters at San Carlos. As we strolled across the paddock beside the sheep sheds, a short figure waved to us and shouted, 'Good morning, gentlemen. I'm Eric Goss, the farm manager of Goose Green.'

'How's it been with you?' I asked.

'Pretty tough. I've had a pretty hard night with these chaps. I was on to Alan Miller at Port San Carlos last night, raised him as the first contact with the outside world after two months being pinned down here. We were able to get in touch with British officers and they spoke to the forces nearby, and after lengthy discussions I presented the Argentinians with a piece of paper as to why they should give up and save lives.'

'Has it been bad for the women and children?'

'Yes, it's been pretty rough. They've been held as captives in the main recreation hall. Their houses have been filthied, and their property stolen. I'm very glad to see you fellows this morning. I hope you can remain with us for some time to come and we will remain British for ever.'

Later Eric concluded the conversation with the invitation, 'Would you like to come into my house and have a cup of tea and talk things over sensibly?'

Because of his position as manager, Eric had been allowed out of the community hall to his house. One hundred and fourteen settlers of Goose Green had been locked into the hall on 1 May after the first Harrier attack with cluster bombs. Initially they were given no meals for hours, but they were later allowed facilities to cook for themselves. Those in charge of the catering were taken under escort to fetch food. In the hall, blankets were slung from the ceiling as partitions and babies and grandparents, the old and the sick slept side by side on mattresses. One old lady had been without her false teeth for a month because the Argentinian officers who wanted her house took her away without warning. Many of the garrison soldiers had quarters in the schoolhouse, where they had died in the attack by 'C' and 'D' Company in the battle.

In Eric Goss's house I found his wife Shirley and the family of their relatives from Port Stanley who had headed out to Goose Green at the time of the Argentinian invasion. Nannie McCulloch was too infirm to move from her armchair and sat in it throughout the battle. Panicky young Argentinian soldiers had driven a pickaxe through the door as she sat by the window. The soldiers wanted to break into the cellars to shelter from the attack. Eric explained how the Argentinians had arrived and commandeered everything from farm tractors to Land Rovers and sheep which they killed inexpertly for mutton. One of the settlement's shepherds, Brian Hewitt, had been sent out by a group of Air Force officers to bring in sheep from the pastures to be killed for meat. As he set out across the camp on his motorbike, accompanied by his two dogs, an Argentinian helicopter dived and opened fire. The pilot landed and told the shepherd he was a spy and would be shot. Arriving back at the settlement, he was about to be marched away when Hewitt recognised the officer who had signed his permit to go into the fields and he was spared the further attentions of the helicopter pilot.

After tea and bread and cheese, Eric took us on a tour of the settlement. Between the houses we could see the paratroopers moving in single files carrying their rifles cocked in case they were ambushed by snipers, but they had cleaned the camouflage cream from their faces and were wearing their maroon berets. Eric showed us one house where young Air Force officers had been staying. A bedroom was piled with tinned food which they had been hoarding, while the conscripts were living off broth and one full meal a day. In another room, plaster ornaments had been smashed wantonly and in a third bungalow the occupants had spread excrement in every room and along the walls. The lack of hygiene was one of the main problems with the younger, untrained soldiers, according to Eric. Others stole useless articles, and the store was looted, a pile of debris and soiled goods strewn along the shelves and floors.

Some officers, particularly the small Naval party, had been kindly towards the settlers. After about three weeks in Goose Green, the garrison commanders decided to play by the book, offering receipts and freshly minted British Falkland Island currency for everything they took. The money had been brought from Argentina in suitcases. Amongst the items they took was lubricating oil, which they used for the guns and Pucara aircraft. 'They made it clear they would take all the stuff anyway, with force if necessary and they insisted in throwing receipts and bits of paper at us,' said Eric Goss.

At the community hall, the settlers had raised the Union Jack. There were a few cheers and children wandered between the paratroopers carrying tins of sweets and boxes of biscuits. There were cups of tea in souvenir mugs for the wedding of the Prince and Princess of Wales with the words 'Falkland Islands' printed on the side. The soldiers looked tired as they had been without sleep for three nights; they treated the settlers with almost alarming politeness. Tony Anderson, one of the farmers, said he had got 'Pretty fed up with the Argies after shutting everybody up for twenty-nine days.' He said most of the soldiers did not know why they were there. 'They were told they were going on an outing, for an exercise. They've stolen the food from the store and most of the vegetables from the gardens, so we've got a tough winter ahead of us. Out around the paddocks all the fences have been removed and put up elsewhere. It'll take about a twelve month to put the place straight.' Mrs Pat Grey added that the food shortage had become serious in the last few days. 'With all the looting it was getting shorter and shorter, and we could only get scraps in from the store.'

'What happened when the paratroopers came in?'

'I cried. I couldn't hold it any more. The tears came streaming down my face. I was so pleased and relieved. It just felt as if a ton brick had been lifted off us.'

Many of the settlers were showing symptoms of shock, laughing and crying as they handed food, tea and beer to the soldiers. The settlement had been converted to an armed camp with pack howitzers between the barns, the anti-aircraft gun on the headland by the sea and rocket pods lashed to spars and fences, even the slide in the children's recreation area. Some of the paratroopers were beginning to organise the prisoners into working parties to clear up the debris scattered between the houses and woolsheds. On the foreshore, soldiers were letting off steam firing captured rifles and submachine-guns into the water. Amongst them was Rev. David Cooper, who said he needed some target practice and wanted to see what the Argentinian weapons were like.

Goose Green had a perfect natural setting. It nestled in its own bay, a dozen white-walled wooden houses, the black sheep sheds and the ship tied to the jetty. The grass appeared as green as any as I have seen in Ireland, but not even the most optimistic islander could call the pasture lush. Closer inspection revealed that the colour came from mosses, hardly rich fodder for the descendants of the cattle Darwin once saw crossing the isthmus to Lafonia.

Eric and Shirley Goss provided a roast lunch, thick, coarse mutton with rich gravy, a pleasant change after nearly a fortnight of nutty, apple flakes, curry and porridge. In the afternoon, Eric and I drove out to look for the kit I left behind at the Gorse Line. Only my helmet was there. Everything left behind on the hill had been dumped with the belongings of the dead.

In the settlement, the Battery Commander said I had received some post. It was a cheque book I had asked to be sent to the *Canberra*, possibly the most useless item I was to carry across the Falklands.

I was heading back to Eric Goss's house when Tony Rice ran towards me telling me to grab my kit and get on the Gazelle that would be flying to San Carlos. 'The Brigadier has sent it for you to get back to the anchorage. You must go now.' I had been too exhausted to think about writing a despatch till then. The pilot told me to get in beside him. 'I haven't got an observer,' he yelled, 'keep a look out for Pucara and give us a shout if you see one.' We took off in the late afternoon and flew over the houses of Goose Green and across the gorse banks which were still alight and gushing smoke into the sky.

IV. AFTER THE BATTLE

Two days after the battle at Goose Green there was still no possibility of broadcasting to London in voice. Following the surrender by Air Vice Commodore Pedrozo and Colonel Pioggi, I flew into San Carlos and took a choppy ride in a rigid raider across the anchorage to the Satellite Communications Centre at Ajax. This was in a tent swathed in camouflage netting, tucked under the rocks well away from the Refrigeration Plant where Rick Jolly and his men had set up their

hospital. Between the sheds and the tents there were still signs
of the bombing raid three nights before, which had killed five
men and wrecked ammunition dumps and weapons stores.
The hospital still housed two 400-kilogram bombs which had
failed to go off.

The signallers told me there was no chance of a voice link to
London. I would have to write the despatch about Goose
Green in block capitals and it would then have to be encoded
and sent to the Ministry of Defence. I went away to look for
some tea and 'scoff' in the hospital area, where I met Rick
Jolly. He had been handling the casualties and the dead from
the battle all day, and said that no one who reached the
hospital area alive had died yet. Lt.-Col. Bill MacGregor of the
Royal Army Medical Corps had apparently carried out a
remarkable throat operation which took half the night. Space
in the hospital was now restricted to half the area originally
taken up by the operating tables and beds for convalescence
because of the two unexploded bombs which the RAF Bomb
Disposal Team wanted to leave until the area could be cleared.

The Unexploded Bomb Team was led by the forthright,
blunt-speaking Flight-Lieutenant Swann. He told me he was
angry that the press had revealed that many of the Argentinian
bombs dropped over San Carlos on 21 May had not gone off.
He said he had heard references to these reports on the press
reviews on the World Service, so the information must have
been freely available in London. Had it come from a journalist
with the Task Force? I said I did not think so, as we were told
to be careful in reporting what had happened to the *Antelope*,
where one of the flight-lieutenant's colleagues, Sergeant Jim
Prescott of the Royal Engineers, had been killed defusing the
bomb that had hit her amidships. In the raids over San Carlos
on the evening of 27 May, when Ajax and San Carlos Settlement had been hit, the Argentinians had used different bombs,
the French-designed bombs retarded with parachutes, and
these had gone off, said Flight-Lieutenant Swann.

'Well, don't blame this one, mate,' said Rick Jolly. 'He's
been at the Goose Green punch-up. It's probably one of those
civil servants again, leaking it to the defence correspondents,

just to show they're in on the act and have got balls as big as aircraft tyres.'

Back in the Satellite Communications tent, I was told there was no chance of a call to London and I began writing the description of the surrender and battle at Goose Green in long-hand. My hands were frozen and my vocabulary seemed wholly inadequate to describe what had happened. Towards the end, I struggled with the word 'heroic'. Was it over-blowing the description to call the battle heroic? Had I lost my sense of perspective? In the end I decided what was good enough for Leonidas was good enough for 'H' Jones, and described his action as 'heroic'. In an act of great kindness, the MOD press officer at Ajax, Alan Percivale, offered to transcribe my script and make sure it was sent by telex.

As Alan and I were discussing the problems of transmitting the script and getting a ride on a landing craft back to San Carlos, there was a call on the secure telephone line from Fleet Headquarters at Northwood. The duty watchkeeper had been woken up there and was told to find out how 'H' Jones had been killed. I told him all I knew, then asked the young officer in Northwood if there was any way he could record my voice on that line. He said it was impossible, so I asked if he could telephone the BBC to expect a despatch from me. 'Do you think I've got a public call box here?' he replied, and said he was now going back to sleep.

The following morning Major-General Jeremy Moore and his staff and the commander of the 5th Infantry Brigade, Brigadier Tony Wilson, came ashore. They held a staff meeting in the cowsheds of one of the farmyards at San Carlos. Never before can East Falkland have seen so many red tabs and woven cap badges in one spot. I went to the farmyard to ask Julian Thompson what he thought had happened at Goose Green and why the enemy's numbers had been so badly under-estimated. Staff officers tried to move me away; my scruffy, unshaven face and muddy clothes must have contrasted oddly with their neatly pressed trousers and shiny green wellington boots, which seemed to be *de rigeur* for the 5th Infantry Brigade officers. Brigadier Thompson asked me what I thought had happened and why the Argentinians had given up. I replied that their intention seemed to have been to make sufficient show of fighting to be able to say they had surrendered with honour. I added that there must be concern now that the civilians in Port Stanley had been shut up in the same way as those at Goose Green and wondered if there was any way of finding out. I thought it might be a way of getting through to the Argentinian commander in the Falklands capital, and establishing whether they would be prepared to negotiate withdrawal rather than have a bloody fight to the finish in the streets of the little port. The brigadier said he would think about this and we would discuss the matter further.

As we talked, I noticed the bright eyes and sharp features of a small man wearing a peaked cap like that of the Afrika Korps. He listened eagerly, not saying a word, his thumbs stuck in the straps of a hiker's knapsack. This was General Jeremy Moore, the Royal Marines' most decorated officer, who had won two Military Crosses and an OBE on active service, and who set off to war with the Bible and Shakespeare's sonnets in his knapsack, which he seemed to keep with him always. I was introduced briefly to the general and the much larger figure of Brigadier Tony Wilson of 5th Infantry Brigade who stood beside him.

Later General Moore told me he had decided to move ahead of the 5th Infantry Brigade and get ashore as soon as possible, 'to take the political pressure off Julian's back'. The break-out from the San Carlos beachhead had been ordered suddenly on Wednesday 26 May, the day after the loss of the *Coventry* and the *Atlantic Conveyor*. Julian Thompson had wanted more time to build up supplies and establish logistical support for the units that would now have to march across the mountains to Port Stanley. On the afternoon of 26 May, the brigadier was called from San Carlos to the secure line to Northwood at the Satellite Communications Centre at Ajax and told in unequivocal terms to move immediately, an order which must have been approved first by the Prime Minister. 45 Commando and 2 Para set out for Douglas and Teal and 2 Para were sent south to attack Goose Green.

Had he known what he was to discover later about the enemy strength in Darwin and Goose Green, Julian Thompson says he would have sent two battalions to attack the Argentinians there and two batteries of guns. Quoting 'B' Company commander of 2 Para, Thompson describes the battle fought by 'H' Jones's men as the 'Come as you are party'. He says he had no idea of the true strength of the enemy in the Darwin Isthmus until the prisoners were counted following the surrender.

If Julian Thompson had little idea that there were about fifteen hundred Argentinians in Goose Green before the battle, there is now incontrovertible evidence that members of the Defence Staff did. Earlier in the campaign, Signals Intelligence intercepted a message from General Menendez in Port Stanley to General Galtieri in Argentina. It was an appreciation of his military position and the disposition of the main Argentinian forces in the Falklands, explaining the deployments round Stanley to the west and east of the port, and saying that the second strongest force was in Goose Green. General Menendez knew that he was in difficulty because of his lack of helicopter facilities, which meant he could not move more than a company or two at a time. General Menendez's appreciation of his position was circulated amongst Intelligence Officers in London but security clearance was not given for it to be transmitted to either Brigade Commander with the Task Force, Brigadier Thompson at San Carlos or Brigadier Wilson, whose men were now moving in by sea from South Georgia aboard the *Canberra* and the *Norland*. Though the brigadiers were not being informed of the enemy numbers in Goose Green, at least one newspaper defence correspondent was, on the day of the battle.

The morning that Major Chris Keeble, Major Gullan and their party were to set out to negotiate the surrender of the Argentinians in Goose Green, Saturday 29 May, the leading report in the *Daily Telegraph* stated: 'British paratroopers have captured the key East Falkland settlement of Goose Green, with its airstrip, and Darwin, the Defence Ministry announced last night. Casualties were light and some Argentinians were taken prisoner.' Apart from the fact that at the time of going to

press Goose Green had not been captured, it is the fourth
sentence of the story which is the most intriguing. The report
goes on, 'The capture was made by the 700-strong Second
Battalion Parachute Regiment which had advanced 25 miles
from the San Carlos bridgehead. About 1,000 Argentinian
troops were stationed in Darwin and Goose Green.' At the
time that 'H' Jones led his men into battle, senior members of
the Defence Staff seem to have had some idea of the real
strength of the enemy in Goose Green, but neither the Brigade
Commander nor the Battalion Commanding Officer knew. By
the evening of the battle, the defence correspondent of the
Daily Telegraph knew that there were about a thousand men in
Goose Green. The rule of thumb in an assault of this kind is
that the attacker tries to gain superiority in numbers of three-
to-one. In the event, 2 Para faced three-to-one against them.
The muddle by which vital intelligence information was not
transmitted to 3 Commando Brigade before the attack on
Goose Green seems one scarcely bettered by Lord George
Germain in the loss of the American Colonies. The failure to
communicate information about the Argentinians defending
the isthmus invited the most heroic defeat of a British unit in
an assault on an enemy position since the Charge of the Light
Brigade.

'In the evening we buried the dead from the battle at Goose
Green. A large pit had been dug above the field hospital at
Ajax Bay, by the Royal Engineers' earthmovers and bull-
dozers. Company Commanders, a few officers, NCOs and men
of 2 Para were flown in from Goose Green in Sea Kings. They
had not been told that they were going to a funeral. They were
told it would be a memorial service, and David Cooper was
furious at the lack of courtesy. The Company Commanders,
the Battery Commander and Major Chris Keeble carried the
bodies of 'H' Jones, Jim Barry, Chris Dent and Richard Nunn
and laid them side by side in the earth. The men and NCOs
carried the bodies of their comrades, to crisp, quiet commands
from RSM Simpson. The 23rd Psalm was said. David Cooper
read the roll of the dead and the RSM scattered a handful of
soil across the grave. There was no encomium, nor bugles, nor

firing parties. Two hundred men stood round the grave in no particular order of rank, General Moore with his knapsack in the middle. It was a glorious afternoon of late autumnal gold. In the anchorage, a frigate swung slowly, her guns trained skyward against air attack. We turned away, and Royal Marine volunteers began to pick carefully through the top soil to remove all stones before the shovels and diggers began filling the grave.

The following morning I hitched a ride from San Carlos back to Goose Green. First in the queue for the helicopters was Brigadier Tony Wilson, the 5th Infantry Brigade Commander. He said he would set up his Brigade Headquarters at Darwin and move towards Stanley from there. I asked him how the Gurkhas would fare in the cold, damp conditions. 'I'll wrap them in so many layers of clothes, they'll look like little penguins,' the Brigadier told me. 'I want them for offensive trench patrolling round Stanley. They'll be excellent for that.'

In Goose Green, parties of prisoners were being escorted by the paratroopers to clear up the mess between the houses. Argentinians were coming in from the fields to surrender days after the battle. A burial party working near Port Darwin had found a severely wounded Argentinian in a trench, one side of his face torn open and gangrenous as he lay beneath his dead comrades. He was shipped out to the Ajax Bay hospital immediately and his life was saved despite multiple fractures to his lower limbs. Piles of artillery and anti-aircraft ammunition lay strewn between the sheep pens and the woolsheds now bearing the symbol POW in untidy white letters.

In the evening, a delegation of Argentinian officers came to Chris Keeble to express serious misgivings, as they put it, about the treatment of the prisoners by the paratroopers. The young Naval lieutenant with the toothy grin and heavy moustache, whom we had met at the surrender, said he would be the interpreter. Major Keeble asked me to stay in the room in case there was trouble with the translation. The Argentinian lieutenant-commander began explaining that the Argentinian soldiers were angry that the paratroopers seemed to have such little respect for the dead they were picking up on the battle-field. They were concerned at the apparent lack of sanitation in the woolsheds, surprising in view of the mess that they left in the houses. Many of the Argentinians were sick with colds, 'flu and dysentery. They also wanted to know when they would be going home; after all, this had been one of the conditions agreed at the surrender. This at least is the gist of the discussion, but the talking went round and round like an elaborate dance, never quite touching the main point. The Naval officer was flanked by two Air Force men and a Special Forces lieutenant sporting the soft, light-green beret of his unit. By the end of the conversation I was quite convinced he understood English perfectly from his reaction to each remark by Chris Keeble, and he did not open his mouth once except to say goodbye at the end. The Special Forces units appeared to be the most politically motivated of the Argentinian ground forces.

After some questioning, it was clear that the prisoners were worried about the matter that they mentioned least; they feared that they were in a forward fighting zone and were likely to be bombed by their own Air Force as they remained corralled in the sheep sheds. They did not believe the para-troopers when they said there were not enough helicopters to ferry all the prisoners to San Carlos immediately. Major Keeble said that doctors would return to the sheds that evening and that the diet would be improved. The delegation felt it had made its point, and left.

Respect for the dead seemed particularly important to the Argentinians. They had laid the grave out beautifully for Lieutenant Nicholas Taylor, RN, whose Harrier had been shot down on 4 May. The grave stood next to those of Argentinians killed in the air raids, and it had a headstone with an inscription of the pilot's name and rank. In several of the houses, letters and diaries of the Argentinians were discovered praying for an end to a senseless war.

Farming, with a little fishing, was the main source of income for Goose Green and, as in the Highland crofts, for most it was a way of life. In the lands round the little village, sheep and small, tough breeds of cattle, like the Kerry and Welsh Black, roamed and were killed for their meat. At each settlement stood a gallows for hanging out the carcasses of the sheep and beef animals to bleed them. Much of the farming land was owned by the Falkland Island Company, which had an elaborate hierarchy of managers and farm managers, elaborate, that is, for so small a community. Some of the managers might own parcels of their own land, and in parts of the islands tracts would be owned by the established names of Falklands history, 'the sheepocracy' as they are called, like the Alazias and the Pitalugas. Shepherds were hired hands who could have a sharecropping interest in their produce. The managers had tight control of the community through the Falkland Island Company Stores, which was almost solely responsible for bringing supplies to the remoter communities and settlements in camp.

Eric Goss was the farm manager in Goose Green, but the senior representative of the FIC was Brooke Hardcastle, the manager at Darwin. On an expedition to search again for my tape-recorder on the Gorse Line, Chris Keeble and I called on the Hardcastles in their white-walled house in the middle of Darwin. It had been nicked by three canon shells from Harriers, and another raid had deposited two unexploded bombs a hundred yards from the house. The house was surrounded by the rough grass, cinder paths and tracks which criss-crossed most settlements in the islands, of the kind you would find in many of the Western Isles of Scotland or western Ireland. Step inside the Hardcastles' house and you might believe you were somewhere in the leafier parts of Surrey, with its conservatory, modern heating and extensive fitted carpetting. Several helpers were cleaning the place when we arrived and we were asked to remove our boots. The Hardcastles insisted on this rule, and officers as well as men had to obey.

The Hardcastles' daughter, Janet MacLeod, had been one of the cooks for the community locked up in Goose Green's recreation hall. She had been to school in Argentina and spoke fluent Spanish. Later she discovered that the wife of one of the officers billeted in her house had been at her school in Buenos Aires at the same time. Janet's husband Bob was the village plumber and handyman and an amateur radio enthusiast. He was the radio ham who broadcast to England for two days after the Argentinian invasion under the code name of 'Bob the plumber'. Once the Argentinians arrived in Goose Green, they took away Bob's radio transmitter and aerials and set them up in the Darwin Boarding School, the building which exploded under the attack of 'C' and 'D' Company in the battle. 'They had beautiful radio equipment,' said Bob, 'but they didn't know how to use it. One of their operators had been a radio amateur for only four months and that was his entire training.'

With replacement aerials flown in from Port San Carlos, Bob was able to resume his transmissions on the amateur wave-bands. We helped him haul the aerials up in half a gale. Snow was covering the mountains in the distance. Janet MacLeod is a slim, attractive woman with long, blonde hair and the look and complexion of a Scots Highlander. She said she was sure the Argentinians had two observation posts in the mountains from which they could see the British attack on the isthmus, spotting targets for the guns and mortars. Across the saddle of Mount Usborne, a cream and red building could be seen distinctly, and the paratroopers prepared to assault it with helicopters. The attack was delayed several times and in the end it fell to the Gurkhas to search for enemy observation posts in the mountains to the north and the hills of Lafonia.

That morning, Janet MacLeod gave me a graphic description of what happened to the little community of Goose Green in its twenty-nine days of captivity in the hall.

'They came round to the houses and said we were to go to the hall. Some people were just pushed out of the door. They didn't have time to get their coats, they were in their bedroom slippers, some of them. It was about nine o'clock in the morning. They said we were going to have a meeting for security, about what to do in case of another Harrier raid, as this had occurred just after the first bombing of the airstrip.

'They shut the door and left us there till about seven o'clock in the evening, before anyone turned up. They then brought us some food, tinned beans, ham and stuff like that, which we rationed out very strictly because we didn't know when they would bring us any more.

'We were left there for a month. The first night nobody had any bedding. We just slept on the floor in our clothes; and the following day we did manage to get some bedding from the store and some of the houses.

'One certain person had to open the door when they knocked and if any other person showed their face, they said they would shoot.'

'Did they treat you badly at any particular times?'

'Well, we did not see much of them. We chose a committee and if anyone wanted anything they had to contact the committee to pass on the requests to the Argentinians. We would knock on the door and ask the guard at the door, who stood there all the time with his bayonet fixed. It was just a case of not being able to contact them until they came to see us.'

'Could you describe the day of the battle? What was happening in the community hall that day?'

'We had prepared ourselves to get under the floor if necessary. We could see what was going on from the windows, and some people watched the whole thing throughout from the windows. We could see the British soldiers coming over the gorse hedge at the top of the hill, and it looked to be about only fifty of them and the Argentinians were shelling them very, very heavily. We saw two Pucaras come over and fire rockets at them, and then bank away. Later, when I was under the floor, somebody else saw another Pucara attack and it was shot down.'

'Did you think you were going to get out alive?'

'No, we didn't think we would get out alive. We only saw fifty [soldiers] coming over the hedge. We imagined there would be more coming round from the other side, but we couldn't see them. We certainly saw them getting a lot of shells up that way. Then, at nightfall, everything went silent. We didn't know what had happened because there were still Argentinians walking round outside, still with their guns. And we thought that perhaps all the British had been captured or killed.

'All that night, because we didn't know it had finished, we were under the floor just in case small arms fire came. The walls are very thin and the bullets would have come straight through, although nothing touched the hall where we were. Some of the houses with people in, did have bullets through them.'

'When did you realise it was all over?'

'Our manager came up at ten in the morning and told us it was over, but we didn't believe him at first. Then all the Argentinians were lining up on the Green and getting a political speech from their lieutenant-colonel. Then they went back to the house to pick up their kit.

'We'd been home while they were lining up to put the kettle on for the British soldiers. We'd seen Bob's radio and it was all right then, although there was a grenade taped to the aerial wire. When we came back after they'd taken their kit away, it was smashed.'

'How did they treat you, as somebody who spoke Spanish and was one of the organisers in the community hall?'

'The officers tried to keep the Spanish-speaking people away from the soldiers as much as possible, because we were hearing the BBC after they let us have a radio. They didn't want the soldiers to know what we thought was going on.

'The soldiers used to take us across to the galley to cook; two women used to go across there each day. There would be three or four soldiers with us in the kitchen.

'One of the soldiers told us that even in the settlement here they were only given one meal a day. Some of the soldiers used to come in from the field, and were looking for food, asking for meat and bread. We couldn't give them anything otherwise they would all have come in for food. One of the soldiers that did ask us for meat two days before the surrender was one of the officers who first came here with them to Goose Green, about two months before. He really

looked terrible: I hardly recognised him. His eyes were really
sunken in, his cheeks were hollow and he really looked a
mess.'

Much of the wrecking in the houses and store carried out on
the morning of the surrender seemed to be an act of petty
malice. Settlers had radios and ornaments smashed. Few were
threatened physically. Radios were smashed because the
Argentinians feared what they might learn from the BBC. The
Hewitt family said they were particularly grateful for what the
World Service had done; in the community hall it was the only
link with what was going on beyond the settlement, and they
managed to listen to news bulletins regularly on an old radio
that had been rebuilt under the floorboards. All his two-way
radio equipment had been smashed or stolen, said Dave
Hewitt, the father of the family. Furniture had been smashed
in his house and pictures and decorations damaged, the wear
and tear of any occupation by troops. In one drawer, scratched
with the point of a nail, was the slogan: 'The Malvinas are
ours, and will remain ours always.' For the patriotic
Argentinian, the Argentinian Malvinas was not so much a
legal, territorial question but a mystical dream of fulfilling
their country's nationhood.

On the day of the battle one man did have a nasty experience
in which he was physically manhandled. In the morning,
Denzil Clausen, a shepherd, had returned to his house for
clothes. A guard caught him fiddling with a radio and music
centre and accused him of trying to signal to the British fleet.
He was shoved on the ground close to a position from where
they were firing rockets. 'It nearly burst my ear-drums,' he
said. He was marched to a house and accused of being a spy,
and was threatened with shooting. They put him in a hut, tied
his feet and hands with a *caparesto*, a leather piece of harness
for leading a horse, his feet strapped so that he could not relax
or the thong would pull on his hands. He lay there throughout
the battle, with rockets and howitzers going off all round him.
At one stage the guard put a gun to his head. In the evening,
the fighting died down and the guards dragged him to another

house with his feet tied. In the yard he could see men carrying
ammunition up to the pack howitzers. Eventually they untied
his hands and gave him some food – wafer biscuits and thin
chocolate. He thought he had lost all sensation in his hands.
They kept him awake most of the night, kicking him if he
seemed about to sleep, and in the early hours of the morning
an officer speaking fluent English said, 'You can go home
now.'

Some of the Argentinians had been helpful to the settlers.
Others were unpleasant and vindictive, but nearly all the
people I spoke to in Goose Green remarked on the fear and
suspicion between the different elements of the Argentinian
garrison. Young professional officers had obvious contempt for
the grubby conscripts in their limp, thin, olive-green uniforms.
Sergeants and corporals would kick and hit men going about
fatigues, and one NCO was seen prodding the stragglers in his
patrol with a bayonet.

I was standing in the house now serving as the battalion headquarters of 2 Para, waiting for a helicopter to take me to San
Carlos to make a broadcast, when there was a loud bang. It
seemed as if some mines had detonated close to the houses, or
an unexploded bomb had gone off. We ran out on to the Green
and saw a black streak of smoke rising behind the sheep sheds
containing the prisoners, and heard screams and shouts and
the rapid pop-popping of small arms ammunition. Someone
shouted for medical orderlies, 'Get the fire extinguishers. Has
anyone got his morphine handy?' The paratroopers carried
morphine capsules in their helmets, and we went indoors to
get them. Returning to the shed, I saw the body of a prisoner
lying perfectly still, blood oozing through the legs of his
trousers, his torso twisted. The medical orderlies were
covering him up. They told me to get away unless I could do
anything, as they feared more ammunition was about to erupt
in the fire.

The prisoners had been moving ammunition away from the
huts. This is against the letter of the Geneva Convention, but
the prisoners wanted to do it for their own safety. A stack of

shells had exploded, killing two men and injuring four others with terrible wounds to legs, face and upper body. One Argentinian lost his arms and his legs and his abdomen was on fire. A British medical orderly drew a pistol and shot him through the head. I did not witness the deed myself; I was on the other side of the buildings at the time, but no one in 2 Para made any secret of what had happened and no shame was felt about it. There was a full Board of Enquiry about the event before the paratroopers left the Falklands. It found that the injured man was likely to have been dead by the time he was shot. It was an act of humanity, and the orderly seems to have had singular presence of mind and courage to do it.

As I went to get into the helicopter, David Cooper asked me if I would speak to the Italian priests, who were worried about the prisoners' welfare. I said I would, but that there was a helicopter waiting. 'No, you go,' said David, 'that's much more important.' I had still not reported in voice what had taken place at Goose Green, and the battalion wanted their families in England to know.

Goose Green had the most beautiful setting of any settlement I saw on the Falklands during the campaign. The white houses clustered on the spit of land sticking out from the Darwin Isthmus, the land round a changing patchwork of green, yellow, gold and brown. The mountains to the east now had snow on them. Geese continuously flitted across the water to the islands whose misty outlines coould just be seen further out to sea. The community received a bigger shock than almost any other in the two months of Argentinian occupation. The people had suffered air raids and bombardment, and a day of battle, and they had endured twenty-nine days of captivity during which the threat of what might happen was worse than any physical deprivation or violence. Many of the settlers had suffered a far worse ordeal than they realised at first and were showing symptoms of delayed shock and disorientation. By the time I left many had yet to come to terms with the violence and fear stirred up by the campaign, and the sense of community was fragile.

Janet MacLeod realised immediately that the Argentinian

invasion and the fighting had changed the village of Goose Green irrevocably. Janet is a Falklander born and bred. Three days after the battle, she said: 'I honestly don't know what is going to happen. Obviously I'd like to stay here. There's going to be more development with oil and fishing and that sort of thing – at least I hope so. The place will never be the same again.' At this point she was interrupted by a long burst of heavy machine-gun fire from the wharf where the paratroopers were clearing Argentinian weapons. 'They'll have to keep soldiers here to keep the Argentinians away, or obtain an agreement from them that they are not going to attack. Otherwise people won't stay, if there was any chance of the Argentinians coming back.'

'What would you do?'

'If they came back? I would go. I would leave here. I wouldn't stay if they came again. I might go to England. I spent some time in New Zealand and I might go there.'

7. Across the Mountains

I arrived back at San Carlos from Goose Green as darkness fell. By the jetty I found a marine with a rigid raider, who addressed me with all the cheer of Charon. He informed me that a ride across to Ajax Bay would be on a one-way ticket. The raiders would not be coming back to Blue Beach as the Commando Brigade Headquarters was being set up at Teal. The trip across to Ajax was the bumpiest I ever encountered, as the wind had whipped up quite a swell, topped with sharp, white waves.

At Ajax I went to the hospital to find some food and tea. Rick Jolly looked even more tired than when I had seen him two days before, and his beard was now a thickening hedge of black. He was not in his customary ebullient spirits. He had just lost two patients in the operating theatre, both victims of the ammunition explosion at Goose Green. The night before, he himself had carried out a major leg amputation on one of the injured from the battle.

One of the Argentinian casualties from the ammunition accident had arrived by helicopter at Ajax Bay with both legs blown off and his pulse down to forty. 'We did everything we could,' said Rick Jolly, 'clamped everywhere that appeared to be bleeding, and shoved pints and pints into him, but then we realised his brain had died.' Some of the victims of the explosion were barely recognisable. The surgeons called for more blood supplies and stocks in the blood bank were dangerously low. Lt.-Col. Ivar Helberg, the C.O. of the Commando Logistics Regiment, went across to the prisoners' compound and asked to see Lt.-Col. Pioggi. Pioggi was nicknamed 'Kojak' by the guards because of his lack of hair and his carefully cultivated tough-guy image. Until now they had found him the least co-operative of the senior Argentinian officers. Ivar Helberg asked him if he could provide at least thirty blood donors from the prisoners. To convince him, Colonel Helberg escorted Pioggi to the operating theatre to show him the gravity of the injuries to the Argentinians. According to Commander Jolly, Pioggi looked as if he was about to vomit and then immediately offered the required number of donors. He also volunteered information about the way live ammunition had been stacked at Goose Green. Rick Jolly says it was evident that the colonel thought the ammunition had been booby-trapped. I cannot be sure that this was so. Much of the ammunition was old and in poor condition and thrown down across the yards between the sheep sheds at Goose Green. Men of the Royal Artillery and Tony Rice's battery had made safe some of the fuses of the 105 mm shells for the pack howitzers but they said the ammunition was unstable. The immediate circumstances of the explosion will never be known; the blast and fire afterwards so maimed those closest at the time that they had no chance of survival, despite the efforts of the surgeons and medical orderlies.

The next day the *Canberra* arrived in the anchorage to discharge units of the 5th Infantry Brigade which she had picked up from the *QE2* at South Georgia. As we climbed up the ladders from the landing craft, a company of Welsh Guards was preparing to go ashore; some seemed amazed to see such scruffy herberts coming aboard. Captain Burne ordered a breakfast of bacon and eggs for us and allowed us priority over everything but the most urgent military traffic on the Marisat telephones to transmit the tapes from Goose Green. At the end of the two-hour session there was the seemingly obligatory question from the interviewer – 'How has it felt? I mean, have you felt frightened? Have you felt exhilarated?' Four days after the battle it was hard to recall the emotions of the morning and afternoon on Coronation Point and swimming through the gorse up on the Bower above Darwin. My whole endeavour that day had been to feel as little as possible, particularly when the bombardment was closest. It was virtually impossible to put into words the sensations I felt at the news of the death of 'H' Jones and those who died with him, and realising that we would be 'stonked' wherever we went, from morning till dusk.

The transmission over, I requested a helicopter back to

Goose Green and 2 Para. Captain David Nicholls said none was available and I would now go to 45 Commando about to march from Teal Inlet to Mount Kent. It was the neatest hijack I have experienced. 2 Para was now part of the 5th Infantry Brigade which had the BBC television team and Michael Nicholson of ITN with them; and 3 Commando Brigade wanted the other broadcasters to go with them. I was mildly annoyed, as 2 Para had asked me to move up to Fitzroy with them, but there was no way of getting a helicopter back to their battalion headquarters.

On the *Canberra*, Captain Burne had told me something of the ship's visit to South Georgia to pick up the Guards from the 'Black Pig', as the P and O staff called the *QE2*. The Welsh Guards and 2nd Battalion Scots Guards were transferred to *Canberra* while the 1st Battalion 7th Gurkha Rifles moved to the *Norland*. Captain Burne described the snowy mountains and huge sweeping glaciers of South Georgia as one of the most magnificent sights in all his years at sea. Later in my travels to and from the *Canberra* I found some letters to me from Helen Hawkett and Lauraine Mulberry of the old coffee trap describing the transfer of the Guards. The first from Lauraine Mulberry is dated 27 May.

> We are off the coast of South Georgia. Have seen two icebergs, whales and penguins – a busy morning! Awaiting the arrival of *QE2* and we and *Norland* are preparing to cross-deck her troops and transfer *Ardent* survivors from us, and *Antelope* survivors from *Norland*, plus some of our patients. About 6 or 8 patients went on *Hydra* [HMS *Hydra*, a survey vessel used as an ambulance ship], who came alongside us in a nasty swell the day before yesterday. She toddled off – a very small ship in a very large sea – to find *Uganda*.

There was another letter from Lauraine dated 29 May:

> 36 hours in South Georgia. *QE2* finally arrived about 6 p.m. on 27th and we embarked the Welsh Guards up to 1.15 a.m. (*QE2* was 2 hrs forwards to us!). 28th was spent taking on 5th Brigade/Scots Guards, 825 Squadron and various other units – along with compo rations and other stores. Chaos reigns – it's Southampton all over again.

Wait till you see us. We are bristling with guns on Prom and Games decks – really are a warship now. Really heavy weather and brilliant sunshine today – plenty of seasick troops.

On the same day, Helen Hawkett wrote:

Hello Foxy – How are you? Keeping your head down I hope. We hear that 2 Para have been doing great things down around Goose Green – hope your legs aren't giving you too much bother with all that walking. The radio tells us you've taken 1,200 prisoners – where on earth do you put them all!

We've had a nice wee cruise to South Georgia to pick up the troops off *QE2*. South Georgia was rather pretty, when it could be seen through mist and darkness. Imagine 'darken ship' at 2.00 p.m. – it's uncivilised. We gave the *Ardent* boys a good send off, with much cheering and waving, with the band playing on the Promenade Deck. All really quite moving. I hope they get back to England quickly.

So now we're off back to Falklands again – wave if you spot us from a distant hill.

Look after yourself – all these battles are a nasty business. See you soon.

And then on 30 May:

P.S. Just heard your piece on the news – must have been quite some day. So very sad about Col. Jones. Let's just hope it's all been worth it.

I spent the night aboard HMS *Fearless*, now the Clapham Junction for the through traffic of staff officers of General Moore's command, 3 Commando and 5th Infantry Brigade. Outside the wardroom there were notices asking officers returning from the field to remove muddy boots and coats. In the wardroom itself I met Max Hastings and the television crew and journalists. Max had just scored a coup by moving with an SAS patrol on the forward slope of Mount Kent and filing copy through their secure radio link to Hereford; though it took days for the MOD censors in London to clear the copy and even then the piece appeared in truncated form. The SAS had decided they needed a little more publicity, so that the work of the men that had died in the helicopter accident on HMS *Intrepid* might be appreciated. However, not every man in the unit approved of the higher publicity profile.

The SAS had been patrolling the area of Mount Kent, which was to be the springboard of 3 Commando Brigade's assault on the high ground immediately to the west of Port Stanley. 3 Para and 45 Commando were already moving to Teal. 42 Commando would be flown in to take Mount Kent and 40 Commando had been left to guard San Carlos against a counter-attack from the West, much to the chagrin of the unit C.O., Malcolm Hunt. Amateur historians were looking for analogies to the way the campaign was now developing. 'H' Jones had feared that the San Carlos beachhead might prove another Anzio, with hard fighting all the way to Stanley if the break-out was not quick enough. One of the SAS officers thought Mount Kent could be the Monte Cassino, where stubborn defence could stall the march on Stanley for weeks. Malcolm Hunt, with his talk of 'attriting' the enemy Air Force, might well have thought that 40 Commando's sojourn at San Carlos was like being stuck behind the lines of Torres Vedras in Wellington's Peninsula campaign.

In the event, Mount Kent turned out to be clear of heavy concentrations of enemy when elements of 42 Commando were flown in on 30 and 31 May. They were led to the crest by SAS patrols where they expected to find an Argentinian company. They found the trenches abandoned by the men flown to reinforce Goose Green. The weather turned to snow, with a wind-chill of $-12°C$. 'Hanging on in Arctic conditions,' was the signal Lt.-Col. Nick Vaux sent to Brigadier Thompson as his marines dug in.

The SAS and other specialist units were carrying out what is termed, with the euphemism of military jargon, 'aggressive patrolling' in the high ground around Port Stanley, though they do not appear to have penetrated the garrison in the port successfully. They talked of 'malleting' everything in sight, as the paratroopers wanted to 'banjo' the enemy, and the marines 'welly' them. There was some irritation at the SAS activities as orthodox forward infantry patrols from many of the marine and paratroop officers, who felt their units had perfectly suitable patrol companies for the job. With their peculiar command structure and direct access to the UK, the SAS did not come under the orders of either Brigade Commander on the Falklands.

The Argentinians seemed hardly capable of mounting counter-patrols across the mountains. One troop of special forces was parachuted to Top Malo House, inland from Teal and Estancia. The troop commander omitted to post sentries, and his men went into the house at Top Malo to cook a sheep which they had killed. These activities were observed by Captain Rod Boswell, who commanded the Royal Marines Mountain and Arctic Warfare Cadre. Rod was one of the most cheerful and loquacious souls on the voyage from Ascension in *Canberra*. He was to tell the story of how he 'bagged' the Argentinians at Top Malo over and again. When the Mountain and Arctic Warfare Cadre attacked, the Argentinians got up from their meal and ran out of the house where they were ambushed. Rockets from a Carl Gustav 84 mm launcher were fired through the windows of the building. Seven men came out with their hands up, and those that tried to run were killed. Finally the commander emerged, yelling excitedly (and with a distinctly Italian accent, by Rod's telling of the story) *'Perfecto! Perfecto!'* And congratulating him on a brilliant operation, he presented Rod Boswell with his bandana.

Not long afterwards, Rod's patrols averted a near disaster when the batteries of 3 Commando Brigade nearly opened up on two companies of 2 Para as they landed on high ground above Bluff Cove to secure the advance of the 5th Infantry Brigade along the southern route to Stanley.

Chris Keeble had decided to move to Fitzroy as soon as possible after the capture of Goose Green. On the suggestion of the Darwin manager, Brooke Hardcastle, he sent forward John Crosland's 'B' Company by helicopter to a settlement at Swan Inlet, half-way between Darwin and Bluff Cove. Finding there were no Argentinians at Swan Inlet House, a phone call was put through to the manager at Fitzroy Settlement, Ron Binney, to discover if there was an enemy garrison there. The brigadier,

Tony Wilson, was sceptical about the ploy at first. 'You simply can't go and just ring up the enemy to find out if they are there,' he is reported to have remarked. Part of the problem was that the southern route could be well observed from look-out positions in the Mount Usborne range and from Mount Challenger, which stood between Bluff Cove and Stanley. The paratroopers thought the risk of being observed worth taking and decided to secure the high ground above Bluff Cove on Wednesday 1 June. When the one Chinook helicopter rescued from the *Atlantic Conveyor* began ferrying Gurkhas to Goose Green, Chris Keeble asked the pilot to fly a company of his men to Bluff Cove, with an escort of two Scout helicopters armed with missiles. The Chinook pilot said his instruments had broken when he hit the water the day before, and he could only make one journey with forty men aboard at most. After an altercation with the load master, Chris Keeble crammed eighty men into the helicopter and it took off. At that moment, 'H' Jones's replacement as unit commanding officer, Lt.-Col. David Chaundler, arrived at Goose Green. Chris Keeble asked to carry on as an operation was under way and left in one of the escorting helicopters.

The Chinook was seen landing above Bluff Cove by forward patrols from 42 Commando near Mount Kent. 3 Commando Brigade had not been told of the plan and concluded that the Chinook must be Argentinian; the Argentinians had two or three still in service on East Falkland. Two batteries were ordered to prepare to fire with four times the fire-power covering the British battalion attack at Goose Green. It was only when Rod Boswell saw that the roundels on the Chinook were the blue and red of the RAF and not the white and light blue of the Fuerza Area of Argentina that the guns were checked. If they had opened fire, one company of 2 Para would have suffered more casualties in a few minutes than the whole battalion did in the entire campaign.

On the morning of Thursday 3 June I took off for Teal Inlet in a Wessex helicopter accompanied by Max Hastings and David Nicholls. We were to join 45 Commando, which would march from Teal to Mount Kent to prepare to take Two

Sisters, the next mountain close to Stanley. The Wessex dipped over the hills and inlets, sometimes ploughing through cloud less than fifty feet from the ground. The Wessex pilots were flying up to nine hours a day in similar conditions. Helicopter assets were still short, though we were surprised to see a row of about ten Wessex 5s squatting in a gully like sleeping grasshoppers. We were told there were not enough pilots to keep them flying all the hours of daylight.

Teal Inlet resembled a rural Army camp and a wreckers' yard, with snow vehicles and tractors churning up the mud, now the texture of thin chocolate. One of the Landing Support ships was unloading ammunition and rations. Local farmers were digging trenches with mechanical diggers on their tractors. The manager is reported to have been so incensed at the desecration of the turf of his home paddocks that he threatened to sue the Army for compensation.

Beyond the manager's house, 45 Commando was forming up by companies to march off in single file towards the mountains. We were told to dump heavy kit and take enough for a night in the open and the rest would be brought up by the BV tracked vehicles. I had not met many officers or marines of 45 Commando before, and they were very much a take-me-as-you-find-me unit. They were based in Arbroath in Scotland and had a strong bias towards Mountain and Arctic Warfare training. 'We're the punishment battalion, mate,' one marine told me as we set out, 'so you won't hear as much about us as the other commandos.' We were given some hurried introductions to the second in command, Major Rupert Van Der Horst, a gaunt man with a diffident manner of speech. Our guide was the schoolmaster, or 'schoolie', Lieutenant Eddie Bairstow, RN, a friendly and helpful adviser, and of all the schoolies I met on the Falklands he was the one who was most accepted by the rest of his unit as one of them. Walking across the hills, he kept up a bright conversation about the difficulties of both his job and mine.

Our aim for the day was an eight- or nine-mile 'yomp' to a point south of Estancia House, where we would turn inland to Mount Kent.

'Yomping', the most celebrated piece of arcane military slang to emerge into general usage from the Falklands campaign, is an expression the marines use for a cross-country trek on skis in Arctic warfare. 45 Commando yomped most of the way across East Falkland, as 3 Para 'tabbed' most of the way from Port San Carlos to Port Stanley. On the march, the commando was a long black snake, stretching for up to two miles. As the cloud lifted that afternoon and the sun came out, we crashed through streams and up bluffs of peat and rock. There were air raid alerts, and the column rested for ten minutes every hour, the standard practice for the British Army on the march for centuries. As we rested, the more energetic made brews, while the rest of us chewed 'nutty', Rolos and the sickly NAAFI glucose sweets. We seemed to live off sweets for days on end, giving the Army and Navy dentists work for years ahead.

The march was strenuous but not crippling. The principal discomfort was damp socks rubbing against boots causing blisters, and at rest times the marines were almost carelessly generous in handing round sticking plaster to bind the feet. The *Sunday Telegraph* correspondent, Charles Laurence, was to suffer badly from infected blisters. He had come all the way with the commando from Ajax, a popular figure with the marines, with his colourful and slightly camp turn of speech, anything good being 'blissful' and possibly 'divine'. His travelling companion was Ian Bruce, the defence correspondent of the *Glasgow Herald*, who according to Charles Laurence made the most 'blissful' porridge in the business.

Charles's most attentive critic was the RSM Pat Chapman, who claimed to be an avid reader of the *Telegraph*. Pat carried an aura of power hardly matched by any officer in the commando. He had been RSM of 41 Commando before it was disbanded and unusually had a second opportunity as RSM with 45. He was a mountaineering warfare specialist, a 'mountain leader', one of the men who would lead the troops in a mountain assault, moving ahead of the main force and securing the dangerous parts in the climb. He had sandy hair and moustache, and the keen expression of one of the moorland creatures in the tales of Beatrix Potter. I felt he was scrutinising carefully everything one did or said, like an animal watching which way its prey was reacting. His refrain was: 'I came to the Falklands with the Marines in '62. I came back again in '72 and now I'm here again in '82. Don't ask me where I'll be in '92, because I'm getting out next year.'

In the afternoon the weather brightened to the north and the east as we dipped towards the coast. For a few minutes we saw thin white strips in the sky – the vapour trails of the covering Harrier patrols. For part of the way I chatted to Max, an impossible creature to keep up with. Covering the ground with his long, loping stride, he waved his walking-stick animatedly as he talked to Rupert Van Der Horst.

After several hours, the straps of my rucksack biting my shoulders were causing greater irritation than the fast-developing blisters on my feet. The sun glistened on the tongues of sea reaching into the land, picking out the rock slides on the hillsides which in the distance appeared a pure white. For miles the only living creature seemed to be the snake of the commando on the march. Orders were by word of mouth, and there had already been some misunderstandings to match any caused by the same method in the trenches in the First World War. Marching from San Carlos to Teal, the leaders of the column had shouted, 'Air Raid Warning Red.' When the message was passed to the rear of the column, those in front were astonished to see the men on the hills behind them hoisting rifles and berets into the air. After a mile or so, 'Air Raid Warning Red' had become 'Galtieri's dead', and the signal for general rejoicing.

More than anything it was the sucking peat pulling the soles of the feet that made the march so exhausting; and the mortar-men and machine-gunners had the weight of their weapons and ammunition bowing them down. As the track took a turn up a narrow pass, we saw a cluster of tents tucked beneath the ridge. Outside one was Sergeant Pennington, he of the penguin stew and Buffalo Bill survival techniques aboard the *Canberra*. 'Everything OK?' he grinned through his gums. 'Come on, Tommo, keep going. You haven't started yet.'

The column stopped at dusk and was told to scatter across the moorland. We constructed a bivouac for the four of us hacks. Max and I shared a tin of curry and listened to the World Service before turning in, though it was barely audible. There were a few sharp commands about showing lights or smoke from fires and we slept.

The morning was dreary, foggy and cold. We were told there was no time to make breakfast and that we had to move quickly, an order soon rescinded as we heated a mess tin of porridge and dried apple flakes, with hot chocolate to drink. 'Blissful,' Charlie Laurence said, and commended the chocolate as the best of the powdered drinks in the ration packs. Charlie's blisters were really beginning to cause trouble and Ian Bruce had spent most of the night shivering and awake as the waggons had not arrived with his sleeping-bag. After the night on the Gorse Line at Goose Green, I had resolved never to be parted from my quilted under-jacket and sleeping-bag again. We wished Ian Bruce had woken us so we could have leant him any spare clothing we had. Later, Charlie had to be helicoptered back to the sick bay in *Fearless*, with 'cellulitis' causing a high fever, and Ian returned to Teal at the weekend with influenza.

Despite the worsening weather, the morning's march seemed less arduous than that of the day before. We turned south into the mountains, muddy tracks and rockfalls. Often we splashed through green, fast-flowing water of mountain brooks, hoping to run fast enough across stones in the river bed that the water would not seep in through the soles of our boots. During one break, four light tanks of the Blues and Royals came roaring in from the direction of our march. Out of one popped Robin Innes-Ker. 'I say, Max,' he shouted, 'what do you want me to do with this bloody typewriter of yours? I've had it in the back of my vehicle for days now.' Ever the master of the logistics of hackery, Max had asked the tanks to take his typewriter to Estancia. But now the troop of Scorpions and Scimitars was being switched to support the 5th Infantry Brigade at Bluff Cove in the south, and after ten minutes of chat they roared off to the west.

The next rest was taken in some rocky hills. The commando had bunched up. There was little need to hurry, as the column was a mile or so from its destination and the battle would not be till the following day at the earliest, though there were already rumours of a further postponement because the mist had again delayed helicopters bringing up artillery ammunition. As we rested, two Gazelle helicopters flew in from Teal with messages from Brigade Headquarters. There was a shout for a journalist to go back with one of the pilots. Max immediately volunteered, as it was likely there would be no battle for several days, but it was made clear that it was me the pilot was sent to take back to Teal or HMS *Fearless* on the command of General Moore himself. I never found out precisely why he wanted me to go back. The marines looked like a very long stick of soldier ants stretched out across the hillsides as the helicopter put its nose down and headed for Teal.

At Brigade Headquarters at Teal I met Colonel Tom Seccombe, who looked flushed and agitated. 'Hello, Foxy,' he said, 'sometimes I think we are being used by the press. Not all of you, of course.' After a while he recovered his good humour. 'Awful lot of marines round here,' he said, as a couple of platoons passed him saluting. I suggested that perhaps they were doubling back behind the hedge, as a plot to keep his saluting arm busy. The reason for the colonel's anger was that after journalists had attended the brigadier's planning meeting that morning, one had made a phone call revealing much of what the brigadier had said to another journalist at Estancia House. Most of the telephone system in the Falklands is on single wire circuits, so a third person can listen to a conversation between any two points on the line, and there was a chance that the Teal-to-Estancia line did pass through enemy-held land, and could be overheard there. The two hacks were certainly overheard by signals surveillance of the phone line at Brigade Headquarters. Brigadier Thompson thought of sending the two journalists home, and radically altering his plan of action; later it was found that the line had been cut well before Port Stanley and the enemy was unlikely to have listened to the call. But the incident meant a radical change in policy towards the press, which had become gradually warmer and more informal as the campaign progressed. No journalists were allowed to attend any Orders Groups thereafter.

Brigadier Thompson said that leaflets had been drawn up to be dropped over Port Stanley asking the Argentinians to give up honourably as their position was now hopeless. An intelligence officer who had seen the leaflets said they were crude and unlikely to persuade anyone to surrender. After talking to Julian Thompson, I was introduced to General Moore's deputy, Brigadier Waters, a big man with heavy glasses, who seemed bemused by the whole scene at Teal. He asked me about the surrender at Goose Green and wondered if the Argentinians in Stanley would agree to a surrender on similar terms. I said I was no expert on the way the Argentinians thought, but considered it vital to ensure that the civilians were being treated well. Contact should be made with the command in Stanley to establish this. Brigadier Waters paused and then asked me if I enjoyed myself wandering all over the world. How well did I know the British armed forces? he asked. I said I had been with the Navy in the '76 Cod War, and had worked for the BBC in Northern Ireland where I had seen a considerable amount of the Army. He said that if I enjoyed an adventurous life wandering over the world so much, I should join the Army. 'At approaching thirty-seven,' I replied in a horrified screech, having long qualified myself for the club for the least military-minded person in the world, 'you must be joking.'

The plan for the attack on Port Stanley was changing. Instead of an assault on the northern route by the 3 Commando Brigade units alone, with the 5th Infantry Brigade in reserve in the south and ready to move up the road from Bluff Cove, it was now to be a divisional attack with units of both brigades involved in the capture of the high ground to the west of the capital. A divisional attack meant even more ammunition had to be brought up for the guns, a thousand rounds for each artillery piece and not five hundred rounds as originally planned. At least five batteries were to be available at all times; this was the lesson of Goose Green, said Julian Thompson. In any attack, a commando or battalion was to be able to call on the fire support of at least two batteries, or twelve guns, in an emergency. 45 Commando had made good time in their march from Teal to the foot of Mount Kent, but to little avail. The attack they expected the day after their arrival, Saturday 5 June, was now put off for four or five days at the minimum. Julian Thompson and Jeremy Moore were determined that there were to be no more 'come-as-you-are parties'. The attack on Stanley was to observe the full etiquette of British infantry tactics.

We decided to go back to HMS *Fearless*. David Nicholls seemed to scrounge a Gazelle from nowhere. It was hidden by some bushes behind the Brigade HQ, and the pilot was a friend of his. He volunteered to be the navigator, and donning the most decrepit pair of spectacles I have seen in a long while, lenses cracked, bridge stuck with plaster, he began studying his much scrawled over map. As we arrived on the flight deck, we met General Moore leaving for the 5th Infantry Brigade. 'See you tomorrow,' said the general, 'come and have a chat then.'

That weekend was spent crossing the anchorage to the different ships to file reports about the build-up of the attack on Stanley. One evening we were abandoned on a metal raft with a storm raging overhead. The swell was too high for the boats to land passengers at the transports and ferries; a large landing craft might pitch five or six feet as it was thrown against a ship's side. On the raft I clambered into a Land Rover for shelter with two Gurkhas and a Royal Engineers colonel who told me he thought he had arrived a bit early. He said his job was to rebuild the airfield at Port Stanley and restore the electricity and water facilities in the town there.

The trickiest manoeuvre in the travels across the anchorage was getting back aboard the ferry *Norland*. She was about to set sail for Montevideo to return the prisoners captured at Goose Green. We were allowed to visit the prisoners and use the Marisat in the ship. To come aboard we had to swing by rope from one of the smaller landing craft into the port through which I had left the ship for the landings of 21 May. Sliding into the landing craft with full kit was far easier than the Tarzan swing we had to do now, ending with a twenty-foot slither across the steel decking. All the prisoners were put in cabin space, some three or four to a two-berth cabin, because quartering them on the car decks below the waterline was considered too dangerous if the ship was attacked. In the officers' space we were allowed to talk to Lt.-Col. Italo Pioggi and Air Vice Commodore Wilson Pedrozo, the commanders from Goose Green. The colonel was as tough as ever, assuring us that Argentina would win and the British would have a hard time attacking Port Stanley. The Air Vice Commodore looked as shifty as ever and did not particularly want to talk about the battles to come, but, he told me, he wanted to make a vigorous complaint about Britain's violation of the Geneva Convention in the treatment of the prisoners from Goose Green and he handed me a document he was registering with the Red Cross. It was drafted very carefully and quoted several of the relevant clauses of the Convention. It complained that prisoners had been handling live ammunition, and that they had not been taken to safety away from the War Zone. It then went on to protest about the removal of his briefcase, his wallet, his personal documents, his watch, his fountain pen, his radio and his calculator. Twice as much space was devoted in the document to the minutiae of his missing effects than the conditions of his men.

I was astonished to learn on the *Norland* that British negotiators were thinking of using Pedrozo as an intermediary to establish contact with the Argentinian commanders in Port Stanley. He seemed the least stable of the few Argentinian officers I had seen at Goose Green, and when I saw him in the *Norland* he seemed to be very depressed.

Earlier in the week there had been a long and pretty public debate aboard the *Fearless* about whether a surrender could be negotiated before it came to a battle in Port Stanley itself. After the failure of Rod Bell's ploy in the marine attack on Fanning Head just before the San Carlos landings, attempts at 'Psy Ops' had been abandoned. After the campaign, Julian

Thompson told me that he considered the lack of understanding of the mentality of the enemy, particularly the enemy command, the biggest single weakness in the British forces' operations on the Falklands.

The key to any negotiations, I argued, was the civilians. Little was known about them, where they were in Port Stanley and whether they were being locked up as at Goose Green. The consultations on the short-wave radio with the doctors each morning had indicated that no one was seriously ill in the port itself. The plan was to establish contact with the garrison commanders to discuss the safety of the civilians if it came to a battle in the capital itself. From these contacts discussions would broaden to the terms of a possible surrender or a negotiated withdrawal of Argentinian forces from the islands. At one point there was a project to get a party of British officers into Stanley under the white flag to see the civilians, and I volunteered to go as a civilian witness representing the British press as at Goose Green. In the discussions about surrender or withdrawal, the British officers would concentrate on the sense of isolation that the Argentinians must now be feeling, with their supply lines virtually cut completely from the mainland of Argentina. It was still thought that the garrison's food was low, that the troops were suffering all manner of diseases from liver fluke to dysentery, and that the conscripts could not stand up to the rain and cold. This picture turned out to be exaggerated. Hercules C 130 flights were still landing at Stanley airfield every night, and a supply ship managed to slip through the British blockade one night in the fog, carrying containers of rations, some far superior to the ration packs the British were getting. The other point that some of the British negotiators wanted to emphasise was the natural friendship between Britain and Argentina. One officer went as far as suggesting that the quarrel between the two countries should be patched up as quickly as possible so that they could resume the fight together against world communism, a bizarre notion which seemed to overlook the nature of the regime in Argentina, taking a strange 'what's a fascist regime or two between friends' approach.

At this stage it appeared that the British Government was not interested in further negotiations, possibly because of the protracted rounds of talks via the United States and through the United Nations in April and the early weeks in May. Eventually approval was given for a negotiating team to be set up with Rod Bell as the interpreter. The team chose as an intermediary one of the Air Force commanders from Goose Green and set off by helicopter to Estancia to try to phone through to Port Stanley. They arrived there only to find the line had been cut two days before.

With the failure of the telephone as a method of contact, the team chose to use the medical conferences on the short-wave radio each morning. At the end of one consultation, Rod Bell would ask the doctor to make contact with a senior officer on General Menendez's staff to discuss the safety of the civilians. As this method of approach was being prepared, by an extraordinary coincidence, it was reported in London that General Moore had made a public broadcast for the Argentinian garrison in Port Stanley to give up, and that a fluent Spanish-speaking Royal Marine officer had voiced the general's appeal. This was so near the truth that the negotiators thought that their plans had been ruined, and no contact was made with Port Stanley for two days to come. Much of the report, which appeared first through the Press Association and in the *Daily Telegraph*, was intelligent conjecture by defence correspondents. They had heard that some form of negotiation might be conducted, that a radio broadcast might be involved, and that leaflets had been prepared for drop by Harriers over the positions round Port Stanley. The Press Association quoted 'a senior Ministry of Defence official', so somebody must have been describing something of the operation being planned by General Moore's staff without explaining its sensitivity because it had yet to take place.

Eventually contact was made with one of the doctors left in Stanley, Dr Alison Bleaney. Two other doctors from England, Daniel and Hilary Haines, had been taken off to house arrest at Fox Bay on West Falkland on the instructions of the man in charge of the political policing of the occupation, Major

Patricio Dowling. Alison Bleaney contacted the Deputy
Military Governor of the Malvinas, Air Commodore Carlos
Blumer-Reeve, who was a popular and trusted figure with
most of the islanders in Stanley. He sent a member of his staff,
Captain Hussey of the Argentinian Navy, who like Blumer-
Reeve had spoken English since childhood, to listen to the
messages being conveyed by Rod Bell on the medical radio
net. It appears that the British intelligence officers on the
Falklands knew little or nothing of Blumer-Reeve or Hussey.
Information about General Mario Menendez was scanty; one
intelligence adviser told me that when they asked London for
the general's political biography all they got back was a page
and a quarter on his military appointments of the kind that
might be discovered from any equivalent of *Who's Who* in
Argentina.

Both Carlos Blumer-Reeve and Captain Hussey are said to
have played an important and courageous role in the surrender
when it finally came. It was apparently they who told
Menendez he had to give up rather than go on consulting with
Buenos Aires, for fear of hundreds of Argentinians and
islanders being killed in the town of Stanley itself if the
fighting resumed. But at first Captain Hussey did not trust the
British when they attempted to appeal for negotiations on the
radio. The thing that made him most suspicious was the use of
the intermediary. He spoke fluent English and he realised Rod
Bell spoke fluent Spanish. Why did they need a middle-
ranking Air Force officer captured at Goose Green to act as an
intermediary? Was there a trick somewhere? Several times
Hussey apparently came to the radio and listened without
replying.

The one positive result of the contacts made through Alison
Bleaney's radio was that once the Argentinians' defences began
to collapse round Port Stanley on the morning of 14 June, the
British knew immediately who to contact and who to negotiate
with. But an intriguing question remains: if the negotiating
team had been established earlier, and if its aims and the
identity of the garrison commanders like Blumer-Reeve and
Hussey were more clearly established, could a negotiated with-

drawal by Menendez's forces from the Falklands have been achieved without the night battles in the mountains round Stanley in which dozens of British, hundreds of Argentinian and three civilian lives were lost?

Two weeks after the San Carlos landings, Britain appeared to have almost total control of the seas round the Falklands. Five nuclear submarines were on active service in the area, and one conventional diesel-electric submarine, HMS *Onyx*. One night aboard HMS *Fearless* I took a walk on one of the upper decks to see the *Onyx* alongside, a huge black slug with the moonlight gleaming faintly on her casing. Men hurried up and down her narrow decking, carrying stores and equipment. The engines of the *Onyx* were far quieter than those of the nuclear-powered boats, and made her much harder to find with sonar. This made her particularly useful for close inshore work, and she may have helped in the operation on the mainland in which the Sea King helicopter ditched on the Chilean coast. Coming into San Carlos one day she hit an underwater pillar of rock, denting her bows, but the damage was fortunately not so severe as to need her withdrawal from patrol.

The activities of the Argentinian Air Force were becoming less intense, too, by the end of the first week in June. On Sunday 6 June we were about to leave *Fearless* for the *Norland* when an Air Raid Warning Red was given. Calmly the ship's captain, Captain Jeremy Larken, RN, told the ship's company to be prepared for a missile attack, as two enemy aircraft had been spotted coming in high over Pebble Island. There was a clang and a thud and the mortars on the upper decks fired 'chaff' to decoy the missile's radar. Captain Larken announced that the destroyer HMS *Exeter* was about to fire her Sea Dart missiles from a position on the *Fearless*'s beam in the anchorage. There was a rumble and roar like an express train. From the bridge of HMS *Fearless*, the *Exeter*'s missile-launchers were enveloped in black smoke, leaving burn marks on the destroyer's foc'sle. From as far away as Teal Inlet, the missile could be seen taking off, one of them exploding against the approaching aircraft in a rose of pink flame. The other, as Jeremy Larken put it, 'cooked', blew up before it reached the

target. Sea Dart was the main air-defence missile carried by
surface ships in the Task Force. It did not have a great success
in the Falklands, though it was by no means the complete dud
some critics made out. It is for striking against aircraft attacking from a high altitude, and much of its success depends on
good early-warning radar. It was not designed primarily to
combat low-level attacks of the type carried out by the
Argentinian pilots over San Carlos and in Falkland Sound. A
Royal Navy missile expert succinctly summed up the difficulties with Sea Dart: 'The trouble with Sea Dart is that it is
underautomated in some respects, and this is being looked at
now. The trouble with Sea Wolf was that it was too automated
for some of its tasks in the Falklands campaign.'

The air attacks were renewed with unexpected ferocity on
Tuesday 8 June. The frigate HMS *Plymouth* was bombed and
hit five times as she approached San Carlos Water in the
morning. An LCU landing craft from HMS *Fearless*, *Foxtrot
4*, was attacked by a Mirage as she made her passage from
Goose Green to Fitzroy carrying important signals equipment
for 5 Brigade Headquarters. She was hit by a single missile,
her stern blown off and five marines in her crew killed, includ-
ing the Coxwain, Colour-Sergeant Brian Johnston. In the
afternoon, two raids by Skyhawks bombed the Landing
Support ships, the RFA *Sir Galahad* and the RFA *Sir
Tristram*, which were unloading two companies of Welsh
Guards with their equipment at a bay near Bluff Cove. The
Welsh Guards sustained the worst casualties of any single
British unit in the campaign; over forty men aboard *Sir
Galahad* were killed and twice as many wounded.

I saw the walking wounded from the ships and the 1st
Battalion the Welsh Guards come aboard HMS *Fearless* that
evening, their faces and hands red and raw, running with
weeping lymph from flash burns. They said they had been
attacked out of a clear sky, with only thirty seconds' warning.
The ships had been unloading for nearly six hours in broad
daylight and the first contingents of the Guards, the RAF
Rapier operators and the Field Ambulance, had not begun to
disembark.

The sequence of events leading up to the disaster at Fitzroy is complex. Brigadier Tony Wilson wanted to get the main units of 5th Infantry Brigade to Bluff Cove as quickly as possible in order to join the final attack on the positions round Port Stanley. A column of vehicles had set off from San Carlos Settlement with the Guards' equipment but it had bogged down after a few miles. Helicopters were not sufficient to fly the two Guards' battalions to Bluff Cove to join 2 Para, already at Fitzroy; and the Gurkhas had to be moved up from Goose Green. The only means of moving the troops round was by sea. In true 'Grand Old Duke of York' fashion, the Scots Guards had been marched up the hill to Sussex Mountains after landing at San Carlos and now had to march back down again to embark in HMS *Intrepid*. On the morning of Sunday 6 June, HMS *Intrepid* arrived in the dark off Fitzroy. Her four landing craft, the LCUs, set off with the Scots Guards aboard, and were guided to Bluff Cove by Major Ewan Southby-Tailyour.

'It was the worst night of my life,' Ewan told me later. 'It was blowing a gale and the journey took seven hours. When we got to Bluff Cove we were observed by the enemy from Mount Challenger. They started firing star shells. Then the artillery and mortar fire came raining down. Fortunately it was out of range.'

As the Guards approached Bluff Cove, the landing craft were shipping gallons of green sea water over the bows. Conditions in the boats had been so cramped that the guardsmen had difficulty in getting their waterproof clothes on, and most only managed it after the rest of their clothing had been soaked thoroughly. Once ashore, they stood in the driving rain in the lee of the sheep sheds. The C.O. of 2 Para, David Chaundler, asked what they were doing there, and was told they were waiting for their unit C.O., Lt.-Col. Mike Scott, for orders. Chaundler decided to take matters into his own hands and with his RSM, Malcolm Simpson, ordered the men to move away from the buildings and dig in against air attack.

The following night it was decided that the Welsh Guards should move round from San Carlos aboard HMS *Fearless* because HMS *Intrepid* had trouble with a bearing in her main driving system. *Fearless* had only two of her four bigger landing craft, and the other two were already deployed in Choiseul Sound. The plan was for her to move to a point off Fitzroy, launch the two craft with her and wait for two more to come out from Bluff Cove guided by Ewan Southby-Tailyour. When *Fearless* arrived, the boats from Bluff Cove were not there to meet her. Ewan had sent a signal that a dawn rendez-vous was the earliest he could manage. Because of the peculiar topography of Bluff Cove and the shield of the mountains behind, winds can gust across the inlet at speeds of more than seventy miles an hour, and this made it impossible to get the landing craft out in time to meet *Fearless*. After launching her two remaining LCUs with two companies of Welsh Guards aboard, *Fearless* departed to reach San Carlos by daylight, and it was decided that the remaining two companies of guardsmen should move round to Fitzroy and Bluff Cove in the RFA *Sir Galahad*.

The inexplicable part of the story is why the *Galahad* and *Tristram*, and Sergeant Johnston's *Foxtrot 4*, were allowed to move round to Bluff Cove to discharge in daylight. It was known that the enemy still had observation posts on the mountains to the north of Bluff Cove, and probably further west overlooking Choiseul Sound from Mount Usborne and Wickham Heights. That very morning a Gazelle helicopter was shot down taking the southern route to Bluff Cove from San Carlos, killing all four men aboard, two signals officers and the pilot and navigator. The Royal Navy was told not to risk another escort by bringing a destroyer or frigate for air-defence close inshore at Bluff Cove. The Rapier batteries had only been established at Fitzroy that day, and by now it had been recognised that the Rapier systems needed twenty-four hours to settle down before they were fully operational. An officer of 2 Para watching from Fitzroy Settlement said he was astonished to see the ships sitting in Fitzroy Bay for five hours with equipment and ammunition being moved ashore before the men. 'I couldn't understand why they didn't line the ships' decks with machine-gun crews all the time to fire against any air attack. They must have known they were in a vulnerable position.'

The first attack, a wave of five Skyhawk A-4s, came in at 17.15 hours GMT, 1.15 p.m. local time. Major Chris Keeble saw the planes approach from the *Galahad*'s stern, two of them together, and drop one bomb in the sea and one right in the middle of the ship. It landed in the tank deck and killed nearly all of the Welsh Guards' mortar platoon. A large raft was alongside shifting stores and ammunition. Some troops watching from the shore said that the planes seemed to pull up and toss their bombs into the ships as they released them to make sure they fused correctly. By the time the second raid took place half an hour later, the *Tristram*, which had also been hit, but which was largely empty of men and stores, and the *Galahad* were burning fiercely, thick black smoke pouring skywards. The attacks were filmed by Bernard Hesketh of the BBC who had been taking general views of Bluff Cove and Fitzroy minutes before the Skyhawks arrived. He filmed the entire rescue operation as the helicopters beat their way to the flight decks of the ships through dense smoke. Time and again the Sea Kings returned to the ships. Some lowered strops to pick up men struggling in the sea, and they moved in close over the sea to sweep the life-rafts away from the blazing ships with the down-draught of their rotors. Some of the lifeboats were rowed to the shore at Fitzroy with the guardsmen singing 'Men of Harlech'. More than 150 men suffered burns and bruises of some kind, and were showing signs of severe shock.

Aboard the *Fearless*, officers and men of the Guards and the crew of the *Galahad* gave me their account of what happened when the ship was bombed.

Second-Lieutenant Johnny Strutt had a dislocated arm and flash burns on his face and hands. 'I was on the top deck and thrown ten feet backwards,' he said. 'My shoulder was dislocated. I was grabbed by someone who threw me into a lifeboat. There's all I remember of the explosion itself.

'We knew we were vulnerable, any ship standing in daylight is bound to be. But we had no warning of the attack.

'I saw two Skyhawks come in extremely low, and get a bomb

right into the tank deck of *Sir Galahad*. In all there were 350 men aboard. I can't comment on the number of dead and serious casualties.

'We've got no fighting equipment now, but we'd be prepared to go back and sort this mess out.'

Ken Adams, the Chief Engineering Officer of *Sir Galahad*, said there had been no warning of the attack. 'The first I knew of it was the roar of the aircraft, and two bangs within two or three seconds of each other. I was on the upper deck by the Second Engineer's Office. With the second bang I went straight through the door by his office and went to sleep on the outer deck, and woke up later to find smoke pouring all over the place.

'It was a superb rescue job: the Sea King helicopters managed to get many, many men from the foc'sle head as the after area was engulfed in smoke. The helicopters were coming in within six inches of the obstructions on the deck to winch stretchers and injured men on cargo slats. There was a very efficient dressing station at Fitzroy where a lot of our Chinese crew were suffering major shock and burns and we tried to wrap them in blankets to keep them warm. But the fire wasn't the trouble: we were getting explosions from the machine-gun ammunition and the aviation fuel tank went up. There were a lot of internal explosions.'

Third Officer Andy Gudgeon was one of the youngest officers aboard: 'I heard the sound of a jet. There was a pipe "Action Stations" and then two explosions. The deck seemed to come up and the door caved in. I was dazed and made my way out through the surgery, crawling around.

'When the captain piped "Abandon Ship", we all went out to help clear the lifeboats. I asked the captain if we should make a search, and I had to make my way back to the accommodation area to get the breathing apparatus and make my way back. A soldier with a gas mask said there was still someone in the accommodation area. I couldn't get this fellow out, and the soldier with the gas mask on couldn't breathe any more. The ammunition started exploding with the "pop, pop, pop" of rifle ammunition. I couldn't get the fellow out and the ammunition was still bursting.

'I had to go outside to breathe and by this time all the lifeboats were gone. I had to climb down the ladder on the side of the ship and just jump in. I was drifting down the side of the ship and I had all the gear on, my boots and so on. A helicopter lowered a strop, but it was dangling and whirling round and impossible to get hold of. I was winched aboard a Sea King eventually from a life-raft and then put into Fitzroy dressing station.

'There were lots of horrible wounds in the hospital there, mainly flash wounds from the initial heat of the blast, and people walking round with drips sticking into them. The noises from the hospital were not very pleasant.'

Second Officer Ian Povey timed the attack precisely. He had been listening to the World Service News at 17.00 GMT and it had just finished. He helped the captain lower life-rafts and lifeboats. 'Abandon Ship' was ordered almost immediately as the captain knew his ship had been crippled. He got ashore on the Mexeflote that was unloading the equipment at the time of the attack. He went to the hospital at Fitzroy to look for the Chinese crew, most of whom did not speak English. 'The injuries looked nasty but were mainly flash burns.' Seeing the Chinese crew, he went to help. 'We were just trying to keep the burns hosed down with water all the time. The medical teams were fantastic. They were spot on.' Ian Povey said the ship's company thought they had seen the worst when she was hit in San Carlos Water and was abandoned temporarily while two bombs were defused. *Galahad* had been a very happy ship, he added, 'She was a good ship with a marvellous feeling among the crew.'

Despite the five hits she had suffered when she was attacked approaching San Carlos, HMS *Plymouth* had a remarkable stroke of fortune. Two fire-fighting parties were sent from HMS *Fearless* and with the frigate's own teams they had all the fires under control in two hours. The frigate came into the anchorage with smoke and steam pouring from her funnel. The ship's captain, Captain David Pentreath, had put fire damage control drills into operation immediately the ship was hit and they had worked brilliantly, only five members of the ship's company being hurt. A Type 12 Rothesay-class frigate, she was one of the oldest escorts with the Task Force and yet she stood up to heavy air attack better than many of the more modern frigates and destroyers. Within three hours, all her main weapons systems were working fully, and she had managed to shoot down one of her attackers, a Skyhawk, with a Sea Cat missile. Captain Pentreath's control of the emergency aboard the *Plymouth* won the warm congratulations of Jeremy Larkins and the company of HMS *Fearless*.

In the raids on 8 June the Argentinians lost seven aircraft. One had hit the sea after the second attack on the LSLs *Galahad* and *Tristram* at Fitzroy Cove. The casualties inflicted on the ships and the men aboard them from the Welsh Guards, the Medical Corps and Fleet Auxiliary were the worst shock of the land campaign. One of the minders said we could report the disaster, but had to mention the 'good news' first, that seven planes had been shot down. But he was too old a hand not to know that the loss of the ships and the men could be slipped into the despatch almost as an afterthought.

In moving the ships to Fitzroy by daylight, the planners had taken one risk too many. The Argentinian Air Force had not been active for some days before, but it was known still to have plenty of strength. It was known, too, that there were well-placed enemy observation posts above Bluff Cove. The strangest part of the drama is why the Welsh Guards commanders waited for more than five hours before disembarking their men.

In Britain the government delayed announcing the full casualty figures as they 'did not want to give comfort to the enemy'. The propaganda radio in English from Argentina said the casualties ran into hundreds and would delay the British attack on Port Stanley for weeks. The setback to 5th Infantry Brigade had quite the reverse effect on General Moore, who was determined to get to Port Stanley all the quicker. Max Hastings and I were told to get to Mount Kent on Thursday 10 June, the day after filing our reports and the interviews with survivors of the *Galahad*. The assault on the positions guarding Stanley to the west were to begin on Friday 11 June. Charles Laurence was left aboard *Fearless* still suffering from high fever caused by his infected feet. It was less than the just desert for one of the two hacks who had yomped furthest across East Falkland.

8. Into Port Stanley

I. NIGHT BATTLES

The weather had turned a somersault by the time we flew to
Estancia House, with bright and warm sun like a day in spring.
Crossing San Carlos Water, it had been low cloud and mist.
The helicopter stopped at San Carlos Port to refuel and behind
us two Harriers pulled up, hovered and then put down at the
edge of the field. The airstrip, which had a tarmac apron, was
now fully operational as a refuelling and rearming base,
though the Harriers returned overnight to the carrier group at
sea.

At Estancia, Max Hastings and I were greeted by Lt.-Col.
Hew Pike, who gave us a guided tour of his headquarters area.
He had a billet in the farmhouse and the Quartermaster,
Captain Norman Menzies, nicknamed inevitably 'Norman the
Storeman', had his echelon in one of the barns, probably the
best supply operation in the entire British Land Force on the
Falklands. In one corner of the field a sign saying 'Rumour
Control' pointed the way to a dugout with all the fittings –
wooden rails for roof props, overhead cover made from corrugated iron, poles and sods of peat on the roof. Inside there
were festoons of Union Jacks, portraits of the Royal family
and, proudest exhibit of all, a headed letter from Downing
Street expressing the Prime Minister's thanks for the letter of
support she had received from the boys of 3 Para, though alas
not signed by the lady herself.

Outside Hew Pike showed us a model of Mount Longdon
which his men had made of earth and sand, indicating the
disposition of enemy forces on the feature. Colonel Pike said
he thought there might be two enemy companies at most on
the long ridge of the mountain, with others in the area.
Broadly, his object was to get the enemy off the crest of the
ridge in the dark and make sure his own men were not

vulnerable in the daylight to harassing artillery fire from Port Stanley.

As we talked, two paratroopers walked to the cooking area carrying three brace of Upland Geese which they had shot further up the inlet. Someone shouted out, 'You've shot the wrong sort, you silly sods. You don't want the white ones; they taste terrible. It's the brown ones, the females, that cook well.' Major Pat Butler of 'D' Company greeted us from a passing convoy of BV tracked vehicles, and said that his recce patrols had passed several interesting nights recently, and Corporal Jeremy Phillips, the sniper we had met on the *Canberra*, had a particularly successful outing on the rear slopes of Longdon the previous night. Hew Pike said he was sorry we were not coming with him and 3 Para and we set off in a tracked vehicle to Julian Thompson's 3 Commando Brigade HQ further up in the mountains.

Brigadier Thompson was about to give the battalion commanders their final orders before the series of attacks on Mount Longdon by 3 Para, Two Sisters by 45 Commando, and Mount Harriet by 42 Commando. The 3 Para attack was to start first, to be followed at half-hour intervals by 45 on the twin peaks of their objective and 42 on Mount Harriet. If the attacks went through quickly, the units were to 'exploit forward', the paras to Wireless Ridge and the commandos to Tumbledown and Sapper Hill. Earlier in the week, the paras had nearly jumped the gun and had set out for Mount Longdon, encountering heavy artillery shellfire on the way. Julian Thompson arrived by helicopter to give his equivalent of Sir Colin Campbell's orders to the Argylls, 'the thin red line' at Balaclava: 'Steady the 93rd. Damn all that eagerness.' The brigadier told the paras to stop until the full brigade attack could be mounted.

Max and I asked if we could attend the briefing. Julian Thompson was friendly but quite adamant; no press could attend 'Orders' before any action at either brigade or battalion level. In the clear sunshine, Tom Seccombe offered us a slug of whisky, and asked if we had enough tabasco for our curry; he said he always kept a small bottle handy when he was out in

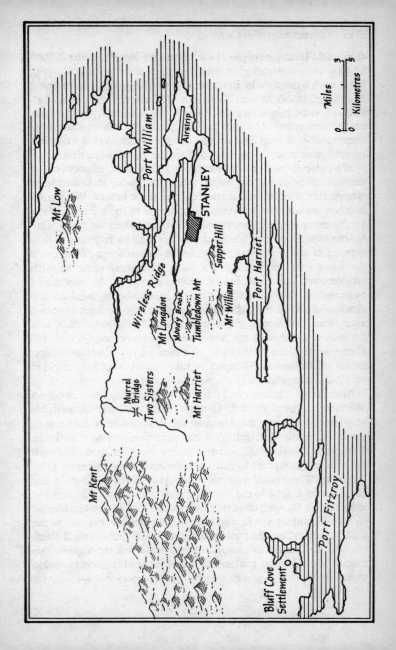

Mt Low

Port William

Airstrip

STANLEY

Wireless Ridge

Mt Longdon

Moody Brook

Sapper Hill

Tumbledown Mt

Mt William

Port Harriet

Murrel Bridge

Two Sisters

Mt Harriet

Mt Kent

Bluff Cove Settlement

Port Fitzroy

Miles

Kilometres

0 3 5

the field. To my surprise, I saw Major Tony Rice, the 2 Para Battery Commander. He said that 2 Para was now moving back to 3 Commando Brigade and would be in reserve for 3 Para's attack on Mount Longdon. He introduced me to Lt.-Col. David Chaundler, 'H' Jones's replacement, an impressively quiet man. The tact and skill with which he took over command of 2 Para was one of the most remarkable exercises of authority and diplomatic skill in the Falklands crisis.

We camped in a pass strewn with heavy slabs of rock on the western slope of Mount Kent, where 45 Commando had been stopped on their march from Teal the week before. We built a bivouac which had us sleeping at an angle of forty-five degrees. In the morning, the waterproof covers and the long grass were laden with frost and ice, and snow gave the hill-tops a thin coating of white powder. We gazed at the stillness of the scene for some minutes until a Sea King helicopter came in with ammunition and blew our kit across the valley. As Max and I approached the colonel's Orders Group, being held in the shadow of an outcrop of rock across the pass, we were gestured away and told not to come near until it was over. Max was furious and decided to have nothing more to do with 45 Commando if they could not give him a proper welcome, and he set off to find a helicopter to take him further up the ridge to 42 Commando HQ.

After the orders had been given, Lt.-Col. Andrew Whitehead, the C.O. of 45 Commando, introduced himself. He was cordial but distant. He said I was welcome to come with the commando, but, initially, he wanted me to stay with the Battalion Main HQ. Clearly there was still widespread suspicion of the press following the telephone incident at Teal. Andrew Whitehead was the quietest of the C.O.s in the Brigade, and very likely the toughest. He was an outstanding skier and in the exercises in Norway excelled in the biathlon, a twenty-kilometre skiing and shooting event. He was one of the best 'yompers' in the business. As with 'H' Jones and 2 Para, his whole manner of command was reflected throughout his unit, and there was a pleasant lack of school-boy braggadocio about it.

The convoy of tracked snow vehicles in the commando HQ set off to take a position on the forward slope of Mount Kent in the late morning. I was offered a ride in the colonel's vehicle along with two minor casualties from the units patrolling on previous nights. One of the marines said he had damaged eardrums from the discharge of a 66 mm rocket close to him. When a rocket is about to be fired, the operator is supposed to shout out 'Sixty-six' so that those near him can block their ears. His fellow marine did this the first time but the rocket failed to go off; when it happened the second time, he forgot to shout the warning. The other casualty had twisted his leg on a night patrol. As the vehicles turned to move up the main track to Stanley to reach the forward slope of the mountain, the engine faltered in our BV. The driver tried to clear the fuel pump, and we waited while he fetched some tools from the gun battery nearby.

Before us we could see the guns bedded into piles of peat turf on their gun-line. They were in wide open country, a valley more than a mile across. The guns, the stacks of ammunition boxes and the tents of the gunners were covered with green camouflage nets interlaced with grass and bracken from the mountains. Looking from paths above the gun positions, it was surprising how well they were concealed in that bare country. We could see one of the guns being upended and levered out of the line with poles; it could have been a scene from *War and Peace* at Austerlitz as the weapon was hauled back, first tail up, then muzzle up, by the gunners. 'We've had a bit of trouble with one of the guns. It's defective and has been firing short; they're trying to get a new one into the line to replace it,' one of them explained. Dropping shells short by a couple of hundred yards at such ranges could mean hitting your own rifle companies as they went into attack. The peat was a real hazard for the gunners and the mortarmen. Guns might have to be relined completely after as few as six shots as they dug into the soft earth. Mortars cracked their base-plates and buckled bipods as they fired with supercharges of explosive; mortarmen stood on the plates to keep them steady and some even knelt, knowing full well that it could mean broken ankles and legs.

While the waggon was being fixed, we decided to walk up
the valley towards Stanley to reach the HQ position before
dark. In front of us to our left was the bumpy spine leading up
to Mount Longdon. Over the rise directly in front were the
Two Sisters and round the flank of Mount Kent to the south
was Harriet. On the ridge leading to Longdon, a Chinook
helicopter was lowering supplies to 3 Para and as it ducked
below the crest we could see rising puffs of black smoke as the
Argentinian artillery started again. Further along the valley we
saw the burnt-out shells of two Argentinian helicopters, a
Chinook and a Huey Iroquois, which had been strafed by
Harrier attacks; we were told not to go near them as the area
might be mined. Then the shelling began, sporadic at first, the
rounds dropping several hundred yards before us and aimed at
the left-hand side of the valley to our direction of march. After
a few minutes it stopped. As we picked our way through a bog,
we heard the distinct single, low note of an incoming artillery
round. 'Get down,' yelled Captain Ian Ballantyne, who was in
charge of our party, and before he could finish the command I
was flat on my face in the mud. The shell burst fifty yards
behind us. Quickly we picked our way to the right-hand side of
the valley and two minutes later saw a round land at the exact
spot where we had flattened ourselves into the bog. At dusk we
pulled into an outcrop of rock with the HQ vehicles and
decided to stay there for the battle rather than expose the
waggons and their signals equipment to further shelling.

We cooked our supper as darkness came on and huddled in
the waggons waiting for the attacks to start. After midnight I
was told that 45's attack was likely to be delayed as the leading
company, 'X-Ray', had not reached the start-line. The plan
was for 'X' Company to move with heavy weapons' support
across the saddle from Mount Kent to assault the enemy
positions, thought to be held by a company, from the west
side. The other two companies, 'Y' and 'Z', were to try to
move round the Two Sisters, cut the enemy off from the rear
and move on to Tumbledown if the way was clear.

I saw nothing of the details of the battles for Stanley that I
did at Goose Green, but from the 45 Commando positions I

had a grandstand view of the fighting across the mountains in the night. I climbed to a small plateau above the vehicles tucked in by the rocks. It was frosty and in the dark the marine sentries moved like Red Indian ghost dancers. Because of the dark, all three battalion attacks were late that night. First to open up was 3 Para on Mount Longdon to our left. I could see tracer being pumped back from the crest into the British forces attacking, the paratroopers replying and the accompanying crash of mortar and artillery. Out to sea, the deep boom of the Naval guns began, and over the battle the Argentinians started firing bright yellow and white flares from their mortars.

The 3rd Battalion the Parachute Regiment were to take the heaviest casualties of any British battalion on the Falklands in battle. The fighting went on well into daylight. Twenty-three men were killed and forty-eight injured; six of the dead lost their lives in heavy shelling from the enemy 155 mm guns the following day. Colonel Hew Pike had thought there were two enemy companies at most on the ridge itself. It turned out later that the paras had faced a full company of the Argentinian 7th Infantry Regiment, which had been reinforced by a company of special forces and marines, with part of another company of infantry sent in to back them up during the fighting. The plan was for the paras' 'A' Company to move to a spur jutting out of the Mount Longdon spine, which had been codenamed 'Wing-Forward'. 'B' Company under Major Mike Argue was to take the main ridge, moving platoons from both sides of the spine in a silent night attack, which would 'go noisy' on contact with enemy, which would mean it could bring in covering mortar and artillery fire. 'C' Company was in reserve to move forward to Wireless Ridge if the enemy folded quickly.

Major Mike Argue's 'B' Company bore the brunt of the attack and sustained the most casualties. Two platoons of his troops had to cross the River Murrel to the south of Longdon in the dark, a difficult job in which the whole battalion had to use an aluminium ladder at one point. His attack 'went noisy' much earlier than expected, and the battalion was constantly under heavy barrage from enemy 120 heavy mortars, three howitzers further east along the valley near Moody Brook and two batteries of pack howitzers on Port Stanley racecourse to the west of the town. Besides this there was heavy fire from the machine-guns and grenades from the top of Mount Longdon itself.

On the north side of the ridge, 'A' Company was caught by machine-guns and accurate shooting by a string of snipers well concealed behind a long slab of rock, who were to keep up their harassment till dawn. 'A' Company could not dislodge them with machine-guns for fear of overshooting the target and hitting 'B' Company, attacking from the other side. As 'B' Company casualties increased, 'A' Company moved in to take the objectives along the top of Longdon as day broke. In daylight, the shelling from Port Stanley became heavier. Under the bombardment it became difficult to handle the prisoners and some Argentinians were reported to have been shooting British wounded as they lay on the ground. Both 3 Para and 42 Commando in the first phase of the battle, on the night of 11/12 June had trouble with Argentinians appearing to surrender and then continuing to fire once the British troops had exposed themselves to view. In the daylight on the following two days, 3 Para suffered the most intense artillery bombardment of any British forward unit in the campaign. By this time the Argentinians had brought forward their 155 mm guns, the heaviest calibre artillery piece on the Falklands, and in one morning's shelling 3 Para took nine casualties from one of these weapons alone.

As day came on, the reserve company 'C' Company was moved up to 'Wing-Forward'. The company commander, Martin Osborne, could see the Argentinians on the rocks of the next three features running east to Moody Brook and the inlets from Berkeley Sound. He was also facing the fire of an Argentinian recoilless artillery piece.

'I can see them all standing around like bunches of grapes,' he radioed back to the C.O., Hew Pike.

'Curb your natural enthusiasm. Dig in,' was the reply.

The 'H' hour for 45 Commando's attack was delayed some two hours to about three in the morning GMT because of the difficulty 'X-Ray' Company had crossing the scree from

Mount Kent, burdened with heavy weapons, Milan and Carl Gustav rockets. Colonel Andrew Whitehead had realised that the enemy was very well established round the two huge pinnacles of rock from which the Two Sisters get their name; there was also the likelihood that the area was mined. The natural cover afforded by the rock-falls should have made the positions well nigh impregnable to the kind of night attack the commandos were now preparing.

Over the radio we could hear Colonel Whitehead's voice speaking to his company commanders in turn. It was a remarkable performance, cool, never ruffled, always giving the impression that he and his men had plenty of time for what they had to do. It astonished even those officers who knew him well. The other remarkable feature about Colonel Whitehead's command that morning was that he managed to change his plan of attack as the battle was about to be joined and now deployed all three rifle companies to attack the two pinnacles of rock. He was also quite frank, in subsequent conversations about the battle, about the initial underestimation of the enemy's position. His unhurried voice guided each step by the fighting men. 'Good,' he would say, 'move there, do that, wait for a minute, pause, well done,' always encouraging and giving praise where necessary.

It was a hard-fought assault. From our position on Mount Kent, we could see the rifle companies inching up the slope, the tracer from the rifles and machine-guns licks of flame like tiny salamanders. The Argentinians poured fire down the hill and a machine-gun on the right-hand peak seemed to have a sweeping command of the British approach. We could see the artillery bursting in front of the advancing marines, asterisks of white flame as the shells burst against the rock. One of the six guns was firing consistently short, and it was dangerously close to the forward companies. At first I imagined it was the gun I had seen levered out of the line as we set out with the BV vehicles earlier in the previous afternoon, but then I realised it could not have been. That gun was on the right end of the line, and the one dropping short was at the left of the pattern of shells on the mountainside.

The artillery was supported by fire from a mortar line near the Murrel Bridge. By dawn, only one of the eight mortar tubes was still working, so intense had been their activity. The peaks of the Two Sisters were secured in daylight. Running down from one of them, there was a series of rock shelters, sangers, built with the durability of Stonehenge, from which the Argentinians had fired heavy machine-guns, bazookas and grenades from rifles. In the attack, the commandos had five men killed and about a dozen wounded. As the battle died down, they took about thirty prisoners.

42 Commando suffered the lightest casualties that night, with two killed, one of them during a reconnaissance patrol to establish the line of attack. Lt.-Col. Nick Vaux's commando had spent more time on Mount Kent than the other units in the assault. His plan of operation for taking the next feature east, Mount Harriet, had been long thought out, but in the end it turned on a brilliantly simple trick. The strength of the enemy seemed to consist of two companies of the Argentinian 4th Infantry Regiment, and they had been placed on the north and west sides of the mountain waiting for an attack to come up the track from Goose Green to Darwin. Colonel Vaux decided to move two of his companies, 'K' and 'L', much further east than the line of the track, through an area known to be mined, and to attack the ridge of Harriet much closer to Port Stanley than the enemy expected.

Two patrols, one led by Sergeant 'Jumper' Collins, established a route free of mines to a start-line facing the eastern tip of Mount Harriet. One of them ran into a patrol of Argentinians. Flares were fired and the Argentinians yelled at them, thinking they were Argentinian stragglers moving back to Stanley from the other battles. A company of Welsh Guards, who were in reserve for the attack, were to help secure the start-line, but they did not meet up with the commandos until two o'clock in the morning GMT, which meant that 'H' hour was delayed for at least an hour. As 'K' Company were forming up to launch their attack, Mike Norman's 'J' Company from further to the west started creating a diversion, firing machine-guns and hurling grenades. To everyone's consternation, the Argentinians put up flares and illuminating rounds from their mortars and Colonel Vaux thought that his trick had been discovered. Nothing happened. 'K' Company began the assault and were only spotted by the enemy when they were within 150 yards of the summit. After some fierce exchanges with the enemy machine-guns, 'K' Company had overrun the position held by the headquarters and command of the units on Mount Harriet and among the prisoners was the colonel of the 4th Infantry Regiment, who, contrary to reports circulating soon after the battle, had stayed with his men throughout the fighting.

'L' Company set off about an hour after 'K' Company and swung left along the ridge, rolling up heavily defended machine-gun and mortar positions. Milan and Carl Gustav 84 mm rockets were used for 'bunker busting' as the anti-tank missiles had been at Goose Green. The crash of the Milans and the 66 and 84 mm rockets was deafening and Captain Ian MacNeill in his report on the battle wrote, 'The demoralizing effect of even near misses must have been considerable; most members of "K" and "L" Companies closest to the explosions testified that they too speedily got their heads down, such was the impact of the missiles exploding.'

Kim Sabido, in a gesture of the most careless courage by any reporter with the Task Force, moved with one of the rifle companies. A man next to him was hit and had to be casevaced, and Kim said it was one of the most frightening experiences of his life to witness an intense small arms fire-fight at night at such close quarters.

By the morning, Lt.-Col. Nick Vaux had an unexpected problem, more than three hundred prisoners. He had hardly enough men both to supervise their movement back to POW cages at Teal and to hold the top of Mount Harriet in the daylight.

During the night, 42 Commando used four batteries of artillery at times in support, a 'full regimental shoot', as it is termed, possibly the heaviest concentration of British artillery fire in action since the Second World War. They also had the Naval bombardment from HMS *Yarmouth*. Other warships supported 3 Para and fired shells into Stanley airfield. One of them, the Country Class light cruiser/destroyer HMS *Glamorgan*, moved close to the shore and was hit by an Exocet missile fired from a shore installation on a bluff between Port Stanley and the airfield to the east. Max Hastings, standing by 42 Commando HQ on the south-west tip of Mount Kent, said he saw the missile 'move like a red-hot lance from the shore and hit the ship, the explosion and clouds of smoke clearly visible'. *Glamorgan* was built of steel and her hull was more durable than that of the Type 42 destroyers like the *Sheffield* and the *Coventry*, and she managed to sail away safely to be patched up off South Georgia. Twelve of her crew were killed.

As dawn approached, the command vehicles of 45 Commando were ordered to move to a position forward of Mount Kent and north of Two Sisters where the River Murrel is crossed by the track from Estancia to Stanley. The Murrel Bridge was a rickety wooden structure supported by concrete slabs and two girders. It was here that ammunition was to be brought to replenish the rifle companies and the casualties picked up by the helicopters to go back to Ajax Bay or Teal. Helicopters had been flying throughout the early hours of the morning ferrying the wounded back. Many of the pilots had no night-vision aids, which were scarce throughout the British forces. The commander of the Argentinians on Mount Harriet, the colonel of the 4th Infantry Regiment, congratulated the commandos for their tenacity and courage, and said that his men might have done better if they had the night-vision goggles that the British had. When the RSM told him that the marines had only their eyeballs as a vision aid, he refused to believe it. It was reported in the United States, too, that much of the British success in the night battles could be ascribed purely to their use of night-vision aids. The Argentinians believed that the British had far more helicopters than they, though it is now clear that this was not so.

We walked slowly down the track to the Murrel Bridge, looking for mines on either side of the ruts made by farm tractors. Ahead, artillery fire was becoming more intense as the Argentinian gunners were firing on the grid reference for the bridge. Once over the bridge, it became so hot that we pulled into the right under a long spur of rock and peat, where we were ordered to dig in as mortars and artillery crashed against the rocks ahead. RSM Pat Chapman arrived from the battleground and seemed to be doing five jobs at once, organising the ammunition dump out in the open where the shells were landing, calling up helicopters for casualties, supervising the provost party to handle the prisoners, shouting for the HQ group to keep their heads down and making sure rations were sent up. 'I'm bloody proud of those lads. They did bloody well. The C.O. was fantastic,' enthused Lieutenant Richard Passmore, the Intelligence Officer.

In the first hours of daylight we saw 2 Para march across the Murrel Bridge, clinking like a mule train. They stood by the track as the shells began churning up the peat and then moved off to the left to back up the 3 Para. 'I knew we were going through a minefield,' said David Cooper, 'but I didn't mind. Anything was better than that shelling.'

Above the rocks, the first dozen prisoners were brought down from the mountainside under the command of Colour-Sergeant Eades.

'By the centre, Mr Fox, here's a to-do,' he bawled at me in his best parade-ground voice, grinning from ear to ear. 'What are we going to do with them?'

'Never mind,' said Colonel Whitehead in my ear, 'they say he asks his wife for a cup of coffee by numbers, too.' The colonel had come to see his HQ, and explained that it was impossible to move on from the Two Sisters as the artillery between the peaks in the daylight had been so heavy and there was a danger of minefields on the forward slopes.

Sergeant Eades tried to make the prisoners do PT to keep warm. Some were whimpering. One said he was only sixteen. A second-lieutenant with a smashed lower leg said he could not walk. I hoisted him so that he could put his arm on my shoulder. He was about 6 foot 4 inches tall and felt almost one and a half times my weight. I asked him how badly he was hurt. '*Agua, agua,*' was all he could whimper in reply. We laid him on the ground and managed to get a helicopter to take him away; he seemed to be suffering from shock more than any physical wound.

In the afternoon I went up to look at the battlefield with Colonel Whitehead. He said the strength of the enemy positions was remarkable, great piles of rock from which they fired heavy machine-guns, bazookas and grenades, and there were stacks of projectiles for the bazookas still left. In the sangers there were thick stains of black where the marines' rockets had exploded. The marine commandos, organised into burial parties, were taking out the dead Argentinians and laying them out to be placed in a mass grave. Many of the dead were regular soldiers, the NCOs who had manned the machine-gun posts in the rocks. The first prisoners to come in were the regulars, too, as the conscripts had run first and run furthest. I looked down between the two pinnacles of the mountain to see a mass of peat, like a ploughed field, where the enemy had put down about a hundred artillery shells since the morning.

Colonel Whitehead said the attack would not be resumed till the following night, Sunday 13 June, as 5th Infantry Brigade needed time to prepare the assault on Mount Tumbledown, which lay between Two Sisters and Stanley. 2 Para would take Wireless Ridge, which led into Moody Brook. He said he was worried about his men not having their packs and sleeping-bags up on the rocks of Two Sisters, and ordered them to find blankets, food and sleeping-bags from the Argentinians' kit. 'Some of it was quite good, actually,' he remarked.

I picked my way slowly down to the rocks by the Murrel Bridge, a walk of about three-quarters of an hour, much longer than I expected. It was like a stroll over Exmoor, with springy moss and heather, squelching bog and rock. At one point I came across a box of American mines, with no sign of whether or not they had been scattered. In the distance I could see the ugly, spikey, black clouds of air-burst artillery shells exploding over the paratroopers on Mount Longdon. Two waves of Harriers came gliding up the valleys, bobbing through the gaps in the mountains on their way to bomb the airfield and the artillery park in Port Stanley.

'Hey, come and look at this,' shouted Richard Passmore, the Intelligence Officer, as I arrived near the bridge. He had a bundle of maps and notes which he said he had taken from a prisoner's briefcase. The prisoner was an artillery major. His maps had all the defensive fire zones marked for the Argentinian artillery and on one piece of greased paper he had the positions of all the major infantry units marked in black crayon. I tried hard to memorise their deployment. The positions of the 3rd, 4th, 6th and 7th Infantry Regiments to the west of Port Stanley were clearly indicated. The stronghold of the 5th Marines was Mount Tumbledown, the next piece of high ground to be attacked. The marines were one of the few units of entirely professional soldiers landed by the Argentinians on the Falklands. Another was the 25th Infantry Regiment, which was placed to the east of Stanley, guarding the airfield and the beaches against an amphibious assault moving into the capital from the south and east, which General Menendez expected till the last.

Richard Passmore and I built a 'basher' together for the night and prepared to cook an all-in-one curry-and-everything supper. I went down to the brook by the Murrel Bridge to wash the mess tins. The sheep dips were frozen over where the gun-lines were being set up. As I was washing, four of the light tanks came down the tracks and clattered over the bridge, followed later by the recovery vehicle known as the Sampson. It is much heavier than the tanks, and as it inched forward, the bridge began to creak. A soldier guided it forward; the bridge cracked, the slats fell down on one side, and the tractor turned over into the stream. 'Andy, Andy, for God's sake,' screamed one of the young soldiers with the Sampson, 'are you all right? Are you all right?' It was the only display of complete panic that I saw by a British soldier on the Falklands. An NCO told him to get a grip of himself and the driver, Andy, eventually crawled out of one of the hatches. I went to ask him if he was all right, and the crew shouted for me to get away as the vehicle was packed with fused ammunition. Two medical orderlies came down and tended the driver, who seemed only a little dazed.

That night I went to sleep with several layers of frost on the waterproof of the tent. A couple of hundred yards away, two gun-lines and a line of mortars boomed and cracked through the darkness. I never slept better in my time on the Falklands. In the morning, the Murrel river was frozen and we had to kick the ice before washing the mess tins. The hills around were a dull red, and I felt no urgency at all to do anything that day. It was particularly relaxing to be the only hack with a forward unit. My presence did not seem to bother most of 45 Commando too much, although there were exceptions. We were examining a heavy 50-calibre Browning machine-gun the breech of which a sergeant of the Heavy Weapons troop was trying to unblock.

'How will you be able to use it in another battle?' I asked innocently.

'Bloody civilians,' he replied. 'Why do we need bloody civilians?'

Despite my lack of urgency, the Adjutant, Mike Irwin, had ordered a helicopter to take me back to Brigade HQ to file reports on the battle so far. The HQ was in a series of heavily camouflaged netted tents against a bluff off the track from Estancia to Stanley, two to three miles west of Murrel Bridge. No sooner had I arrived than David Nicholls said I should return to 45 Commando. The 5th Brigade attack on Tumbledown would take place that night. 2 Para under the Commando Brigade would take Wireless Ridge. 45 Commando should be ready to move in to Sapper Hill, the last line of defence outside Stanley itself, and 3 Para would move through 2 Para to Moody Brook. We could watch the battles from the former Argentinian Observation Post on the edge of Two Sisters. I would take the ITN television crew with me and Charles Laurence would come back to rejoin 45 Commando.

There had been an Air Raid Warning Red since I arrived, but it was only sporadically observed. Machine-guns pointed lazily out of peat sangers and the sentries glanced casually at the sky. I went to the hacks' tent to get some post and started back to the helicopter landing-site, chatting idly to Charles

Laurence. I was reading a letter from my brother in which he was expressing general anxiety for my safety and well-being, which I thought rather overpitched, when there was a scream of jets. Someone shouted, 'Get down. Here they come.' Charlie and I threw ourselves behind some rock, which gave little cover. I clearly saw the markings on the underside of two olive-green Skyhawks. They seemed to swing into the side of the valley. Machine-guns opened up and there were flashes of flame from the guns, and two small bombs came gliding down with white parachutes dragging from their tails. Peat and flame erupted about fifty yards below us, and then the planes headed off down the valley across the broad plain by Estancia House. They seemed to climb casually above the settlement, pull round in a shallow curve and then sweep along the far side of the hill, their shadows like two swallows swooping for flies. Ahead, across the pass, they pulled up sharply and started a second run. There was a loud explosion as a Blowpipe missile was fired, to no effect. Again there came the sight of the lighter-painted underside of the aircraft, forty or fifty yards from our heads, and another eruption of peat and shrapnel as the bombs hit the earth.

'That was a bit bloody close,' said a figure emerging from one of the tents wearing only his vest and trousers, his face half covered with shaving soap. 'Bit bloody mean to come just then. I was having a good Sunday morning shave. I had to hide under the wheel of the nearest truck.' This was Captain Eames of the Air Corps, who had controlled the brigadier's helicopters through the land fighting and had been with 2 Para at Goose Green.

General Jeremy Moore could be seen striding between the tents wearing his helmet, an unusual sight, as he preferred his Afrika Korps-style peaked forage cap. Julian Thompson emerged from his tent, too, telling the pilots to move the helicopters parked in the valley. He thought they were too close to the tents and the Argentinian pilots had spotted the sun glinting off the perspex of their cockpits. 'We'll have to move Brigade HQ now,' added the brigadier. 'They know we're here now and they'll try to get us again.'

The flight of Skyhawks nearly killed the general, the brigadier and knocked out the headquarters of 3 Brigade at one blow. It is not clear whether they had found the tents by seeing the sun on the helicopters or whether they had located the target by surveillance of the radio signals coming from the area. It was later discovered that they had excellent radio-surveillance equipment, better than much of the equipment with the British forces, and ironically some of it was made by a United Kingdom firm. They also had very good low-level local radar of German manufacture.

The flight of Skyhawks had already bombed positions west of where 2 and 3 Para were lying up round Mount Longdon. They did not make a third attempt to attack Brigade HQ. After the second run, they climbed high over Teal, and one was shot down by Rapier. By now both Teal and Bluff Cove had the second-generation Rapier, 'Blind Fire', which was radar-controlled and could shoot at night and in cloudy weather.

That evening we set up a flimsy bivouac on the side of one of the pinnacles of rock on Two Sisters. For the early part of the night it snowed, sleeted and rained continuously. The outside and inside of the tent were dripping. At midnight, Lieutenant Andy Shore came to guide us round the forward slope of the peak, along a goat track to a niche in the rock which the Argentinians had used as their Observation Post. It gave a view from Longdon in the north to the lights of Port Stanley in the east and Tumbledown, William and Harriet in the south.

The battle that night was even harder to read in the dark than the assaults on Longdon, Two Sisters and Harriet two nights before. The attack on Wireless Ridge by 2 Para seemed to go remarkably quickly. The lights of Port Stanley, dull orange and a few brighter white ones, had been extinguished for half an hour, at about ten o'clock local time (for Port Stanley), one o'clock GMT. The 2 Para attack was planned to be noisy from the start. Artillery, mortar and ships at sea started pounding in the distance, sometimes all six guns of a battery discharging together. Tracer bounced along the peaks of Wireless Ridge itself. Illuminating shells burst to the north and to the south over Tumbledown. Out towards Berkeley Sound there was a bright-red glow of an explosion in the sky, which broke into three parts and flaming debris floated downwards; it appeared that an aircraft had been knocked down by a missile. The moon was filtered through clouds throwing a strange rainbow corona round it. Suddenly I could see machine-gun tracer firing across the water into Stanley Harbour. It appeared that 2 Para had taken their objective in little more than an hour.

It was not 2 Para firing across the water. I later found out that it was 'G' Squadron of the SAS, 'doing their own thing' as a paratrooper put it. The SAS men had been observing Port Stanley from high ground north of the town for some days, and now decided to mount their own infantry attack. 2 Para took till daylight to clear the enemy from the ridge.

Their plan was an attack in four phases with two batteries of artillery giving support. 'A' and 'B' Companies were to fire from the south onto the first line of hills making up Wireless Ridge, while 'D' Company was to hit the enemy positions along the spine of the ridge. The pattern was to be repeated on the second line of hills with Patrol Company, 'D' Company, eventually securing the last peak above Moody Brook. As Major John Crosland of 'B' Company put it, 'If Goose Green was the come-as-you-are party, Wireless Ridge was the classical infantry tactic of the night battalion attack, an almost formal affair.'

'It was a beautiful plan, of almost Germanic simplicity,' said Major Chris Keeble.

The operation went as planned from the first. 'D' Company began pushing the enemy back along the hillside, but was then pinned by heavy airburst shelling. The Argentinians had brought one of their 155 mm guns right into the town and placed it behind the school, making it difficult to detect and counter-bombard. 'A' and 'B' Companies attacking across the ridge succeeded in overrunning positions where they found field telephone and radios still switched on, indicating that headquarters positions had been taken with much the same tactic by which 42 Commando had stormed the headquarters of the units on Mount Harriet two nights before.

As Lt.-Col. Chaundler regrouped the three companies after taking their first objectives, the four tanks of Robin Innes-Ker's troop of the Blues and Royals began pouring machine-gun fire into enemy positions with surprising effect. They doubled the fire power of the Machine-gun Platoon. 'Bloody fools, though,' said one paratrooper. 'They stuck themselves above the skyline and just kept blasting away. They could be seen quite clearly and all hell was let loose when the enemy artillery started coming in and bursting round us.' Artillery fire killed all three of 2 Para's dead that night. Seventeen prisoners were taken, but the Argentinians were beginning to move off the hill in hundreds, as Phil Neame's 'D' Company pushed along the second spine of high ground, which is Wireless Ridge itself.

As day broke, the enemy mounted their first and only counter-attack from Moody Brook. A platoon of regular Argentinian paratroopers started charging up the hill, only to be broken by artillery thrashing down the Moody Brook Valley and fire from 2 Para above. 'They didn't stand a chance,' remarked David Chaundler.

Despite the collapse of the Argentinians on Wireless Ridge, well-controlled Argentinian artillery fire was still troubling the leading companies of 2 Para. The weather was too misty to strike against the enemy guns, but twice Scout helicopters fired their SS11 missiles at the guns firing from the other side of the valley by Moody Brook.

As he came forward to reorganise his battle plan just after the counter-attack by the Argentinians had failed, Colonel Chaundler looked down from the eastern promontory of Wireless Ridge. 'I saw the Argentinians pouring down the hill into Stanley. They were like hundreds and thousands of black ants, pouring back.' His battalion prepared to follow, but first Brigadier Julian Thompson came to size up the position and then gave 2 Para permission to move down the road into Stanley. With them was 'C' Company of 3 Para, which had acted as reserve for the Wireless Ridge operation. The artillery Forward Observation Officer with 'C' Company threw his arms round Major Osborne, shouting, 'Don't you realise it's all over, and we're still alive!'

To the south, the Second Battalion Scots Guards had what General Moore called 'a bloody hard grind' taking Tumbledown. From the position on Two Sisters, I could see tracer bouncing round the mountain, the woodpecker hammering of the machine-guns hardly pausing. Illuminating rounds went up from the enemy mortars. In my radio commentary on the battle I remarked, 'Two brilliant flares shoot into the sky and I can see the edge of the objective covered with snow.' Fire was bouncing in from three directions. 42 Commando on the edge of Mount Harriet were firing the Argentinians' heavy mortars and 50-calibre machine-guns they had captured two nights before. The machine-guns had a distinctive deep throb. 'It's good to see it going back at them,' remarked Lieutenant Shore.

The Scots Guards had the misfortune to be attacking the best regular Argentinian unit, the 5th Marines. They had been led to their start-line up a narrow path through a minefield. From Two Sisters we could see a heavy small arms engagement at the bottom of Tumbledown which lasted at least half an hour. Artillery behind us, up to three batteries at a time, stonked Tumbledown and Mount William, the objective to be taken later by the Gurkhas. Tumbledown in the flares and shellbursts looked like a giant macaroon with its covering of snow. The Guards had to fight through snow, sleet and fog, and one of their stretcher-bearers, Guardsman Williams, was to lose his way in the dark, to hide for more than a month, not realising that hostilities were over.

After six hours' fighting, the artillery lifted and the Guards stormed the top of the mountain with a bayonet charge. Artillery then concentrated on Mount William and the Gurkhas took it in daylight, without suffering the loss of a single man. The Scots Guards lost eight men killed, among them one of the most senior NCOs of the regiment, WO2 Daniel Wight. The Argentinian marines had not expected the Guards to take the line of attack they did, and could not believe that they would fight with such courage up the narrow track to take the mountain. It was when they saw the Gurkhas coming in behind the Guards, also on an unexpected line of attack, that the Argentinians broke and retreated to Sapper Hill and Stanley. A Gurkha officer reported them falling back 'in regimental strength'.

In the early hours of the morning I had seen a helicopter swing round the rear of Two Sisters and drive towards the battle. It was carrying General Jeremy Moore to his forward troops. It was in the spirit in which he had won his first MC in Malaya as a platoon commander, a time when he was being continuously restrained by his superiors 'for overdoing things'.

Once the Argentinian retreat looked like becoming a rout, Jeremy Moore took control. 'I told Julian Thompson to go forward to see what was happening,' he told me afterwards. 'At that moment I had to grab the radio and do it all myself. Harriers were due to drop laser-targeted cluster bombs on Sapper Hill. I was told they could not be recalled as they were less than ten minutes away from target. In fact we stopped them with under three minutes to go.'

Returning from Two Sisters to the Murrel Bridge, I knew nothing of this. We could hear the firing of small arms behind us as the Gurkhas closed with their objective. Reaching the rock stack by the Murrel Bridge, Richard Passmore said, 'No time for breakfast, we've got to move. Be ready in half an hour. Hot pursuit. They're falling back and perhaps we'll get them on Sapper Hill.'

We made a quick brew and some porridge. RSM Chapman supervised the loading of machine-guns and ammunition on the waggons. David Nicholls appeared from the mist and said: 'I'm coming with you.' The BV 'bandwaggons' revved their engines and lumbered forward. It started to snow again.

II. THE ROAD TO PORT STANLEY

'The white flag has gone up in Stanley,' shouted a marine radio operator from the back of one of the vehicles.

'Does that mean it's over?' we shouted back.

'Don't know, but I hope so.'

At the back of the column some marines started singing and shouting. One unfurled a Union Jack on a stick, the kind you buy on a beach to stick into sandcastles. He said he had brought it with him from the United Kingdom.

'All call signs to make best speed to objective,' came the next order from the radio. Then, 'No more opening fire.'

The snow came driving in from the sea and the vehicles lurched through the ruts in the track. The column stopped and there was a shout of 'Minefields Ahead.'

'Make safe all weapons,' came the final order from brigade and there was a cheer, as rifles were emptied and their springs eased. Now everyone knew it was over. At the head of the convoy we could see the assault engineers plodding quietly across the ground they said was mined. One placed two sticks on either side of the track, tied white tape to them and then lit a flare which gushed a cloud of purple smoke across the snow-covered ground. The vehicles began moving forward again.

The radio operator reported that the paratroopers were now moving up the road into Stanley and were halted at the race-course. The collapse had been sudden, and in the daylight retreat had become rout. What made the Argentinians break so dramatically that morning is not clear. They thought there were many more British troops than there were attacking them. The Argentinian infantry on the high ground, Wireless Ridge, Tumbledown, William and Sapper Hill, were being squeezed back into the town along wide-open ground. In the Moody Brook Valley the British artillery officers could see the Argentinians standing in the open like herds of startled cattle, while airburst shells from the guns crashed overhead spreading shrapnel in their ranks. The artillery Forward Observation Officers shouted down their radios, 'Check. Check. Check all firing.'

The artillery fire had been ferocious for two days and nights before with about twenty thousand rounds fired at the western side of the little port. In the bombardment, three settlers had been killed. They were three women who had gone to their houses at the edge of the town. Mistakenly, General Moore's staff had believed that the houses on the road leading to

Moody Brook Camp had been abandoned. For some days the Red Cross had tried to establish a secure zone round the church in the middle of the town, but this was never agreed.

Besides the effect of artillery and the Harrier strikes, it was the unexpected success of the paras on Wireless Ridge and Longdon, and the Scots Guards on Tumbledown that finally broke the enemy's will to hold the high ground guarding the port. It was the sheer tenacity of the Guards that amazed the Argentinian marine regulars. 'The Scots Guards had a bloody hard grind on Tumbledown,' said Jeremy Moore, 'but they were still ready to go, being well trained.' An Argentinian officer said it was the sight of the Gurkhas advancing on an unexpected line of attack on Mount William that convinced him that his position was hopeless.

In the early afternoon the 45 Commando convoy was ploughing through deeper mud as it approached Moody Brook. There was a heap of mangled metal across a field, like a huge scrap-merchant's yard. Lorries lurched on their sides, farm tractors and jeeps up to their axles in mud. This had been the main supply base for the Argentinian forces. On all sides the peat lay hurled in every direction as if a tribe of drunken giants had decided to have a ploughing contest.

Along the valley, smoke rose from fifty fires among the houses, and there was the sweet smell of burning peat. The town looked something like I had expected, but the scale was much smaller. It was little more than an outsize fishing village by Scottish standards. The grey, wintry sky, the columns of white and blue-grey smoke, the wrecked vehicles, the troops plodding down the road with their weapons on their shoulders, had the qualities of a painting by Paul Nash of one of the rear positions on the Western Front. It was a pattern of deep grey, blues and browns, and the black, black peat which caked our faces, hands, vehicles and our food.

Suddenly we were on metal road, for the first time in two and a half months. The vehicles roared off, leaving the column behind. David Nicholls and I clung on with arms and legs as the 'bandwaggon' bounced across shell pocks in the road. We were ordered to halt opposite Sapper Hill, where 45 were to dig in. The paras further ahead had been told to stay on the edge of the town while negotiations were under way. Max Hastings had left 2 Para to move into the centre alone. Two settlers saw him by the war memorial, a garish art nouveau construction, and embraced him. Max was the first man with the Falklands Land Force to walk into Stanley. He made some interviews with the settlers and then had the presence of mind to ask Brigadier Thompson for a helicopter to San Carlos and so managed to get the news through to London that the Argentinian resistance had collapsed and British paratroops had reached Port Stanley.

The vehicles churned up the slope to Sapper Hill across a field littered with field guns, mostly the Italian-built 105 mm pack howitzers. Some had muzzles pointing skyward, some into the ground, others had been thrown sideways and backwards into the earth by the British artillery bombardment. Shells and shell-cases lay scattered round the carefully constructed walls of peat turves of the shelters. As we hauled up over the bluff to where the commando was to bivouac for the night, I told David Nicholls we had to go into the town, and he could not insist on preventing journalists from moving in to talk to the settlers now. He understood this immediately and said, 'Do you mind if I come with you?'

We walked back through the artillery park. I counted more than thirty field guns and there must have been others buried in their turf bunkers. Across the road was a hangar made of corrugated iron with enormous red crosses plastered all over it by the Argentinians, though they appear to have used it as an ammunition and supply dump. The Beaver Seaplane which had been housed there previously had been thrown down on the beach like a discarded toy. Inside were the men of 42 Commando drying out their clothes. Among them, and seeming to be one of them with hardly a sign of rank or status, was the neat figure of Julian Thompson puffing casually on his pipe.

'Hello, Foxy,' he said. 'What are you up to now? Lurking again I suppose.' He told me he had to wait on the edge of the port with the rest of his brigade while the negotiations started.

He had come forward to the 2 Para position just after dawn. He found Lt.-Col. David Chaundler standing in the open donning his maroon beret. The brigadier took cover behind some rocks and hauled the colonel behind him. As they did so, the last salvo of Argentinian artillery shells in the entire Falklands campaign landed in front of the paratroopers' positions. It was then that David Chaundler again asked permission to march down the road to Stanley and it was granted.

Further up the road, men of 2 and 3 Para were organising billets for the night in the houses on the shore road, and by the war memorial we could see the white helmets of the Argentinian military police trying to marshall retreating troops.

In one of the modern bungalows with large picture windows now cracked and shattered from the artillery fire of the previous days, men of Major Pat Butler's 'D' Company of 3 Para were settling in. They were being welcomed by the owners Ian Stewart and his wife Hulda, who had just returned to inspect the damage to their home. Ian is the manager of the Cable and Wireless station, and his wife a teacher, two important figures in the community, particularly among those that stayed throughout the Argentinian occupation. Ian is a short, sprightly Scotsman, with a nervous speech delivery in which every sentence is punctuated with the word 'actually'. As they made jug after kettle after pot of tea and handed round biscuits and cake just baked that day, the Stewarts told me of their experience.

'When did you know it was over?' I asked.

'Probably about an hour ago,' replied Ian. 'Earlier we had gone up to the Secretariat to ask Commodore Blumer-Reeve what the state of play was because nobody seemed to know what was happening. He said there was a cease-fire in effect and that at four o'clock [19.00 hours GMT] there would be a meeting between British and Argentine forces, and then we would know what was going on.

'That was the first time that I had been out on the street today. There were some of them going along singing in English, "We're going home". It was pretty obvious they had packed in, mentally if not physically. I believe there was a lot of arms being chucked away and that sort of thing.'

'How have they treated you?'

'It's been a mental thing more than physical. Some people have been treated badly. There has been a tremendous amount of looting, actually, from day one, actually, when we were told about respect for property and persons; that's been about the biggest lie that there has been. Something like seventy or eighty houses have been completely gutted.'

'Many restrictions on your movements? There's a lot of barbed wire lying about, I notice.'

'Yes, there were quite a few restrictions. We weren't allowed on the beaches. We weren't allowed to go up past the Beaver Hangar, actually. Down towards the airport, that's been a no-go area. Till recently you could go to camp, but as soon as the British line started moving in they weren't very keen on anyone leaving town.

'The curfew was instituted a few weeks ago. It originally started at six o'clock in the evening until half-past six in the morning. Then it was tightened down, actually, and it became four o'clock in the afternoon until half-past eight in the morning.

'Most of the soldiers were a danger to themselves with their own weapons. They just didn't seem to know what they were doing. They were very badly treated by their own people; some were only sixteen or seventeen. It was obvious they were going round absolutely starving and it was nothing unusual for people round here to be asked all the time for food.'

'How did you survive the bombardment?'

'We decided to cut a hole in the sitting-room floor and hide down there. There were six of us in there on Saturday morning. But when the windows started blowing in and the shrapnel started arriving in the kitchen, we decided to call it a day and clear out.'

'What of the future?'

'I think there's tremendous prospects for this colony, always has been. We'll have to be safeguarded or we'll have to call it a day. Speaking personally, I'll stay.'

His wife had held classes for a dozen children in their house as the contract teachers had left by plane not long after the Argentinians arrived. Hulda Stewart said that the area where her nieces had once picnicked everywhere round the capital seemed to be mined. She summed up the experience of the dwindling number of islanders who had stuck out the occupation of Port Stanley: 'Today is like coming out of a long, long nightmare. It's marvellous. I just can't thank everybody enough.'

I walked up the shore road to the centre of the town and met a nurse, Marina Felton, and her boyfriend.

'How's it been?' I asked.

'Pretty noisy, but it's really nice now. I am really happy. It's got a bit rough with the shelling, but it hasn't been too bad.'

'A lot of the houses have been shot up,' said her boyfriend.

'Yes, they've held up old people at gunpoint to get food,' said Marina. 'I think we'll stay now; I think we owe it to the British forces to stay.'

Between the main public jetty and Post Office building in Port Stanley there is a long, low row of buildings with white fronts, similar to stonebuilt farmhouses in the west of England; indeed, they were designed by an architect who hailed from Devon and Somerset. Three of these buildings make up what has become one of the most celebrated hotels in the South Atlantic, the Upland Goose. Throughout the Argentinian occupation, the proprietors, Mr and Mrs Desmond King, had Argentinian military priests and special forces billeted on them. They were still there when I arrived on the evening of the 14th. Mrs King seemed to find the quiet courtesy of many of these professional officers easier to tolerate after the four days of bombardment than the raucous behaviour of the hacks who had now settled in the front bar. In the kitchen the family were preparing supper and listening to the BBC's special 'Calling the Falklands' programme. Alison King, Desmond King's daughter who helped run the hotel, and her boyfriend, Graham Bound, the editor of the *Penguin News*, the islands' weekly newspaper, told me something of what had happened in the last days of Argentinian rule in the capital.

'They didn't respect property from the word go,' said Graham, 'but some of the soldiers were quite well disciplined. They've been bewildered, and had no real direction from the officers.'

'The officers don't seem to have been with them; the officers were in the town while the soldiers were in the trenches without sleep and sometimes without food,' added Alison King. 'They looked pretty miserable on the whole, the young people. The older, more mature soldiers seemed to think they were going to win, but the younger ones just wanted to go home.'

One of the group in the Kings' kitchen said that he had seen some Argentinians mutiny in the town that afternoon: 'The officer told us to move on for our own safety, and the troops turned on their officers and started machine-gunning the houses. I know my father's house was hit.' Graham Bound told me that fourteen prominent citizens of Port Stanley, including the two doctors, Daniel and Hilary Haines, and their children had been shipped out to West Falkland where they were thought to be held at Fox Bay. Others in the group were members of the Falkland Island Committee and the local Falkland Defence Force. No news of them had been heard since they were removed by Major Patricio Dowling's military police. I said I would see if the matter could be raised before the cease-fire negotiations were concluded.

The talks were being conducted in a grey plaster building standing back from the shore road, the main administrative centre of the Falklands government, known as the Secretariat building. It was just after eleven o'clock local time, 20.00 hours GMT. I asked to see General Moore and was shown into a room with a long table which was filled with Marine, Army and Naval officers trying to look busy. At the table itself were two Argentinians whom I later identified as Carlos Blumer-Reeve and Captain Hussey. There was also a special forces colonel who had seen himself as the chief British negotiator. I asked to see the general again and was promptly asked to leave. Only two minutes after my arrival, General Menendez signed the surrender document. The British officers, Tom Seccombe leaning on the window-sill holding a telephone and Commodore Clapp with his elbows on the table, seemed to be rehearsing some tableau like the photographs of Montgomery's staff at Luneburg Heath.

Earlier that afternoon the negotiating team that had made the radio contact with Captain Hussey through Dr Alison Bleaney had re-established the link. Alison Bleaney played a vital role in ensuring Captain Hussey got through to General Moore's team and they flew in by Sea King helicopter from HMS *Fearless* shortly before four in the afternoon, local time. The talks had been difficult in two respects, the disarming of the thousands of Argentinian soldiers in Port Stanley and how they should be repatriated, and whether the troops on West Falkland should surrender at the same time as those on the east island. It was agreed that officers should keep side-arms and should be responsible for marching their own units out of the town over the next day or so to lay down their arms at the airfield, and they would bivouac there until transport could be arranged to ship them home. The surrender of West Falkland was taken formally by Lt.-Col. Malcolm Hunt at Fox Bay and Port Howard, though General Menendez did say he agreed to the surrender of all forces under his command on the Falklands when he signed the surrender document in Port Stanley that night.

After the signing was over, General Moore came into the room where I was waiting and said, 'You wanted to see me, Robert. What can I do for you? I have just this minute signed the surrender document.' He looked remarkably fresh considering he had spent half the night watching the Scots Guards and the Gurkhas advancing in the snow. I said we had better do an interview. There were only three hacks there, myself, Leslie Dowd of Reuters, and Pat Watts, the Falkland Islands' Broadcasting Officer. There was also a Navy lieutenant with a video camera from HMS *Fearless*.

The tape-recorder jammed the first time, and we started again. General Moore calculated he had 11,000 Argentinian prisoners in the Port Stanley area alone and the Argentinians would move out in the morning. 'Now, happily, the killing will stop,' he said, and then praised the training and skill of his own forces. 'They've had a jolly hard slog and are just as fit as ever. One might say the logistic achievement on top of the achievement in sheer fighting and guts is absolutely colossal. The way the Navy has kept the stuff coming, despite its losses, and the way the stuff has been got over this very difficult country has been a tremendous effort by all sorts of people like the helicopter pilots very bravely getting casualties and moving logistics through the day and night.'

'Somebody said to me last night that instead of being a four to six battalion attack, the assault on Stanley should have been by three divisions. Would you dare echo the Duke of Wellington and say that it had been a damn near-run thing?'

'Logistically, it was a damn close-run thing. Some of my guns this morning that started four hundred rounds a gun were down to twenty.'

Pat Watts asked the general if he would like to see some of the people in the town, and we climbed into Pat's old Marina, the general sitting in front hugging a bottle of whisky and Leslie and myself in the back. We stopped at the West Store, where 150 people had been sheltering from the shelling and bombing.

'Best blooming faces we've seen in ten weeks,' said an old lady.

'Lovely to see you.'

'I gather the buzz hasn't got around,' shouted Jeremy Moore. 'At nine o'clock your time General Menendez signed for me the surrender of all Argentine forces on both East and West Falkland. When the Navy comes in tomorrow, the Argentine Navy and Air Force won't attack them. So I think we're now in the happy position where we are going to have a bit of peace again.'

The hall burst into clapping, cheers and song. 'God save the Queen. Well done the British,' shouted the old people. This was the first they knew that the fighting was over. After a chorus of 'For he's a jolly good fellow', the Loyal Toast was proposed.

'The Queen,' said the islanders, drinking from plastic mugs and beer cans which glittered in the candle-light.

A boy of about twelve with the lilting speech of the true kelper spoke of the memories of that day: 'I've seen the helicopters, but didn't see the soldiers. I heard about the tanks coming down the Darwin road. The shelling was right around our house, a lot of them nearly hit the house.'

General Moore then decided to visit the hospital where Alison Bleaney was supervising the night work. In the long, low building children played, and Dr Alison nursed her baby at her breast. Her husband, Mike, who works for the Falkland Island Company, told me, 'I'm glad it's all over but I don't feel as elated as I thought I would. I'm very sad about the number of people who've died here. We're all very sad about the number of people who've had to die for this territorial thing. Generally they haven't been too bad to us, not depriving us of our food, but depriving us of our liberty. They've treated their own conscripts shamefully, and sometimes they haven't looked after their own wounded.' That evening we had found two dead Argentinians lying in the road covered with iron sheets, and left there with convoys of military police passing up and down the road by them.

Mike Bleaney explained the difficulty in which the Falkland Island Company had found itself faced with the invasion. 'They were very polite at first. But they took everything and then apologised later. We had strict instructions from Coalite, the parent company in England, no profiteering from the enemy, and we didn't.'

'You seem very depressed.'

'Me? I'm not depressed. I'm delighted to see you fellows here. I'm unhappy because the place I wanted to bring my children up in has been spoilt, spoilt by this invasion. The lifestyle I came down here to find is gone. It's gone forever. As my wife said, we'll never be able to walk on the beach again for fear of treading on a bloody mine.'

As we left the hospital, General Moore said he was going to find his quarters in Government House. Pat Watts invited us to stay with him. Shortly after we parted from the general's

company, we heard explosions along the waterfront. 'They've
set the ammunition on fire,' an islander shouted. 'There's
loads of ammo in there and fuel and gas in cylinders.' There
were no fire pumps available. Young Argentinian soldiers
stood round in the timber yard, now well alight; others
huddled in a long file up the main street past the Post Office.

'We've got to get them out,' another islander yelled. I asked
the officers to move the men because they were in danger. An
Argentinian asked me if I was a British officer, and I said,
'No.' I realised they had not seen any British soldiers yet.
They asked me if I was British, and I said, 'Yes.' Still the
Argentinians wouldn't move with the bullets crackling and
popping in the fires behind them. I was asked again if I was an
officer, and finally shouted, 'For the purposes of tonight, yes.
Move your men for their own safety, you bloody fools.' All
sense of discipline and respect between officers and men in this
group of Argentinians had broken down. I went into one of the
houses threatened by fire and found young Argentinian Air
Force officers turning in for the night. I told them they had
better get out. They took with them an odd collection of
objects, including notebooks and pens taken from the houses.
On the floor were brown boxes of rifle ammunition stamped
'Naval Party 8901', the marines Mike Norman had commanded in the battle on 2 April.

The fire burnt itself out and was smouldering in the
morning. Port Stanley was awash with rain and mud as the
Argentinians began trudging to the airfield. Later in the
morning we took a jeep ride the three miles to the airfield
where men of the Argentinian anti-aircraft units and the
infantry left to guard the beaches to the east of the capital were
now forming up. The sea was wild with booming rollers
roaring up the shoreline between the dunes. The prisoners
were huddled inside their clothes, soaked with rain and stiff
with mud. At the gate to the airfield they threw down helmets
and arms and then walked the mile and a half to the air
terminal, now an empty shell riddled with bullet scars. All the
other buildings were gutted, the turf ploughed up by the
Harrier bombs. Pucara, Aermacchi fighters and some of the

islanders' private planes were lined up along the runway, some still in working order, though they were to be sabotaged later. The runway itself was unmarked down one side, and there were signs of only one hit by the Vulcan bomber from Ascension, and the crater had been carefully filled. We knew that Argentinian pilots had been flying their own Hercules C 130 transports until the very last night of hostilities, coming in with no navigation lights. Among the last passengers out were signallers carrying special codes, and a television crew led by Buenos Aires's most famous war reporter, by the reporter's own account. He had stayed at the Upland Goose, and according to Desmond King did not seem too keen to see the Argentinian troops out in the trenches. Round the airfield the prisoners were beginning to make shelters of blankets and thin waterproof capes. The wind was bitter and that night gales blowing from the Antarctic had a chill factor of $-18°C$.

Back in town I had the last piece of censored copy I wrote from the Falklands passed by David Nicholls. 'Great,' he said, 'You must get back to the ships to transmit this. You've been out of touch with them for quite a time.'

Wandering towards the landing-site on the soccer field I saw Robin Innes-Ker standing by his tank. 'I'm supposed to be a road block,' he said, 'stopping troops moving into the town. But how the hell I'm meant to do it I don't know.'

'How did you get on in the battle?'

'Oh, that was terrific. We fired away all our ammunition, twice over. It really worked.'

The helicopter took me back to the *Canberra* where I filed my report on the surrender, the last engagements in the hills and the interviews with the settlers.

'Fine,' said my editor, 'we knew you'd get there in the end. We heard you were in Stanley interviewing people. You've been away quite a time. You gave us a bit of a fright.'

I realised I had not spoken to London for six days, and hardly noticed the passage of time in the mountains, where in the quieter moments I had felt thoroughly at home.

9. Prisoners

'Our brave troops have been outnumbered by a technically superior enemy,' stated the propaganda radio in English from Buenos Aires on the morning of Tuesday 15 June. 'Our troops have continued a fierce struggle fighting in the suburbs of Puerto Argentino [Port Stanley].' Later the radio announced that a 'cease-fire' had been declared. The announcement was made over twelve hours after General Menendez had surrendered all his forces on the Falklands.

It was now the overwhelming number of prisoners that was beginning to worry the staff of Rear Admiral Woodward at sea and Major-General Jeremy Moore, who now became the British Military Governor of the Falklands. 'If we are not allowed to get the prisoners home quickly, we could face something of the proportion of a natural disaster,' said Commodore Clapp, who was now preparing to move his headquarters to Port Stanley, aboard HMS *Fearless*. He had been to see the prisoners taken by 40 Commando at Fox Bay and Port Howard on West Falkland. Some at Port Howard, he said, had been starving. Settlers reported them scooping up feed put out for chickens and bones left for the dogs. Some units would have well-fed platoons and some in the same company who were almost starving. The weather conditions on the airfield at Stanley were bleak. Exposed at the best of times, it was now getting the force of gales from the Antarctic, some gusting up to eighty miles an hour, bringing with them chill factors of nearly twenty below zero.

There were now some four thousand prisoners on the airfield. Others were being rounded up in fatigue parties to clear the mess in the town. Some prisoners had wrecked the school, burnt two houses and spread the floors of the main post office and hall with excreta. 2 Para's RSM commandeered two

pressure-hoses and put a party of POWs to work for a morning
to clear the mess from the floors. The presence of about four
thousand British troops with not too much to do was beginning to be felt, too. They took over billets in the empty houses
and helped themselves to the Argentinian food in the row of
cargo containers lining the shore road to the west. 42
Commando at Moody Brook was still short of rations from
their rear echelon, and they testify to the excellence of much of
the Argentinian rations, with tinned meat, spaghetti and other
pasta and canned fruit. The men of 42 had to contend with a
plague of rats in their quarters, which were some of the
buildings bombarded by the Argentinians when they first
invaded on 2 April. There was also a degree of 'proffing',
stealing, or 'liberating' equipment and food from empty
houses by both armies. The Falklands vet, Stephen Whiteley,
whose wife was killed by an artillery shell in the last days of the
battle, had his collection of gold coins stolen while he was
being treated in hospital.

On the airfield, some of the regular Argentinian units had
organised themselves efficiently. The anti-aircraft unit of the
5th Marines had a field kitchen, cooking ravioli and spaghetti
throughout the day, and brewing the most common beverage
for the soldiers, maté. By the field kitchen I met a Lieutenant
Gonzalez, who spoke good English. I asked him if he was
looking forward to going home, and he replied by asking when
that would be. I said I did not know but it depended when the
authorities in Buenos Aires gave permission for the *Canberra*
and *Norland* to land prisoners at an Argentinian port.

'But we are not prisoners,' he countered, 'there has been no
surrender.'

'There has. It was signed by General Menendez on Monday
night.'

'Does that really mean we are prisoners?' he seemed
completely surprised by the notion. No one had told him what
exactly had happened and that he and his unit were now
protected by the Geneva Convention's rules about prisoners of
war. He asked me to explain this to his superior, a lieutenant-
colonel.

'It seems incredible. But I think I believe you. I think the
BBC always tries to tell the truth. We've heard that Mrs
Thatcher doesn't always like the BBC, at least not over what
they've said about the Malvinas,' said Gonzalez. He said his
country's forces had been overwhelmed by superior numbers.

'How many British troops do you think came against you in
the last battles on the mountains?' I asked him.

'About fifteen thousand.'

'You'd be about right if you thought of a third of that
number.' The lieutenant thought that about ten British ships
had been sunk, which was not such a wild exaggeration. Many
of his fellow officers were truly convinced that HMS *Invincible*
had been sunk. Captain Rod Bell took twenty minutes to
assure a colonel he was escorting to the negotiations the
previous day that the carrier had not been destroyed. The
colonel was desolate when he realised the marine was telling
the truth: 'Why did they lie to us all the time? Why?'

There is evidence that the Argentinians ran a sophisticated
propaganda campaign among the troops on the islands.
Broadcasts were organised by a group of Italians who said they
were military priests. I saw the first edition of a Spanish-
language newspaper printed for the troops on the Malvinas. It
recounted the events of the first week in May. It was fairly
accurate, though it omitted the death toll from the *General
Belgrano*, and concluded with a piece of bombastic doggerel
about 'the honour and blood of our young men being tested in
battle. We will never yield the Malvinas, and Argentina will
rule from where the Condor flies in the Mountains, across the
Southern Seas.'

As I was waiting to catch a helicopter to return to the
Canberra, by now anchored in Berkeley Sound waiting to
embark prisoners, I spoke to another Argentinian officer who
was in a group of NCOs and officers formed up by the football
pitch, waiting to be moved to the ships. He, too, seemed to
have an extraordinary idea of the number of British soldiers in
the field.

'I think we killed many British soldiers out there,' he said.

'How many?'

'About six zero, zero, zero,' he said. His English was not as good as that of Gonzalez on the airfield. He went on to recount how many Argentinians there had been fighting, how many killed, how many injured. But by the time he finished, the 'zero, zero, zero' game had quite baffled me.

Two days after the surrender the rain lifted, and the sun came out. The men of 2 Para came marching up the road to the Anglican church in the little port, which has the rather grandiose title of the 'Cathedral'. 'I thought they all wanted to reflect a little on what they've been through,' said David Cooper, 'before they go home and forget all about it.'

The little church was packed with paratroopers standing at the door. As they marched to the gate, islanders waved and cheered, others stood mute, tears pouring down their faces, the signs of deep shock and sheer relief. Inside, David Cooper prepared to give the most surprising sermon most of us had ever heard, part stand-up comedy routine and part simple straight-talk. It was the second part of the sermon begun on the *Norland* on the night of 20 May when he told us all we were about to go out and face death.

After praising 2 Para, which brought the roof down with cheers and applause, David Cooper reminded the congregation of the night on the *Norland* and continued:

Now what I would say to you now, before the war stories start, before we get back to the 'shot' [Aldershot] and start punching the lights out of the crap-hats [any unit not wearing red berets], what I would like you to remember is what you felt when you thought you were going to die and what was important to you then. It may have been your wife, it may have been your girlfriend, it may have been your dog [laughter, as the Cooper dogs are famous on the Bisley ranges] – it may even have been your life itself.

But remember, when the chips are down, that's what's important. And when life becomes easy again, and these realities become obscured, just remember that when you did have your back against the wall, spiritually, mentally, when things did cause you to think very, very hard, about what really mattered, remember how much God figured in that. And don't forget. Remember who was important to you. And when you get home and you've been back home four or five weeks, and you're beginning to take your wife, or your girlfriend or your dog [laughter] for granted, well just remember – 'think on', as they say in the part of the world that Colour Gerrard and I come from – what is important and try to model and mould your life on that because if that is what's seen you through to this, then it won't do you any harm in seeing you through the rest of your life.

I'm not going to beat my gums much more. I just want to say to all of you personally thanks for all your support. It's meant a lot to me.

Outside the church, the cars and jeeps were beginning to drive on the left for the first time in two months. Marines and paratroopers had taken over the smart Mercedes jeeps left behind, and the SAS were particularly impressed by the French Panhard armoured cars, though how these wheeled vehicles were expected to navigate the Falkland bogs is hard to imagine.

In his office in the Secretariat building, Julian Thompson seemed to be a commander with little to do. The movement of men and ships was now the responsibility of the Harbour Master and Commodore Clapp's men. Jeremy Moore was now the Governor, and the men of 3 Commando Brigade were now being shipped to *Sir Bedivere*, one of the LSLs tied up at the main wharf, for a shower and a night's rest. Julian Thompson asked me and Patrick Bishop of the *Observer* for a cup of tea and some lugubrious-looking fruit cake from the West Stores. We talked about his first reflections on the campaign.

He said the most surprising aspect was the low loss of life. He thought the quality of the enemy Air Force, particularly that of their pilots, had been high. They had been technically ingenious, with local radar surveillance, and the construction of land-launched Exocet missiles which we had seen on flatbed lorries and a concrete launching pad on the road to the airfield.

They had excellent night-vision goggles, many of which had been smashed by retreating troops. There were simple lessons for British ground forces from this in the future, he said, such as the need for better shoulder-launched missiles for infantry like the American 'Stinger' used by the SAS. There was a need for better radio-interception equipment, and secure radio nets. Few of the British artillery radio nets were ever secure; the crew of *Canberra* say that they followed the progress of the last land battles by listening to the Battery Commanders and Forward Observation officers calling to the gun-lines.

Brigadier Thompson said the success of the attack on the capital was due to the simultaneous attack by two brigades at night, covered by accurate artillery fire. 'They realised they were malleted then,' he said tersely. The Rapier missiles had done their work at San Carlos and had allowed the time for the logistical build-up. Logistics appears to have been one of the biggest single weaknesses in General Menendez's forces; there was never enough support for the number of troops he had on the island, which must have been somewhere in the region of 12,000, though I never saw a final assessment of how many Argentinian ground troops were on the islands at any one time.

'The psychological moment was Darwin and Goose Green,' continued Julian Thompson. 'We engaged their forces on the ground and beat them, and showed the Pucara could be dealt with by infantry from the ground. But above all it was our ability to fight at night and move quickly over the ground on our feet that they had not bargained for. Take 42 Commando on Mount Kent and Mount Challenger. They could fight at night and keep up aggressive patrolling in the day. But then the whole thing would have been different again if we had a fleet carrier with us.'

By the end of the week, *Canberra* was given permission to disembark 4,000 prisoners at Puerto Madryn in Chubut Province of Argentina. I booked my passage with Captain Burne and Captain Scott-Masson, and was surprised that only one other journalist, Leslie Dowd of Reuters, and Tom Smith, the *Daily Express* photographer, wanted to see Argentina. The others wanted to wait for Prince Andrew to come ashore to phone home from the RFA *Sir Bedivere*.

Before sailing, I took a helicopter from *Canberra* at anchor in the outer harbour to HMS *Fearless* and to the shore to collect kit and batteries. I left *Canberra* at breakfast time to arrive ten minutes later on HMS *Fearless* in time for lunch. *Canberra* was working to local time, which was three hours behind GMT, or Zulu, still the rule with the Navy. It was possible to take a quarter of an hour helicopter ride round Stanley harbour and suffer from jet-lag.

The prisoners aboard the *Canberra* were guarded by Major Martin Osborne's 'C' Company of 3 Para, and the Prince of Wales Company of the Welsh Guards commanded by Major Guy Sale. The Crow's Nest Bar stewards, Geoffrey and Taffy, tried to give us a semblance of *Canberra* life before the landings at San Carlos by opening a bar in the Card Room on the games deck. 'Ooh, what a smelly lot,' Geoffrey was over-heard to remark as the prisoners came aboard. 'Not like my young men at all.'

Geoffrey was right; everywhere the prisoners went was pervaded by the smell of peat, cheap Argentinian tobacco and maté. It was a quite distinctive aroma; one whiff of it conjures up the whole Falklands episode in an instant.

The Guards and the paras set to organising a rota for showers and laundry; and they managed to give each man two showers on the duty and wash his kit once. Relations between prisoners and guards were remarkably cordial, and were helped by the services of the Anglo-Argentinians as inter-preters. On the huge paper rubbish sacks, the paras scrawled: 'Putto el rubbisho in el sacko, por favor. Gracias.' The prisoners admitted frankly that they liked the respect they were shown as individuals by the British officers, and when they left, little notes were found all over the ship thanking the paras and Guards, written in broken English and often on the back of messages the Argentinians themselves had received in the field from their families at home.

Interpreting the Geneva Convention was something of an ad hoc affair; the commander of the prisoners' guard was Lt.-Col.

Andy Keeling, a Royal Marine who had been hoisted out of a course at the Defence College, Latimer, to join the Task Force. A major from the Army's legal branch had joined us and he spewed out the relevant chapter and verse of the Convention like a computer.

The prisoners' conditions were checked by a member of the Red Cross, a charming Swiss called Hugo Berchtold. He was a quiet man with a sly sense of humour. He told Captain Burne that when he had left Switzerland to join the *Uganda*, he had imagined he would get ashore at San Carlos, find a hotel room there and be able to drive round the islands. He is now a specialist in African affairs but had spent several years in Argentina, experience which yielded an unexpected bonus in handling Argentinian complaints.

The most senior prisoner aboard was a Major Carlos E. Cariso Salvadores. Hugo suddenly realised they had met before. Three years earlier, the Red Cross tried to get the Argentinian military authorities to acknowledge the rights of the Geneva Convention in the military camps for political detainees. He had visited a particularly harsh camp outside Buenos Aires a year later to inspect conditions there. The commandant was Major Cariso, who by Berchtold's account showed no interest whatsoever in the rights of the Geneva Convention as far as his prisoners were concerned.

In the evening we went to the sick bay where there were about twenty young Argentinians lying on mattresses, some the wounded from the first engagements at Fanning Head on 21 May. The P and O crew who had looked after them from that day, and possibly saved the lives of one or two of them, were preparing to cook them a farewell supper of steak au poivre. It was a strangely silent meal, and most of the people in the room did not want to think too much about the morrow. The steaks were cooked by Frank and Anna Taylor and Franco Tamburini, who had attended the young prisoners from the first.

'We're really worried about one or two of them,' said Major Robert Ward, a kindly Rupert Bear of a figure who had been the *Canberra*'s staff officer throughout the campaign, a job he discharged with an efficiency carefully concealed by his bon-homie. 'The one we call Stumpy – he's got terrible frostbite, and he lost a leg – is really worrying. We don't think he'll last the journey if they have to go miles by road. And there are one or two others as bad.'

Later that evening we met up in the Card Room Bar, which notwithstanding Geoffrey and Taffy's efforts was a far draughtier place than the Crow's Nest despite the scaffolding pergola and creaking timbers holding up the forward flight deck there. In our company was one of Admiral Woodward's staff officers, Lieutenant-Commander Bill O'Shaughnessy, a fluent Spanish speaker. He expressed the irritation of many of the Navy men at what they considered to be the slowness of General Moore's land campaign. He attacked the press with some bitterness, too, and when he vented his spleen on the way the *Canberra* was run, he was politely put right by the ship's accountant Helen Hawkett. His irritation was understandable. The difficulties of the carrier group at sea, probably the most vulnerable part of the Task Force, were not appreciated deeply by most of the troops ashore.

The company of *Canberra* had become quite a united group by this time. In the morning Captain Scott-Masson gave Leslie Dowd and myself an impromptu press conference in which he expressed his relief that his ship had survived the campaign so well. He paid tribute to the regular P and O crew aboard and the contract crewmen embarked for the deployment, par-ticularly those who had served as auxiliary nursing staff in the sick bays. The ship had been on her longest voyage without stopping, over 30,000 miles, tying up twice only, at Freetown for fuel and now at Puerto Madryn in Argentina. Maurice Rudderham, the Purser, and Nigel Horn, Deputy Purser, and Helen Hawkett compiled for me one of those lists of statistics in which aficionados of the *Guinness Book of Records* delight. Maurice has calculated that 646,847 meals were served aboard during the deployment of 94 days, including 27,848 for prisoners of war. Eleven tons of eggs, 65 tons of meat, 11 of cold meat, 460,000 cans or pints of beer were consumed and 38,750 half-gallon sachets of tea or equivalent were used. Statistics for tomato sauce and brown sauce are not available because supply could never meet demand.

Although the figures were never published, the cost of taking *Canberra* up from service must have been in the region of £100,000 per day.

The sea was a flat calm, on a beautiful, clean, winter's morning, when the *Canberra* sighted the Patagonian coast. Albatrosses and gulls had announced previously that land was near. The prisoners were exercising on the promenade deck, walking slowly and gazing over the rails. There had been a little trouble among the prisoners the night before when they were told that Leopoldo Galtieri had fallen from power. There were cheers and catcalls and then fights broke out with the hardline supporters of the old regime, but these soon died down.

Puerto Madryn is an aluminium-smelting town on a bay called the Guelfo Nuevo. As the ship approached, we could see the entrance to the bay. A destroyer approached at speed on the *Canberra*'s port bow. '*Canberra, Canberra,* do you receive me? This is the destroyer Delta 2. I am here to give you guidance and support. Proceed directly to Puerto Madryn at speed of your convenience,' said a fluent American voice over the tannoy.

'Delta 2, this is *Canberra.* We will comply and inform you of alterations of course and speed.'

The destroyer was the *Santissima Trinidad,* one of the two British-designed Type 42s, and the year before Lieutenant Commander O'Shaughnessy had served aboard her as a Liaison Officer. 'She looks in terrible shape,' he remarked, watching from the bridge, 'no wonder their Navy didn't come out to try their luck after the sinking of the *Belgrano.*'

Argentinian officers serving aboard their two British-designed destroyers, the *Hercules* and *Trinidad,* had been trained at Portland. There had been quite a number of contacts between the Navies and Armies of the two countries, and Bill O'Shaughnessy had spent eight months with the Argentinian Navy in 1981. At Goose Green the paras had gathered film from Argentinian prisoners' cameras and looking at the prints back in Aldershot three months later, a sergeant was examining some shots of the different units that had been garrisoning Goose Green. 'I know those two,' he said, pointing at two soldiers facing the camera, 'they were in the recruits' platoon at the depot [Aldershot] several years ago.'

The voyage to Puerto Madryn was a home-coming for one of the prisoners, Milton Rhys, whose family ran the annual eisteddfod at Trelew up the Chubut Valley from Madryn itself. He was a twenty-year-old kindergarten teacher, waiting eventually to go to the University of Wales, Cardiff, to study Welsh Language and Chant, when he was recalled for military service to serve on General Menendez's staff as a translator. 'My ancestors came here in 1865 with the first two hundred Welsh colonists in the little ship called the *Mimosa*. They came here to Puerto Madryn, now full of aluminium factories. It is now a sanctuary for sea animals, for sea lions, sea elephants and the Wright Whale.

'At Trelew we have two eisteddfods, the youth events and the bigger eisteddfod. We receive visits not only from Wales but from choirs from all over South America. In the last years cultural and study exchanges have increased between Wales and the Colony. This is getting stronger and more of the Welsh children are going back to study in Wales.'

'How did you come to the Falklands?' I asked him.

'I had already done my year's military service. But they were looking for translators to work over there.'

'Did you stay in the town of Stanley? Did you manage to get out into the field?'

'I stayed as a translator with General Menendez's staff in town. I went once to Bluff Cove and Fitzroy to buy food, to buy sheep. I also helped sorting out problems in the hospital, translating for them there.'

'What happened when the British came in?'

'It was quite surprising. It was over in a day and a half. We didn't expect a fight in the town. We got quite scared, ran a bit until everything settled down. Government House is quite near Moody Brook, on the edge of town. Some mortar bombs landed quite near. A piece of shrapnel hit me on the shoulder; it was just a small piece.'

'What were you told was happening?'

'The officers took their radios to another part of town. The translators were told to go out towards the airport, so we don't know what happened at the end. We only know that two hours after the shelling stopped, we were told there was a cease-fire. Our weapons were down, as we were told British soldiers were coming in by Moody Brook and we were not to fire.'

'As a Welshman who is a citizen of Argentina, how do you reflect on this experience?' I asked him finally.

'I have a strong religious belief. I don't care what nations are in conflict, Britain and Argentina, and Iran and Iraq, Israel. Whatever nations are in conflict, I think war is out of line. I think there must be a better way than throwing bullets at each other.'

I also met a nineteen-year-old conscript from the 7th Infantry Regiment whose name is as English as Milton Rhys's is Welsh. He did not want me to use his name for fear of repercussions on his family. But he did want to tell me of his experiences, and those of his friends in the battles on Mount Longdon.

'I was called up just after my schooling in Buenos Aires. I have done service now for thirteen months, but only had four weeks' basic training and had no contact with guns apart from that. We had a week to prepare to move and we flew into Porto Argentino from Rio Gallegos. We had to walk to our position on Mount Longdon. We stayed there for about two months. We were cold but that wasn't the major problem. We were more or less well fed. It could have been better but we managed to survive. We did have hot food. We had maté in the morning, at midday hot food, and at night, soup. We didn't have bread or biscuits and we drank water from the earth; we didn't have our own water. I was in a mortar section. The first time I was sent to use a mortar, I had no idea what it was about. We weren't properly prepared.'

'What happened when the fighting started round Mount Longdon?'

'I could see the tracer ammunition, and I heard English soldiers shouting in the dark and I was very afraid. We spent all the night listening to the battle. One section of my company was sent to reinforce the other company of the same regiment that was fighting. Forty-six men went and the next morning only twenty-one came back. They told us all about it. It was terrible.

'We retreated to Port Stanley. We were told to get back into a shed. We had headed to the airport but we turned back and spent the night in the sheds as prisoners. Sincerely, I was relieved; I realised the British were superior and if we hadn't surrendered it would have been terrible because a lot of people would have been killed.'

'How have conditions been on the *Canberra*?'

'I think it would be correct to tell you, in the name of the Argentine company here, we really didn't expect this kind of treatment. It's really excellent; everybody thinks the same. The sick are being looked after. We are having showers. We are eating properly. I think the British are very well organised in every aspect. No, I'm not surprised. They've shown themselves to have been great fighters, and they're great people in treating their prisoners of war. I don't know if it is because of the Geneva Convention or what. It's incredible.'

The pilot came aboard as the *Canberra* headed towards the brown concrete jetty. On some bollards and ledges half-way up the wharf a family of eight baby seals basked in the sunshine. On the quay stood a hundred sailors, ambulancemen and nurses, junior Air Force, Naval and military officers and men in the light-brown uniforms of the Coastguard Service. A line of trucks and coaches stretched back along the pier to the main road. There was only one photographer, who showed little inclination to use the cameras round his neck; innocently I thought he must have been from the official press. On reflection I think he was official all right, but from the Interior Ministry. A man with a long, sad Frankie Howerd face stood in a camel-hair coat clutching a bundle of files, one containing questionnaires and lists of the main clauses of the Geneva Treaty. With him were six or seven men and women from the International Red Cross.

First down the aluminium gangway was Major Cariso. He saluted the representative of the Staff in Buenos Aires, a man with silver hair and sunglasses, wearing olive-green fatigues and a peaked forage cap, Brigadier Garai. They shook hands. Then the prisoners started clattering down the two gangways in groups of a hundred. There were some handshakes and salutes. The atmosphere was frosty. There was almost no sign of emotion until a ripple of polite clapping for the young officers of the Special Forces in their soft-green velvet berets tugged forward in a raffish way. One older officer on the quay embraced his son with the tears pouring down his face. NCOs and officers were picked out of the lines and cross-examined by men with clipboards. The official in the camel-hair coat looked grimmer; he turned out to be the representative of the Foreign Ministry preoccupied with the Geneva Convention. The brigadier turned away and went into a building. It appeared that it was the first time that the officers of the reception committee had begun to comprehend the scale of the Argentinian defeat on the Falklands and they were numbed by what they were now seeing.

Some of the conscripts had been ordered to bring the officers' kit bags off the ship, and as they reached the buildings by the customs' shed, and thought they were out of sight of their superiors, they kicked the bags gleefully onto the ground, booting them to the water's edge on the other side of the pier before running, laughing and jumping, to the lorries.

Down one of the gangways the injured were beginning to be moved. Some could hobble on crutches. Others were lifted on stretchers. On the quay, the psychiatrist, Lieutenant-Commander Morgan O'Connell, supervised the transfer of the stretchers. The ambulance teams came forward and quietly and swiftly took the injured men away. One had lost an eye, another a leg and an arm. Most were suffering cruelly from frostbite and their toes and feet were thick lumps of black skin. Captain Burne shook hands with those on the stretchers that passed him. Frank and Anna Taylor and Franco Tamburini had persuaded all the medical staff to sign P and O *Canberra* menu cards for the worst injured, in memory of their supper the night before.

'Good luck. Good luck. Good luck, Miguel,' shouted Anna. 'Give us a wave before you go.'

'God, I hope he's going to be all right. He won't if it's more than twenty miles in that Army truck,' said Major Bob Ward.

Some were so badly injured that they had to be eased through one of the galley ports onto the quay itself across bridges of cargo slats By twilight, 4,104 prisoners had been transferred. Brigadier Garai thanked Captain Burne and Colonel Keeling for the way the men had been looked after. There was a brief ceremony on the promenade deck with the brigadier, Colonel Keeling and Chris Burne signing an agreement that the transfer had been completed. The *Canberra* sailed in the dark, all her lights blazing for the first time in the voyage, escorted by the British destroyer of the Argentinian Navy, the *Trinidad*.

The candour with which the Anglo-Argentinian prisoners had spoken underlined the daft side of this conflict. These were boys who, if I was fifteen or twenty years younger, I might have met at university or on study exchanges. We spoke the same language and were of the same culture. This irony was underlined in a conversation I had with another Anglo-Argentinian who did not want his name published for family reasons. His father carries a British passport and is a businessman in Buenos Aires. He himself is an Argentinian studying at university.

He was recalled from studies on 9 April, having left the Army after a year's national service on 9 March. He said that in his year's national service there had been some preparations for the Falklands. 'When I was called back I didn't want to go. I thought they should have solved this diplomatically,' he said. 'I was sent to Mount Longdon and spent sixty days in a hole waiting for you. I ducked my head into the hole, I couldn't shoot. I couldn't do anything about it. I did get involved in the battle, it was a terrible experience and I don't want to talk about it. I want to forget it.

'I'd like to say we've been very well attended here; and we didn't expect it. We've had food, showers. We've been comfy and had everything we couldn't have in the sixty days on the islands.'

'Being Argentine but with an English cultural background through your father, how do you look on the Malvinas question?' I asked him.

'Well, I think the war could have been avoided. I understand your soldiers, sure, because we speak the same language. People might say, "But he's got an English father." No, I'm Argentine. I can't do anything about that and I do what my government says. Now I just want to go back home, start studying and forget all about this thing.'

10. 'These quiet little islands of ours' Past, Present and Future

The *Canberra* returned to Berkeley Sound exactly a week after the surrender in Port Stanley. The inner harbour and the outer waters of Port William were filled with ships and boats of all sizes, landing craft, whalers, Mexeflotes, huge container ships from which Harriers were being extracted from their giant black polythene bags. Overhead the helicopters churned to and fro, nets of supplies, guns and Rapier batteries swinging under them. There were the frigates and destroyers and the LPDs, *Fearless* and *Intrepid*, probably more ships of the Royal Navy since the Second World War when Commodore Harwood's squadron assembled here for the Battle of the River Plate in 1939. The oldest-looking ships were the newest recruits to the fleet, the rusty-hulled trawlers now being used for ocean-going minesweeper operations, each of the three of them and their tender flying a white ensign in almost mint condition.

The activity in the skies and across the waters of the harbour at Stanley was the sign that the leading elements of the Task Force were beginning to wind down. Preparations were being made for going home. By the end of the week, the Royal Marines of 3 Commando Brigade were to leave on the *Canberra* and the *Stromness*, and the two parachute battalions in the *Norland*. There was an air of relaxation among the islanders, too. Members of different units extended invitations to visit them for supper in their billets, though as likely as not the menu would consist of Rats Arctic and Rats GS, with a piece of 'proffed' Argentinian corned beef thrown in as an extra luxury.

The islanders were beginning to get their houses in order too, though the water supply and faltering electricity were continuing to break down throughout the day and evening. The mess made by British vehicles and troops spreading mud across the roads was as bad as anything brought in from the fields by the Argentinians, and deserted houses suffered further dilapidation. One hazard was turning out to be far worse than first feared – mines.

The Argentinians had littered nearly every approach to the capital with minefields. Those laid by professional engineering units were marked beautifully with barbed wire and notices, as Convention requires. The idea of a minefield is to delay troops. They are not intended to be infantry killers in themselves. Argentinian engineers among the prisoners of war had been helpful in lifting the fields they knew and understood. They were paid the regulation allowance according to the scale laid down by the Convention in 1949; this came to about £10.00 per week, which they spent on such great luxuries as soap, toothpaste and washing powder in the West Store. The real problem was caused by the patterns of mines laid by the infantry units, usually unmarked and very often undetectable. The mines still lying in their thousands across East Falkland range from heavy metal American anti-tank mines from the Second World War to a variety of anti-personnel mines, which have done the most damage in shattering legs and feet, many of them after hostilities have ceased. The most difficult to detect are the Italian plastic anti-personnel mines which have no metal in them if the detonator ring is removed. Completely new techniques of mine-lifting will have to be developed to remove these, and many sapper units in the field had to abandon their work while these are being perfected.

On the edge of Stanley airfield I saw a party of 59th Independent Field Squadron Royal Engineers demonstrating techniques for removing the mines, finding the most reliable method was using the metal prodder, something like a park litter collector's stick. I had come across 13 Delta Recce Troop at Goose Green, where they were led by Staff-Sergeant Terry Collins. There they had bedded down for the night after the fighting died down in the middle of the minefield. One of them woke up in the morning and said, 'Those shell marks look strangely regular to me.' They noticed there were mines buried between the two trenches they had dug and one of the team had placed his sleeping kit right on top of an anti-tank mine.

The squadron was led by a tall, thin, articulate man, Major Rod MacDonald, who looked like a younger brother of Chris Keeble. He had helped to draw up the map of the known minefields posted each day in the Secretariat building. Each day the area of red grew so that there was hardly a space of moorland between Mount Kent, Bluff Cove and Stanley which they knew for certain was completely clear of mines.

'Their Army sappers didn't tell their Marine sappers where they'd put minefields,' Major MacDonald summed up. 'And the infantry scattered mines indiscriminately over areas they wished to defend.

'I honestly don't think we'll ever be able to find all the mines in this minefield. If you bear in mind we're still lifting mines in Britain from the Second World War, and these are all detectable, that gives you some idea of the enormity of the problem here. I am very angry that they have been scattered so indiscriminately. We observe rules stringently when we lay mines, and now I'm having my men badly injured after hostilities are over.'

'What do you think will happen now? What do you think can be done for what used to be these quiet little islands of ours?' said Pat Watts, my companion on most of my travels round Stanley. Pat had been the man in charge of the broadcasting station before, during and after the Argentinian occupation, a native islander who was devoted to the place he had grown up in.

Temporarily, these 'quiet little islands' were under the control of Major-General Jeremy Moore, due to retire within weeks of his return to the United Kingdom. He should have left the Marines in February of 1982, but for the IRA bomb that blew up the car of the corps' commandant-general, Lieutenant-General Sir Steuart Pringle, in which he lost a leg. In a sense, the whole of Jeremy Moore's career had led to the

Falklands campaign, and a surprising amount of that career had been spent working with the man whose brigade went ashore first and whose troops arrived first in Stanley, Brigadier Julian Thompson.

There is nothing of the stereotype about these two modern generals. Both have more than a touch of the intellectual about them, with a passion for history, and not just military history. Jeremy Moore is characteristically frank about why he became a marine: 'At school in the war I wanted to join the Fleet Air Arm. My housemaster wrote to my father saying "an honest plodder like Jeremy" would not make a career as a Naval officer, so he said perhaps I should join the Marines as a last resort.' He says he is glad he did so and gave up flying soon after as he would certainly have killed himself by now.

As a platoon commander he won the MC in Malaya and a bar to it in the Brunei Revolt of 1962. He particularly enjoyed the challenge of the Borneo campaign, where he was on the staff of Major-General Peter Hunt: 'A marvellous campaign, with a wide-ranging border of 1,000 miles where the characteristics of the brigade areas were very different.'

He won his OBE in Northern Ireland in 1972 in Operation Motorman to clear the no-go areas in Londonderry. In that tour he set about training his men to appear on television. 'After Bloody Sunday [when paratroopers killed thirteen civilians in Londonderry], the other side scored a stunning propaganda coup. The Public Relations side of our operation hadn't got its act together. The Ministry of Defence PR Operation didn't get its act together in this operation either. But I'm not fussed by it.'

In a draughty sitting-room I asked him about his reflections on the campaign and the men he had worked with.

'What was needed was speed but not being bloody stupid. The Israelis would have done it much faster, but with many more casualties. Speed isn't just lots of activity. We needed a reasonably successful major battle. That's what 2 Para did at Goose Green. We surprised the enemy because they didn't believe we'd marched there, which you can do with the quality of troops that we had.

'Then we came to the battle on the night of the 12th and the bloody hard grind of the Scots Guards on Tumbledown. But they were still ready to go, being well trained. The guns were the vital part, too. Because of the weather at Goose Green, there was only half a battery. I determined after that, that a three-brigade attack should be able to call on the support of at least five batteries [thirty guns].'

'And what about air cover?'

'We broke the classic teaching that you should attempt no amphibious operation without superiority or at least local air control. Well, I would say that where the Grace of God came in was that those very brave pilots went for the escorts on 21 May [at San Carlos] and not the amphibious ships. That might have stopped us altogether. From then on, it was a slow climb up. No one had taken Rapier in a ship for 8,000 miles before and they took time to settle down. But they shot down fourteen or fifteen planes. The main enemy aircraft destroyer was the Sea Harrier, the SHA. They could only hit the enemy planes after they had delivered their ordnance. The Harriers gave us the whip hand.

'As you know, you could never discount the enemy aircraft. You may remember we learnt this when they bombed us at brigade [above Estancia] the day before the last battle.'

Both Julian Thompson and Jeremy Moore paid tribute again and again to their men. 'They were remarkably easy to handle right up at the front. Obviously with the Guards on Tumbledown we soon knew we were in the saddle position,' was Jeremy Moore's assessment of his last command in battle.

'They're more inquiring now, they want to know the reasons for things before moving now,' said Julian Thompson, who proudly boasts of his recce troop commander, who was a barrister, and another platoon commander with a degree in Arabic. 'Very few old sweats these days. I wasn't surprised but very grateful for the response I got. This was much harder, longer and more difficult than Suez.'

Jeremy Moore heaped praise on Julian Thompson, antagonising members of 5 Brigade for declaring him 'The man of the match'. Later he explained his reasons for saying this.

'Julian inspires immense confidence, so all they did, they did with conviction. His brigade fought the first battle, and set the pattern of what happened in the mountains. Julian set the pattern. I had to get ashore at San Carlos as quickly as I did to take the political pressure off Julian's back so he could concentrate on the battle ahead, which is what he did.'

At fifty-four, Jeremy Moore was the most successful British general since the Second World War, and he would return to a hero's welcome and redundancy. As we chatted in that freezing sitting-room, he talked of his other enthusiasms, ballet and literature. He could as happily talk about Tolstoy's powers of description of young soldiers coming under fire for the first time in *War and Peace*, of the letters of Abelard and the theology of Bonhoeffer as the nuts and bolts of modern soldiering. He spoke of the rediscovered pleasure of making elaborate models with his son Andrew, who, never the greatest speller in the world, had sent a letter concluding with a sentence which summed up most of our apprehensions and fears: 'I hope we are going to win Daddy. I think we will but I'm not shore.'

As the first troops prepared to leave, islanders came in from 'camp' to retrieve their belongings and clean out their homes. The Bowles returned from Goose Green, thankful that only a few ornaments and windows had been cracked in their smart bungalow in the middle of town. In the Upland Goose, the King family served hot lunches and dinners, a considerable achievement given the amount of fresh vegetables uprooted from the gardens by the hungry Argentinians. Mrs King looked exhausted from the work and strain of the occupation. Even more tired was Commander Rick Jolly, who had come in from Ajax. I saw him walking up to Government House, his face green with fatigue; he was like a sleep-walker as he lurched into the low privet hedge without realising it. He and Lt.-Col. Bill MacGregor had now set up the surgery in the Civilian Hospital, where Argentinians and British troops were still being tended and patched up to be moved out to the hospital ships *Uganda* and *Bahia Paraiso* to take passage for home.

With the return from camp, tension was rising between the settlers who had stayed in Stanley and those who had moved out. Some of those that left thought those remaining had been virtual collaborators, and many of those that stayed thought some of their fellow citizens had just cut and run. One of those who had stayed was one of the most notable expatriates in the capital, Jack Abbott, who had passed his seventy-eighth birthday in lonely isolation in a snugly constructed wooden house at the top of the hill in Stanley. Jack had been married to an islander, and when she died he decided to make his home in the Falklands. A great benefactor of anything from the Scout Troop to the port's recreational facilities, he had earned the nickname 'British Abbott' for his patriotism and love of Britain. Part of his almost romantic love of Britain came from the fact that he is half-American by birth, had lived a life of hardship and adventure in the twenties and thirties, including a spell lumber-jacking and trapping in Canada, and had served as a sergeant in the Second World War. His nickname was emphasised in the month of tension before the Argentinians arrived. Several of the islanders told him that if Argentina did use force, they doubted if Britain would do anything by force of arms to help the islanders. Jack said, 'I never doubted Britain or Mrs Thatcher for a minute.'

'They're a strange lot, these people, sometimes,' he told me, one of the mildest understatements I heard on the Falklands. He explained the division between native islanders and the expatriates, the settlers who had come from Britain. This cost him his position on the Falkland Islands Committee. When I saw him, he had the commanding officer and the second in command of 2 Para, David Chaundler and Chris Keeble, as his guests in his house. 'It makes me very proud to have such men staying here, but they wouldn't come, you know, until they had seen all their men properly housed.'

Jack's story is one of the sheer loneliness of those islanders that stayed behind in Stanley when the British troops started to close in from the mountains to the west. From a population of about 1,000 there were now about 150 to 200 remaining, according to Jack. His only contact with his fellow citizens was a daily visit to Les and Peggy Halliday down the hill for a cup of tea each afternoon before curfew.

'No Argentine ever came into this house,' he told me. 'I don't understand it. I declared my 410 shotgun, no one came to collect it. No one came near me – until they broke in. One afternoon I left here at twenty to three, and came back here at a quarter to four. The place was in a shambles. Every bit of food in the house had been removed. They took my binoculars, clock, wrist-watch. Every drawer had been pulled out. But they did nothing unpleasant as they did in so many other houses.

'The second occasion was after the big attack on Stanley when the house was broken into twice in one morning. They shot the lock off my back door. I'd only been down the road for a very short time. I came back and said, "What the hell's all this?" And men came out from all directions and I said, "What the bloody hell are you people doing in my house?" And they went out, too. You know, I've had a very good life, and no one was going to shove me out of my house. I got seven of them out, and then minutes later twelve more came and I persuaded them not to come into the house. I felt sorry for them in a way: there were parties drifting all over the place. They didn't know what to do.

'The worst night I had was when the British were trying to get a big artillery piece that the Argies had on the hill not a hundred yards from here. The Argies used to move this around every day. That last night they moved it into the road immediately above my top fence and that fired all night. I have nothing but contempt for a nation whose armed forces put their artillery between the houses. We were now all worried about street fighting in Stanley.

'The only thing I succumbed to finally was intense loneliness. I was alone here from four in the afternoon to eight-thirty in the morning. Actually I found great comfort in watching the Royal Wedding on video throughout the bombardment.

'In my opinion there were many brave acts. Take the plumber, a man called Place. His wife left before the invasion, seriously ill, but he wouldn't leave because he knew he was needed. The hospital kept going magnificently. John Leonard, an American, did a great deal of organising the people here. More and more, as the days went by, they tried to put increasing pressure on us. In the end I went to see the doctors and Dr Alison said I was suffering from acute loneliness. So I spent the last night in the Colony Club. I woke up the next day and saw two fellows wearing camouflage trousers. I said, "You fellows British?" They said they were two reporters from the *Daily Express* and another paper. Well, then we really went to town.'

On a dull, grey, wintry afternoon we went back to Darwin Hill to dedicate a simple memorial to 'H' Jones and the men who fell with him. As we waited by the racecourse to get a lift in a Chinook helicopter, we saw a Wessex helicopter staggering and lurching across the grass like a racehorse with a broken leg. It bucked and jumped for about a hundred and fifty yards and then settled down, its body twisted and a rotor blade dangling down. It had caught a plastic bag in its rotor as it took off and had nearly rolled over. 'God, that was bloody close,' said a white-faced Ewan Southby-Tailyour emerging from the hold. 'If the sodding thing had rolled it might have blown up.' I had spent dozens of hours in helicopters throughout the campaign and not really bothered about the danger; the machine-guns drooping through the open doors had become a familiar sight, taken completely for granted. This was the nearest to a helicopter accident, quite apart from war damage, that I saw. The ride in the Chinook was very uncomfortable. We were cramped and enclosed in the beast's belly, and the sight of the Wessex on the racecourse had made us think how lucky we had been in having so few mishaps with the helicopters.

The settlers drove up from Goose Green in their trucks and tractors and parked by the Gorse Line. On Darwin Hill stood a plain iron cross on a cairn of local stone; the simple brass plate was dedicated to the memory of Lieutenant-Colonel 'H' Jones and the men who died with him at Goose Green on 28 May 1982. The company commanders and men of 2 Para stood bareheaded. With them stood the captain and officers of the *Norland*, Brigadier Thompson, Brigadier Wilson, the gunners, sappers and signallers and a patrol of SAS who dropped their weapons behind the men. David Cooper gave a simple address and Chris Keeble read the lesson. Brooke Hardcastle from Darwin laid a wreath, as did Eric Goss for the people of Goose Green. A Gurkha bugler played reveille and the Last Post and a Gurkha piper played the lament 'The Flowers of the Forest' near the gully where 'H', Chris Dent, David Wood and Corporal Mick Melia had fallen. The hills were continuously changing as clouds slid across the sun, green, brown, yellow and deep red. A flock of Upland Geese scudded over the water as a patrol of Gurkhas marched along the shore track to Goose Green. They had just had a man killed by a hand grenade, filling in trenches at Burntside.

This was the battalion's farewell to the ground where 'H' and his men had died. Other regiments held their memorial services. At Bluff Cove the hulk of the *Galahad* was dedicated as a war grave. The roll of honour of those that died on 8 June was read, and the Guards sang 'Land of My Fathers'. Later the ship was to be taken out and sunk. The young women were buried in Port Stanley after a funeral attended by General Moore, and at which the Anglican and Catholic priests officiated. Then the soldiers started packing up. Most of the paratroopers shifted their kit to the *Norland* and the commandos embarked, most of them, in the *Canberra*.

I went across to the *Canberra* the day she sailed, to collect clothes and spare recorder batteries. There were a few drinks, handshakes, and 'See you in Southampton' greetings. I left the ship in the coaster MV *Forrest*, which the British had claimed earlier they had sunk when it was manned by the Argentinians. Calling at HMS *Plymouth*, we collected the Argentinian Air Force men who had been arrested at the weather station at Thule on the South Sandwich Islands. They threw me their kit, which I helped stack. They also expected me to lift it aboard the ferry *St Edmund* when they went aboard her, clearly thinking I was not of the officer class. They were smartly dressed, with flashy orange foul-weather suits and uniforms. They were clean and tidy, but still had that characteristic stink of peat, tobacco and maté.

As they disembarked at the Sealink ferry *St Edmund*, some Scots Guards wearing camouflage kit and glengarries on their heads came aboard the coaster. They were the pipers led by Pipe-Major Jimmy Riddle. They were late, they said, and standing at the stern tuned their pipes, playing a wilder and wilder reel as the vessel ploughed through a rainstorm. Ashore, they formed up and marched in the dusk to Government House. The noise of the pipes was drowned again and again by the clatter of helicopters. It was one of the most evocative musical renditions I have heard. At Government House they halted and played reels, jigs and slow marches. Several hours earlier, the former Governor Rex Hunt had returned to an enthusiastic reception on the playing field, to take up residence in the shambling Victorian mansion. He came to the door, and I asked for a few words as the Scots Guards played a haunting melody.

'A great day?' I asked the new Civil Commissioner.

'I am delighted to be back,' said the former Governor, 'but I'm freezing at the moment because Don's gone off and he's locked my coat in the gunroom.'

After our brief chat, in which the Civil Commissioner paid tribute to the British servicemen and the islanders, the pipers swung down the drive and up the shore road. 'The Bonnie Lass of Fivie' was drowned by two small helicopters chattering across the harbour in unison.

The following morning there was a press conference in Government House in which Rex Hunt talked of the future of the islands. The opportunities for development are limited, he explained. There is an acute shortage of housing, and any new settlers would need to be prepared to pay their own passage and build their own house on the islands. Expansion of the farming industry might be difficult, though studies were being made. Kelp (seaweed) harvesting was another possibility, though the attempt by a British concern to do this in the fifties and sixties had not met with success. An American consortium was now interested as the Falklands had some of the best kelp-beds in the world, matched only by those round New Zealand and Australia. Kelp can be used as a base material for a range of pharmaceuticals, particularly for iodine extracts. But the Americans would use a factory ship, not employing many islanders. Fishing is another possible growth industry, but exploration for oil round the islands had yet to yield any substantial finds.

I was particularly anxious to know when Mr Hunt had first realised that the Argentinians intended to invade the islands. There was now growing suspicion in the islands themselves about the conduct of the British Foreign and Commonwealth Office throughout the emergency, and throughout the years leading up to the crisis. Since the beginning of the year, many of these kelpers, among them at least four members of the Falkland Islands Council, felt that the British Government was given warning signs that the Galtieri regime was about to use force to resolve the Malvinas issue, and for various reasons the Foreign Office chose to ignore these. The critics do agree that Argentinian generals had threatened invasion before, but by the beginning of March, they argue, there was clear evidence that the whole tone of the threats being made by the Galtieri junta was harsher than anything heard in recent years from Buenos Aires on the Malvinas question.

'I first knew that they were sending a fleet just twelve hours before they actually invaded,' Mr Hunt told me in Government House. 'We got a signal from the Foreign Office at 3.30 that Thursday afternoon and that was the first clear evidence that the Argentinian task force was heading towards Stanley.'

This kind of development is just what many islanders had feared for years. In late 1980, Nicholas Ridley, Parliamentary Under Secretary at the Foreign Office, visited Port Stanley to consult islanders about the future status of the Falklands. Asked about protection from invasion, he assured a public meeting that Intelligence would give sufficient warning for British forces to counteract any serious attempt by Argentina to take the islands by force.

In December 1981, the new head of the Argentinian junta, Leopoldo Galtieri, made a threatening speech about the

Malvinas. At the end of February, British and Argentinian delegations met at the UN in New York to discuss the future of the Falklands. The delegation was led on the British side by Nicholas Ridley's successor, Richard Luce. In the delegation were two of the Falkland Islands councillors, John Cheek and Tim Blake. It has never been made entirely clear what was discussed at this meeting, and there are many different versions of what was said. Other matters were talked about besides the sovereignty question. It is said that the Argentinian delegation indicated that they wanted regular monthly meetings of the Falklands Council to discuss the transfer of sovereignty within a year. This story is referred to constantly by councillors in the Falklands today. A similar timetable for the transfer of sovereignty was mentioned in the government-sponsored propaganda radio broadcasts from Buenos Aires in English. ('They shouldn't have done that,' said Rex Hunt, 'because it broke the confidentiality of the talks in New York.') The timetable is not mentioned, however, in the position document at the beginning of the talks at the UN on the weekend of Friday 26 and Saturday 27 February 1982, nor in the final communique. The communique referred merely to more regular meetings to discuss the question of the Falklands or Malvinas.

There is no doubt that some of the senior officers in General Menendez's command felt that warning had been given at New York. 'Why are you so surprised to see us?' the Deputy Governor, Commodore Carlos Blumer-Reeve, is said to have remarked to the Harbour Master Les Halliday. 'We did give you warning in New York.' Another Argentinian officer told Ian Stewart, head of Cable and Wireless in Stanley, 'You were told in the corridors of New York during the talks that we would invade.'

Returning from New York, the two councillors, John Cheek and Tim Blake, grew alarmed at the tenor of the propaganda broadcasts and the government-inspired editorial in the Buenos Aires press. On the instigation of the Falkland Islands Council, the Foreign Office sent a diplomatic note to the Galtieri junta over Lord Carrington's signature. It stated bluntly that there could be no further negotiations about the Falklands, 'in the present atmosphere of threats'. The mystery is how the Foreign Office could have sent a note saying this, yet continue indicating publicly that at this time there was nothing in the threats that had not been heard before; and on these occasions it had not come to the use of force by the Argentinians. Councillor Tim Blake was telling people in Stanley privately that if it came to a fight he did not think Britain would send a fleet to the Falklands to oppose the Argentinians, despite the assurances of Nicholas Ridley just over twelve months before.

Two other councillors, Tony Blake and Ron Binney, decided to hold meetings in settlements out in camp to warn the settlers of the deepening crisis. Meetings were held at Fitzroy and North Arm Settlement. At one of the meetings, according to a witness, the proposition was debated that 'the next time we meet with the Argentines we'll have to discuss the transfer of sovereignty'.

I asked Tony Blake what made him call the meetings out in camp. 'There were the media threats,' he said, and earlier that year one of Buenos Aires's most authoritative commentators, Iglesias Rouco, had written in *La Prensa*, 'This year Buenos Aires will recover the islands by force'. 'It was nothing specific,' Tony Blake went on to assure me. 'There was a general sense of threat which I thought we should discuss.' After some more questioning, he replied, 'Look, there was a sense of threat and there seemed to be no preparation. I don't want to delve into it too deeply. It's a thing of the past, and there's now a very big future ahead of us.'

On 16 and 17 March, the last Falkland Islands Council meeting was held, as it turned out, before the Argentinians came. On 19 March the Davidoff scrap-metal merchants raised the Argentinian flag on South Georgia. On 20 March HMS *Endurance*, the Antarctic Survey ship, was despatched to South Georgia. In the last week of March, Governor Hunt called together his senior civil servants to discuss the Argentinians' activities on South Georgia. Many of the same group met after the invasion to request the removal of all civilians during hostilities under a 'protective power' arrangement laid down by Convention. This was rejected because, the civil servants in the ad hoc committee were told, the evacuation would not be temporary and their claims would be weakened.

Whatever the strength of the threats before the invasion, and the misunderstandings of what was being said and not said at New York and in the government-inspired editorials and the propaganda radio from Buenos Aires, it is clear that there was a huge misassessment of General Galtieri, his government and his military staff.

I put the question to Rex Hunt: 'You had a new man at the top in Argentina, Leopoldo Galtieri, who had taken over from General Viola and it seemed that he was going for a more aggressive foreign policy, and this was read by the commentators quite early?'

'Yes, again, I didn't think he would be so foolish as to commit the Argentines to armed aggression in the Falklands as he did.'

John Cheek, one of the councillors at New York, said that he did have an inkling in March that the Argentinians were seriously contemplating invasion. 'But,' he told me, 'I got the timetable wrong. I thought they would come in July or August, the beginning of our summer and not in the winter as they did.'

A diplomat working in Buenos Aires at the time the crisis broke said that General Galtieri had brought into power with him a new government and a new military staff. Little was known about the key personalities in both structures, a comment which seemed to be borne out by the lack of detailed information about the command under General Mario Benjamin Menendez in his military governorship of the Falkland Islands.

The claims, counter-claims and suspicions about the events and miscalculations that led up to the conflict on the Falklands seem to have left deep scars in the community of the kelpers. Throughout the invasion and occupation, and the battles to liberate Stanley, some of the leading public servants struggled to keep some semblance of continuity in the lives of the islanders; among them were the doctors, like Alison Bleaney, her husband Mike working at the Falkland Islands Company, the Kings at the Upland Goose, the Post Office staff, the plumbers and electricians, Ian Stewart at Cable and Wireless and Hulda at the schools drained of contract teachers and then children leaving for camp, Steve Whiteley the vet, Les Halliday the Harbour Master and Pat Watts the Broadcasting Officer.

Pat Watts had been my companion round town for the two weeks I spent in Stanley. We had swapped tape-recordings for the BBC and the Islands' Broadcasting Service, for which he was both engineer and producer-cum-broadcaster. He is the same age as me and is working in a similar job. He has educated himself, as there was nothing beyond GCE 'O' level standard tuition on the islands. Throughout the crisis he managed to keep broadcasting to the islanders in the hours before invasion to the moment of surrender.

He drove me out to the airfield to get the Hercules flight to Ascension. 'On the night of the invasion my only thought was to do what I could for the people of the islands until I could do no more. I asked the Governor, "What do you want me to do, Sir?" And he said, "Stay in the radio all night. Keep me on the air, when I want to be on the air, and stay there until you feel you must go home to the safety of your own house to look after your children." I did this until the Argentines finally walked into the radio studio. It took them a long time. I kept thinking, "when the hell are they coming here?" I'd had phone calls from all over town saying Government House had been taken, the flag was up there and the soldiers had walked into people's homes, given them flags and had told them what they could and could not do. When they came in, I just about collapsed. I felt that the place was no longer mine.

'Immediately they went into the radio station, they said, "We know who you are. We've got your name down here. We want you to carry on to be the Chief of the Radio. We're going to increase your salary. We don't want you to leave. You can have holidays in Buenos Aires whenever you want." I had to make the decision, "Would I stay or not?" But then I thought

I could still be of use to the community of the islands, especially those in the outer settlements who had no idea of what the Argentines were doing. I thought somehow my voice would reassure these people.

'It hurt me greatly to call it Radio Nacional Islas Malvinas, and I tried to avoid referring to Port Stanley as Porto Argentino. I called it "the capital" or the "largest settlement on the island".'

Pat Watts persuaded the Argentinians to allow the re-broadcast of BBC World Service Sports programmes. 'We all have our favourite soccer teams here, and I told them if there was no sport broadcast they'd have serious civil unrest. They got a bit angry when we slipped in the odd news bulletin in the sports programme. One official burst in when there was an item about a rugby match with the Argentine team being cancelled because of the Falklands crisis.'

The man who burst into the studio on that occasion was Major Patricio Dowling, the Argentinian of Irish extraction who had been involved in police operations leading to 'disappearances' in Argentina over several years.

'He did such extraordinary things,' explained Pat Watts. 'He came in and asked to see all the records, and sat down and played all the well-known Irish tunes on the gramophone, "I'll Take You Home Again Cathleen" and "When Irish Eyes are Smiling", things like that. He was obviously here to clean up the place, to get anybody who was going to start any form of sabotage, or any resistance movement.'

'What does the future hold for you and your family?'

'Well, it's a pretty good mess, and the Royal Engineers are doing a good job to clear it up. But that's not the problem. The problem is "Where do we go from here?" I lived here, and I'm an islander, because I liked the peace and tranquillity of the place, the freedom of life I had here, a time to think, as I always said to myself. I don't know if I am going to have time to think in the future, and whether my children will have time to think. It's going to be different, and we have to expect it. We want to be free of the Argentines, and we have to accept the military. But how can I take my children to those beaches over there? However good the job by the Royal Engineers, there's always the fear that there's something on those beaches hidden away and my children or I might step on it. Even the simple fact of going to my peat bog to cut my peat for my fuel, a job I enjoyed, a healthy job, well I asked the Royal Engineer officer, "Is it safe for me to go there?" And he said, "According to my map it's safe, but for God's sake don't go near it because we don't know ourselves what could be on your peat bog or anybody else's." We've still got freedom, but I think we've lost the peace of these islands. Maybe I'll have to look for another place to find the peace that I've always enjoyed here.'

The blue-grey Hercules plane roared down from the rain clouds, seeming to hit the runway at an angle of forty-five degrees, its fat tyres bending under the impact, spurting steam and spray as it braked to a halt. I said my farewells to Pat and lugged myself and my bergen onto the ramp of the aircraft, crushing myself between forty bulky SAS men for the eleven-hour flight to Ascension, then to Britain and another reality.

11. Aftermath

In July the troops began arriving home. First of the major units to land in England were the two Parachute Regiment Battalions, who came into the RAF station at Brize Norton in Super VC 10s from Ascension. Their Colonel-in-Chief, the Prince of Wales, was there to greet them, and a cheering crowd of two thousand wives, parents and children. The tension broke with tears, smiles and embraces. 'I'm going to have a great meal tonight,' RSM Malcolm Simpson told me. 'My abiding memory of that place is days without food and tons of water, then days of rations arriving in plenty with no water to cook them in, and miles and miles of peat.'

Colonel David Chaundler spoke again of the image that stuck most in his mind from the battles, 'The hundreds and thousands of Argentinians pouring off Wireless Ridge like ants, pouring back into Stanley to surrender.'

Canberra returned in much the same wave of nostalgia that she left, bands playing Elgar, streamers and banners festooning buildings and cranes along Southampton Water. Hundreds of small craft bobbed around her on the blazing July morning as she brought the commandos home. Prince Charles paid a short visit by helicopter, and then withdrew discreetly, leaving the men to meet their families. Some of the officers seemed inordinately tired, still recovering in feet, hands and minds from the epic 'yomp' across the mountains to the night battles for Port Stanley.

As exhausted as the men were their wives and mothers who had at least as testing a time as the men on the Falklands themselves. It is hard to appreciate the anxiety and apprehension of those waiting at home, for those whose men did come back as well as those who lost sons, husbands, fathers and lovers out in the peat and on the seas. Though the campaign was relatively brief, three months from the invasion by Argentina on 2 April to the final surrender, two hundred and fifty-five British and about seven or eight hundred Argentinians lost their lives, and well over a thousand troops were injured. The psychological damage appears to be as great as the physical injury. 'You bloody journalists out there don't understand what hell we went through back here, we wives,' one paratroop officer's wife said to me. 'You're so bloody condescending because you've been out there. Can you honestly know what it was like looking after all the wives? To tell one with two babies crawling round her and her stomach out two feet expecting another, that her man isn't coming back? You have to look after her, and see to the mundane things as well, like making sure she has money coming in to tide her over for the next four or five days, before you can get her her proper welfare allowance.'

It is hard to understand such sorrow and anxiety. In the field the moments of apprehension were the worst. Was that plane heading your way? Were the Argentinians going to shell and mortar again, or throw Pucara and Skyhawk at you as you walked the wide open moorland? Were the tracks, the beach, the fords in the stream mined? When it happened, the stonk at Goose Green, the coal-shovel clatter of heavy artillery shells smashing the rocks, the A-4s bombing the Brigade Headquarters in the mountains on that clear, bright, last full day of hostilities, it either happened so suddenly or was so concentrated an experience that you did not have time to think of anything much except whether you would make it through the next half-minute or so of firing. Once the silence returned, one was in command again, and the campaign was marked by simple certainties, that you would get rations, that your companions would see you through, and you would probably be able to sleep at night.

Reporting the war was a strangely difficult experience. It was an enclosed, remote and relatively brief episode, with far less scope for vicarious experience of it by those at home than in the television campaigns in the Middle East and Vietnam. The way we moved in the fields, mostly on our feet, gave it an oddly old-fashioned quality. Much of the language of the troops was the same as in the trenches of the Western Front and the land campaigns of the Second World War, with 'stonking', 'brews' and 'scoff'. It was a campaign that called for the descriptive skills of Evelyn Waugh, and much of it did resemble scenes from the *Sword of Honour* trilogy more than a disciple of Tom Wolff's New Journalism. The hacks who had covered other, bigger, noisier wars seemed infected by the brilliance of Michael Herr's *Dispatches*, the cult work of New Journalism on the Vietnam War. But this was war on a more lilliputian scale, and there were no PXes, telexes or Inter-continental Hotels, only the Upland Goose and a succession of 'bivvies' and 'bashers' across the island. It was at once an intimate and remote experience. Intimate because we lived so close to the soldiers and shared their thoughts and worries with them. The last day I visited him in the Secretariat building in Stanley, Julian Thompson asked me, 'Well, do you think they'll attack us again, have one more go with the aircraft at Stanley once the prisoners leave, to salvage some glory?' He did not expect me to reply with anything sensible, I imagine, but it was a matter of sharing his anxiety. It was remote because it was so old-fashioned; some of the officers spoke in the gentlemanly way that their predecessors might in the Desert War or the Battle of Britain.

The Falklands Campaign is quite likely to prove the last small war fought for a British imperial colony. There was much of the whole setting of the episode that had overtones of nineteenth-century gunboat diplomacy, or Fashoda and the Agadir Crisis. Paradoxically, it could be argued that a judicious use of the presence of gunboats at the right time might have avoided bloodshed. In the antique flavour of the campaign, and the train of events leading up to it, lies its greatest lesson. The whole crisis was compounded by a lack of communication, information and intelligence which had some echoes from the crisis leading to the Crimean War, the last European war to be declared by ambassadors. Communication failed at all hands, and is one of the most serious questions arising from the conflict. Failure to communicate the right information about Argentinian intentions led to General Menendez's forces putting their men ashore at Stanley virtually unopposed. In the field, vital intelligence information did not get through to the commanders, such as the true numbers of the Argentinian garrison in Goose Green before the battle, and the background and identity of the men in General Menendez's staff, which was vital information for the preparation of negotiations. Units moving up for the last battles round Stanley had frequently to use intelligence photographs weeks old. Artillery drones with cameras could have been used, giving photographic information on enemy positions an hour or so before the battle was joined. I remember the Intelligence Officer of 45 Commando receiving his latest batch of pictures of the Argentinians on the Mount Kent and Two Sisters features the day after Two Sisters had been taken by Royal Marines.

'Was it all worth it?' I am now asked frequently, and it is a question I find impossible to answer. One feels mildly affronted for it to be suggested that such an extraordinary experience, which so nearly cost me my life, was worthless. The days in that wild landscape, the companionship of many of the men in the field, was enjoyable more often than not; fear and danger were exhilarating too. Our curious isolation made me do things I would not normally have contemplated, and I think for a time it made me shed the selfishness which many of us hacks wear like a carapace. For me it was an existential dream. For others, the victims, the terribly injured mentally and physically, their families, and the families of the dead, it was a nightmare. That nightmare is far from over for many of the islanders of the Falklands themselves. Fragile communities recovering from occupation and confinement, as at Goose Green, will have to be treated gently if they are not to fracture. Most of the islanders can hardly welcome being the hosts to garrisons of soldiers, sailors and airmen several times the size of the settler population for the next few years.

At the end of *In Patagonia*, the story of his travels in Tierra del Fuego in the mid-1970s, Bruce Chatwin describes his departure from Punta Arenas: 'There was a boy from the

Falklands in a seal-skin hat and strange sharp teeth. "'Bout time the Argentines took us over," he said. "We're so bloody inbred.'" Ironically, it was the Argentinians who had given the islanders the most practical route of escape from their isolation in recent years. With their LADE service they had established an air link to Comodoro Rivadavia, whence trips could be taken to Buenos Aires and beyond. Much of the sheep-rearing and ranching life of Patagonia dove-tailed with that of the Falklands. The great sheep interests were intimately linked, the Fox enterprises in West Falkland and Tierra del Fuego and even the Menendez ranches. Falkland breeding sheep were more prized than Spanish and European in Patagonia. The Falklands sheep and those of the Chubut Valley in Patagonia provided the purest naturally bleached wool in the world, I was told by a Dutchman who used to buy wool in Tierra del Fuego for the concern of Hartwool which still has its head offices in Buenos Aires. And sheep and cattle do seem to be the best hope for the immediate future of the Falklands economy. Kelp-harvesting might bring in a little extra income but will not absorb labour or provide a growth industry on the islands themselves. In 1974, exports grossed £2,678,000, 99 per cent earned from unprocessed wool. All wool was sold at auction in London. 'Now the London markets are gone, with the decline in the wool industry, so the only future for the Falklands is to sell their wool either on the Buenos Aires or Montevideo markets,' said the former executive of Hartwool. There is, then, a natural economic and social affinity with Patagonia; but temporarily the links between the Falklands and Chubut, and Santa Cruz provinces and Tierra del Fuego, are now severed. The possibility of economic expansion from oil discoveries and tourism in the Falklands seems, for the moment, to be a pipe dream.

The war in the Falklands was fought for the principle of the islanders having the right to determine their nationality and citizenship on the one hand, and of a claim for territorial sovereignty which had almost mystical connotations for the sense of nationhood of Argentina, on the other. Yet if the Falklands are to hold any stable future for their present inhabitants, some more modern dimension and more modern currency must be given to the dispute between London and Buenos Aires than the claim and counter-claim of imperial colony and territorial sovereignty in the name of the strident nationalism in which Argentina was born in the last century.

There was a principle for which Britain fought, and one suspects that if the invasion force of General Galtieri's junta was permitted to stay once it had landed, it could have set a dangerous precedent for other parts of the world, not least for Britain's disputed colonies like Gibraltar and Hong Kong. Yet a considerable number of voices in the international community dismissed the conflict and its causes as 'irrelevant' or 'wrong-headed'. In the three months following my return from Port Stanley, I was surprised at the number of people I know with close dealings with United States government officials and politicians who have told me that in their own view and that of their American friends the Falklands conflict was 'meaningless'. Experts on international strategy and military tactics immediately began to argue that the real test-ground for modern close-combat weapons and missiles was in the Middle East War in the Lebanon. One former member of the International Institute for Strategic Studies said on radio, 'The whole of the Falklands War was based on Second World War tactics, with no electronic decoys for missiles, no use of anti-missile missiles, all low-flying and iron bombs,' a caricature which borders on the absurd. The Falklands saw the success of the Harrier, the VSTOL aircraft, for the first time in full combat, the use of air-defence missiles as a principal in providing air cover, and the vulnerability of the surface ship to sea-skimming missiles like Exocet.

The evidence is that the Americans and the Russians did not see the conflict as irrelevant whatever their more public spokesmen may have said. Despite a few blasts initially against British imperialism, there is little to show that the Russians helped the Argentinians with material and intelligence despite the watch kept over the Task Force by spy ships, satellites and long-range reconnaissance aircraft. Russia seems to have been more worried about the implications for the Antarctica Treaty due to be renegotiated soon, if Argentina held the Falkland Island Dependencies, than the British phenomenon of the 'Empire Strikes Back'. America, too, turned dramatically from President Reagan's initial 'even-handed policy towards two equally friendly nations', to offering assistance on a generous scale to Britain, so much so that the American electronic media and the newspaper press have now suggested that it was American equipment, such as night goggles and the Sidewinder missile, the loan of the airstrip at Ascension and intelligence information which in the end won the war for the British. Little remarked on is the American offer of a battalion of their own troops to help the British, according to Ministry of Defence sources, once the CIA had made the assessment that sooner or later Britain's forces would win in the Falklands. One would like to understand more about the motives behind that offer. Perhaps the Americans realised that the Falklands battle does have important implications for ground force and Naval tactics for conflict in theatres other than the Middle East and the plains of Central Europe.

The lessons being most widely discussed in the immediate aftermath are those for the British armed services, particularly the Navy. Some of the equipment worked surprisingly well. The Sea Harrier exceeded all expectation and gave the Argentinian command its biggest surprise, according to Argentinian pilots who were taken prisoner, and Sea Wolf and Rapier missiles worked well. Ship design of the Type 42 destroyer and Type 21 frigate was shown to have weaknesses and so too did missiles like Sea Dart and Blowpipe. The Navy knows that the future of the surface fleet is even more debatable now that the power of the sea-skimming missile, Exocet, has been felt and it is said that the Soviet equivalent, the SS9, is even more powerful. The Navy is fighting hard for a 'Blue Water' strategic role, one beyond the NATO deployment of guarding the eastern Atlantic. The Army and RAF argue for concentration on the 'Continental Commitment' in the Central European sector of NATO. Following the Falklands campaign, some of the paratroopers and marines are arguing for Special Forces Divisions including airborne and amphibious forces for rapid deployment, and not just inside NATO. The marines particularly are concerned about the scaling down of the amphibious warfare training and capability of British forces. 'We simply cannot legislate for one kind of warfare in one theatre,' Brigadier Thompson told me when we were discussing the reduction of amphibious warfare units and the phasing out of the two key ships *Fearless* and *Intrepid*.

One major lesson for all the armed forces is communication – how they communicate internally, between each other, and with the world at large. The Navy still may imagine that such conflicts should be fought without the attentions of the press. Some military commanders have suggested that the civilian press officer should not be allowed in theatres of active service. But the real muddle over censorship and press policy was caused by lack of practice (many of the regulations dated from the last World War) and sheer confusion, rather than human perfidy. There were so many different policies emanating from different quarters – Fleet, the Ministry of Defence, the Task Force and Brigade Commands – that regulations and rules would be changed as arbitrarily and frequently as Humpty Dumpty altered the meaning of the words in *Alice Through the Looking Glass*.

In the end, much depended on the trust between individuals in the field. All three armed services functioned because they were professional, trained men. The ground forces ran smoothly on the skills in command of the NCOs, the sergeants and the corporals. I now realise why Tolstoy in his conclusion to *War and Peace* placed so much emphasis on the corporal as the key figure in a land army. In the way the soldiers and the sailors went about their jobs there was a surprising lack of jingoism. There was a bit of 'Let's sort out the Spics' immediately before and after a battle, but most felt sorry for the bedraggled troops who became prisoners at Goose Green and on Stanley airfield.

'What a pathetic lot,' said one of the paratroop officers, seeing a particularly sickly bunch of young prisoners straggle away from the surrender at Goose Green, 'you can't really want to fight kids like that.' Another senior officer said, 'I think it was right to do what we did, but it's a sorry kind of victory to crow over.' Individual Argentinian units fought well and bravely, artillery, mortarmen, special forces, the machine-gunners, the pilots of the Air Force. 'But,' said David Chaundler, C.O. of 2 Para, about the final battles on the high ground, 'most of them just stood there and waited for us like frightened rabbits in the headlights of an approaching car.'

Now the defeated Argentinians face an uncertain time in the turmoil of their country's politics following the defeat. I do not know how long it took the prisoners disembarking from the *Canberra* at Puerto Madryn to get home, men like Milton Rhys and his companions, but we did hear reports that they were being detained in isolation camps for several weeks afterwards.

The real difference between the two armies was the cohesion of command between officers, NCOs and the ranks. The British appeared to be truly professional soldiers in the post-Oliver Cromwell tradition. The Argentinian generals had tried to mix a little soldiering with their politics in the Malvinas adventure. The British left the politics out of the soldiering, even the inter-unit and regimental rivalries were laid aside when the campaign began in earnest, and for that, several of us who went with them are grateful for our lives.

Postscript

On Tuesday 12 October, twelve hundred men and women involved in the Falklands campaign marched through the City of London to Guildhall. In the fine drizzle they paraded behind massed bands of the Royal Marines, the Guards, the Gurkhas and the Parachute Regiment. Many of those marching sported the new South Atlantic Medal, with its garish ribbon of blue and white with a streak of yellow, oddly resembling the national flag of Argentina. Behind contingents of soldiers came trucks towing the equipment that proved so vital in the campaign – rigid raiders, the 105-mm light gun and the Rapier missile.

The salute was taken by the Lord Mayor of London, Alderman Sir Christopher Leaver, with the Prime Minister at his side. Michael Foot, the leader of the Opposition, was a guest at the luncheon, but no member of the Royal family was present. The idea of the parade had been the Lord Mayor's, and it was paid for from private funds. Many were offended at the idea of a 'Victory Parade', and technically it was described as 'a gesture of thanks to the Task Force'. It has been pointed out that there were no similar parades after the two great World Wars. Looking across to the Bank of England and down to the saluting platform in front of the Mansion House, there did seem to be again that curious Victorian or Edwardian atmosphere which has cloaked so much of the Falklands episode. By the Bank, a Scots Guards band played 'Land of Hope and Glory' and 'It's a Long Way to Tipperary', and the crowds sang with them and, for once, seemed to know the words. It was much the same expression of feeling of nostalgia for a romantic notion of the past which brought the great crowds to the streets of London for the Royal Wedding of the Prince and Princess of Wales and the Queen's Jubilee of 1977.

The first contingent in the parade, behind the massed bands of the Royal Marines, Portsmouth, and of Flag Officer 3rd Flotilla, Sir Sandy Woodward, was the Royal Navy. At the head of the column strode Commander Alan West, the captain of HMS *Ardent*, awarded the Distinguished Service Cross for his leadership and bravery in the Falklands. The last time I had seen him was when he had brought his young crew aboard the *Canberra* on the evening of 21 May. The last I saw of his ship was a ball of blue flame in the darkness above the hills on the west side of San Carlos Water.

Commander West's award came with some eight hundred others for gallantry and meritorious service, announced in a special supplement to the *London Gazette* of Friday 8 October. The supplement was not due for release until Monday 11 October, but in one of the greatest orgies of press, television and radio leaks and embargo-breaking, the awards were announced for three whole days from the Friday to the Monday. Margaret Thatcher was reported to be upset, but the 'Falklands Factor', through the strange device of a three-day embargo, had won unexpectedly lengthy coverage.

Awards and honours of all kinds are nearly always controversial; Nobel prizes, the patronage of knighthoods and peerages, even university and college exams and honours, all are almost bound to be disputed. But the 11 October supplement of the *London Gazette* does tell of some remarkable acts of gallantry and service, and of sheer human courage. Many of these stories were almost completely unknown before, except to a tight circle of unit commanders in the Falklands and to those making the citations.

The list was headed by two posthumous Victoria Crosses, to Lieutenant-Colonel 'H' Jones of 2nd Battalion the Parachute Regiment, for his heroic leadership at Goose Green and for his single-handed and single-minded attack on the enemy machine-guns on Darwin Hill, which has been described vividly by his bodyguard, Sergeant Norman, in this book. The second VC was won by Sergeant Ian McKay of 3rd Battalion the Parachute Regiment. He was with Major Mike Argue's 'B' Company on Mount Longdon on the night of 11/12 June.

Two platoons were cut off by heavy machine-gun, artillery and mortar fire. His platoon commander was hit, a section corporal was injured in the legs and a private killed. Sergeant McKay had taken command of the platoon and continued to charge the enemy bunkers alone. He was killed by his own grenades as he took the positions. His citation concludes:

> Without doubt Sergeant McKay's action retrieved a most dangerous situation and was instrumental in ensuring the success of the attack. His was a coolly calculated act, the dangers of which must have been too apparent to him beforehand. Undeterred, he performed with outstanding selflessness, perseverance and courage. With a complete disregard for his own safety, he displayed courage and leadership of the highest order, and was an inspiration to all those around him.

Sergeant McKay's company commander, Major Mike Argue, won the Military Cross, as did Major David Collett for their role in taking Mount Longdon. The NGSFO Willie McCracken won the MC for the same action. Dair Farrar-Hockley and John Crosland of 2 Para won the MC for their parts in the battle at Goose Green, as did Major Kiszely of the Scots Guards at Tumbledown and Peter Babbington for the Mount Harriet action. Interviewed about his award, Peter Babbington recalled the difficulty of handling the three hundred prisoners taken by 42 Commando on Mount Harriet: 'They had some tobacco and quantities of marijuana. I told my men to hang on to the marijuana as we might need it; it was so cold that night.'

Sergeant 'Jumper' Collins won the Military Medal for leading his patrol through minefields on Mount Harriet to take the two forward fighting companies of 42 Commando to the start-line. Corporal Stephen Newland, who also won the MM, scaled part of the mountain by himself to attack enemy snipers and machine-guns.

Distinguished Service Orders were won by the commanding officer of 3 Para, Hew Pike, Mike Scott of the Scots Guards, Nick Vaux and Andrew Whitehead. In the latter's citation, the cool manner in which he directed the attack on Two Sisters was given particular emphasis. The awards are too numerous to give a complete list in this short postscript. Many are too modest, almost shy, men like the award of the Military Cross to Lieutenant Chris Fox of 45 Commando. He led 45 Commando's reconnaissance patrols, and won the award for fighting his way out of a skirmish with Argentinian positions during a surveillance patrol of Two Sisters a week before the main attack went in on the mountain. I saw Chris last on the top of those crags, telling Lieutenant-Colonel Andrew Whitehead about the minefields which lay further east towards Port Stanley. He looked tired and had a slightly apologetic expression as he said, 'Well, you see, we've already found a couple of minefields down there, and I think there are some more. Shall we go and look for them too?' His face was fresh and unmarked and he looked as if he had barely turned twenty. Behind his diffident manner of speaking, however, it became evident very quickly that there was a mind like a razor and a very strong will.

A large number of awards went to the Royal Navy, whose lists included the Royal Marines. DSOs and DSCs went to the captains of the frigates and destroyers that protected the troops landing at San Carlos: Nick Tobin of HMS *Antelope* won the DSC, Captain Jeremy Larken of HMS *Fearless* won the DSO, as did David Pentreath of HMS *Plymouth*. A DSO went to Lieutenant-Commander Brian Dutton for defusing the bomb that lodged in HMS *Argonaut* on 21 May; the job took a week and much of the work was done during air raids and air raid alerts. Captain Harry North of the Merchant Service, who was lost at sea when the *Atlantic Conveyor* was sunk, received a posthumous DSC, as did Lieutenant-Commander John Sephton, who stood on the flight deck of HMS *Ardent* firing a submachine-gun at a Skyhawk directly overhead as his ship's main armaments were put out of action. The civilian NAAFI Manager, Stephen Leake, who was called up with the rank of acting Petty Officer on 15 May, received the Distinguished Service Medal for his firing of the General Purpose Machine-Gun from the *Ardent*.

Several more of the Navy men mentioned in this book received awards and something of their story has been told already. Colour-Sergeant Brian Johnston, whose landing craft *F4* was sunk in Choiseul Sound on 8 June, received a posthumous Queen's Gallantry Medal. Lieutenant Richard Nunn, RM, won a posthumous Distinguished Flying Cross. Third-Officer Andy Gudgeon of the *Sir Galahad* and Chief Engineer Officer Ken Adams of the same ship also received the Queen's Gallantry Medal, and Ian Povey of the *Sir Galahad* received the Queen's Commendation for Brave Conduct. A brother officer, Paul Henry, received posthumously the highest civilian award for gallantry, the George Medal. Second Engineer Officer Paul Henry was trapped below in the *Sir Galahad* as the engine room filled with smoke following the air raids on 8 June. Knowing that he was badly wounded, he handed his breathing apparatus to a junior officer, telling him to make his way out of the compartment and saying that he himself would follow, though knowing he was too badly hurt to move. The GM was also awarded to Able Seaman Dillon of HMS *Ardent*. When the ship was attacked on 21 May, he went to control flood-damage in the dining area and was knocked unconscious. On coming round, he discovered that he was surrounded by falling debris and that 'a fire was raging in the area'. Though badly wounded by shrapnel, he managed to rescue another man from the burning wreckage. He dragged the man into the water and, after a struggle, both were hauled up by a helicopter crewman.

That crewman was Surgeon Commander Rick Jolly, who received the OBE, as did Lieutenant-Colonel Bill MacGregor, who led the team of surgeons at Ajax Bay. Among those manning the civilian ships, Captain Christopher Burne, Captain Dennis Scott-Masson, Captain Don Ellerby and Captain John Morton won the CBE. Commander Chris Esplin-Jones and Commander Andrew Ritchie won the OBE, as did Major Ewan Southby-Tailyour for his work on planning and carrying out the landing operations themselves.

In the London parade the most spectacular element was the fly-past, with Harriers and Victor tankers in tight formation, the Hercules, the VC 10 and the three Vulcan bombers, and the helicopters of the RAF, the Navy, the Army and the Teeny Weenies, the Royal Marine Air Squadron. A number of awards were made to flyers of all services. John Greenhalgh won the DFC for his extraordinary night casualty evacuation from Goose Green, and the man who led the vital Harrier raid in that battle, Squadron-Leader Jerry Pook, also won the DFC. He had flown twenty-three missions in the Falklands.

The RAF bomb-disposal expert, Flight-Lieutenant Alan Swan, was awarded the Queen's Gallantry Medal for defusing a bomb at Goose Green while being in imminent personal danger. His colleague, Sergeant Jim Prescott of the Royal Engineers, won the same decoration posthumously for his work in trying to defuse the bomb on HMS *Antelope* which eventually caused her destruction.

There were a number of civilian awards, too, of which some twenty or so were to islanders of the Falklands themselves. Dr Alison Bleaney won the OBE for her work in looking after the dwindling community in Port Stanley under Argentinian occupation, and for persuading the Argentinians under General Menendez to give up before more lives were lost in the town itself. The two priests, Monsignor Daniel Spraggon and the Reverend Harry Bagnall, were also given the OBE. My friends Pat Watts and Steve Whitley, the plumber Denis Place and the policeman-turned-pathfinder for the 3 Para 'tab' across East Falkland, Terry Peck, won the MBE. Nurses, shepherds, tractor-drivers were all recognised for their bravery and help to their communities. Eric Goss, the farm manager at Goose Green, was awarded the MBE.

Three names should be given special mention at the end of this book, all receiving some recognition in the honours and awards. Major Chris Keeble, the modern crusading Knight Templar and second in command of 2 Para, won the DSO for his direction of his battalion at Goose Green. The Reverend David Cooper, 2 Para's padre, and Steve Hughes, the 2 Para doctor, were mentioned in despatches. I am grateful to these men for their help and their company during the campaign and in the odyssey of putting this book together.

Unusually, the honours list gave citations for a number of

men of the SAS. Major Cedric Delves won the DSO for the retaking of South Georgia and for surveillance work round Port Stanley. Captain Gavin Hamilton won a posthumous MC for taking enemy fire to allow the rest of his surveillance patrol to escape near Port Howard on 10 June. In many respects, the SAS had worn quite a public face in the campaign and its aftermath. The role of the SAS men as the strategic intelligence-gathering element for the Task Force was vital. Yet in the longer perspective it is intelligence and communication, and the lack of it, that will arouse increasing controversy as the Falklands campaign and its origins are examined.

The crisis broke into armed conflict in April, May and June 1982 because intelligence on Argentinian intentions at all levels was lacking, inadequate or, for what little there was, poorly transmitted. A defence expert who had considerable experience of the operation of military intelligence suggests that the trouble really began in the mid-seventies. In Harold Wilson's last administration, so this expert claims, it was decided that military intelligence was too costly to operate on a world-wide basis. Britain's defence was becoming increasingly concentrated on NATO, Europe and the North Atlantic. British military intelligence activities were virtually withdrawn from a number of countries in 1976, and one of these was Argentina.

Much of the intelligence which helped Rear Admiral Woodward's tactical deployment had to come from Britain's allies and friends in interesting places. One of the most vital signals came from the Chilean Naval Command in Punta Arenas in the last week in April. A message was sent from the admiral controlling Punta Arenas, through an intermediary, to the British Military Attaché in Santiago. The message in English read, 'A1 information. One heavy unit, two light units at sea. 13.00–14.00 Zulu, latitude 54° 00′ south, longitude 65° 40′ west. Steering evasive course 335 degrees. Speed 18 knots.' This was the information that the cruiser *Belgrano* was moving round the Total Exclusion Zone to the south. It is now thought that she was part of an elaborate trap for the Task Force. Two Argentinian frigates already inside the Total

Exclusion Zone would tempt the British carriers south, and they would then be pounded by the *Belgrano*'s guns and the Exocets of the cruiser and her two escorts. Meanwhile the Argentinian carrier group, with the *Venticinco di Mayo* leading it, would move round the north of the Falklands and cut off the retreating British force. Alternatively, the *Belgrano* could have moved east to bombard South Georgia and cut off the islands there from re-supply.

The decision to sink the *Belgrano* was one of the most critical of the campaign. Once taken, it meant that there would be a fight all the way to Port Stanley. The antique cruiser, one of the few survivors of Pearl Harbour, as the USS *Phoenix*, posed the biggest single naval threat to the British Task Force. Her sinking may well have turned on a note in perfect English sent by a Chilean staff officer based in Punta Arenas.

London
14 October 1982

Epilogue

The clouds made a jagged screen of black over the mountains towards Van in the east, as the helicopter blades began to turn in the fields of wheat, thick green in the early growth of spring. Aboard the machines, the twin-rotored Chinooks of the RAF, the men of 45 Commando Royal marines were about to make an unofficial entry into northern Iraq to protect the refugee Kurds who had fled Saddam's forces by the million in the weeks before. As the machines ducked low for the run across the border marked by the arms of the Tigris, crewmen cocked their machineguns slung out of the cargo doors – to dissuade any passing Iraqi sniper from chancing a pot-shot.

At the moment the machines crossed the frontier into Iraq, the sun heralded their arrival by bursting through the clouds, bathing the valley in the limpid light of early spring. With little ceremony the helicopters dumped their human load at a little village beyond the town of Zakho which guards the main highway south from Diyarbakir and the Silk Road to Mosul and Baghdad. The Marines quickly took up position by their new home, the village schoolhouse, where classrooms were still littered with textbooks extolling the omniscience and virtue of the great leader Saddam Hussein. Beyond the school the flat houses, characteristic of all Kurdish villages, were stacked like layers in a sponge cake.

The schoolmaster, one of the very few to have stayed behind in the face of the physical and psychological terror of Saddam against the Kurds, descended the path to shout a greeting in fractured English to the Marines' commander, an austere steel-haired man in green camouflage.

The men of 45 Commando busied about cleaning up the headquarters for their new assignment – 'Operation Safe

Haven' in which they were to shepherd the Kurds from their mountain refuges in Turkey back to the plain, where they were to be fed, sheltered and given medical attention. Altogether some 5,000 British servicemen and women would be involved, mostly from 3 Commando Brigade Royal Marines.

The commandos confessed it was an unusual exercise, in fact an operation quite unlike any other they had experienced. But no one was grumbling – at least not officially. There was a real job to be done. Up in the mountains under the torrential rain of late winter the Kurds were dying by the hundred, if not the thousand, each day and each week. At least a million and a half had to be brought back from the Turkish border alone, and another million had fled to the mountains of Iran – the biggest single movement of refugees in modern times. Most Marines believed the rescue of the Kurds was a job for which they were suited, and that British soldiers will have to be trained for such tasks in the future.

The last time I had seen 45 Commando in the field was when he walked into Stanley together as the snow was falling on 14 June 1982. Since then we had gone our different ways, 45 Commando to the regular round of arctic warfare training in Norway and tours in Northern Ireland. The Marines had missed out on the Gulf deployment and Operation Desert Storm and Desert Sabre, or in the more prosaic British version Operation Granby. Life as itinerant reporter had taken me to the desert. With the Command Troop of the 14th/20th King's Hussars earlier in the year I had already made one unscheduled break-in into Iraq as witness to the great allied armoured thrust to expel Saddam's troops from Kuwait.

The reunion with 45 Commando was in exotic surroundings none of us could have envisaged nine years before when we were heading into the South Atlantic. Some of the faces were familiar from those days, though most were not. Quite a high proportion of Marines and Paras quit within two years of the Falklands campaign – a quite common phenomenon in the circumstances: they had tasted the action for which the years in training were a preparation, and the aftermath was an anticlimax.

One of those recognised immediately was Andy Salmon – a section commander in 1982 – now the Officer Commanding the Reconnaissance Troop. Together we liberated the village of Batufa guarding the eastern approach to the plains of Zakho – much to the chagrin of the American General, who seemed as uncomfortable about the press as he was about his entire mission with the Kurds. In the village we met a handsome young Kurdish woman in a yellow dress – she was already the mother of three children though she could not have seen her twentieth birthday. She was from a well-to-do family of Batufa, who had decided to say behind in their large modern house of many airy rooms. We were offered fine aromatic mint tea, and regaled with tales of the destruction and woes of the village. The Iraqi troops had come to the houses on wrecking and looting forays, said the old grand-father, a grizzled gentleman with a grave face topped by a tight turban. The family showed us smashed trinkets and ornaments, broken mirrors and pieces of furniture. On the whole the house had got off lightly – probably because it was occupied.

Further up the street we encountered a patrol of Iraqi soldiers, who seemed completely disorientated. They grinned and posed for photographs, one waving a rocket-propelled grenade launcher in an alarmingly unprofessional manner. They told us they were Shi'ites from the south, doing enforced military service. One said he believed his parents had died in the fighting round the Shi'ite holy cities of Najaf and Karbala. There the destruction had been fright-ening, he said, and as bad as anything seen in the port of Basra, which had suffered from two Gulf wars before Sad-dam's troops wrought a hurricane of vengeance on the rebellious Shi'ites.

The roads out of Zakho were littered with straggling soldiers, some carrying strange booty – the favourites were bits of ornately carved beds and mirrors – as they pulled back from facing the allied troops trying to protect the Kurds. By contrast with the confusion of refugees and retreating Iraqis, the Royal Marines moved with purpose and precision, though several confessed that they had little idea what to expect over the next hill. One dreary day of incessant fine mountain rain, a party set off in three or four decrepit British trucks to get some infirm and sick Kurds from the high passes – the walking wounded who might not make the journey back home without assistance.

Halfway up the mountain we came to a narrow valley which looked like a huge breakers' yard. Cars, trucks, tractors had been abandoned as they broke down or ran out of fuel in the Kurds' headlong flight from Saddam's helicopters which had been firing gas and ordnance into their villages and towns along the northern valleys. This was 'Car City', the last stop before the big climb over the mountain ridge into Turkey. A man in a pin-stripe suit with a prosperous belly asked the marines commander to fetch his old mother from further up the mountain; she was ill and would die there if no help came. Colonel Thomson agreed to the mission. A soldier's soldier, in his mid-forties he seemed old for his command. In the Falklands he had led the Special Boat Squadron to great effect, and with a good deal more professional restraint in dealings with the press than his more garrulous counterpart commanding the SAS at the time. Unusually he was now serving a second tour as Commanding Officer, this time with 45 Commando. Parsimonious in words, he held the immediate trust and respect of those serving above him and below him – a rare phenomenon in the office politics of modern service life.

The colonel confessed himself bewildered by the scale of problems presented by the Kurds. As we struggled to shove his Land Rover up a steep glissade of mud, the refugees filtered slowly through the trees on the mountainside. Most were young women and girls, mothers with babies at the breast and girls of nine or ten barefoot carrying younger brothers and sisters on their back. About one in every three adults was pregnant; this was a population explosion on the march.

We found the old woman eventually in a circle of tents and old vehicles by a mountain track which coiled round a jagged peak and into Turkey. She seemed frail, but in reasonable health, and barking at her son with the tetchiness of a confirmed matriarch. She was a tribal queen, used to getting her way. 'I think we may have been conned,' muttered Colonel Thomson, 'but you never know. This is part of the job we've come to do – and we must try to get the old people off the mountain.' The Kurds were a law unto themselves, a typical mountain society where feuds and rivalries followed the lines of the valleys and passes dividing the communities. The Marines, like the other soldiers in the allied force, had to deploy a delicate balance of diplomacy and cajolery to get the Kurds moving to safe areas, and even to follow the most basic rules of hygiene.

More familiar to the Marines were the tasks of advancing to establish forward positions against the vagrant bits of Saddam's rag-bag army. Most spectacular was their leap forward to secure the airfield by one of the Iraqi dictator's summer palaces at Sarsank – an architectural pot-pourri of Castle Doom and a Butlins Holiday Camp. The airfield itself had been comprehensively cratered by allied bombers during the offensive of Operation Desert Storm and hardly a building nearby had escaped the blast damage. The Marines landed from their helicopters on the edge of the vast apron of tarmac – and filed off like a patrol of ants, labouring under their heavy packs.

At Sarsank they were to confront a makeshift garrison of secret police and Republican Guard – whom they saw off in a gentle exchange of fire a few days later. Three days before 45 Commando took up residence, I had arrived with a band of two colleagues and a television crew in a mustard-coloured Land Rover. The Republican Guard commanders gave us tea, admonished us, and said they contemplated despatching us immediately to Baghdad. A doctor of dubious medical ethics said he worked with the garrison and did not like the English as he knew they had tortured and killed their prisoners of war in the desert campaign two months before.

The commandos were in northern Iraq to keep the peace and allow the Kurds to go home – a diplomatic show of strength which is now an increasingly important role for the armed forces of senior western allies such as Britain and France. The most theatrical performance came only a few days after first landing inside Iraq. For several days the Iraqis had been moving secret police – Mukhabarat – and Republican Guard in plain dark olive-green uniforms into Zakho to intimidate the population and deter the allied efforts to help the Kurds in Operation Safe Haven. The allies decided to accept the challenge and face down Saddam's men. One blazing afternoon a company of Royal Marines, advertising themselves with their green berets rather than steel helmets boarded huge six-wheeled US Army trucks and roared across the bridge over the tributary of the Tigris into Zakho. Rifles were cocked and the heavy calibre machineguns were readied in their cradles atop the trucks. The children cheered and waved, the Republican Guards were astonished. The temporary residence for the company was to be one of the town's three hotels – or rather would-be hotel for it had been trashed to little more than a shell before it could be completed. In less than a day it had been cleaned of filth and rubbish and the Marines were patrolling the streets in the standard six man 'brick' pattern adopted for patrols in Belfast. Their colleagues from the US Marines followed at a discreet distance to learn how the job was done.

'Well it's just the same as we've always done in Northern Ireland,' observed a ginger-haired commando. 'We've had plenty of practice as we've just come from a tour in South Armagh.'

Life in training and operations had followed a fairly familiar path in the years after the expedition to the South Atlantic in the middle of 1982. But the story of the place they came to liberate, of the Falkland Islands themselves, was to show some surprising departures and breaks with the past. Within a very few years the main holdings and business on the islands was to become less the preserve of the Falkland Islands Company and the big farms, many owned by absentee landlords. Larger holdings were broken up into family-sized units, and sold to owner-occupiers on heavy mortgages. At the time of most of the sales in the mid-eighties, the prices of wool on world markets were depressed. The Falkland Islands Company was sold by Coalite to Anglo United, and began to take less interest in the Islands and the future. Fortunately in the early nineties the price of wool picked up, and the high natural quality of Falklands samples became a real prospect once again.

The story of the conflict had aroused the British government to action in providing funds for public works and infrastructure which the Shackleton Report of 1976 had identified as an urgent necessity. Shackleton made further recommendations in late 1982, and these unlocked the door to payments of about £50 million by the British Government of the next six or seven years in the form of grants and compensation for war damage. The Falkland Islanders showed a semblance of personal wealth they could only dream of ten years before. They became a society addicted to video; they had a telephone system which linked the main settlements, and which could be dialled direct from the United Kingdom. The population began to rise steadily towards the magic figure of 2,500 – the optimum number of inhabitants the authorities said the economy could sustain. In addition the islanders had a new airport at the military base of Mount Pleasant, home of a garrison of about a thousand service personnel and support staff.

The biggest source of wealth was the boom in offshore fishery. Licences were granted to ships of a dozen nations to use harbour facilities at Port Stanley and ride at anchor in Berkeley Sound. The islanders provided victuals, medical services and other assistance – at a price. Attempts to get a local fishery going were less happy, and public funds of nearly £9 million for such projects mysteriously went astray. Another mirage was the persistent report that the islands were rich in oil reserves. Oil and fossil fuels are likely to prove a very distant prospect. The Malvina Basin between the Falklands and the Argentine coast is known to be one of the biggest reserves in the region. Yet it will be generations before it becomes technically and commercially viable – and then operations will have to be conducted, in cooperation with the Argentines, from Argentina itself.

Two years after the conflict the Islands were struck by an appalling accident. On a blustery night in April 1984 the King Edward Memorial Hospital in Stanley burnt down. Eight people died in the fire; in the conflict only three civilians had lost their lives. The King Edward had been built in time to receive the wounded from the Battle of the Falklands in December 1914. It was a wooden structure, in much need of repair – or better still replacement altogether. Conditions had been made more difficult by the need to share with a large medical staff for the garrison which then had not moved out of Stanley. Relations between the two teams of doctors and nurses were not harmonious – the Army doctors and nurses were used to hierarchy, whereas the civilians epitomised the friendly informality of island society. Just before the fire a new military clinic had been opened in prefab cabins next to the hospital itself, where new fire hoses were left unconnected to the water supply. Afterwards the circumstances of how the fire started were never fully explained, despite a legal inquiry – arson was never entirely ruled out.

Many islanders found the presence of the garrison irksome, but this produced yet more confusion in the minds of the more thoughtful. Some said they felt both grateful and guilty about the soldiers and that it had needed such effort and sacrifice in action to wrest their homes back from the Argentines. Yet the islanders have been assiduous in keeping the memory of the conflict green, carefully marking the anniversary of invasion and liberation each year.

Over the years almost every aspect of the campaign, its conduct and its reporting, have come under scrutiny and reappraisal. The books and articles continued to pour forth in their hundreds, and still do so. Perspectives change with time and as more information comes to light. On a number of points of fact and interpretation I realise the account in this book is wrong – though I have kept the narrative intact as even the mistakes are a faithful reflection of how the experience of the campaign appeared to me at the time and in the weeks of the immediate aftermath.

Not all the subsequent debates and differences of opinion can be rehearsed here – some have become almost tediously academic – but it is worth reflecting on how my views on some of the events recorded here have altered.

The planning of the landings at San Carlos seems now to have been bolder and braver than I realised at the time. It was realised from quite early on that the cover from Combat Air Patrols of pairs of Sea Harriers would be limited, and the aircraft would have devoted much time to the protection of their own groups of ships. A lot would depend on the missiles and anti-aircraft fire of the frigates and destroyers escorting the landing force. The decision to place a handful of them, *Antrim*, *Plymouth*, *Ardent* and *Argonaut*, out in Falkland Sound to draw fire away from the amphibious ships, and the *Canberra*, *Norland* and *Elk*, carried a high risk. They were to be like a screen of decoy ducks on a lake, and a sharp Argentine pilot might have realised this, ignored them and concentrated on the more valuable – and vulnerable – landing ships and transports. The trick worked brilliantly; it had a truly Nelsonian flair. As I record here, the picket got a bashing – *Ardent* sunk, *Argonaut* immobilised and *Antrim* with a bomb through its Sea Slug missile launcher – but the *Canberra* and her sister ships were untouched. This touch of tactical cunning I ascribed at the time to Admiral John Woodward: I was wrong as it is now evident it was the work of Commodore Mike Clapp, who did not receive subsequently the praise he deserves for this bold stroke.

The biggest confusion remains in my mind about what happened at Goose Green, how exactly Colonel Jones died in the attempt to save his battalion as it stared disaster in the face, and how so few men could unlock the battle, and then surround and defeat an enemy almost three times as large and with the defensive advantage. There are almost as many different versions of the events as there were people on the battlefield that day: some have been quite outlandish; some have carefully rearranged key events for the historical record; and none of the instant histories in the ten years after succeed in recreating the atmosphere and drama of that extraordinary engagement.

The officers of 2 Para carried out an exercise which should make any journalistic commentator or contemporary historian think twice before rushing to judgement on such matters. In the months after the battle the two commanders of the battalion, David Chaundler and Chris Keeble, asked anyone who was there at the time to write down on a sheet of foolscap paper what they thought had happened during the action, to them and to those around them. Looking at the different offerings, the officers came to the conclusion that nobody actually knew the whole story at the time or afterwards – though David Chaundler thinks he has managed to piece together now an outline of all the main moves and decisions of the different sub-units.

This is a salutary lesson. Goose Green was on the miniature scale of warfare, with something around 2,000 combatants involved at the most. It rates somewhere on the level of Nibley wood in the Wars of the Roses or Widow McCormick's Cabbage Patch in the Fenian Rising rather than the Granacus, Cannae, Verdun and the Somme. But let no one deceive themselves, it was a real and at times desperate fight, with nearly two hundred casualties and possibly as much as a hundred dead. If it is still difficult to establish what went on during the eighteen hours of battle on that narrow isthmus of moorland one wonders how much laundering has gone into the official accounts of the mass offensives and campaigns of ancient and modern warfare.

Quite soon after this book was written it became clear that the helicopter carrying 5 Brigade's two senior signals officers forward to Fitzroy had been shot down by the Sea Dart of HMS *Cardiff* (p. 238). In the dark the helicopter had failed to respond with an IFF (identification friend or foe) signal, and Cardiff fired but soon realised the mistake. Such was the chaos in 5 Brigade HQ that the ships approaching the islands from the south for gunfire support had not been informed of the planned movements of all the brigade's aircraft. It was to be several years before the information was made public, which proved immensely damaging and distressing for those immediately concerned, particularly the families of the dead.

Accidents of friendly fire are a hazard of any war, particularly in the electronic age. On the day of the landings 'C' Company of 3 Para were mortared by their own battalion outside Port San Carlos because of an inadvertent error over map references. Patrols of 45 Commando collided in the mist during reconnoitering operations into enemy lines forward of Mount Kent, and casualties were inflicted. But it was the controversy over the downing of the helicopter by HMS *Cardiff* which led to a prompt and laudable change of policy by the services and the Ministry of Defence. It was decided that in such cases in the future as much information or possible would be made public – after the next of kin had been informed.

The new policy was tested severely in the Gulf conflict. When two Warrior armoured fighting vehicles of the Royal Regiment of Fusiliers battle Group were hit by American A10 Thunderbolt 'tank busters', killing seven instantly and wounding 11, the commanders acted immediately. The briefing of journalists less than a day later by Brigadier Christopher Hammerbeck, commanding 4 Brigade, was exemplary – and the war had still hours to run before President Bush declared his cease fire. The brigadier told us all he knew, and all we could want to know at the time, killing at a stroke any germinating rumours and conspiracy theories.

The most difficult Falklands controversy still to unravel was the bombing of the LSL transports *Sir Galahad* and *Sir Tristram* as they waited to discharge at Fitzroy on 7 June 1982, which led to some 50 Welsh Guardsmen being killed or severely wounded, and a casualty list of about a hundred in all. At the time in the battle area the whole episode seemed an accumulation of little setbacks which became a disaster: the Guards had not managed to get into Bluff Cove at night because of foul weather and enemy artillery; the ammunition was unloaded from the ships before the men; the Rapier anti-aircraft missiles were not up and running; the attacking aircraft had been spotted after take-off from the Argentine coast but not tracked to their targets. But time and reflection lead to one overriding conclusion. Much was made at the time about decisions, or indecision at the local command level. The most potent criticism is the one now put by Julian Thompson, then Commanding 3 Commando Brigade. The whole sequence of events went wrong because the Fleet Command at Northwood would not allow HMS *Fearless* to go round once more from San Carlos to Fitzroy to disgorge the Welsh Guards, as it only managed to deliver half the battalion at the first attempt. The admirals and their advisers said they were not prepared to risk such a major ship – though it would make passage at night. It was one of the clearest cases of what Thompson calls Northwood's penchant for 'backseat driving'. Superb communications which allowed instant contact with the battlefield commanders by satellite had led to hubris – it gave the commanders and politicians in the rear 8,000 miles away a false sense of omniscience.

The battles for the mountains overlooking Port Stanley, Tumbledown and Longdon especially, were grimmer and bloodier affairs than we heard of at the time. The 2nd Battalion of the Scots Guards fought with the bayonet and only took the heights of Tumbledown at dawn on the 14 June and thus opened the way into Stanley. The Argentine Marines had laid their defences well, heavy machinegun and mortar posts well positioned in the rocks – which on another day and with another command would have made the position well nigh impregnable. But the Marines had planned a withdrawal battle – for they knew there were no reliable reinforcements to hand to ensure they held their position. The Guards were ordered to wear berets and not helmets, to avoid being confused with the enemy, which seems a lunatic decision given the amount of shrapnel and rock splinter flying about. That Tumbledown was carried in the end was largely due to the courage and decisiveness of Major John Kiszely, OC Left Flank Company, and one of the outstanding company commanders of the entire conflict. His men took the last major enemy position – on the way up he found that one Guardsman Mackenzie had obeyed orders to follow him up the mountain even though he had run out of ammunition.

Longdon two nights before was equally difficult, a long action followed by a day's heavy counter shelling from heavy guns round Stanley inflicting more casualties than were taken in the battle itself. The attack was supposed to be 'silent' – it had to be because the gun batteries were needed on fire missions elsewhere as the Marines were preparing to take Mount Harriet and Two Sisters. But after Corporal Milne trod on a mine at the start line by the Murrell Bridge, the enemy knew the Paras were there and it developed into an eleven-hour slog through the positions across the rocky spine that was Longdon. Recoilless anti-tank guns, mortar machineguns and phosphorous grenades were fired at minimum range. A vivid portrayal of the battle is the recently published *Excursion to Hell* by Vince Bramley, then a Lance Corporal in the Machine-gun Platoon, one of the best of all the first-hand accounts of the campaign. He describes how the momentum of high emotion of some of the Paras went on after the firing had died. One NCO is said to have shot a group of American mercenaries out of hand, though they had laid down the weapons. The incident is not yet closed, and at the time of writing it is being examined and considered at the highest level in Whitehall.

Within two or three years, the Falklands campaign and its implications became a distinctly unfashionable topic for discussion. Discreetly the battles and actions were examined and debated in the military academies. At the Staff College the favourite was Wireless Ridge where the light reconnaissance vehicles of the Blues and Royals were used to full effect for the first time. 2 Para took only three killed and they probably fell from friendly artillery fire. The battle plan disrupted the enemy decision cycle entirely, and the Argentines' feeble counter attack mounted in the early hours of daylight on 14 June petered out after it had barely begun.

The irony is that the action was commanded by Lt Colonel David Chaundler, the only CO who led his troops into battle who did not get decorated for the Falklands – it was an astonishing oversight, probably due to the whims and vanities of politicians, because the planning and execution of his battle plan is now thought to have been about the best by all the battalion commanders.

In a way, though, the Falklands became a form of private guilt in the tribal family of the British armed services. Senior officers and politicians liked to hint that it was something of a strategic red herring, and Britain's security and defence priorities lay in a completely different direction. It would be hard to envisage Britain mounting another such amphibious operation a long way from home again. It smacked of a global 'blue waters' strategy for which the romantics in the Navy hankered, but which was quite inappropriate to the limited military and economic resources of a second rank power like Britain. No, the choice had to be against 'blue waters' in favour of 'the continental commitment'. Britain's defence priority, so the established view of the mid-eighties went, lay in collective security with our European and North American allies in NATO to face the threat of the big red arrow – the serried ranks of the forces of the Soviet Union and the Warsaw Pact. This was certainly the thinking behind the 'Way Ahead' Defence Cuts of 1981 ordered by John Nott, Defence Secretary at the time of the Falklands: he believed the Navy and Air Force should be trimmed in favour of nuclear and conventional forces committed to NATO in Europe. A year after the Falklands campaign he retired from politics, his views unchanged.

But in 1986 came Gorbachev and the thaw. Three years later the Berlin Wall fell and massive cuts in conventional military forces in Europe (through the CFE process) were in prospect. Barely eighteen months after the end of the division of Berlin, the Warsaw Pact had melted away and soon the Soviet Union showed every sign of coming unstuck with the armed forces the cat's-paw of the warring parties. Since there was no longer a threat from the east, no more big red arrows on the map, conventional forces in the West could be hacked to the bone. The era of the peace dividend was at hand, and NATO cast about for a new strategic doctrine to keep it in business.

Commanders and strategists in Britain and America were accused of inventing new threats to replace the old ones to justify the armed services and their own careers. Powers of fiction and invention were scarcely needed, however, for new threats were emerging. The strategic map of Europe and its neighbourhood has become infinitely complex in the aftermath of the Cold War.

Dramatic as were the changes in Europe itself, nothing was to be as sudden and surprising as the crisis generated by Saddam Hussein and the war in the Gulf. With the invasion of Kuwait on 2 August 1990 a vital strategic lifeline was threatened – and that week Saddam's tanks could have roared on unopposed to take the vital oil ports of Saudi Arabia on the Gulf. This would have thrown the world economy into cataclysm, affecting rich and poor, First World and Third World alike. Yet the anti-militarist left were opposed to action, and as eight years before, they were prepared to give dictatorship the benefit of the doubt. Once more they had picked a particularly poor candidate as Saddam's regime has one of the worst records on human rights abuse in the region – however much the indulgence of him in the Iran–Iraq war forbore the West to ignore it.

Once more, in just over eight years, Britain prepared to despatch an expeditionary force overseas, albeit as a junior partner to the United States. Nearly 40,000 personnel from all three services were involved, and the operation was mounted with ill-disguised effort and strain. It took the resources of the entire British Army of the Rhine, nominally some 55,000 strong, to equip and deploy a light armoured division of two armoured brigades (tank and infantry) and an artillery brigade. A third armoured brigade could not be sent as there were not enough working Challenger tanks to go round. In Germany the Rhine Army was left with only a dozen working Challenger tanks. 'The trouble is that for

years we ran our forces on the ground in Germany on a third
party, fire and theft basis,' said Major General Rupert Smith,
who commanded the 1st UK Division in the desert, 'but
when we got to the Gulf we suddenly wanted a fully comprehensive policy.'

Going to the desert as an accredited correspondent of a
British Operational Force, donning camouflage fatigues
(though this time in delicate shades of sand), I felt like a
repeat offender. As I went up to the 4th Armoured Brigade
on the ranges north of Al Jubail in the last week of January,
faint echoes of the same experience eight years before aboard
Canberra and *Norland* came drifting back.

Many of the mundane preoccupations of daily life were the
same, hanging on to kit (a losing battle again), the round of
stand-to at dawn and dusk, the heart-attack-on-a-plate
breakfasts, keeping the 'green worm' sleeping bag dry and
out of prying hands. The weather was just as variable, and
surprisingly cold in the desert where on several mornings we
found ice round the Challengers and Warriors and the heavy
rain produced a carpet of fine grass across the sand.

But much was different from the Falklands experience –
the sheer scale of the desert campaign for one thing. We were
aware at all times that the British Division was quite a small
cog in a very large machine – one of the smallest of the
seventeen divisions the allies were deploying along the Saudi
borders with Kuwait and Iraq. Even a brigade on the move
would require a procession hours on end of hundreds of
vehicles, wheeled and tracked kicking up typhoons of sand
and dust. Overhead the skies would be full of parades of
aircraft, tankers, F-15 and F-16 fighter bombers, the occasional British Tornado, Wild Weasel jammers, planes with
anti-aircraft or land searching radars, and the ugly Warthog
A-10 tank-busters painted with the pearly teeth of sharks.
The Falklands was the all-British come-as-you-are party.
Desert Storm was a much more formal business.

The formality embraced the way the journalists were run –
and many of the restrictions came from the Americans who,
on the whole, believed the hacks were best kept at arms'

length. In the Falklands the rules for the accompanying journalists were rough and ready, and largely a matter of improvisation on the spot. Since much depended on whether individual soldiers or reporters happened to get on together, the experience was much more productive for both sides than the media pundits and armchair commentators claimed afterwards with the gift of 20-20 hindsight. The big encumbrance was distance, access to satellite phones and the double censorship brought in by the MoD in Whitehall. The regulations for the British hacks in Operation Granby in the desert were rigid, and so more conducive to frustration and bad temper. In the field we were hindered from moving around from unit to unit and between the two brigades of the armoured division. Initially we were discouraged from living with the battle groups. I misplayed my hand from the start and within days was accused by the 4 Brigade Press and Information Officer of 'always trying to fish for information'. A facetious remark about that being a pretty good job description did not improve relations which went from grumbling argument to silent hostility.

My rescuers from boredom and idleness were knights in camouflaged, if not shining, armour – the 14th/20th King's Hussars. I could not have picked a better bunch to go to war with in the circumstances. The 14/20th are a family regiment, most come from a tight radius round Oldham, Manchester and parts of the Lancashire coast. This was to be the regiment's third invasion of Iraq this century – they had gone up the Euphrates to Baghdad in 1917 and 1941, both times as part of the Indian Army. They had a wonderfully relaxed attitude to all that life could throw at them, and they were the epitome of Lancashire phlegm. This did not conceal their skill and understanding of what they had to do – at their best they were as good as any unit I came across in the Falklands. Being the only armoured regiment of 4 Brigade – the other armoured brigade had two cavalry regiments with Challenger tanks – they had an extra burden of duty and responsibility in providing the tank firepower to support the infantry.

The spirit of the regiment was summed up by Lt Colonel

Mike Vickery, their commander in the Gulf, describing how the regiment's forebears in the 14th Light Dragoons captured their most famous trophy, a solid silver chamber pot given by the Emperor Napoleon to his brother Joseph, at the battle of Vitoria in 1813. 'As part of the Ragged Brigade the 14th Dragoons managed to sneak round the back – I suppose you call it "asymmetric warfare" today – and fell upon the baggage train. They found the pot in the coach of the King of Spain. We've always been pretty good at sneaking round the back in war.' In the Second World War the regiment, by then the 14th/20th, spent the early part in Iraq and the Middle East, joining in the Italian campaign later. Its last engagement was at Medicina in the Lombard Plain in April 1945 where the regiment was commanded by Colonel 'Freckles' Tilney. His son Godfrey was the second in command in the Gulf, the third generation to serve the regiment. His grandfather had committed the solecism of ordering a beer in the mess after a hard afternoon on the polo field in India – since the flavour of the day was Swipes Beer, he was known as 'Swipes' Tilney ever after.

Since I was to travel to war in the Battery Commander's Warrior observation vehicle my home became the jumble of camouflage nets and assorted tracked vehicles known as the Command Troop. There my guide, counsellor, critic and friend was Corporal Steve Redgrave, the gunner of the Colonel's tank, baptised the 'Emperor' after the regiment's most famous trophy. Steve was a small man who looked like an upturned pudding basin on legs (as he himself put it) under his enormous helmet. He was half my age, almost to the year, but that merely added to the caustic wit and criticism. He was sharp and bright, a natural soldier, but in deference to his wife who was finishing her art degree in Manchester he was quitting the colours. In fact he should have left months before, but he lied to his family and stayed for the campaign. The least pompous of men, his reasons for signing up for the desert would shock any cynic of the post-modern age: 'I decided I couldn't let my mates down. It was a bit of queen and country, I know, too. But I always thought in the end the UN would sort something out. I never thought it would come to this, but now I know we are going to war.' Our relationship was one of harmonious rancour – he was my streetwise guide in navigating the intricacies of regimental politics. To him I was merely 'the fat-gutted bastard' of the press.

On occasion he would save us from the mind-numbing routines and exercises in that cold winter desert. One night we were setting up camp after an aimless exercise in 'passage of lines' through American forces in preparation for breaking into southern Iraq. As the tank's engines died in the freezing night air, Steve stood up on the turret to deliver the perfect epigraph on that fruitless day's work: 'I'm that happy, I could shit', he intoned in his Lancashire accent. To which rejoined the voice of the adjutant from the bowels of the tank, 'said a highly placed military source.'

The presiding genius was that of Colonel Mike Vickery. At forty-two he was comparatively old to have command – it was, though the same age at which H. Jones commanded 2 Para when he died. We met as the tanks were bombing up for the first time with their battle ammunition before moving up to the concentration areas west of the Wadi al Batin from where they would move into Iraq. A silver-haired elegant figure, though with the stomach of a polo player who has enjoyed the all-round entertainment of the game, he has a slightly curved nose, not at all unlike the famous Hohenzollern eagle of the regimental badge – affectionately known as 'the shite hawk'.

He explained to me that first day that he thought the regiment would have quite a long wait before battle. 'I want to raise their readiness by a notch each day. I don't want to get them too fired up now, because they'll find it hard to keep their sharpness – I want them to have enough in reserve so they'll be ready on the day.' As the days turned to weeks in the sand, we got to know each other well, and he extended to me and my colleagues the trust that many of his superiors seemed unable or unwilling to. He would introduce informal tutorials on some of the mysteries of armoured warfare and made sure I got to know the regiment and its support elements, particularly the REME, mechanics of genius who had nothing to declare but their brains and their toolboxes. Such generosity was not without cost – Brigade Headquarters and the chief censor thought we were continuously trading deep secrets. Most of the plotting was entirely innocent – indeed, the great reporting coup of this long waiting period was to get the eve of battle mess night of alcohol-free beer and compo gazetted in the 'Court and Social' pages of the *Daily Telegraph*. Mike Vickery was not a man for the soap box or the great eve of battle speech, but when he said simply at the last regimental orders group, 'Gentlemen, I am about to order the 14th/20th into battle for the first time since the Second World War,' the effect was electrifying. At the more or less repeatable anecdote (in mixed company) he is a master. He is a great encourager – two of his favourite epithets to subordinates and equals are 'outstanding', or 'trif'. As a host, formal, military and informal he was outstanding, and became a friend for life.

During the waiting game in the desert, the Falklands revisited in strange ways. During a brief call on the Royal Scots, a wonderfully carefree bunch of tartan bother, I was ushered to a tent to see a video on 'Battle Shock', and 'Battle Stress'. Suddenly it was yesterday in San Carlos. Rick Jolly was talking volubly to the camera about the effects of stress and shock on battle casualties. Jabbering nineteen to the dozen Commander Morgan O'Connell was telling us that war's most significant wounds were psychological. Morgan, I remember, claimed that the journalists would prove the group most vulnerable to psychological disorder as we were a mob of uncooperative loners and individualists – in that case now on my seventh campaign, I must have long passed the point of no return.

The other tenuous link to the Falklands was the Commander of the 1st UK Division, Major General Rupert Smith. He had been a close friend of H. Jones in the Parachute Regiment – indeed I first met him in the Jones house playing charades at a party in December 1982, he was then about to command 3 Para. Rupert Smith was the outstanding British commander of the Gulf operation, and possibly one of the most accomplished commanders of the whole alliance in the field – incisive, bold, and trusted implicitly by those he commands. His intelligence is one of the most disconcerting of anyone I know – his brain seems always to be laying ambushes.

His approach to the press was highly individual for the modern age. For the most part he did not believe in talking to them – that was for others to do, and he had two brigade commanders who were not unaverse to publicity and advertisement, anyway. When I did catch up with him days after the cease fire, he managed to derail the interview after a few minutes by stating, 'I don't think I accept the premise of your question.' Later he turned the tables by asking what I thought the risk of instability in Europe was from the flood of migration that appeared to be coming from the Maghreb and the eastern Mediterranean, a subject he knew I was writing about. As we departed for a gourmet compo lunch he said quietly, 'I wanted to make sure that nobody under my command suffered the lack of fire support that you and H. endured at Goose Green. That sort of thing was not going to happen again if I could help it.'

Helped it, he had. The hours and days of careful planning and preparation by Rupert Smith and his staff ensured that the British Division could move as far and fast as any unit in the desert. Each sub unit commander, of battery, squadron, company and platoon, knew his mission. At one point General Smith cut the logistics tail for nearly ten hours so as not to impede the advance of the British and the American 1st Infantry Division. The result was that after a pursuit battle of three days and nearly 150 miles through Iraq into Kuwait, the British was the only one of 17 allied divisions capable of advancing to the gates of Basra, if need be.

When the battle came in the desert, it proved theatrical, nasty and brief. There had been a night of storm before the tanks of 4 and 7 Brigade moved to pass through the defensive dunes into Iraq on 25 February 1991. As we halted the sky turned the colour of pea soup from the fumes of oil fires set by the Iraqis to the east and a gathering thunderstorm. Suddenly on the horizon a regiment of guns began firing into the gloom, flashes from their muzzles cutting the gloom as supply vehicles scurried in between like herds of frightened buffalo. In pyrotechnic arcs of light the multi-launch rockets punched towards the thunder clouds which replied with jagged shafts of lightning.

The advance into Iraq was a stop-go affair – advance a few hundred yards, stop, wait for orders then go again. The battlefield seemed an infernally crowded place. The satellite navigation system became confused, and visibility was down to a few hundred yards in the thick oily rain. The tanks opened fire with a roll of sharp cracks. The Iraqi tanks burst open their targets like cans of processed food. Turrets were hurled yards away by artillery and the high explosive and kinetic rounds of the allied tanks. Most devastating were the salvos of multi-launch rockets, six hundred and sixty bomblets in a matter of seconds, wiping out whole companies in an instant. But the Iraqis did not want to fight; they had been abandoned by their commanders, and their leader Saddam Hussein. In the early hours I could get out of the Battery Commander's Warrior – to witness an astonishingly theatrical scene. The sky was deep purple, lit by artillery illumination shells. Before a huge berm, a defensive sand dune, crouched a hundred Iraqi prisoners looking like slaves in Nabucco, waiting for a party of Grenadier Guards to escort them to the cages.

In the morning we again descended from the Battery commander's Warrior to see the plain of hard sand dotted with burning tanks – fortunately many of them had been abandoned by the Iraqis desperate to surrender. By noon the first sequence of actions was over. Across the field surged Iraqis waving white shirts and clothes, moving in a panicky dance trying to surrender. All night few had wanted to stand and fight. A man with a thick beard showed us where he had buried his Kalashnikov rifle and his food, which he implored us to take – it was a bag of dried dates.

By evening several hundred prisoners had congregated round the tanks – the crews giving as much food and water as they could spare. They looked cold and hungry, but showed little fear – but they shunned the ones in funny uniforms, obviously the Ba'ath Party men and the secret police. Again that evening the tanks joined in a long chase into the positions guarding the western border of Kuwait along the Wadi al Batin. For a few minutes some Iraqis chose to fight, they had the superior G5 artillery pieces designed by Gerald Bull, architect of the infamous 'super gun'.

After another morning of replenishment, on Wednesday 27 February, the British and American tanks set off on another chase towards Basra – all were aware that time was running out, and that the politicians might cry halt and the Republican Guard, the principal military objective, might get away. The tanks charged line abreast like an ancient battle fleet across the sand. At one point they fired on vehicles two miles off – two air defence artillery tenders – setting their aluminium hulls ablaze. Fortunately their crew had dismounted at the time to answer a call of nature.

Another night and an early start this time to cut off any Iraqis pouring back from Kuwait City. But on the edge of the shallow ravine known as the Wadi al Batin on a battered plastic transistor radio we heard President Bush intone his declaration of cease fire. The ground war of a hundred hours was over. Miraculously shampoo bottles poured forth whisky and toasts were drunk.

Later we drove into Kuwait itself under a sky which heralded the apocalypse. Black clouds of soot from the hundreds of fires set by the retreating Iraqis compounded with thunder and rain. A few days later we came across the detritus of the last action – on the main road cutting the Mutlar Ridge which skirts the bay of Kuwait City to the north. Here American tanks, aircraft and helicopters had caught the remnants of the Iraqi garrison in the city scurrying away in any vehicle they could, tanks, trucks, stolen cars, rubbish trucks, fire appliances and buses. With them went their incongruous booty from stolen washing machines and televisions to knick knacks, furniture and jewellery. Three to four hundred must have died in that terrible storm of ordnance, but many more appear to have escaped. Even greater was the destruction of the armoured divisions guarding the northern border between Iraq and Kuwait on the last night of the war. 'When we saw them in our night sights we could pick them off like a game of space invaders,' an American officer remarked laconically.

Days after on lonely tap line roads through the oilfields we would come across scenes of strange domestic savagery. At one spot an armoured carrier and a truck had been caught in full retreat – the remains of their occupants later scattered for hundreds of yards around, victims in an instant of the hyperbolic violence of modern weapons. They had been abandoned by their commanders and colleagues in the field, and sacrificed by the cruel leadership in Baghdad.

That was a war ago. Only weeks later came Operation Safe Haven to help the Kurds. In the summer the simmering feuds of Yugoslavia burst into civil war. The conflict has been a terrible vendetta in the cornfields of the Danube and along the coast of Dalmatia where Dubrovnik, Byron's 'Pearl of the Adriatic' has been a hostage of siege by predatory Serbs and Montenegrins. The conflict has been a study in military incompetence by the former Yugoslav Federal Army (JNA) once said to be the best trained and equipped in eastern Europe, but now little more than a heavily-gunned Serb militia. The deficiencies in handling weaponry by the Croat and Serb irregulars has been alarming for any third party in the vicinity.

For all the crudity of the fighting, the Yugoslav conflict has produced a new kind of war, and one that the rest of Europe and its allies will find it hard to ignore. For it is not a war involving governments and armies acting on behalf of the people – in the way the father of modern strategy, Clausewitz, depicted. It is a war by the people, among the people. The army has become a faction of its own like the various sects and parties and putative political authorities of the

Serbs and Croats. It no longer claims to be a people's army under the old marxist-leninist doctrine of Tito's communist Yugoslavia, for it is now making war on part of the people that it was supposed to represent – the Croats and Slovenes.

Europe will be affected because of the upset caused by the mass movement of refugees, fugitives, exiles and asylum seekers. Millions of Yugoslavs live abroad in the immediate European neighbourhood in countries like Italy, Hungary, Austria, Switzerland and Germany. Millions of Europeans live in Yugoslavia – Italians, Germans, Hungarians, Czechs, Ukrainians, Ruthenians, Gypsies to name but some.

But Europe is likely to become involved – later rather than sooner – for another reason. The warring factions in Yugoslavia are symptoms of a new form of brigandage or banditry now abroad in southern Europe. These elements are a law unto themselves. If Europe and America threaten sanctions then Zagreb and Belgrade could become capitals of rump, mafia statelets which live by drugs and arms trafficking, money laundering, organised crime and terrorism. In short we may have connived by inaction at the creation of a little Lebanon inside Europe.

If some form of military operation has to be mounted for Yugoslavia, or elsewhere in southern Europe – if only for very low level humanitarian objectives – the lessons of launching and supporting a force from the Falklands and Safe Haven are likely to prove more valuable than anything learned in the Gulf. Desert Storm and Desert Sabre, for all the high tech and precision weapons, was a strangely old-fashioned war – an experience unlikely to be repeated. It showed, for example, that the 70-ton main battle tank, will soon be a thing of the past – for it can only work in open terrain like desert or steppe. It is unlikely that such a coalition will mass again to fight for such a limited and clearly defined objective as the liberation of Kuwait.

In the aftermath of Desert Storm and the upheavals in eastern Europe the Ministry of Defence and the government in Britain, and their counterparts in the United States, once more seem to have taken a false step in their programme of defence cuts. The 'Options for Change' programme of cuts (largely to satisfy the Treasury Department) confirmed in July 1991 has ominous similarities to John Nott's ambitious 'Way Ahead' defence review of ten years before. With the end of the Cold War, some measure of defence reform and reduction of expenditure and manpower is not only desirable but necessary. The defect of 'Options for Change' is that it has no coherent view of what British forces are likely to be required for. Cutting the Army (including the Marines) to 104,000 will make the soldiers hard put to fulfil present commitments, let alone meet new demands. The cuts programme seems in no danger of producing the balanced force capable of mounting flexible, mobile responses to meet new demands and threats emerging round the fringes of Europe. Nor is a genuine peace dividend likely, as no real cut in the defence budget can be expected before the end of the twentieth century; we are likely to end up with forces that are very expensive for what they can do. The slogan of Tom King, the Defence Secretary who launched 'Options for Change', was that Britain would get 'a smaller but better army'. Such has been the effect on morale, said one Gulf veteran, 'all we are getting is a smaller but bitter army'.

At the time the Falklands campaign may have looked like Britain's last colonial war. But for what is to come the military experience gathered there will prove more helpful than the march and counter march of NATO exercises in Germany which so preoccupied the British Army command over the past forty years, and the deployment of the 1st UK Division to the Arabian desert. The Falklands expedition and the Commandos' Mission to help the Kurds may give a far better pointer to future operations, given the alarums and instabilities now emerging from Britain and her allies in the European backyard.

Robert Fox,
London, November 1991

Further Reading

War in the South Atlantic, Max Hastings and Simon Jenkins, London 1983; the best account of the war on the front and in Whitehall so far.

Signals of War, Laurence Freedman and Virginia Gamba-Stonehouse, London 1989; an intriguing analysis of the diplomatic war.

Above All Courage, Max Arthur ed, London 1985; gripping first-hand accounts of combatants given in interviews.

Operation Corporate, London 1985, revised as *Task Force*, London 1987 by Martin Middlebrook; a steady if rather sterile account of the campaign from the British side.

The Fight for the Malvinas, London 1989, by Martin Middlebrook; the view from Argentina, somewhat incomplete.

The Royal Navy and the Falklands War, by David Brown, London 1987; an excellent account of naval actions.

Falklands – The Air War, by R. A. Burden, M. I. Draper, D. A. Rough, C. R. Smith and D. L. Wilton, London 1986; comprehensive cover of the air war.

Air War South Atlantic, by Jeffrey Ethell and Alfred Price, London 1983; controversial, punchy early account of the air war.

The Land That Lost Its Heroes, by Jimmy Burns, London 1987; intriguing account of the Argentine build-up and propaganda.

Excursion to Hell, by Vince Bramley, London 1991; a powerful first-person account by a member of 3 Para.

Glossary

Aircraft: Argentinian: A-4 Skyhawk fighter bombers. Mirage fighter bombers Dassault 111 and Israeli-built Dagger. Canberra British-built jet bomber. Super Etendard delivery Exocet.

AW: Amphibious Warfare; Comm. AW: Commodore Amphibious Warfare (Commodore Michael Clapp, RN).

BC: Battery Commander.

BMA: Brigade Maintenance Area.

Brew: Any drink brewed in the field.

Brigade:
> *3 Commando Brigade:* 40, 42, 45 Commando and Logistics Regiment, Royal Marines, 3rd Battalion the Parachute Regt attached for campaign and 2nd Battalion for battles of Goose Green and Wireless Ridge. Commander: Brigadier Julian Thompson, RM.
>
> *5 Infantry Brigade:* 1st Bn Welsh Guards, 2nd Bn Scots Guards, 1st Bn 7th Gurkha Rifles, and 2 Para from 1 to 10 June.

Camp: All Falklands outside Stanley, from Spanish *campo.*

CAP: Combat Air Patrol.

Carriers:
> British: *Invincible* (throughdeck cruiser) and *Hermes.*
> Argentinian: *Venticinco di Mayo* (ex-*Venerable*).

Casevac: Casualty Evacuation (moving the injured by helicopter).

CLFFI: Commander Land Forces Falkland Islands (Major-General Jeremy Moore, RM).

Cruiser: Argentinian: *General Belgrano* (ex-USS *Phoenix*, laid down 1935); 15×6-inch guns, 8×5-inch, Sea Cat and Exocet missiles; sunk 2 May.

Destroyers:

British: Type 42 – Sheffield class armed with Mk 8 4.5-inch gun (115 mm) and Sea Dart missile. *Sheffield* sunk 10 May, *Coventry* 25 May. Type 22 – Broadsword class armed with Sea Wolf anti-air/anti-missile missiles. County Class destroyers, e.g. *Antrim* and *Glamorgan*.

Argentinian: Two Type 42s, *Santissima Trinidad* and *Hercules*.

FAC: Forward Air Controller.

FGA: Fighter Ground Attack.

FIC: Falklands Islands Company.

FIGAS: Falkland Islands General Air Service.

FOO: Forward Observation Officer.

Frigates:

British: Type 21 Amazon Class using Sea Cat and Mk 8 Naval gun 4.5-inch. *Ardent* sunk 21 May and *Antelope* 24 May. Type 12 Rothesay Class, *Plymouth* and *Yarmouth*, Sea Cat missiles and twin 4.5-inch Mk 6 (semi-automatic gun). Leander Class, various, e.g. *Argonaut, Penelope* – Exocet ships.

FRs 1/SHA: Sea Harrier armed with Sidewinder air to air missiles and Ferranti Blue Fox radar.

GPMG: (or 'gimpy') General Purpose Machine-Gun, used in support of British troops using 7.62-mm ammunition.

GR3: Ground attack aircraft, using guns, and CBU cluster bombs.

Grott: (as in grotto) slang for cabin, Navy refer to 'pit'.

Hack: journalist (noun); to hack, military slang for 'to succeed', i.e. 'I can hack it.'

Helicopters:

British: Naval Lynx, Wasp, Sea King and Wessex 5. Scout and Gazelle light helicopters. Chinook twin-rotor heavy lift.

Argentinian: Huey Iroquois, Augusta Bell 109, Chinook and Puma.

LCU: Large landing craft, carries a company or vehicles; four to *Fearless* and *Intrepid*.

LCVP: Landing Craft Vehicle Personnel, carries a platoon or Land Rover and trailer, also four to *Fearless* and *Intrepid*.

LPD: Assault ships, 12,500 tonnes, *Intrepid* and *Fearless*, carries 500 troops, and vehicles for launch in landing craft from dock astern.

LSL: Landing Support Logistics Ship, the *Sir Galahad* class landing support ship, 5,670 tonnes carrying troops and vehicles.

Marisat/Inmarsat: Secure maritime satellite for phone calls to world.

MAW: Mountain and Arctic Warfare Cadre, Royal Marines.

Minders: Ministry of Defence Press Officers looking after hacks, after TV series 'Minder'.

Missiles:

Sea Dart, sea to air very high level attack.

Exocet sea skimmer, ground-, air- and sea-launched.

Sea to air – Sea Cat; Sea Slug; Sea Wolf (and anti-missile).

Land-based – Rapier ground to air; Milan: man carried, fire from stand, anti-tank but used for 'bunker-busting'.

Blowpipe shoulder-launched anti-air missile, man-guided to target.

Stringer US shoulder-launched heat-seeking on 'fire and forget' basis.

NGS: Naval Gunfire Support, principally from twin Mk 6 4.5-inch semi-automatic guns and single Mk 8 4.5-inch automatic.

NGSFO: Naval Gunfire Support Forward Officer, man who guides Naval guns ashore.

PNG: Passive Night Goggles, for helicopter night flying.

Proff: To profiteer, i.e. steal.

RAS: Replenishment at Sea, and 'rassing' also means 'getting hold of'.

RFA: Royal Fleet Auxiliary.

Rifles:

British: SLR (Self Loading Rifle), 7.62-mm calibre.

Argentinian: Belgian-designed FN, 7.62-mm calibre.

Rockets:

66-mm shoulder-launched; once only with throw-away launcher, used for 'bunker-busting'.

84-mm Carl Gustav (Swedish); the 'Charlie G' as above,
fired from stand, anti-tank used for 'bunker-busting'.

Mortar: basic infantry 81-mm used by both sides, also
heavy 120-mm used by Argentinians.

SAS: Special Air Service, recruits from Army unit.

SBS: Special Boat Squadron from Royal Marines.

Scran/Scoff: Food.

SNO: Senior Naval Officer, Chris Burne SNO *Canberra*,
Chris Esplin-Jones, *Norland*.

Submarines:

British: Five nuclear hunter-killer – *Valiant, Conqueror,
Courageous, Spartan, Splendid*. One patrol conventional
sub – *Onyx*.

Argentinian: Two modern German coastal 'Salta' class,
two WWII ex-US 'Guppy' class; the *Santa Fe* crippled
at Grytviken 26 April.

VSTOL: Vertical/Short-take-off/Landing aircraft. The first
operational aircraft of this kind in the world was the
Harrier.

Yomp: To march across country, paras use 'tab'.

Index

A Selected List of Non-Fiction Available from Mandarin

☐ 7493 0109 0	**The Warrior Queens**	Antonia Fraser	£4.99
☐ 7493 0108 2	**Mary Queen of Scots**	Antonia Fraser	£5.99
☐ 7493 0010 8	**Cromwell**	Antonia Fraser	£7.50
☐ 7493 0106 6	**The Weaker Vessel**	Antonia Fraser	£5.99
☐ 7493 0014 0	**The Demon Drink**	Jancis Robinson	£4.99
☐ 7493 0016 7	**Vietnam – The 10,000 Day War**	Michael Maclear	£3.99
☐ 7493 0061 2	**Voyager**	Yeager/Rutan	£3.99
☐ 7493 0113 9	**Peggy Ashcroft**	Michael Billington	£3.99
☐ 7493 0177 5	**The Troubles**	Mick O'Connor	£4.99
☐ 7493 0004 3	**South Africa**	Graham Leach	£3.99
☐ 7493 0254 2	**Families and How to Survive Them**	Creese/Skynner	£5.99
☐ 7493 0060 4	**The Fashion Conspiracy**	Nicolas Coleridge	£3.99
☐ 7493 0179 1	**The Tao of Pooh**	Benjamin Hoff	£2.99
☐ 7493 0000 0	**Moonwalk**	Michael Jackson	£2.99